THE EVOLUTION OF
A MANUFACTURING
SYSTEM AT TOYOTA

THE EVOLUTION OF A MANUFACTURING SYSTEM AT TOYOTA

Takahiro Fujimoto

New York   Oxford

Oxford University Press

1999

Oxford University Press

Oxford   New York
Athens   Auckland   Bangkok   Bogotá   Buenos Aires   Calcutta
Cape Town   Chennai   Dar es Salaam   Delhi   Florence   Hong Kong   Istanbul
Karachi   Kuala Lumpur   Madrid   Melbourne   Mexico City   Mumbai
Nairobi   Paris   São Paulo   Singapore   Taipei   Tokyo   Toronto   Warsaw

and associated companies in
Berlin   Ibadan

Published by Oxford University Press, Inc.
198 Madison Avenue, New York, New York 10016

Oxford is a registered trademark of Oxford University Press

Library of Congress Cataloging-in-Publication Data
Fujimoto, Takahiro, 1955–
    The evolution of a manufacturing system at Toyota / Takahiro Fujimoto.
        p.   cm.
    Includes bibliographical references and index.
    ISBN-13 978-0-19-512320-3
    ISBN 0-19-512320-4
        1. Automobiles—Design and construction.   2. Toyota Jidosha Kabushiki
Kaisha—Management.   3. Industrial efficiency.   4. Operations research.
5. Toyota automobiles.   I. Title.
    TL278 .F83   1999
    629.2'34—dc21   98-38201

Printed in the United States of America
on acid-free paper

PREFACE AND
ACKNOWLEDGMENTS

What is the real source of lasting competence for manufacturing? This book is an attempt to explore organizational capabilities embedded in a typical high-performing company of the late twentieth century—Toyota Motor Corporation. In these pages I will discuss, in detail, the concept of system emergence and evolutionary learning, which gradually formed a highly complex and competitive manufacturing system over time.

Indeed, the book itself "emerged" from a series of papers that I wrote for various conferences and book projects in the first half of the 1990s, including the Third Prince Bertil Symposium on the Dynamic Firm (June 1994, Stockholm School of Economics, Sweden); the 33rd Zushi Conference of the Tokyo Center for Economic Research (March 1995, Kanagawa, Japan); Tokyo University Research Institute for the Japanese Economy Conference on Business History of Enterprise Systems and Entrepreneurship (January 1993, Shizuoka, Japan); the First GERPISA International Colloquium on "Trajectories of Automobile Firms" (June 1993, Paris, France); the 21st International Conference on Business History (January 1994, Shizuoka, Japan), "Innovation in Japan" project of the Japan Centre for Economic Research; and the 3rd International Conference on Assembly Automation and Work Organization (October 1995, Ca' Foscari University of Venice, Italy). Although these papers were written for separate reasons and disciplines, all of them had a common theme: a focus on the evolution of a competitive manufacturing system from both functional and historical points of view.

The Evolution of a Manufacturing System at Toyota is in many ways a direct consequence of my previous study on automobile product development during the late 1980s with Kim B. Clark of Harvard Business School. In this study, we focused mostly on comparison and explanation of product development performance by automobile makers worldwide—a typical functional analysis of effective manufacturing systems. I have maintained my research interests in competitive performance and organizational capabilities in this highly complex and international industry, but it was natural for me to shift attention from static or cross-sectional comparisons to intertemporal research on the competitive dynamics of this sector. On the one hand, as we continued to accumulate comparative data of automobile product development in the 1990s, our focus shifted to the ways these firms built competitive organizational capabilities on a global scale. On the other hand, while investigating a highly complex system of effective product development routines in a few Japanese auto firms, I became increasingly interested in how such a complicated system was formed in the first place. To me, it seemed intuitively impossible to explain it as purely managers' deliberate planning and foresight.

My interest in the evolution of manufacturing systems goes back even further to the early 1980s, when I was a researcher-consultant at Mitsubishi Research Institute in Tokyo, conducting a series of automobile-related projects for various clients. This was the time when I started to witness intensifying competition for organizational capability-building among the auto firms worldwide. I was then heavily influenced by a work by the late William Abernathy, *The Productivity Dilemma*, which unequivocally explained the dynamics of the early U.S. automobile industry through a thorough historical analysis of its product-process systems. I was also fascinated by his insights and personality, since I met him in 1981, when he was a professor at Harvard Business School, and eventually I decided to apply to the school in 1984.

Further back still, my investigation of emergence in a sociotechnical system began in the late 1970s, when I was doing field research on agricultural irrigation systems for my undergraduate thesis, under the supervision of Moriaki Tsuchiya of Tokyo University. I was comparing two water distribution systems for rice paddies in Japan—a modern closed-channel system that had been deliberately planned by the water resource development authority, and an old open-channel system in which various formal and informal rules for water distribution emerged out of coalitions and conflicts among villages. One thing that fascinated me was how the emergent village system, although its physical facilities were relatively poor, tended to be more effective than the planned one in maintaining facilities to achieve a given level of rice harvests. Since then, I have been curious about why an emergent system can sometimes outperform deliberately planned systems.

Because of this book's diverse origins, it has been a challenge for me to make something reasonably coherent out of the diverse elements—or multiple emergent paths—of my existing works. In general, my intention has been to describe this complex phenomenon as such. Because of that, I may have sacrificed some simplicity in my conceptual arguments; the empirical and historical materials that I gathered were overwhelmingly complicated and difficult to interpret from any single theory's point of view. Any criticism or advice for improving the theoretical brevity of my current interpretations is quite welcome, if it can still preserve the richness of what I have observed.

It is also very difficult for me to specify every person who, directly or indirectly, helped me write this book. Please note that I limit these acknowledgments to a rather small number of people who directly assisted me. First, I would like to thank all of the organizers of the conferences and projects mentioned above, including Alfred Chandler, Peter Hagström, Örjan Sölvell, Hideshi Ito, Akio Okochi, Haruhito Takeda, Robert Boyer, Patrick Fridenson, Michel Freyssenet, Haruhito Shiomi, Kazuo Wada, Akira Goto, Hiroyuki Odagiri, Giuseppe Volpato and Arnaldo Camuffo, who gave me opportunities to explore these ideas in papers that later became the building blocks of this book. I received insightful comments from many participants at these conferences, as well as at subsequent seminars: Giovanni Dosi, Richard Nelson, Benjamin Coriat, Kim Clark, Martin Kenny, David Hounshell, Wes Cohen, Banri Asanuma, Koichi Shimokawa, Masahiko Aoki, Ulrich Jürgens, Charles Fine, Michael Cusumano, John Paul MacDuffie, to name a few, as well as anonymous reviewers of the first draft. Paul Adler of the University of Southern California was also kind enough to spend some time as an "informal reviewer" of my manuscripts. Appendix B2 is virtually a joint work with Akira Takeishi of Hitotsubashi University, who I worked with on many projects while we were both working at Mitsubishi Research Institute.

For financial support, I wish to thank the Abe Fellowship Program of the Social Science Research Council and the American Council of Learned Societies for funds provided by the Japan Foundation Center for Global Partnership, which gave me an opportunity to do part of this research and write the manuscript during my stays in Europe and America. Harvard Business School (Kim Clark), INSEAD Euro-Asia Centre (Arnaud de Meyer), and Lyon University (Yveline Lecler) provided me with logistical support during my stays there in 1996–97 as a visiting professor/researcher. Needless to say, the staff of Tokyo University Faculty of Economics, my home base, have given me constant financial and logistical support since 1990. I thank many of my colleagues in these institutions, who gave me numerous ideas in daily conversations.

On the empirical side, I owe thanks to at least a few hundred practitioners at Toyota Motor Corporation and other automakers and parts suppliers in the world, all who have provided me with valuable materials and insights during the past several years. I acknowledge the key people in the book wherever possible, but they represent only the tip of the iceberg; for reasons of confidentiality, I can't disclose the names of many others. I greatly admire the professionalism and knowledge of these cooperative engineers and managers.

Throughout the writing process I received professional supports from a number of people. Editor Martha Nichols converted my redundant and complicated manuscripts into a readable and concise one. Keiko Shiroki and Morgan McCurdy helped me with secretarial support at Tokyo and Harvard Universities, respectively. Herbert Addison of Oxford University Press, as well as several other staff, gave me continuous encouragement and advice. This book was a particularly difficult one for me; without their support, it would have been impossible to publish it.

Finally, I want to thank my wife Kozue and my son Ryusuke, who were always supportive while I was working on this book, at my office at Tokyo University, at home, in Europe, and in America—a traveling writer who never forgot their efforts or inspiration.

Tokyo
April 1998

CONTENTS

Part I

EMERGENCE AND
FUNCTIONS OF THE TOTAL
MANUFACTURING SYSTEM

1

AN EVOLUTIONARY FRAMEWORK
FOR MANUFACTURING

Even in today's uncertain and highly competitive markets, some manufacturing firms consistently outperform their rivals over a long period of time. One of the best examples of such a high performer is Toyota Motor Corporation. Founded in the 1930s, Toyota started off by assembling five trucks per day. In 1950, it produced only about ten thousand units; but by the 1980s, this Japanese company had evolved into one of the largest automakers in the world, producing 3 to 4 million cars and trucks domestically. As of the late 1990s, rapid growth of overseas production has pushed Toyota's annual world-wide production up to almost 5 million units. Toyota has led the domestic passenger car market since 1963. Additionally, it has not recorded an operating loss since it officially started to measure its profits in the 1940s. Toyota is known as one of the world's best performers in both manufacturing quality and productivity in the past few decades.[1]

The Toyota story, ballyhooed by the Western business press and academic researchers since the early 1980s, is one many other manufacturers have tried to emulate. By now, there's a general consensus that the Toyota production system (often just called TPS) and total quality control (TQC) have provided a definite source of competitive advantage, along with the company's product development capabilities and its effective relationships with suppliers. Under the more challenging business circumstances of the 1990s—the flagging Japanese economy, an aging labor force, the catchup of Western automakers, and growing social demands for environmental protection—Toyota remains one of the most profitable large companies in Japan; internationally, its manufacturing system is still quite competitive. While some other auto firms have been more profitable than Toyota at certain points in time, Toyota has stood out for the last few decades because of its consistently high manufacturing performance.

Much of the hype about Toyota is justified, but even this firm has made mistakes or encountered problems. Its history has not been that of smooth progress and perfect decision making. In 1950, for instance, Toyota faced major labor strikes and was at the edge of bankruptcy, one of the only times the company has recorded a pre-tax loss. In the early 1990s, in the wake of Japan's postbubble recession, its operating profits per sales ratio dipped below its normally strong 5 percent. So what's the key to Toyota's resilience? And why has its success been so hard to replicate? Toyota has many versions of its official history, but they all tend to explain the company's growth in terms of a series of deliberate, well-thought-out steps, rather than as the result of trial and error or inevitable muddling through.[2] Meanwhile, Western media commentators have touted a Japanese style of work and manufacturing as the basis for Toyota's impact. Academic researchers have honed such popular assumptions by proposing that "lean producers"[3] like Toyota possess a set of firm-specific and difficult-to-imitate resources and routines—often called *organizational capabilities*—that bring about high competitive performance.

There's some truth to all of these explanations. The capability-based view of the firm, in particular, lends itself to Toyota's operations. But even a focus on organizational capabilities leads to further questions about how a successful company evolves. First, how do we describe the structural content of a capability itself, thereby avoiding the tautology of inferring capability from high performance and then saying that such performance is caused by the capability? Second, how do we analyze a detailed mechanism through which a certain capability creates high performance? Third, how and why was such a capability formed in the first place? Through cool and rational calculation? The visions of an entrepreneurial genius? Pure luck?

In *The Evolution of a Manufacturing System at Toyota*, I address this triad of questions. The book is mainly an empirical work, based on years of field research at Toyota and other Japanese and Western automakers. But to add conceptual depth and coherence to the Toyota story, I use an evolutionary framework, combining a functional analysis of how certain organizational routines result in competitive advantages with a historical analysis of how this company has developed its formidable manufacturing capabilities. Evolutionary views of business systems have increased in popularity since I began this study; by presenting my own framework, I intend neither to debate its theoretical novelty nor to apply neo-Darwinian concepts in a lockstep fashion. (See appendix A for a more detailed discussion.)[4] I have chosen this perspective simply because it fits a basic, observable fact: although Toyota's manufacturing system looks as if it were deliberately designed as a competitive weapon, it was created gradually through a complex historical process that can never be reduced to managers' rational foresight alone.

This book highlights what I call Toyota's *evolutionary learning capability*:[5] an organization's overall ability to evolve competitive routines even in highly episodic and uncertain situations. Such a dynamic capability encompasses making good decisions, learning from mistakes, and grasping the competitive benefits of unintended consequences. Manufacturing companies that survive for decades don't succeed just because they implement the right systems or routines at a certain point in time; they also have a long-term ability to generate effective routines even without prior knowledge of their competitive effects. Neither a result of deliberately planned business strategy nor random chance, then, Toyota's manufacturing system has evolved since its beginnings through a complicated interplay of forces: entrepreneurial vision, historical imperatives and crises, unanticipated events, regional competitive pressures, and global transformation of the industry and market. More than anything else, I will argue that this company's superior evolutionary learning capability has made a decisive contribution to its high and stable performance.

To my knowledge, few previous studies have looked at the rational and emergent aspects of the Toyota system in a balanced way. A mountain of business research has been generated on the competitive strength of Japanese automakers since the late 1970s.[6] But these mostly Western observations have concentrated on routinized aspects of capabilities vis-à-vis competing firms at a certain point in time: how Toyota and others, for instance, have achieved superior productivity, manufacturing quality, or delivery through a set of distinctive practices and routines. While there have been many studies on the history of TPS, as well as Japanese automobile manufacturing and supplier systems in general, few have drawn explicit connections between analyses of competitive performance and routine capabilities at the level of the total manufacturing system.[7] And even if there's been much discussion of certain dynamic capabilities—namely, company-wide continuous improvements—such analyses tend to cover only routinized processes of organizational learning and problem solving. How a company exercises the dynamic capability to build these routinized capabilities themselves has not been tapped.

To that end, *The Evolution of a Manufacturing System at Toyota* discusses the Toyota story from two additional angles. It reinterprets a firm's total manufacturing system from an information/knowledge point of view; it also presents a three-layer model of a manufacturing firm's organizational capabilities, one that includes routinized manufacturing and learning capabilities, as well as the evolutionary learning capability to build such organizational routines. The core of my empirical work involves the Toyota-style manufacturing system, whose three basic components are production, product development, and supplier systems. Therefore, the studies included in this book range from the overall manufacturing system to specific product development processes, to a detailed case of a supplier relationship called the *black box parts system*, to a new assembly system implemented by Toyota in the 1990s. For each case, I examine both the competitive functions and the evolutionary patterns of a given system.

Under the economic and social conditions of the 1990s, most Japanese automakers have restrengthened their manufacturing capabilities, simplified their product lines, globalized their operations, tried to make their workplaces attractive to employees, and started to develop new product technologies that are environmentally friendly (for example, direct injection, a lean-burn engine, an advanced electric vehicle, or a hybrid vehicle). Yet many have suffered from poor financial performance since the beginning of the 1990s. "Japanese-ness" no longer seems such a magic bullet, and it's now clear that the organizational capabilities of individual companies—especially Toyota— make a real difference.

Linking Manufacturing with an Evolutionary Framework

When a certain stable and complex pattern, be it a biological species or manufacturing practice, changes and survives in a competitive environment, we can analyze such a dynamic phenomenon in evolutionary terms. An evolutionary framework is particularly useful when it is obvious the system was created as more than someone's deliberate plan for survival. The history of Toyota's manufacturing system fits this evolutionary view very well. Although the system turned out to be quite competitive, its elements were not always intended at the start as competitive weapons.

Claiming that human behavior has unintended consequences is by no means new. Robert K. Merton, in his classic book *Social Theory and Social Structure*, says, "[T]he distinctive intellectual contributions of the sociologists are found primarily in the study of unintended consequences . . . of social practices, as well as in the study of anticipated consequences."[8] Anthony Giddens notes, "Human history is created by intentional activities but is not an intended project; it persistently eludes efforts to bring it under conscious direction."[9] Henry Mintzberg, advocating his well-known concept of emergent strategy formation, argues, "An organization can have a pattern (or realized strategy) without knowing it, let alone making it explicit."[10] Similar statements have been made by past philosophers, anthropologists, sociologists, and economists, including Emile Durkheim, Karl Popper, and Claude Levi-Strauss.[11]

More broadly, in the field of management and economics, notable scholars like Mintzberg, Richard Nelson, Karl Weick, and Robert Burgelman have applied evolutionary ideas to organizational, strategic, and economic issues, emphasizing the emergent nature of business-economic system formation.[12] Some say an organization can learn, select adaptive routines, and thereby survive; others believe external environments screen organizations through the equivalent of natural selection, and only the lucky survive. Some appreciate human efforts; others emphasize chance events.

The evolutionists in economics and management clearly have wide-ranging ideas, but they all seem to share at least one notion: the formation of a business system cannot be explained solely by foresight and deliberate planning. As James Collins and Jerry Porras, in their popular book *Built to Last*, put it, "Visionary companies make some of their best moves by experimentation, trial and error, opportunism, and—quite literally—accident. What looks in retrospect like brilliant foresight and preplanning was often the result of 'Let's just try a lot of stuff and keep what works.' In this sense, visionary companies mimic the biological evolution of species."[13]

But in technology and operations management, where I do most of my research, there have been relatively few studies highlighting the role of system formation processes that aren't deliberately planned. Researchers of modern manufacturing management have generally focused on the functional rationality of existing systems. Business historians describing developments of manufacturing systems have also emphasized rational decision-making processes. This bias toward rational explanation is quite understandable, considering the nature of the modern mass-production system—a highly functional mechanism unequivocally designed to achieve superior competitive performance in productivity, quality, speed, and flexibility. Indeed, I believe the primary task of scholars in this field is functional analysis of existing or planned manufacturing systems, the kind of work I have carried out in the past.[14]

Yet even if manufacturing involves well-oiled machines and technical routines, such systems aren't just a product of deliberate planning. While Toyota's official documents may attribute the company's high performance to intentional strategizing, some of its successful routines may have originated unintentionally. For instance, Toyota increased its reliance on suppliers' engineering activities in the 1960s apparently because managers at the time believed that would alleviate the mounting workload for in-house engineers. This specific solution to workload problems, however, had unintended consequences for competitive performance. Relying on suppliers' engineering activities became a major competitive weapon for Toyota and other Japanese automakers by the 1980s, since it enabled them to cut costs through component design for manufacturing (DFM) and to save money and time in product development. In chapter 5, I discuss this phenomenon in further detail.

Because competitive systems don't always result from competitive foresight, this book adopts an evolutionary view in order to capture the complexity of Toyota's manufacturing history. Methodologically, an evolutionary framework offers a dynamic perspective that separately explains an observed system's survival (its *functional logic*) and its formation (its *genetic logic*). For example, the neo-Darwinian or synthetic theory of biological evolution, the prevailing model in this field today, explains a living system's survival in terms of natural selection but its origin as a product of random variation. Armen A. Alchian applies a similar model to microeconomic theory, arguing that "success (survival)—does not require proper motivation but may rather be the result of fortuitous circumstances."[15]

Let me reiterate here that this book is essentially an empirical work; therefore, the evolutionary framework is nothing more than a tool for integrating the collected data. If it had turned out that the genetic and functional explanations for the Toyota manufacturing system were virtually the same—that is, it was created by the intentional actions of people who already knew its competitive functions—there would be no need to employ an evolutionary model. I would have happily adopted the traditional rational decision-making perspective of operations management, if it had fit the facts. An evolutionary framework makes sense only when thorough functional and historical analyses of the same system reveal a significant gap between the two explanations. I will repeatedly emphasize the separation of genetic and functional logic throughout *The Evolution of a Manufacturing System at Toyota* because this, I believe, is at the heart of evolutionary thinking.

Multi-Path System Emergence

The idea that social systems often evolve because of unanticipated events and unplanned behavior is related to *system emergence*, a concept central to my evolutionary framework. Unlike the neo-Darwinian model, however, I don't reduce the historical process that formed Toyota-style manufacturing routines to randomness. Instead I describe it as the interplay of both intended and unintended consequences for the people who created the system. I call this highly irregular historical process *multi-path system emergence*, in which decision makers often don't know beforehand which path will lead to a successful outcome—deliberate planning, environmental imperatives, intuition, imitation, or luck.

The word *emergence* generally means that a certain system trait cannot be explained by the behavior of its constituent parts alone or predicted from the previous states of the system owing to its complexity from the observers' point of view.[16] It has appeared in existing work in biological evolution, sociology, and general system theory, as well as business literature.[17] Across these various disciplines, the nu-

Rational Calculation

activity 2

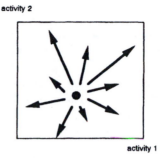

objective
function

current
system

activity 2

Random Trials

activity 2

activity 1

Environmental Constraints

activity 2

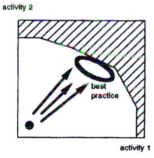

activity 1

Entrepreneurial Vision

activity 2

vision

activity 1

Knowledge Transfer

activity 2

best
practice

activity 1

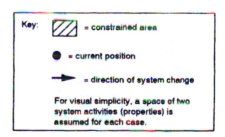

Key: = constrained area

= current position

= direction of system change

For visual simplicity, a space of two
system activities (properties) is
assumed for each case.

Source: Modified and adopted from Fujimoto (1995).

Figure 1.1 Multi-Path System Emergence

ances of this concept may differ somewhat by case. But my interpretation of system emergence in this book rejects the kind of rational optimism that says system change is entirely controlled by purposeful plans that existed prior to the change; it also denies the cynical notion that social system change is merely due to random accidents with little connection to human efforts.

More specifically, system emergence can occur through a number of different paths, and a combination of them may be required to explain a particular change. When looking at manufacturing firms, I include the following paths for system change (see figure 1.1):

- *Random trials.* An organization's outcomes are a matter of pure chance. A lucky one gets a better system, while an unlucky one gets a poor one—so in that case, you might as well try everything.

- *Rational calculation.* Decision makers deliberately choose a new routine that satisfices or maximizes an organization's main objective function—competitive performance that contributes to better chances of survival. They examine feasible alternatives based on their understanding of environmental constraints and capability limits.[18] This is the rational problem-solving approach many managers believe is the only way to create successful change.[19]

- *Environmental constraints.* The directions of system changes that decision makers choose may be constrained by certain limitations imposed by external or internal environments. The constraints may be objective (such as laws and regulations), or they may be "self-restraints" based on managerial perception of the environment. Under some fortuitous conditions, the choices affected by the constraints may turn out to enhance the system's competitive performance even if the decision makers themselves don't have such objectives beforehand.

- *Entrepreneurial vision.* Gifted leaders, based on their vision, philosophy, or intuition, choose a desirable set of activities without much analysis of organizational capabilities and environmental constraints. Objective constraints may prohibit them from realizing their dreams, but the vision itself may trigger certain actions that eventually remove the limits—a "self-fulfilling prophecy."[20]

- *Knowledge transfer.* Certain competitive routines may be transferred from another organization to the one in question.[21] The transfer may happen within the industry (competitor, supplier, customer) or across industries. Also, the transfer may be a "pull" type, in which the adopter-imitator of the system takes initiative based on benchmarking, or it may be a "push" type, in which the source organization is the driving force behind the transfer—often an unintended transfer from the receiver's point of view.

A particular combination of these system emergence paths may affect how organizational routines and capabilities differ across firms and regions. For example, sometimes universally prevalent, region-specific, and firm-specific patterns of manufacturing capability all exist at the same time—a situation researchers of a single international industry often encounter and one that I discuss in the context of the Japanese automobile industry. Consider the following conditions, all of which may affect a company's manufacturing performance:

- *Universally prevalent patterns* of practice may emerge when decision makers share identical objectives and constraints worldwide, when the best practice has been transferred to everyone, and when severe selection environments allow only a particular pattern to survive.
- *Region-specific patterns* of capabilities may emerge when firms share regional environmental constraints or objectives, or when knowledge transfers occur only within each region.
- *Firm-specific patterns* may emerge when each company takes a "random walk" in changing its systems, faces unique environmental constraints, or is led by different entrepreneurial visions; when knowledge transfers between firms are limited; and, above all, when firms have varying levels of evolutionary learning capabilities.

Although pure chance and historical imperatives often play important roles in the system emergence and capability-building process, a company may still be able to build certain manufacturing capabilities faster and more effectively than its competitors through a strong evolutionary learning capability. For example, historical imperatives may explain why the Japanese automakers in general acquired certain regional-specific capabilities, but it does not explain why some Japanese companies like Toyota have had better capabilities than others. In this case, evolutionary learning capability does matter.

The Limits of a Biological Analogy

Since the time of Darwin, of course, evolutionary frameworks have been applied to social, economic, and managerial systems, as well as to biological organisms. Because of the popularity of such analyses, the concept has now become quite equivocal, often creating disagreements among researchers. An "evolutionary model" can mean different things to different people: random system variations, domination of environmental forces as a selection mechanism, a regular succession of stages, or progression to a supreme goal. *The Evolution of a Manufacturing System at Toyota* follows none of these specific interpretations. (For those interested in comparison of evolutionary theories, see appendix A.) This book adopts a broader definition of an evolutionary framework.

The prevalent paradigm in biology theorizes that *variation* (mutation as random changes of genetic information or DNA), *selection* (natural selection caused mostly by different propagation rates), and *retention* (reproduction of genetic DNA information in and across individuals) jointly create changes and diversification of genetic information, which then materialize in living systems through adaptation to changing environments. Among the three aspects, the selection force by external environments is particularly emphasized in this paradigm. The present book also adopts this generic scheme of variation-selection-retention.[22] In order to analyze manufacturing systems, however, I decided not to follow all the specific assumptions of the biological model. For instance, I don't explain a system's variation as a purely random process; I describe it as multi-path system emergence. In this sense, the evolutionary perspective here is rather Lamarckian, in that it recognizes an individual firm's ability to learn or adapt its routines to the environment nonrandomly, although imperfectly.

The present framework also assumes a lenient selection environment because relatively weak organizations, with lower competitive performance, can still survive, at least for a certain "moratorium" during which time they may change their routines. That way, it's possible to observe significant cross-organizational differences in performance at a certain point in time. In addition, selection mechanisms inside an organization may pre-screen the manufacturing routines that have the highest probability of surviving in the external business environment—what Robert Burgelman calls "intraorganizational ecological process."[23]

Finally, I assume only an incomplete mechanism for retention and duplication of organizational knowledge or information in a social system, unlike the relatively strict mechanism of gene or DNA duplication in living systems. To the extent that organizational routines and memories can erode quickly, an organization that evolves would require a reasonably reliable mechanism for knowledge retention, including bureaucratic documentation and work standardization.

Those readers who conceive of the evolutionary model based strictly on the neo-Darwinian concept in biology may find the above framework too broad to be called evolutionary. However, I would argue that, in order to fully exploit the rich insights from evolutionary thinking for a social system analysis, the definition of the evolutionary framework in general should be broad enough to be free from specific assumptions of neo-Darwinism (see appendix A). Although straightforward neo-Darwinian models may be applicable to certain types of business-economic studies, it is not applicable to the dynamic analysis of Toyota-style manufacturing. Thus, the present conceptual framework is meant to be evolutionary in a broad sense, but strictly speaking, it is *not* neo-Darwinian.

Note that this framework also differs from some other versions of evolutionary analyses. Clearly, I'm not advocating a crude social Darwinism that could be used to justify elimination of the "weak." I also don't assume system evolution causes constant progression toward something inherently valuable (so-called progressivism). From my perspective, what the evolutionary process tends to bring about is not progress but simply adaptation to environmental requirements, whatever they may be. As for a linear stage model, while I agree it's often possible to identify distinctive stages of a manufacturing system after the fact, I don't assume such a predetermined sequence. I don't claim that system changes are always incremental, either—that is, evolutionary rather than revolutionary—although I do emphasize the cumulative aspects of system change in the present empirical analysis.

Information and the Total System

The second key to understanding Toyota's consistently high performance is a total system perspective of manufacturing routines. Here information is central for at least two reasons: first, the notion of organizational routines as informational patterns—something like the gene as a unit of DNA "information"—is a logical consequence of evolutionary thinking; second, information is the common element that flows through the product development, production, and supplier systems.

Information is broadly defined here as intangible patterns of materials or energy that represent some other events or objects, rather than tangible objects themselves.[24] By this definition, knowledge, as well as skills, is also regarded as a kind of human-embodied information asset. In the present framework, the information that runs through a manufacturing system is considered *value-carrying information*, meaning that it is expected to attract and satisfy customers when embodied in the product and delivered to them.[25] In this context, a manufacturing routine is nothing but a stable pattern of information flow and asset embedded in a manufacturing system.

Take, for example, a successful product like the Toyota Camry. When a customer buys this car and uses it every day, what he or she consumes is essentially a bundle of information delivered through the car rather than the car as a physical entity. Each time the customer drives it, he or she is aware of the Camry's style, visibility from the cabin, feel of the seat, sound of the engine, feel of acceleration, road noise, squeaks and rattles of the dashboard, and so on. The customer also remembers the price paid for the car, how economically it oper-

ates, its breakdowns and repairs, praise of the car by friends, even re-
actions of people on the street. Therefore, he or she continuously interprets and reinterprets all these informational inputs, which translate into overall customer satisfaction or dissatisfaction.

Now take a piece of value-carrying information: exterior body
styling. Good styling certainly satisfies the customer, other things
being equal. This piece of information is produced and reproduced
through press machines and in body and paint shops at, say, Toyota's
Georgetown plant in Kentucky. Suppose we observe a 4,000-ton transfer press machine producing fenders of the car every six seconds.
What we see is 0.8-millimeter steel sheets supplied one after another
to the machine, in which a series of press dies sandwich them and
mold them into fender panels of identical and predesigned shape.
One could regard this as a physical transformation of sheet steel—the
usual interpretation. In the information view of a manufacturing system, however, we interpret the same process as information transmission from the dies to the material. At each cycle of the press operation
the body-design information embodied in the dies is transferred to the
steel sheets; it is thereby duplicated and multiplied in the form of the
body panels, which are subsequently painted, assembled, and delivered to customers.

Starting from this press operation, we can trace back the stream of
value-carrying information. Behind the press dies, for example, we can
easily identify die-design information stored in the CAM (computer-
aided manufacturing) data file in the production engineering area.
The die-design information was made out of detailed body-design
information embodied in a CAD (computer-aided design) file. Now
we're in the middle of the product development process. By tracking
the information stream further back, we see that the body design information was created by scanning and refinement of a clay model,
which Toyota's modelers sculpted based on body-design information
provided by the company's exterior designers. Finally, even farther upstream, we reach the body information that originally emerged in the
mind of one of Toyota's designers. The journey of the value-carrying
information makes a full circle, starting from the future customer's experience and ending in the present customer's experience—which
then becomes a starting point for the next cycle.

Value-carrying information, then, goes beyond the boundary of the
manufacturing system and circulates between the producer (including its suppliers) and consumers. By looking at what producers and
consumers do from an information point of view, we can identify an
integrated system in which information circulates from development
to production to marketing to consumption and finally back to development, evolving as a complex natural system might—like the mete-
orological cycle of water evaporation and recirculation (see figure
1.2).[26]

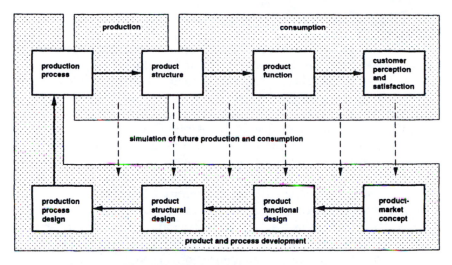

Source: Adopted and modified from Fujimoto (1989) and Clark and Fujimoto (1991).
Note: For visual simplicity environmental uncertainty, supplier systems and sales systems were omitted from the chart.
         ▭ = information asset   ◄──── = flow of value-carrying information

Figure 1.2 Product Development as Simulation and Search of Production and Consumption

This informational approach to manufacturing has broader theoretical implications in the fields of business and organizational research. In recent years, two contrasting views of information processing in organizations have appeared, one that emphasizes information creation, the other information transmission.[27] The information-transmission view (usually just called "information processing") focuses on how an organization transmits the necessary amount of information for executing defined tasks. On the other hand, the knowledge-creation view (or "information creation" in this book) emphasizes how information is created through human thought processes. As Ikujiro Nonaka has said, "creating information is synonymous with creating meaning."[28]

Information transmission and knowledge creation are often considered mutually exclusive viewpoints in the business literature. Yet from my perspective, both are important as far as an effective manufacturing system is concerned. A firm's efforts to satisfy customers are based on a combination of knowledge creation and information transmission. More to the competitive point, only companies that are effective in both aspects of information processing tend to be successful in the marketplace. For instance, without accurate and efficient information transmission from product design to process design—and eventually production on the shop floor—a great product idea would not bring about a great product; and without active knowledge creation in the organization—the continual process of creating meaning—the product's concept would not attract customers in the first place, even if it is precisely engineered and produced.

Indeed, a combined information-knowledge view of manufacturing can provide crucial insights about why the Toyota-style system has not only been difficult for others to imitate but also tough even to specify. Many researchers now believe the tacit nature of manufacturing knowledge makes such routines elusive. I fully agree with this observation, but tacit knowledge doesn't explain the whole story. After all, today's high-volume production systems, be they Ford's or Toyota's, are mostly articulated and standardized. This is the imperative for modern mass production, and Toyota is no exception.

In my view, routines are difficult to identify when they exist in the form of a complex network of intangible elements that encompass the entire manufacturing area, even if each element is not tacit itself. Outside observers have tended to focus on the functionality of individual practices and subsystems, or tangible factors in general, but they may be overlooking these broader and intangible flows of value-carrying information, which have to be consistently managed throughout the manufacturing process. Thus, the Toyota-style manufacturing system is neither a simple sum of individual techniques nor a mysterious whole.

Three Layers of Organizational Capabilities

Let's summarize the following historical phenomena. First, Toyota (as well as some other Japanese firms to a lesser extent) demonstrated significantly higher levels of manufacturing performance in the world auto industry by the 1980s. Second, high performers like Toyota improved faster and more consistently than other firms during an extended period prior to this time. Third, the high levels of performance and pace of continuous improvements appeared to stem from an overall manufacturing system rather than individual techniques or practices. Fourth, the Toyota-style system was not created all at once, but gradually and cumulatively evolved, mainly between the 1940s and 1980s, and is evolving even in the 1990s.

To analyze these basic facts, we need to focus on Toyota's organizational capabilities in manufacturing. However, it's not enough to examine routinized aspects of manufacturing capabilities at a given point in time. We can add Toyota's famous *kaizen* capabilities, a routinized ability for continuous improvements; but this is still not enough because we need to explain why Toyota could acquire such routines themselves.

Given that competitive performance and routine capabilities change over time, it makes sense to analyze manufacturing capabilities from an evolutionary point of view. Yet surprisingly, there have been few studies on the evolutionary aspects of organizational capabilities at Toyota

Table 1.1   Three Levels of Manufacturing Capability

	Basic Nature	Influence on	Interpretation
Routinized manufacturing capability	static & routine	level of competitive performance (in stable environments)	firm-specific pattern of the steady-state information system in terms of efficiency and accuracy of repetitive information transmission
Routinized learning capability	dynamic & routine	changes or recoveries of competitive performance	firm-specific ability of handling repetitive problem solving cycles or a routinized pattern of system changes
Evolutionary learning capability	dynamic & non-routine	changes in patterns of routine-capability	firm-specific ability of handling the sysytem emergence or the non-routine pattern of system changes in building the above routine capabilities

or the Japanese automakers in general. In order to fill in this missing piece, I propose the following three-layer model (see table 1.1):

1. *Routinized manufacturing capability.* A set of organizational routines that affect the level of manufacturing performance at a given time in a steady state of repetitive production, development, and transactions.
2. *Routinized learning capability.* A set of organizational routines that affect the pace of continuous or repetitive performance improvements, as well as recoveries from system disruptions or deterioration.
3. *Evolutionary learning capability.* A nonroutine ability that affects creation of the above routine capabilities themselves through irregular processes of multi-path system emergence.[29]

Although this kind of multilayer framework may not be new in the literature of strategic management and organizational learning, a three-layer approach to organizational capabilities in manufacturing enables us to highlight Toyota's ability to build competitive routines in a more or less nonroutine manner—a previously unexplored key to its success. Conceptually, again, my intention here is to connect detailed process analyses in the area of technology and operations management with previous evolutionary, as well as resource-capability-based, theories of the firm.[30]

Routinized Manufacturing Capability

The first layer of this framework refers to a stable pattern of productive resources, as well as their repetitive interactions, that creates firm-specific advantages in competitive performance.[31] If a factory operates with a consistently lower number of defective parts per million compared to its competitors, for instance, and if certain defect-preventing routines such as *poka-yoke, jidoka, andon,* and 5-S (see Appendix B) are implemented more thoroughly by this factory than by others, we can infer that this set of routines constitutes the factory's routinized manufacturing capability.[32] In an industry where repetitive production is more or less the dominant mode, a stable and relatively high level of manufacturing performance (when the task environment is also stable) means such organizational routines exist.

In addition, from an information point of view, this kind of manufacturing capability can be considered a pattern in a steady-state information system, one in which given product-related information is repetitively transmitted in a more effective, accurate, efficient, and/or flexible manner than that of the firm's competitors. For example, *poka-yoke, jidoka,* and so on are sets of routines that jointly enhance the accuracy of repetitive information transmission on the shop floor, through the production process to the products themselves. Thus, in a stable environment, where it is possible to ignore changes in market needs and internal system disruptions over time, a high level of manufacturing capability would, in theory, be a sufficient condition for a stable level of manufacturing performance.[33]

Routinized manufacturing capability can be defined for each dimension of competitive performance—factor productivity, throughput time, design quality, and so on. But a firm's ability to achieve consistently high performance in multiple dimensions at the same time may be even more important for its survival and growth. For example, as William Abernathy notes, some firms may improve productivity by sacrificing flexibility;[34] others may improve conformance quality while lowering productivity. When such tradeoffs between two dimensions are commonly observed in an industry, a firm that successfully reduces or eliminates such a dilemma may be able to outperform its competitors in both parameters at the same time. I examine the overall manufacturing capabilities of effective Japanese firms such as Toyota in chapter 4.[35]

Routinized Learning Capability

This second layer refers to a firm's distinctive ability to change the manufacturing system in a frequent and regular manner to improve functionality. Frequent incremental changes of a firm's products or processes, which allow it to compete more effectively, imply that it has a certain routinized learning capability. And when a manufacturing company wrestles with many deteriorations or disruptions of its products and processes—yet recovers from these problems more effectively and speedily than its competitors—it's clear such a company has this capability.

Information-wise, a routinized learning capability is a set of organizational routines for repetitively modifying a firm's information assets for better adaptation in a dynamic environment, one in which product obsolescence and disruptions of production processes are common. Suppose that defect rates at one factory, measured by parts per million, are decreasing continually and at a higher rate than at rivals over an extended period, and that there's also evidence this factory installed and implemented TQC (total quality control) and TPM (total productive maintenance) programs more effectively than others over the same period. We can infer that this manufacturing firm has a routinized learning capability.

Routinized learning capability may also be regarded as a firm-specific ability to perform organizational problem-solving cycles more effectively than competitors. In the context of a manufacturing system, a standard problem-solving cycle refers to a heuristic routine that converts problem information (input) into solution information (output). The heuristics of problem solving is discussed in more detail in chapter 4. But in a broad sense, a firm's routinized learning capability consists of the following linked organizational routines:[36]

- *Routines for problem identification.* Stable practices that reveal and help visualize problems, diffuse problem information to problem solvers, and keep individuals conscious of problems.
- *Routines for problem solving.* The ability to search, simulate, and evaluate alternatives; to coordinate knowledge, skills, responsibility, and authority for solving problems; and to diffuse such tools throughout an organization.
- *Routines for solution retention.* The ability to formalize and institutionalize new solutions in standard operating procedures, thereby providing stability for individuals who internalize the solutions.[37]

In an industry where repetitive production of multiple products is common—such as in automobile manufacturing—a firm's routinized learning capabilities can be observed in at least two areas. First, continuous process improvements occur on the factory shop floor. Say, a Toyota group parts supplier has a factory at which just-in-time and visual management are thoroughly implemented so that workers and supervisors can easily find defects in the production process. At the same factory, workers, supervisors, and engineers consistently follow standard steps for incremental improvements (sometimes called the quality control story)—from problem definition to root cause analysis, to shop floor experiments for evaluating alternatives, to decentralized selection and implementation of the revised procedure, to standardization and use of countermeasures to make sure they don't go back to the old way. The company may have a standard format of *kaizen* report sheets and common statistical tools for shop floor workers to apply to their cases step by step, following this sequence.

Second, product development involves repetitive improvements of design quality and product mix. In fact, the product development stages—concept generation, product planning, product engineering, and process engineering—form an interconnected bundle of distinctive problem-solving cycles.[38] At the product engineering stage, for example, informational outputs from product planning, such as product specifications, styling, and layout, become its goals (goal setting); product designs are then developed (alternative idea generation); prototypes are constructed according to the designs (model building); they are tested in proving grounds and laboratories (experiment); and the cycles are iterated until a satisfactory result is achieved, when the final engineering drawings are chosen as a solution (selection).

One could argue that the reality of shop floor management and product development is much more complicated, ill-structured, and less streamlined than what a standard model of linear problem-solving cycles assumes.[39] For explaining the routinized learning capability, however, the standard problem-solving routine remains relevant. Although the linear model may not reflect the actual messiness of the shop floor, an organization that imposes a routinized problem-solving scheme on this confusing reality is still likely to improve its performance faster than organizations that have not established such routines. In other words, a firm with a consistent problem-solving routine throughout the organization is likely to achieve better results in terms of continuous improvement.[40]

Evolutionary Learning Capability

The third layer of this framework is not so easy to observe in the everyday workings of a company. The evolutionary learning capability may be regarded as a certain dynamic capability for capability building, but it is not a routine itself.[41] Therefore, routinized learning capability and evolutionary learning capability, while both dynamic, should be distinguished from each other. The former deals with repetitive or regular patterns of system changes, whereas the latter is related to higher order system changes that themselves are rather irregular and infrequent, and are often connected with rare, episodic, and unique historical events.[42] Routinized learning may turn out to be the path that the organization takes for the next system change, but evolutionary learners on the spot do not even know in advance if this route is open to them. In other words, the evolutionary learning capability is *a firm-specific ability to cope with a complex historical process of capability building—or multi-path system emergence—*that is neither totally controllable nor predictable.

As is discussed in much more detail in the next chapter, the overall Toyota-style manufacturing system evolved over the course of several decades; it is a cumulative result of individual capability building. Unlike the cases of continuous process improvements and product development outlined above, it's hard to find a commonality among these events in terms of patterns and timing. That's because such an evolutionary process is based on a complex network of events that contain random chances, rational decisions, simple responses to environmental constraints, unintended successful trials, unsuccessful trials, and so on.

A firm with superior evolutionary learning capability, like Toyota, is able to manage the system emergence process of routine capability building better than its competitors.[43] As such, this is a nonroutine, dynamic capability embedded in the organization. But what are the organizational processes, structures, and cultures behind this elusive concept? As a start for answering this complicated question, let me compare evolutionary learning with related concepts like problem solving and organizational learning.

While the process of system emergence does include the standard problem-solving cycles discussed above, problem-solving heuristics don't always explain system emergence and a firm's evolutionary learning capability. The regular sequence of problem identification, solution, and retention may not exist; in many cases, trials of solutions precede problem recognition, as James March and Johan Olsen point out in relation to their "garbage can model."[44] As with Toyota's increasing reliance on suppliers in the 1960s, solutions to certain noncompetitive problems may subsequently and inadvertently become solutions for competitive problems.

Evolutionary learning is also connected to organizational learning, but the former covers more ground.[45] Generally speaking, when an organization learns, it changes its routines to adapt better to the environment and/or revises its shared knowledge about the relationship between the routines and their effects.[46] Much has been written about organizational learning itself, but most theorists have assumed implicitly regular patterns of learning (problem-solving routines), repetitions (learning by doing), or overt intention to learn (planned searches for alternative courses of action). Evolutionary learning capability often involves more than these processes; it implies an ability to acquire effective routines *through any path*, even if it is hard to predict which types of learning opportunities will emerge and when. These opportunities may include learning from preexisting theories, others' routines, or planned experimentation.[47] But they may also include learning from the unintended consequences of an organization's own actions—even if the organization later explains what happened in different terms, converting luck into "competence."

The point is, evolutionary learners simultaneously activate two different modes of learning: intentional and opportunistic. That means that evolutionary learning capability has two components:

- *Intentional Learning Capability.* A firm is able to search alternative organizational routines more effectively than competitors in advance of actual trials or establishment of routines. This may include calculating potentially effective trials rationally or using an entrepreneur's intuitive ability to envision effective trials. In any case, creation of causal knowledge precedes routinization.

- *Opportunistic (i.e., ex-post) Learning Capability.* What if a new routine was created for a noncompetitive reason but turns out to increase competitive performance? A firm with an ability to reinterpret past trials or existing routines can still create specific advantages for itself because it grasps the competitive consequences of such emergent routines, shapes a routine to exploit its full potential, and then institutionalizes and retains the routine more effectively than its rivals. Thus, routinization precedes competitive insights in this mode.

Even when competing companies do not differ in intentional learning capability, one firm may still be able to outperform others by possessing better opportunistic learning capability. In fact, the historical evidence presented in this book indicates that opportunistic (ex-post) learning explains a significant part of the evolution of the Toyota-style manufacturing system. One of the objectives of *The Evolution of a Manufacturing System at Toyota* is to explain how such a highly competitive system was developed through a process that was not necessarily driven by rational intention to gain competitive advantages.

I do not deny that social systems are changed mostly by intentional human actions; at the same time, I disagree with purely teleological explanations in which intentional actions always appear to result in intended consequences. An evolutionary perspective recognizes that rational behavior (described by either the "perfect rationalism" of neoclassical economics or the "bounded rationalism" of Herbert Simon[48]) may create organizational changes, but such an approach in a complex system represents only one of many possible paths.

Based on years of empirical research in the world's automobile industry, I conclude that a wide variety of performance outcomes and practices exist at different firms, and that these systems have changed in mostly nonroutine ways over time. Thus, I believe an evolutionary framework substantially adds to our understanding of why certain manufacturing practices have emerged at Toyota. A company's decision makers should certainly attempt to solve problems rationally, but they shouldn't assume that rational plans always solve those problems. The actual process of system change is essentially emergent. And no matter how successful a company has been, it needs to develop an organizational culture of "preparedness." It must convert both the intended and the unintended consequences of its actions, the lucky breaks and the well-laid plans, the temporary successes and the failures, into long-term competitive routines. A company with an evolutionary learning capability is constantly and deliberately searching for more competitive routines; but it is also well prepared for reinterpreting, refining, and institutionalizing those routines that have become established for whatever reasons. After all, Fortune favors the prepared organizational mind.[49]

How This Book Is Organized

The research presented in *The Evolution of a Manufacturing System at Toyota* focuses on the manufacturing-oriented organizational capabilities of successful Japanese automakers during the 1980s, mainly at Toyota; I explain how these capabilities contributed to their competitive advantages and analyze how they evolved over time. My data include first-hand materials collected through field research at Toyota and other firms; original questionnaire surveys; intracompany documents; second-hand materials from academic literature, publicly available statistics, and official company histories; and international comparative data wherever relevant. For simplicity of discussion, I focus only on the single-product situation, as opposed to a multiproduct or multibusiness setting.

The book has two main parts. Part I contains this introduction as well as three chapters that present Toyota's history and a more detailed explanation of my conceptual framework. Chapters 2 and 3, "System Emergence at Toyota: History" and "System Emergence at Toyota: Reinterpretation," extend the discussion of system emergence and evolutionary learning capability. Here I relate Toyota's history as a company and the long-term evolution of its overall manufacturing system; I also present some specific cases of system emergence, such as just-in-time operations (JIT), multitasking with product-focused layout, *jidoka* and flexible equipment, *kaizen* and total quality control (TQC), the black box parts system, and the "heavyweight" product manager system.

Chapter 4, "The Anatomy of Manufacturing Routines: An Information View," returns to the routinized manufacturing and learning capabilities of high-performing Japanese firms during the 1980s—that is, the routine aspects of the Toyota-style production and product development systems. Since a firm's manufacturing and routinized learning capabilities are often complementary, it's difficult to analyze these layers separately in the real world; the two capabilities are often intertwined in an inseparable system, which is why I examine them together here. In addition, this chapter reinterprets key concepts of the resource capability framework in more detail. Core elements of manufacturing systems of effective Japanese automakers will be reframed in terms of information.

Part II of the book focuses on specific cases of evolution by detailing three major subsystems of the overall Toyota-style manufacturing system: production, product development, and supplier systems (or purchasing). In chapters 5 through 7, I have collected and analyzed more original data from Toyota, as well as from other auto and auto parts manufacturers.

Chapter 5, "Evolution of the Black Box Parts Supplier System," explores the functions, origins, and formation of this purchasing system made famous in Japan, in which parts suppliers are involved in the product development processes of car makers. Chapter 6, "Evolution of Product Development Routines," pays special attention to the mechanism of overbuilding capabilities by analyzing a recent phenomenon called "fat design" among the Japanese automakers. Chapter 7, "Evolution of Toyota's New Assembly System," revisits the question of what constitutes Toyota's evolutionary capability, this time detailing a new assembly system developed in the 1990s.

The Evolution of a Manufacturing System at Toyota closes with chapter 8, "Toyota as a 'Prepared' Organization," and two appendices. Appendix A, "The Evolutionary Framework," further investigates some theoretical issues raised by the evolutionary framework adopted in this book. Appendix B, "The Basics of Toyota-Style Manufacturing," acquaints readers who may be unfamiliar with the basic elements and facts of the Toyota-style system—production practices such as JIT, TQC, and continuous improvements, as well as supplier management routines—with each element and discusses its overall performance.

Simultaneously describing how a manufacturing system was formed (its genetic logic), detailing what constitutes its current operational routines (its structure), and explaining how it has realized competitive advantages, and thereby survived over time (its functional logic) is a complex agenda. I don't claim to have all the answers, since one can generalize only so much from a single company. That said, I believe that focusing on a specific firm like Toyota Motor Corporation, which has survived and thrived, can yield rich insights for those interested in this company, in the automobile industry, or in the long-term success of any manufacturing firm.

2

SYSTEM EMERGENCE AT TOYOTA
History

Chapters 2 and 3 analyze the historical aspects of the Japanese automobile manufacturing system as an evolutionary process (see figure 2.1). The main purpose of this analysis is to demonstrate that Toyota's manufacturing capability building process can be described as *multi-path system emergence*, and thereby to highlight the top layer of Toyota's distinctive competence—its *evolutionary learning capability*. The present chapter describes a brief history of the Toyota-style manufacturing system, and the next chapter reinterprets it from the system emergence point of view.

This is a rather challenging task. On the one hand, we have to understand the overall mechanisms of total system evolution; on the other, we need to get into details, examine the genetic processes of major components, and confirm that system emergence is happening at detailed operational levels. We need to explain this complex and elusive phenomenon comprehensively.

That's why these two chapters proceed step by step. In step 1 of chapter 2, I give a brief history of the Japanese automobile industry and the Toyota-style manufacturing system. The purpose is merely to sketch the overall historical process roughly chronologically, without further analysis. In step 2, I extract certain key themes or concepts from this historical description to present the overall picture of system emergence, but I do not yet do any systematic investigation.

In chapter 3, I reinterpret the historical facts from the point of view of multi-path system emergence and evolutionary learning capability. Thus in step 3, I focus on the details of the manufacturing system, presenting some discrete examples of its subsystems' evolution. This section is meant to be the central part of chapter 3, and demonstrates the diversity of evolutionary paths for each of the system's core subsys-

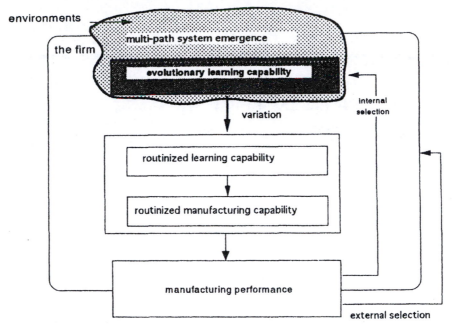

Figure 2.1 System Emergence: The Focus of Chapters 2 and 3

tems. Finally, in step 4, I make a more systematic analysis by applying the framework presented in chapter 1 and thereby confirming the emergent nature of the Toyota-style system's evolution.

My historical analysis in chapters 2 and 3, as well as other chapters, is based on data and materials that I collected on various occasions between the early 1980s and the mid-1990s, including interviews with some key figures behind the Toyota-style manufacturing system: Taiichi Ohno (known as the architect of the so-called Toyota production system), Masao Nemoto (one of the initial leaders of total quality control at Toyota), Kaneyoshi Kusunoki (one of Ohno's first disciples after the 1970s, who initiated efforts for systematic explanation of the Toyota production system), as well as dozens of other executives and managers in Toyota's production, production engineering, product development, purchasing, and human resource management divisions.[1] The study is based also on official company histories, internal documents, memos, and operating procedures that I collected, as well as secondary data including newspapers, periodicals, statistics, academic books and papers, and so on.

It is important to note here that what this chapter tries to accomplish is not purely historical research, but a genetic analysis as part of the evolutionary framework. That is, the ultimate purpose is not to describe precisely the historical events and their consequences per se (which has already been done by many historians in the past), but to explain how the patterns of organizational routines and their performance observed at a certain subsequent period (e.g., Toyota's manufacturing practices in the 1980s) were created historically. Such a genetic analysis tends to start from a present-time phenomenon and go backward, searching for its evolutionary paths and origins.

In this regard, let me emphasize three "stylized" facts that empirical researchers have generally observed regarding manufacturing performance and capabilities of automobile firms from the 1980s to the early 1990s:[2]

1. *Regional specificity (Japan effect).* During the 1980s, Japanese automakers tended to cluster in terms of competitive performance and practices and on average outperformed U.S. and European firms.[3]
2. *Individual firm specificity (Toyota effect).* Despite the regional effect, there were significant differences in performance and practices among the Japanese automakers. Toyota tended to outperform other Japanese firms in many competitive indicators. Thus, region-specific patterns and firm-specific patterns in production and development capabilities and performance coexisted during the 1980s.[4]
3. *Universality (Ford effect).* Some aspects of manufacturing were generic, or common to automobile mass producers worldwide, in that they all introduced elements of the standard Ford system, directly or indirectly. It is a myth that the Toyota system is a unique antithesis of Ford system.

The main question in this chapter is how such region-specific or firm-specific routine capabilities were acquired by certain firms over time. Take the Toyota-style manufacturing system. Was it created all at once by visionary system creators such as Sakichi Toyoda (inventor of Toyoda-style looms and founder of Toyoda Automatic Loom), Kiichiro Toyoda (founder of Toyota Motor Corporation), or Taiichi Ohno? Or was it gradually created as various elements were cumulatively incorporated into the system? Was the system created by a series of rational decisions based on deliberate planning? Or was the company simply lucky to build its capability? Was the company's capability limited by certain uncontrollable factors? Was the Toyota-style system an imitation of forerunners such as the Ford system? Or is it a unique system created by taking a totally different path?

Step 1: A Brief History of Toyota-style Automobile Manufacturing

As the first step, let us outline the history of Japanese automobile manufacturing. Since there are already many books and articles on the his-

tory of the Japanese automobile industry, this history is limited to issues related to subsequent analyses of system emergence.[5]

The Pre–World War II History of Automobile Manufacturing

Although production of four-wheel automobiles in Japan started
around 1910, early work was nothing but sporadic trials by small venture business owners, inventor-engineers, or mechanics. Customers
were mostly limited to a small number of wealthy upper-class people
with curiosity. By 1925, cumulative production not having exceeded
several hundred units, manufacturing virtually remained in the prototype production stage. None of the automobile venture businesses
established during this period are directly connected to today's major
automakers (see figure 2.2)

Knock-down assembly of foreign automobiles, as well as imports of
complete vehicles (mainly European makes), existed by 1920, but the
number of cars produced was extremely small. The Japanese government tried to protect the domestic automobile industry with the Military Subsidies Act of 1918, but before 1925 the actual number of
trucks produced never exceeded 100 per year. Clearly, any influence
of the American mass-production system on the Japanese market was
negligible during this early period.

Japan's automobile market, beyond attracting the curious, formed
in the early 1920s, particularly after the major earthquake of 1923 de-
stroyed trolleys and railways in Tokyo. In response to the breakdown
in its public transportation system, the Tokyo municipal authority decided to import about 800 chassis of the Ford Model T for bus use,
which demonstrated the effectiveness of automobiles as an alternative
transportation mode. Prior to the war, however, the domestic market
continued to be relatively small, with annual sales peaking at only
about 50,000 units, mainly trucks (see table 2-1).

Dominance by U.S. Automakers.   The first significant attempts at automobile production in Japan were knock-down (KD) assembly operations, mostly between the mid-1920s and the mid-1930s, mainly by
Ford and General Motors (GM).

Ford's original plan in eastern Asia was to build a KD plant in
China, which Ford had regarded as a more promising market than
Japan. Because the demand for automobiles expanded quickly after
the 1923 earthquake, particularly for imports from America, which
tended to have shorter delivery times than European vehicles, Ford
decided to establish Ford of Japan in 1925, a wholly owned subsidiary, and to build a KD assembly plant in Yokohama. Although it
was a small and temporary plant from Ford's point of view, it was
equipped with chassis and body conveyer lines, was unusually large,
and thus was a threat to the domestic industry.

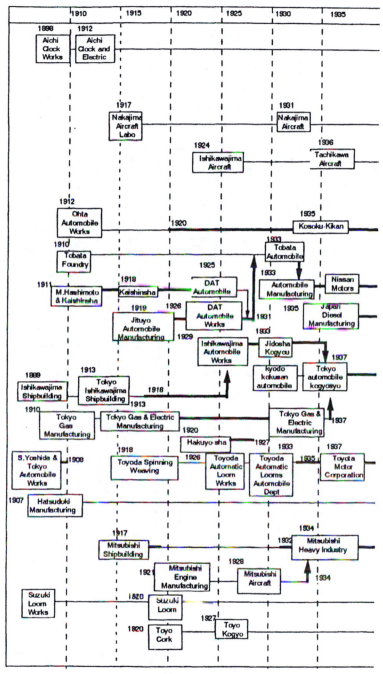

Source: Nikkan Jidosha Shinbun-sha (1996). Modified and translated by the Author.

Note: ▬▬▬ The period when four wheel vehicles were produced.

_____ The period when two wheel, or three wheel vehicle businessed,
or other businesses were conducted.

Figure 2.2 Evolution of Japanese Auto Firms

29

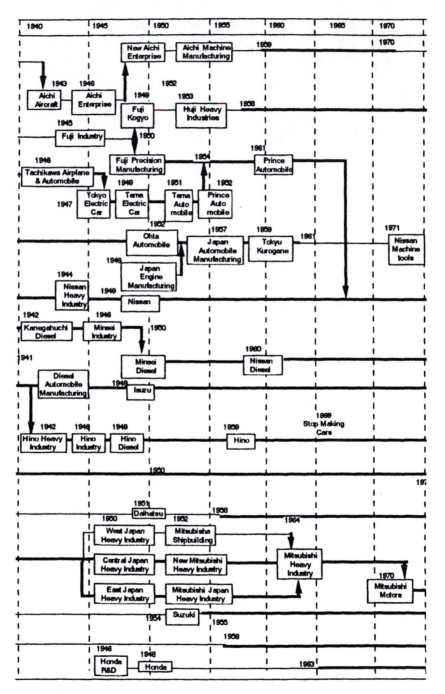

Figure 2.2 (continued)

30

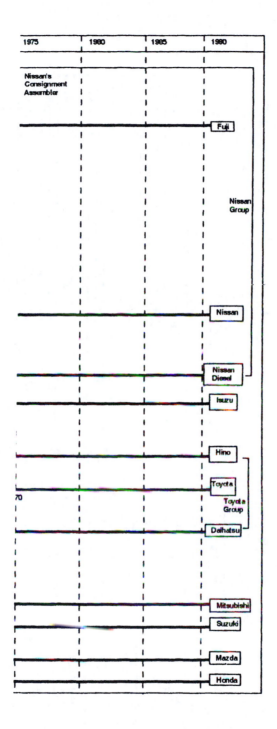

Table 2.1   Selected Statistics

category	vehicle population: passenger cars	vehicle population: commercial vehicles	vehicle population: total	domestic production: four wheel passenger c.	domestic production: four wheel commercial v.	domestic production: total	three wheelers	total (3wlr incl.)	total (only 4 wlr)	knock down (excl.)	Domestic Sales (4 Wheelers): passenger cars	Domestic Sales: commercial vehicles	Domestic Sales: total	Imports: passenger cars	Imports: commercial vehicles	Imports: total	Exports: passenger cars	Exports: commercial vehicles	Exports: total	vehicle popul. per car
1920	9355	644	9999							0				1745		1745				
1921	11228	888	12116							0				1074		1074				
1922	13483	1383	14866							0				752		752				
1923	10666	2099	12765							0				1938		1938				
1924	17939	6394	24333							0				4063		4063				
1925	21002	8162	29164			245		245	245	3437				5202		5202	1765		1765	
1926	27973	12097	40070			302		302	302	8877				11303		11303	2361		2361	
1927	35775	15987	51762			347		347	347	12668				16665		16665	3895		3895	
1928	44660	21719	66379			437		437	437	24341				32571		32571	7883		7883	
1929	52829	27541	80370			458		458	458	29338				34793		34793	5018		5018	
1930	57827	30881	88708	458		458	300	758	458	19878				22727		22727	2591		2591	
1931	41193	56063	97256	436		436	552	988	436	20199				22522		22522	1867		1867	
1932	41457	58784	100221	880		880	1511	2391	880	14087				15964		15964	997		997	
1933	41911	63021	104932	1681		1681	2372	4053	1681	15082				17254		17254	491		491	
1934	44153	68388	112541	2787		2787	3438	6225	2787	33458				37141		37141	895		895	
1935	45580	75346	120926	5089		5089	10358	15447	5089	30787				36810		36810	934		934	
1936	46165	80083	126248	12086	100	12186	12840	25026	12186	31058				44361		44361	1117		1117	
1937	51396	77339	128735	16988	1067	18055	15236	33291	18055	31839				50994		50994	1100		1100	
1938	47866	79087	127053	22538	1850	24388	10685	35073	24388	18093				42981		42981	500		500	
1939	42115	77642	119757	34020	494	34514	8194	42708	34514	0				34514		34514	0		0	
1940	39920	82911	122831	44562	1479	46041	8252	54293	46041											
1941	37374	76228	113602	45502	996	46498	4666	51164	46498											
1942	28043	78063	106106	36499	689	37188	3821	41009	37188											
1943	25030	78366	103396	25646	233	25879	2259	28138	25879											
1944	22350	72275	94625	21743	19	21762	1338	23100	21762											
1945	18113	72668	90781	8167		8167	420	8587	8167											
1946	20375	92111	112486	14921		14921	2692	17613	14921											0.27
1947	26340	123664	150004	11210	110	11320	7432	18752	11320											0.34
1948	30273	150431	180704	19986	381	20367	16852	37219	20367								8		8	0.38
1949	38265	168383	204648	27630	1070	28700	26727	55427	28700								469	13	482	0.44
1950	42588	182909	225497	30003	1594	31597	35498	67095	31597		1953	29554	31507				7	5502	5509	0.51
1951	57333	206817	264150	34879	3611	38490	43802	82292	38490		3812	32243	36055				0	6753	6753	0.68
1952	88354	234502	322856	34129	4837	38966	62224	101190	38966		5250	34147	39397				0	665	665	1.03
1953	114996	264958	379954	40989	8789	49778	97484	147262	49778		7998	38274	46272				1	1096	1097	1.32
1954	138518	296065	434583	55601	14472	70073	98081	168154	70073		12763	47775	60538	5311	1437	6748	1	987	988	1.57
1955	153325	317981	471306	48664	20268	68932	105409	174341	68932		20055	44475	64530	6684	2419	9103	2	1229	1231	1.72
1956	181024	372675	553699	79010	32056	111066	105409	216475	111066		30304	74886	105190	6179	540	6719	46	2401	2447	2.01
1957	218524	463672	682196	134856	47121	181977	107937	289914	181977		43535	116370	159905	5450	1252	6702	410	6144	6554	2.40
1958	259631	557676	817307	137660	50643	188303	98677	286980	188303		48420	117447	165867	5994	1117	7111	2357	7886	10243	2.63
1959	318758	690364	1009122	184216	78598	262814	158042	420856	262814		67040	160469	227509	3540	789	4329	4884	14401	19285	3.44
1960	457333	896193	1353526	316457	165094	481551	278032	759543	481551		145227	262953	408180	4310	866	5176	7013	31796	38809	4.90
1961	663951	1299604	1963555	564371	249508	813879	220595	1034474	813879		173307	317531	490838	5646	6582	12228	11531	45506	57037	7.04
1962	889032	1840272	2729304	721922	268784	990706	144187	1134873	990706		252269	673722	925991	9339	2725	12064	16011	50679	66690	9.34
1963	1233651	2528701	3762352	875701	407830	1283531	117190	1400721	1283531		371076	839442	1210518	12185	728	12913	31447	67117	98564	13
1964	1672159	3316091	4988450	1122815	579660	1702475	80048	1782523	1702475		493536	1000667	1494203	12881	467	13348	65665	84756	150421	17
1965	2181275	4118745	6300020	1178436	697178	1875614	42944	1918558	1875614		586267	1088075	1674342	15244	510	15754	100716	93452	194108	22
1966	2833246	5088126	7921372	1408743	877656	2286399	33364	2319763	2286399		740259	1319863	2060122	14352	519	14871	153090	102644	255734	29
1967	3636409	6192615	10029024	1770731	1375755	3146486	26453	3172939	3146486		1131337	1583434	2714771				223491	138754	302245	38

| 1968 |
| 1969 |
| 1970 |
| 1971 |
| 1972 |
| 1973 |
| 1974 |
| 1975 |
| 1976 |
| 1977 |
| 1978 |
| 1979 |
| 1980 |
| 1981 |
| 1982 |
| 1983 |
| 1984 |
| 1985 |
| 1986 |
| 1987 |
| 1988 |
| 1989 |
| 1990 |
| 1991 |
| 1992 |
| 1993 |
| 1994 |
| 1995 |
| 1996 |

Source: Japan Automobile Manufacturers Association, etc.

33

Similarly, General Motors established its Japanese subsidiary in 1927 and started KD assembly in Osaka. According to a brochure in 1935, the GM Osaka plant employed 900 people (700 in production) and assembled 50 vehicles per day at capacity (eight car models and four truck models).[6] Chrysler and other American models were also assembled by Japanese companies in smaller quantities.

Overall, American cars and trucks dominated the Japanese market · between 1925 and 1935. The peak year for KD plants was 1934, when about 33,000 knock-down kits, or about 92 percent of the total domestic demand, were imported and assembled (imports of chassis and complete vehicles was about 5 percent). The domestic brand occupied only 3 percent of the market, or about 1,000 units, in that same year. There were two main groups in the domestic sector: three Japanese companies (Kaishin-sha, Tokyo Gasu Denki Kogyo, and Tokyo Ishikawajima Zosensho) that were producing mid-size trucks under the Military Subsidiaries Act, and about twenty makers of three-wheelers. Both groups deliberately avoided direct competition with the American subsidiaries, which were mostly making 1- to 1.5-ton trucks.

In the mid-1930s, motivated by its strong market position, Ford planned to build a new and much larger plant in Japan. Thus, the direct transfer of the Ford system by the American automakers was about to take place.[7]

The Protectionist Policy and Japanese Firms.   The situation changed in 1936, when the Japanese government, under the military authority's influence, launched a protectionist policy called the Automobile Manufacturing Enterprise Law. It essentially prevented the operation of foreign automakers in Japan, and shut down the U.S. automobile assembly by the end of the 1930s. Generally speaking, the prewar industrial policies, focusing on protection of domestic truck producers, were motivated largely by this sector's potential for and actual contribution to military purposes.

The same law subsidized three licensed domestic companies for producing trucks (see figure 2.2): Toyota (founded as Toyota Motor Co., Ltd. in 1937), Nissan (founded in 1933 as a result of a merger, renamed Nissan Motors Co. Ltd. in 1934), and Isuzu (founded as Tokyo Jidosha Kogyosho in 1937 after a series of mergers, renamed Isuzu Motors Ltd. in 1949). These Japanese firms started truck production; Toyota and Nissan virtually took over the domestic market, filling the gap created by the U.S. makers' exit. (Isuzu specialized military trucks with a relatively small production volume.) In this way, the direct transfer of the Ford production system was abruptly stopped.

Although small and medium-size enterprises that produced mainly three-wheel vehicles did exist, Toyota and Nissan—the truck producers licensed by the 1936 law—were the only significant domestic manufacturers during the prewar period. In other words, after 1936, the main adopter of the Ford system in Japan changed from the American subsidiaries to the two main Japanese makers. The Ford system (narrowly defined as a production concept) refers to a mass-production system, established by the Ford Motor Company under Henry Ford's leadership, that features large-volume production of identical products or components, interchangeable parts, special-purpose machines, moving assembly lines, and so on.[8]

Although both companies directly and indirectly applied the American production and manufacturing technology, their adoption of the Ford system had to be selective, taking the limits of the domestic market and existing production systems into account. Annual domestic production by those firms just before World War II was about 30,000 units, compared to roughly 5 million units in the U.S. at the same time.

Besides, these Japanese companies generally lacked sufficient technological and financial resources to carry out internationally competitive automobile production, despite the fact that Toyota and Nissan belonged to local or new *zaibatsu* (financial clique), respectively. For example, the Toyota and Nissan products were constantly criticized by the military authority, a major vehicle user in those days, for their relatively poor durability and reliability.[9] Toyota's prewar productivity was estimated to be roughly one-tenth that of the Ford Motor Company.

The Origin of Toyota's Automobile Business.   Toyota Motor Co., Ltd., a spinoff automobile producer of Toyoda Automatic Loom Works, Ltd., was established in 1937, but its project for entering the automobile business had started in the early 1930s, at the parent company.[10] Toyota's original project, led by Kiichiro Toyoda of Toyoda Automatic Loom (son of Sakichi Toyoda, inventor-founder of the Toyota group), was to develop passenger cars, although it quickly switched to truck production after it learned of the government's plan for sector regulation. However, Kiichiro's ultimate vision throughout the 1930s and '40s was to build passenger cars.

Kiichiro Toyoda started engine research and prototyping in a small corner of its facility around 1931, five years before the protectionist policy was launched. Ford and GM were still dominating the domestic automobile market at that time. Kiichiro started with reverse engineering (tear-down and sketches of components) of the Smith motor, a small engine commonly used for motor cycles and three-wheelers, and completed a 4 horsepower prototype engine. His initial business plan was to develop an automobile that would directly compete with some major models of the U.S. firms in those days. When U.S. firms were enjoying an overwhelming market share in Japan, this was quite an ambitious goal.

After getting top management approval to start the Automobile Division of Toyoda Automatic Loom, Kiichiro and some of his staff ordered from Germany and the United States the machine tools for building a prototype, purchased a Chevrolet car, reverse-engineered it, sketched the decomposed parts, and estimated the materials used. Thus, Toyoda decided to design the first prototype by combining elements of the Chevrolet engine that had been regarded as fuel efficient with the Ford chassis, which was robust enough for Japan's bumpy roads.

In 1934, Toyoda started building a pilot plant in the city of Kariya, in Aichi prefecture. As it could not find appropriate suppliers of special steel, Toyoda built its own steel mill next to the prototype shop, imported an electric furnace from the United States, and invited American engineers to assist its operation. At the same time, Kiichiro told his staff to go to the United States, purchase machine tools for commercial production, and learn the American mass-production system by visiting selected factories for half a year. After considerable trial and error, the first prototype engine was completed in the fall of 1934. As for the body, Kiichiro decided to adopt a streamlined design contemporary for that time. As with the engine, Toyoda bought Chrysler and Chevrolet cars, disassembled them, sketched the body components, made life-size drawings and gauges, and built prototype bodies, mostly by hand. The company invited some craftsmen from outside repair shops, from whom Toyoda's technicians learned how to make bodies by hand. Genuine parts from Ford and other American makers were used for most of the prototype's chassis and gear parts. In May 1935, about one year after starting the body prototyping, Toyoda completed the first of several prototypes of the A1 model, a five-passenger sedan with a 3400 cc engine.

While its initial attempts were more or less imitation and a patchwork of American automobile technologies, in both product and process, Toyoda was an active receiver of the technologies in combining them and adapting them to Japanese conditions. Kiichiro did not try to introduce the Ford system directly, but did apply its elements selectively to Japan (small market, bad roads, etc.), in both product and process technology.

Toyoda's Kariya assembly plant was completed in 1936. Its capacity (150 units per month) was quite small by American standards. Kiichiro's goal was to match Toyoda's unit cost of producing 20,000 to 30,000 units per year with that of American models' producing several hundred thousand units per year. Therefore, Toyoda modified the Ford production system for small-volume production. For example, in the production of body panels, it mixed the Ford-style mechanization of press machines with traditional manual work using hammers, in order to save fixed costs for tooling.

In 1937, Toyoda Automatic Loom separated its automobile division and established the Toyota Motor Co., Ltd. (hence called Toyota). In the same year, as production at the Kariya plant reached full capacity,

Kiichiro ordered construction of a much bigger assembly plant in Koromo (now located within the city of Toyota, in Aichi prefecture), completed in 1938. However, the planned size of the Koromo plant (2,000 units per month, 5,000 employees) was still much smaller than that of the average American factory. As a result, Toyota continued to select production technologies deliberately, considering the limited scale of production. (See chapter 3 for details on press and machining operations.)

Toyota also relied on foreign production equipment and parts in this initial stage. For the Koromo plant alone, Toyota imported over 500 machine tools from Germany and the United States. As the Japan-China war started in 1937, though, it became difficult to import special-purpose machines. Toyota then established its own machine tool shop at the Koromo plant and started making multispindle lathes, boring machines, small press machines, and so on. The tool shop became an independent company, Toyoda Machine Works, in 1941. Similarly, the cost of procuring foreign parts decreased to about 12 percent of unit manufacturing cost, or about one-fifth of parts procurement costs, by November 1936; but it was not until 1943 that Toyota's supplier organization, Kyoho-kai, was established.

While Toyota was trying to introduce the American mass-production system in its new Koromo plant, the traditional craft-type system persisted in some production processes, according to anecdotes by employees of those days.[11] A former worker in the machine shop recalls, "Many elements of craft production persisted, and craft skills were required in job shop environments. Workers machined a variety of parts, while sharpening their own cutting tools. Process flows were often disturbed, work-in-process inventories piled up, and lack of balance in machine utilization occurred."[12] An employee in the forging plant of the same period noted that "[t]here was a team of five workers for each hammer machine: one for heating, one for rough hammering, two for shaping, and one for finishing. One in the hammer was called *bo-shin*, who led the team as master and was responsible for production volume and quality. It was said that it would take three years to master heating and five years to master hammering. Craftsmanship of the forging workers was remarkable."[13]

It is difficult to assess accurately how such elements of the craft-type systems affected the subsequent evolution of the Toyota-style system. But as discussed later on, my interpretation of the historical materials of the 1930s to '50s is that, despite the strong influence of the Ford system (also Taylorism), the flexible nature of the early indigenous (craft-type) systems of those days carried over to the early Toyota production system.

Patterns of Technology Transfer: Toyota versus Nissan.   Although the two main automobile makers during the prewar era (also the postwar era), Toyota and Nissan, both adopted various elements of U.S. product and process technologies, the basic pattern of technology transfer differed between the two, however (see also Cusumano, 1985).

Nissan was oriented to bundled technology transfer, or adoption of the U.S. system as a package. The company's original plan was to make a formal coalition (tie-up) with Ford directly. Nissan was therefore rather reluctant to get a license under the new protectionist law, but decided hastily to participate in the arrangement after it found that Toyota had obtained one. Because Nissan was not well prepared to start the auto business without the American alliance, it had to rely heavily on imports of equipment, such as press machines, forging machines, and the entire engine machining line and the casting facility, from Graham Page, a small U.S. company that had abandoned its plan to produce trucks. Nissan also bought the right to manufacture a semi-cab-over truck model designed by Graham Page. Thus, Nissan tended to purchase packages of product and process technologies from small American companies.

By contrast, Toyota tended to rely on existing production technologies and mix them with unbundled technologies imported from America and Europe. In short, Toyota (including Toyoda Automatic Loom in the early stage) was more active than Nissan in absorbing unbundled American technologies and infusing them in its own production base, in which certain traditional craft-type production elements persisted.

A Postwar History of Japanese Automobile Manufacturing

Late 1940s—Recovery and Survival. The Japanese auto industry started producing trucks soon after the end of World War II, under supervision of the General Headquarters of the Allied Forces (GHQ).[14] For the first five years, the main Japanese automobile firms, such as Toyota, did not have financial capability, so they had to live with existing production equipment and models. Production of passenger cars was negligible. The industry-wide production volume didn't recover to its prewar peak. Toyota's productivity was estimated to be roughly one-tenth of the major U.S. makers, such as Ford. Kiichiro Toyoda was optimistic, however; in the fall of 1945, he set a target of reaching the productivity level of U.S. Ford within three years. This turned out to be unrealistic, but productivity at some of Toyota's shops did improve by several times by 1950 and by about ten times by 1955, according to Taiichi Ohno.[15] Incidentally, Toyota's vehicle per person productivity is estimated to have surpassed the average U.S. level by the 1960s (Cusumano, 1985, 1988).

Its financial capability being insufficient, Toyota had to attempt its productivity improvements without much hardware investment. That is, the company had to rely on "soft" and inexpensive measures. Typical examples included standardization of work designs (i.e., introduction of a certain Taylor system), as well as partial introduction of the Toyota production system, such as product-flow layout of machines, multitask job assignment (*takotei-mochi*), and levelization of production pace (*heijunka*). Using low-cost jigs for body assembly was also adopted. Such measures often deemphasized the existing craft-type system, and thus tended to trigger some resistance on the part of craftspeople, but it did not stop the change process. In this early period, the shift was made from an indigenous work system to a Taylor system, and the Toyota production system was partially introduced.

Through such measures in the late 1940s Toyota did increase its productivity rather dramatically without significant capital investment, but at the end of this period the company also piled up finished goods inventories owing to overproduction in the middle of a recession. Facing the threat of bankruptcy, Toyota fired a large fraction of its labor force, which triggered a long strike by the workers. It is also said that conflicts between craftsmen-foremen trying to preserve their traditional power on the shop floor and Toyota's managers introducing standardized production methods (e.g., Ohno) were behind this crisis.[16]

1950s—Laying the Foundation for Toyota-style Manufacturing.   The special orders for motor vehicles by the American Army Procurement Agency (APA) during the Korean War helped Toyota and other Japanese truck makers to recover from the recession. After the labor crisis of 1950, however, Toyota took a conservative policy regarding employment, keeping its number of workers stable so that labor productivity could naturally increase.

Significant investment in new production equipment also started in the early 1950s. In addition to the renewal of prewar machines, there was introduction of large press machines, continuous casting machines, automatic multispot welders, and moving conveyer lines. Development and adoption of Detroit-type transfer machines for engine machining followed in the late 1950s. The large-scale car assembly plants (typically 100,000 to 200,000 units per year) were not built until the very end of the 1950s, though. After all, with an annual output of about 500,000 units, Japan was still essentially a small truck-producing country.

Nevertheless, significant investments were made on the product side. In addition to new models of trucks, Toyota introduced the first passenger car model with a significant production volume, called the Crown, in the early 1950s. While most other major Japanese automakers (Nissan, Isuzu, Hino) at that time imported their passenger car designs through license agreements with European automobile manufacturers, Toyota decided to stick with its own product designs. (Other firms shifted to their own product designs by the 1960s.) In many cases, the early development and production of passenger cars was supported both financially and technologically by the truck business. At this time Toyota, for its development of the Crown, introduced the *shusa* system (or "heavyweight product manager" organization, according to the typology Kim Clark and I created), which appoints a strong project leader and product champion for each product.[17]

As for management techniques, the Japanese automakers continued to learn the U.S. techniques related to scientific management, including training within industry (TWI) and statistical quality control (SQC). The education of first-line supervisors for quality control and continuous improvements (*kaizen*) started also in the 1950s, following TWI. The *kanban* system (a production and inventory control system using returnable parts containers and instruction plates, each of which orders production and parts delivery to upstream stations according to the progress of downstream production units) was introduced in parts of Toyota factories by the late 1950s. On the other hand, neither systematic approaches of technical assistance to the parts suppliers nor company-wide quality management (TQC) had been effectively installed in the 1950s. The focus of supplier management is said to have been on solving problems in the quantity, delivery, and quality of parts.

1960s—Rapid Growth of Domestic Car Market.   Annual automobile production grew dramatically, from about 500,000 units in 1960 to 5 million in 1970. The major engine for this growth in the 1960s (the latter half in particular) was domestic demand: so-called motorization, or the explosive expansion of demand for family-owned passenger cars, which profoundly changed the automobile manufacturing system. (Exports were still roughly 1 million per year in 1970.) Productivity continued to increase rapidly.

After Toyota's first large-scale assembly factory, the Motomachi plant, was built in 1959, there was a rush of startups of large assembly plants. Indeed, over half of the Japanese assembly plants producing passenger cars as of 1990 (excluding consignment assembly plants by vehicle suppliers) started production between 1959 and 1969 (see table 2.2). The large scale of these plants enabled massive introduction of mechanization and automation in machining and metal forming, which resulted in a reduction in the number of the independent automobile manufacturers in Japan, but about ten car and truck manufacturers remained. Almost all of them have survived into the late 1990s, although some of them have been grouped into clusters around Toyota, Nissan, GM, and Ford mainly through minority shareholding.

The volume of passenger cars produced had surpassed that of commercial vehicles by the late 1960s, and Japan had transformed itself from a small truck-producing country to a major car-producing country by the end of the decade. In order to respond to this domestic mo-

Table 2.2   Startup Year of Japanese Passenger Car Plants

Company	Factory	Year	Remarks
Toyota	Motomachi	1959	Toyota's first high-volume pasenger car assembly plant.
Toyota	Takaoka	1966	
Toyota	Tsutsumi	1970	
Toyota	Tahara	1979	
Nissan	Oppama	1961	
Nissan	Zama	1965	Started as a truck plant. Closed in 1995.
Nissan	Tochigi	1968	
Nissan	Kyushu	1975	Started as a truck plant.
Nissan	Murayama	1962	Started as Prince's plant.
Mazda	Ujina	1966	
Mazda	Hofu	1982	
Mitsubishi	Oh-e	1946	
Mitsubishi	Mizushima	1946	
Mitsubishi	Okazaki	1977	
Honda	Suzuka	1960	
Honda	Sayama	1964	
Isuzu	Fujisawa	1962	Stopped car production in 1992.
Daihatsu	Ikeda	1962	
Daihatsu	Kyoto	1973	
Daihatsu	Shiga	1987	
Fuji	Ohta	1960	
Fuji	Yajima	1969	
Suzuki	Iwata	1967	
Suzuki	Kosei	1970	

Note: The year represents the start of the first assembly line where the plant has multiple assembly lines. Consignment assembly plants of vehicle suppliers (e.g., Kanto, Central, Toyota Auto Body, etc. for Toyota) are omitted.

Source: Nikkan Jidosha Shinbun-sha, *Jidosha Sangyo Handbook* [Automobile Industry handbook].

torization, automakers rapidly moved into offering a full line of products. For example, the number of Toyota's basic car platforms increased from two in 1960 to three in 1965 and to eight in 1970. This product proliferation meant that workloads rapidly increased, not only in production but also in product development. Besides, the four-year cycle for making major model changes, uniquely frequent in the world automobile market then, became prevalent among major Japanese passenger cars in the 1960s, which further heightened the product development workload.

Such workload pressures had a profound effect on the car makers' supplier management policies. In a word, outsourcing was expanded, in both production and product development. In production, major first-tier suppliers acquired subassembly capabilities and started to deliver larger modules of components. They also invested in special-purpose machine tools and transfer machines. As a result, the number of first-tier suppliers tended to decrease, many of former first-tier suppliers descended to the lower tiers, and the hierarchy of parts makers got taller, with a rapid increase in third- and fourth-tier suppliers.[18]

In product development, the *black box parts system* (whereby suppliers participate in automobile product development) prevailed, particularly into the late 1960s, and reflected the rapid product proliferation of this period. Accordingly, suppliers began to specialize in certain items as they accumulated the component technologies. Technology imports from Western parts makers also accelerated during this period. At the same time, the technically capable suppliers on the first tier diversified their customer base, and the hierarchy became more open to multiple assemblers as customers—the "Alps" structure, rather than the "pyramid" structure of automakers with dedicated suppliers.

On the quality side, the 1960s was the era of TQC (company-wide quality management), particularly for Toyota. The company adopted TQC in the beginning of the 1960s, won the Deming Prize in the mid-1960s, and started to transfer a company-wide quality control system to its suppliers in the late 1960s. In inventory control, also, a just-in-time delivery system was disseminated after the mid-1960s. Accordingly, many of Toyota's first-tier suppliers dramatically decreased their inventory levels in the late 1960s and early 1970s (Lieberman and Demeester, 1995). Cost control and improvement methods (standard cost, target cost, value analysis, etc.) also were increasingly emphasized in supplier management. Thus a supplier management policy focused on competitive factors (quality, cost, delivery) emerged during this period.

The 1960s was an era of quantity expansion for most of the Japanese automobile firms, but for Toyota it was also when both the Toyota production system and total quality control were installed, and when systematic diffusion to the suppliers was started.

1970s—Export Expansion and Technology Development. Quite contrary to the 1960s situation, domestic production growth was fueled by exports. While production increased from about 5 million to 11 million units per year between 1970 and 1980 (interrupted in only one year by the first oil crisis), exports grew from 1 million to 6 million units. Thus, by the end of the decade Japanese motor vehicle exports had surpassed domestic sales.

The main area of export growth was North America, from about 500,000 in 1970 to about 2.6 million in 1980. Despite this rapid market penetration, Japanese firms faced only sporadic trade friction with the United States. This was partly because there was a fairly clear division of market territories between U.S. makers, who were producing and selling large American cars, and Japanese makers, who were exporting small cars. The small-car segment grew typically as a second car for American households and partly as a growing preference by young baby boomers for small economical cars. Although U.S. automakers started to develop somewhat smaller models after the first oil crisis, such product changes tended to be incremental, within the traditional concept of a big American car. This division of territories by vehicle size between the United States and foreign (mostly Japanese) makers continued throughout the late 1970s.

At the same time, export expansion meant that the number of variations within each basic Japanese model increased rapidly, and differences among the variations widened as domestic plants handled a variety of the world's demands and regulations. At Toyota, for example, the levelization of product mix (*heijunka*, or randomization of assembly sequence) became important as heavy-content cars and light-content cars were handled on the same assembly line.

The 1970s was also when automobile producers became aware of their social responsibilities in terms of vehicle safety, emission control, and efficient energy consumption. In a sense, motor vehicles were increasingly recognized as social goods, and the producers of these goods faced public criticism and regulatory pressures, mostly domestic at that time. The Japanese makers, for example, had to deal with safety disputes on some models by the late 1960s, with pressures for better fuel economy following the first oil crisis in the mid-1970s, and with some of the toughest emissions regulations in the world throughout the decade.

Motivated by social and market pressures, the Japanese automobile manufacturers accelerated their investments in new technologies, ranging from electronic control devices and advanced materials for weight reduction, to catalyst technologies for emission reduction, modification of engine designs, and exploration of alternative engines. The focal point was technological improvement of the small internal combustion engine. It is said, for example, that roughly half of the R&D personnel at Toyota were mobilized for engine technology development in the mid-1970s, which slowed new product development during that period. Various technologies aimed at greater fuel efficiency and emission control were developed.[19] By the end of the 1970s, the main Japanese automakers had built world-class capability in small engine technologies.

Microelectronics technologies also started to be diffused into production processes in the form of numerical control machines and robots. Robotization of body welding was particularly the focal point, an area in which Nissan tended to precede Toyota. Traditional mechanical automation (e.g., engine machining) and manual operations (e.g., assembly) persisted in many areas, though.

As for overall management, the 1970s was when Japanese manufacturers emphasized so-called slim management (*genryo keiei*). With the oil crisis, many practitioners predicted that Japan's era of continuous growth would be over and managers would have to limit production inputs. For example, automakers returned to a conservative employment policy, minimizing any increase in employment from the latter half of the 1970s to the mid-1980s. It turned out, however, that production continued to grow, so labor productivity also grew.

In production management, the 1970s was a time of system elaboration. Although most of the main elements of Toyota-style production had been in place by the beginning of the decade, Toyota continued to refine its system for a sharper focus on continuous improvement in productivity and quality.

In supplier management, also, the 1970s was an era of system refinement and diffusion. The Toyota-style production system and total quality control continued to spread to the suppliers. There was tighter synchronization of assembler-supplier production through just-in-time delivery. Periodic reduction of unit parts cost, with or without an increase in order volume, became regular practice. Thus, both internal production management and supplier management were focused on improvements in manufacturing performance (quality, cost, delivery). A sense of crisis between the first and second oil shocks motivated this thrust; ironically, despite the absence of optimism on the part of producers, both the production and the competitiveness of the Japanese auto industry continued to grow throughout the 1970s, toward the top of the world market.

1980s—Internationalization and Product-Process Refinement. As already described, the 1980s was when the competitiveness of Japanese automobile manufacturers on average, Toyota in particular, was recognized internationally. It is hard to tell when the overall competitiveness of Japanese export cars peaked, partly because competitiveness is a multifaceted phenomenon and partly because of the time lag between reality and recognition, but it would be reasonable to estimate that the peak period included the early 1980s.

It should be noted, however, that strategic changes in the U.S. firms reveal such competitive gaps. Unlike during the first oil crisis, U.S. firms responded to the second oil crisis of 1980 by changing their basic product architecture. They switched from making large American cars smaller (i.e., downsizing of the late 1970s) to renewing most of their product mix, from large American cars (typically body-on-frame architecture and rear-wheel drive) to small and medium cars (mostly unit-body architecture and front-wheel drive). Many of the new American models had to compete directly with the Japanese small cars. There were comparative studies of the Japanese and U.S. small cars, and the Japanese advantages in productivity was first recognized at this time by some American researchers and practitioners.

Japanese exports peaked in the mid-1980s at nearly 7 million units. Despite U.S.-Japan trade frictions at the beginning of the decade, which resulted in voluntary export restraints on Japanese passenger cars, Japanese car and truck exports continued to grow, peaking also in the mid-1980s at roughly 3 million units. Overall, however, increases in exports in the early 1980s were not as rapid as in the 1970s.

The 1980s was also a period of internationalization of production for the Japanese automobile assemblers and major parts manufacturers. Although Japanese firms operated many small assembly plants in the countries that had local content policies (mostly developing countries), overseas operations of large-scale assembly plants (typically with a capacity of about 200,000 units per year and with painting, welding, and press shops) started in the early 1980s in North America, initially in response to trade frictions. With appreciation of the yen in 1985, Japan became a high-cost country and manufacturing facility investments in North America, and later in Europe, continued. By the end of the decade Japanese automakers had a roughly 2 million unit production capacity in the United States (Fujimoto, Nishiguchi, and Sei, 1994). Over 200 Japanese parts suppliers, mostly first tier, also set up North American manufacturing operations by the mid-1980s, responding in part to U.S. regulations regarding parts localization.

As a result of the slowdown in exports, as well as a saturation of the domestic market, Japanese domestic production stayed at around the 11 million unit level throughout the first half of the 1980s. The end of continuous growth was much discussed again. For major Japanese firms, including Toyota, it was estimated that a majority of operating profits were coming from North American operations, owing to a favorable exchange rate, continued productivity and quality advantages, and relatively high retail prices for the automobiles in America.

In the late 1980s, the cost competitiveness of Japanese import automobiles decreased significantly, mainly because of a sharp increase in the yen relative to the dollar. However, major Japanese producers, including Toyota, could maintain the overall competitiveness of their products throughout the 1980s by the following measures: (1) maintaining real-term competitive advantages in such areas as productivity and manufacturing quality (Womack et al., 1990); (2) reducing the margins for U.S. exports, which might have been unusually high in the early 1980s, to absorb cost increase; (3) increasing the capacity of North American transplants to alleviate the impact of exchange rates; and (4) improving total product quality, including product integrity (Clark and Fujimoto, 1990, 1991) to compensate for the loss in cost competitiveness. As a result, the market share of the Japanese firms (imports and local production combined) was generally maintained throughout this period.

On the other hand, as the Japanese economy entered its bubble period in the late 1980s, the domestic automobile market expanded unexpectedly by more than 2 million units per year, whereas exports had already started to decrease slowly. Overall, domestic production further increased to 13.5 million units in 1990, which was the historical peak. In retrospect, this was the last stage of a forty-year period of continuous growth in domestic production (1950–1990).The best-selling book *The Machine that Changed the World* explained the international competitiveness of Toyota's style of production (reinterpreted as "lean production") as an outcome of superior total system management, and the perceived strength of the Japanese auto manufacturing (if not necessarily real) also peaked.[20]

As suggested, the overall competitiveness of Japanese automobiles was generally maintained in the late 1980s, but the source of its strength had shifted by the end of the decade. As appreciation of the yen eroded their cost competitiveness, Japanese firms had to increasingly rely on the quality side of their strength. Real-term productivity growth had been slowing since the early 1980s (see appendix B.2), but total quality (manufacturing quality and design quality combined) continued to increase. Besides manufacturing quality, Japanese firms attempted to improve product integrity at the total vehicle level, apparently targeting some European high-end models (Clark and Fujimoto, 1990). A higher total product quality apparently had both positive and negative impacts on overall competitiveness: it could make up for relatively high retail prices and helped Japanese cars sustain their resale value; it also tended to result in high cost owing to over-quality, or what might be called "fat product design." (We will come back to this issue in chapter 6.)

Another trend observed in both North American and Japanese markets was expanded demand for passenger vehicles other than traditional sedans (e.g., minivans, pickup trucks, sport utility vehicles).[21] Ironically, the Japanese automakers that enjoyed competitive advantages in the sedan segment tended to lag behind other Japanese firms in entering this rapidly growing nonsedan market.

As for production processes and techniques, the 1980s continued with system elaboration. The basic elements of Toyota's production system were in place, but Toyota continued to refine its system. Micro-electronics, computers, and new process technologies arrived on the shop floors, but they did not change the basic pattern of the Toyota-style manufacturing system.

As competitive analyses by the Western practitioners and research-ers of Japanese automobile manufacturing systems deepened, from discovery of individual techniques to comprehension of total system functions, there were significant efforts by the Western automakers for a reverse catchup. Japanese firms, on the other hand, transferred their manufacturing systems to their North American and European plants, with certain local adaptations (Abo, 1994; Fujimoto, Nishiguchi and Sei, 1994).

One interesting phenomenon was a reinterpretation or modifica-tion of the existing Toyota-style system, which apparently occurred in the process of international knowledge transfer. On the one hand, some Toyota managers felt that they had to reinterpret the existing Toyota system, clarify the logic behind it, translate it into English, and thereby give systematic explanations for what it had built up for many years in order to dispel some negative misunderstanding of the sys-tem. Although there had been efforts to give systematic explanations to the Toyota production system since 1970, it is likely that operation of the transplants accelerated those efforts.

Some Western automakers, on the other hand, examined the ele-ments of the Toyota-style system, adopted them selectively when con-vinced of the rationale behind them, and purified such elements when they were convinced of their value, which sometimes resulted in more extreme practices than Toyota's own (see chapter 6).

1990s—Regaining Balance in the Era of Fluctuation.   It is too early to draw any conclusions about the 1990s, but we can note at least four major long-term trends (Fujimoto, 1994c; Fujimoto and Takeishi, 1994; Fujimoto, 1997a). One is the end of the era of continuous growth (1950–1990) and the beginning of volume fluctuations. Domestic pro-duction decreased from about 13.5 million units in 1990 to 10.5 million units in 1995, owing to a combination of postbubble recession, further appreciation of the yen (1993–1994), and an increase in overseas pro-duction. It is thus likely that, following the pattern of mature automo-bile-producing countries in North America and Europe, the Japanese domestic production would start to fluctuate. The Toyota-style manu facturing system, which had been developed mostly during the era of continuous growth, might need to be modified into the one that can handle such fluctuations while retaining its competitive strength.

The second long-term trend has been a change in Japan's demo-graphic structure: after the mid-1990s, Japan's population of youth started to shrink and is estimated to decrease by roughly 40 percent by the year 2010. Considering also that young people tend to have a different attitude toward work, it seems inevitable that Japanese automobile firms will have to make a long-term commitment to creating workplaces that are more attractive to young people, more friendly to the aging whom the new system has to rely on, and more motivating to workers at large.

The third trend is a narrowing of the competitive gap between Japanese and Western manufacturers. Although the Japanese auto industry on average maintained certain competitive advantages into the mid-1990s, it is clear that the gap has narrowed or disappeared in other aspects, and that international competition will be close for a long time, where the capabilities of individual firms matter more than their geographical origins.

The fourth trend is the expansion of automobile markets in areas such as other parts of Asia and Latin America. The impact of these emerging markets and their industries will be multifaceted. They may mean new market opportunities for established automakers, but also new competitors in the world market. These companies may become potential partners for strategic coalition, but may also be sources of further trade friction. As the world automobile market continues to grow, energy conservation and environmental protections will be increasingly important.

In response to these four trends, the Japanese automobile industry will have to modify its manufacturing system. More specifically, the emerging system may be called the "lean-on-balance" system, in an attempt to maintain the core capabilities of the Toyota-style (lean) manufacturing system while gaining certain balances that did not exist during the growth era. The problems that need fixing include the following: an imbalance between customer satisfaction and employee dissatisfaction; an imbalance between lean manufacturing and fat product design; and an imbalance between a firm's ability to handle international and interfirm competition, cooperation, and conflicts (Fujimoto, 1994c; Fujimoto and Takeishi, 1994; 1997). A detailed description of this emerging system is beyond the scope of this book, but part of this trend will be discussed in chapters 6 and 7.

Step 2: Overall Patterns of Manufacturing System Evolution

So far I have presented a brief history of the Japanese automobile industry and the Toyota-style manufacturing system. Writing the overall history of the Japanese automobile industry would require at least a book, which is outside the scope of this work. From the above outline, however, we can identify some basic patterns in the creation of Japanese automobile manufacturing systems.

Cumulative Changes.   The Toyota-style system was not developed all at once by one-time strategic decision making, but evolved during the

postwar period, or even since the 1930s. The historical pattern highlights both change and continuity. On the one hand, the manufacturing system was constantly evolving by taking in new elements and rebalancing the overall system. Even the Toyota-style system of the
1980s, which was often described as a complete one by many researchers and practitioners, is further changing in some important aspects (see chapter 7).

On the other hand, there is some evidence of remarkable continuity, which dates back to the beginning of the company—for example,
the concept of "just in time" stressed by Kiichiro Toyoda back in the
1930s. Although Toyota, which has tended to identify with the tradition of its Toyoda family founders (e.g., Sakichi, Kiichiro) and may be
biased toward such continuity, detailed historical studies seem to
confirm that these basic ideas, if not actual implementation, did exist
from the very early stages of Toyota's history. Overall, the pattern of
change in Toyota's manufacturing system can be characterized as cumulative and evolutionary rather than as a series of revolutionary
changes in which basic traditions were abandoned.

Long-Term Adaptation.   We can interpret the Japanese automotive
industry history as an adaptation process in which manufacturing
systems responded rationally and effectively to crises and challenges
imposed by changing environments. Toyota faced financial and labor
crises in the later 1940s to the early '50s; production expansion and
product proliferation under resources constraints in the 1960s; two oil
crises in the 1970s and '80s; social and regulatory pressures for vehicle safety, environmental protection, and energy conservation after the
1970s; abrupt appreciation of the yen and persistent trade friction in
the 1980s and '90s; labor shortages around 1990; and a decrease in
domestic production in the early 1990s. In the long run, it looks as if
Toyota responded effectively to these problems and corrected the system. The system, as we have observed, seems to be reasonably rational
in its ability to allow the company to compete, survive, and grow in
the changing environments of the 1930s through 1990s.

In the short run, however, there are many anecdotes indicating that
adaptation was not always instant and smooth. Crises sometimes persisted for an extended period. A significant amount of resources and
time were needed for trial-and-error system changes (see, for example,
the case of "fat product design" discussed in chapter 6 and the assembly
line problem described in chapter 7). Thus, even though it looks as if
the company had eventually made effective system changes, it is
difficult to explain the system evolution solely as a series of ex-ante
rational decision-making processes.

Hybridization.   To what extent was the Toyota-style manufacturing
system unique? The historical data in this chapter indicate that the

system was not a unique and original one that challenged the traditional Ford system, despite sharp contrasts between the two system as of the 1980s. In short, Toyota's production organization—during the prewar and early postwar era in particular—adopted various elements of the Ford system selectively and in unbundled forms, and hybridized them with their indigenous system and original ideas. There is an obvious continuity between the two systems.[22] It also learned from experiences with other industries (e.g., textiles). Thus, it is a myth that the Toyota production system was a pure invention of genius Japanese automobile practitioners.

However, we should not underestimate the entrepreneurial imagination of Toyota's production managers (e.g., Kiichiro Toyoda, Taiichi Ohno, Eiji Toyoda), who integrated elements of the Ford system in a domestic environment quite different from that of the United States. Thus, the Toyota-style system has been neither purely original nor totally imitative. It is essentially a *hybrid*.

Forward Adaptation.   As some anecdotes from Toyota's beginnings indicate, the early leaders of the company had great foresight when it came to international competition. For example, Toyota's leaders competitively benchmarked against Ford and thereby set ambitious goals for productivity increases even when the domestic market was effectively protected from foreign makers (i.e., between the 1930s and 1960s). It was essentially *forward adaptation* to future international competition that the managers perceived to be inevitable.

On the one hand, it is reasonable to infer that memory of the dominance of Ford and GM in the late 1920s and early 1930s facilitated the Japanese automakers' tendency toward forward adaptation and thereby toward early competitive improvements. In a sense, Japanese automakers were lucky to have had direct, early experience with the overwhelming competence of the large U.S. automakers.

At the same time, it is still remarkable that Kiichiro Toyoda was rather accurately estimating the productivity level of Ford as early as the fall of 1945, and even tried to catch up with Ford within a short period, although it was not a realistic plan then. Thus, forward adaptation seems to be a result partly of the luck of history and partly of entrepreneurial vision by managers, particularly at Toyota.

Rationalization at the Pregrowth Stage.   My data lead to two contrasting conclusions regarding the impact of production growth. First, the rapid and continuous growth of domestic production, and a large production scale as a result, particularly in the 1960s and '70s, had a profound positive effect on productivity by Japanese automobile makers, largely through improvements in process and job design, mechanization of the process, and increased outsourcing.

At the same time, however, historical analysis also reveals a rapid

increase in productivity already happening at Toyota, even during the
first five years of the postwar period when there was no significant increase in production. Thus, Toyota dramatically improved productivity, if not manufacturing quality, before the high-growth era started in
the late 1950s or '60s, and in a heavily protected market. It seems that
a combination of improvement efforts since the pregrowth era and the
economies of scale and high growth after the 1960s created most of
the productivity advantage enjoyed by the Japanese auto industry.

Compressed Life Cycle.   As early as the late 1940s and early 1950s,
Toyota (at least the production facilities that Taiichi Ohno supervised)
attempted to introduce certain elements of the Ford system and Taylor
system (e.g., work standardization) on its indigenous shop floors,
which had maintained characteristics of the conventional craft-type
systems.[23] This implies that Toyota selectively and partially introduced both the Ford system and the Toyota production system at the
same time. Such early hybridization seems to have had a positive impact on subsequent productivity increases.

A framework that might be applied to the present topic is the
product-process life cycle model proposed by William Abernathy
(1978). This framework shows how an industry tends to develop from
a fluid stage of high flexibility and low productivity to a specific stage
of high productivity and low flexibility. Abernathy argues that Ford in
the 1920s was an extreme example of the specific-rigid production
system. Although this type of linear model cannot be applied to every
case of industrial evolution, it certainly gives us insights in analyzing
the automobile industry. Hounshell (1984) goes further and argues
that Ford's pursuit of ultimate efficiency and rigidity failed as "flexible
mass production," represented by Alfred Sloan's General Motors, took
over the lead position in the industry. Womack et al. (1990) also indicate a historical sequence from the craft-type system (fluid) to the
mass-production (specific) system and to a "lean production system"
(Japanese version of flexible mass production).

In Womack et al.'s three-stage life cycle model, product variety and
process flexibility are high at the first, fluid (craft-type) stage, decrease
during the second, specific (Ford system) stage, and then increase
again at the third stage of flexible mass production. The degree of variety and flexibility is high at the first and third stage, but different in
that the former stage lacks standardization while the latter is based on
standardization of product and process designs. In the latter stage,
product change and variety are absorbed by flexible linkage of standardized product-process elements; in the former stage, lack of standardization itself is the source of variety.

Let us now try to apply this simple model to our historical case.
Toyota, facing a fragmented small market and potential competitive
pressures from the big U.S. competitors, pursued work standardiza-

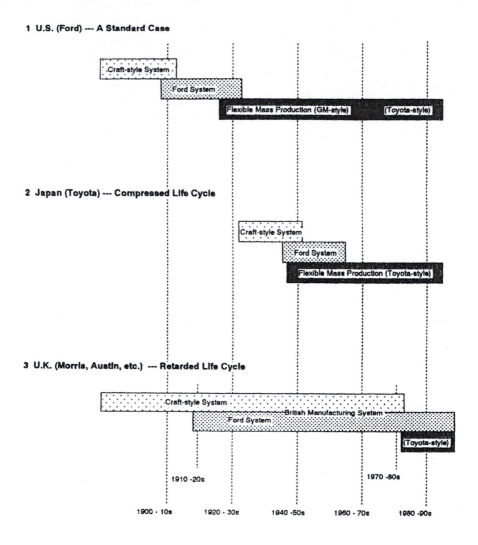

Source: Fujimoto and Tidd (1993).

Figure 2.3 Product-Process Life Cycles in the U.S., Japan, and U.K.

tion and created flexible systems at the same time, thereby skipping
the second stage. We may call this pattern a *compressed product-
process life cycle* (see figure 2.3, case 2). When this direct shift from
the indigenous craft-style system to the flexible mass-production system was implemented in the 1940s and '50s, managers at Toyota did
not regard this emergent system as a way to outperform their Western
rivals, but rather as an imperative for surviving in their small and fragmented market (Japanese exports were negligible then). The flexibility

factors carried over from the indigenous system and retained in the Toyota-style mass-production system, however, became a source of its competitive advantage in subsequent years, when the market size and Toyota's productivity both grew rapidly and major automobile markets worldwide began to emphasize product variety. By the late 1970s, Toyota had found itself achieving world-class flexibility and efficiency at the same time—an unintended consequence.

In the U.S. automobile manufacturing system, by contrast, the classic Ford system was the dominant mode in almost pure form between the 1910s and '20s (see figure 2.3, case 1). The American production system also moved from its pure Ford system to a flexible mass-production production (GM style) system, but the organizational routines and mind-sets for classic mass production persisted and eventually became an obstacle when U.S. companies tried to shift to more flexible and efficient modes of production (i.e., a lean production system) in response to challenges from Japanese automakers in the 1970s and '80s.

Although the above story may be too simplistic to explain the complex reality of industrial evolution, it highlights some important features of the Japanese automobile industry's evolution.

A Comparison with the Evolution of the U.K. Automobile Industry

To clarify further the evolution of Toyota's manufacturing system, let's briefly compare the history of British and Japanese manufacturing systems, mainly focusing on adoption and adaptation of the Ford system from America.[24] In a sense, both systems can be characterized as hybrids of the Ford system and their indigenous (essentially craft-type) systems. The influence of the Ford system was significant in both the British and Japanese auto industries. Competitive performance in the mid-1980s, however, was quite contrasting, with Toyota's productivity higher than that of U.S. Ford, while that of British makers was lower than the U.S. counterparts. Thus, despite the fact that they were both intended as hybrids of the Ford system, what accounts for such a difference in performance and capabilities?

My findings are summarized in table 2.3. Direct transplantation of the Ford system in Japan (i.e., the Ford Yokohama plant) was in fact more successful than that in the U.K. (i.e., the Ford Manchester and Dagenham plants) during the prewar era, as far as their market shares were concerned. The "technology push" approach by U.S. Ford was not effective in the British market, compared to the "demand pull" strategy of domestic mass producers such as Morris and Austin, which absorbed certain parts of the Ford system and competed effectively with Ford U.K. In Japan, by contrast, only strong protectionism by the military and government could stop the dominance of U.S. mass producers in the Japanese market.

Table 2.3   The U.K.–Japan Comparison of Production History

	U.K.	Japan
Peak Market Size	400K	5K
Demand structure	Variety Workmanship Design quality	Car market was hardly developed
Government policy	Relatively open	Protectionistic after 1936
Ford assembly plant	Manchester, 1911 Mostly cars 4% share in 1931	Yokohama, 1925 Mostly trucks 50% share
Top domestic makers	Competitive (Morris and Austin)	Not competitive without protection
Relative productivity to top U.S. makers	1/3	1/10
Relative quality to top U.S. makers	Design quality: Competitive in U.K.	Unsatisfactory
Production system	Modified Fordism (Morris)	Modified Fordism (Toyota)
Shop control	Managers chose indirect control	Oriented to direct shop floor control
Labor union	Almost union-free	Union-free

b. Post-War Period

	U.K.	Japan
Production growth	50K: 1910s 500K: 1930s 2M: 1960s -	50K: 1930s - 1953 500K: 1960 2M: 1965 5M: 1970
Productivity (U.K. vs. Japan)	1955: higher 1960: lower After 1960: Declined	1955: lower 1960: higher After 1960: Grew
Direct shop control, time-based wage standardization	by 1980s	by 1950s
Serious labor problems	1960s and 70s	around 1950
JIT-TQC techniques introduced	1980s	late 1940s - 60s
Managers' efforts to improve production-labor system	Little efforts while growing	Much efforts before growing
Protectionism	Relatively weak	Strong 1930s - 1960s

Ironically, the relative success of prewar domestic automobile mass producers in the U.K. delayed the introduction of such Ford system factors as direct shop floor control, machine pacing, and a time-based wage system. Some major British companies (e.g., Morris) adapted its production system, not only to the smaller market emphasizing variety and design quality but also to their perceived labor environments.

It was largely decisions by British automobile managers, rather than resistance by craft unions, that led to the choice of indirect shop floor control and a piece-rate incentive system, the essential elements of the British mass production system. Backward adaptation, or adaptation of the emerging production system to the past practices of craft unionism, created a pattern of shop floor management that was somewhat similar to the real-craft production (strong craft union, indirect shop floor control, and so on) found in traditional industrial sectors in the U.K.; it was a self-fulfilling prophesy.

The difference in evolution between Toyota and the British mass producers may be described also as compressed versus retarded modes of the product-process life cycle discussed earlier. This helps us contrast the British and Japanese responses to small and fragmented markets (see figure 2.3, cases 2 and 3). As pointed out earlier, Toyota moved directly from old craft-type production to flexible mass production by skipping the pure Ford system stage of inflexible mass production. British makers, by contrast, retained the elements of craft-type production long after they reached the level of mass production. In the interwar period, the British system of mass production attempted to absorb the variety in the market by retaining the flexible aspects of its craft-type system and blended it with the Ford system: a case of retarded life cycle. This strategy functioned well initially, but faced serious resistance when the industry finally started to move to the second stage in terms of labor management.

Thus, Toyota fused its indigenous elements and Ford system elements in its production system for higher competitiveness, while the British caused a "collision" between the craft elements and the Ford system elements, which deteriorated their competitiveness.

This comparison illuminates an important aspect of system emergence: two systems with many similar elements can nonetheless follow divergent paths. Indeed, despite the clear differences between the British and Japanese cultures and the timing of their industrialization, the main automakers in the two countries (e.g., Toyota and Morris) had many features in common historically. The production system of the prewar Morris, for example, had a remarkable competence for flexible production that resembled the postwar Toyota system.[25] And yet their paths had diverged by the 1980s. To a certain extent, one can ascribe this to differences in history and management style, but the complex nature of system emergence also has to play a part.

It would be reasonable to infer from the foregoing analysis that the process of Toyota-style capability building was in fact emergent: the firm continued to attempt rational adaptation to changing environments. This usually worked in the long run, but its efforts were often incomplete, at least in the short run. The foresight of executives played an important part in this evolutionary process (forward adaptation), but the unintended consequences of previous actions, bounded by environmental constraints, also facilitated the evolution. Toyota adopted much of the best practice of those days (i.e., the Ford system), but the hybridization was unique.

This analysis at this point is, however, little more than an impressionistic sketch. In order to tell more precisely if there was system emergence in Toyota's case, we need to get into system details, exploring their histories at deeper levels—subjects for the next chapter.

SYSTEM EMERGENCE AT TOYOTA
Reinterpretation

Introduction: An Operational Definition of Multi-Path System Emergence

Having outlined a history of the Toyota-style manufacturing system in chapter 2, let's now interpret it from the system emergence point of view. The present chapter includes the last two steps of the historical analysis. In step 3, I rearrange the given history to demonstrate how a variety of evolutionary paths created the main components of the Toyota-style system. In step 4, I summarize my historical findings to see if Toyota, in fact, possessed an evolutionary learning capability, by which it created that competitive manufacturing system out of the multi-path system emergence.

To proceed with an in-depth analysis at this step, the multi-path system emergence and the evolutionary learning capability, which I defined conceptually in chapter 1, is operationally redefined as follows (see also figure 3.1): when there is (1) a wide variety of system change patterns (rational calculation, environmental constraints, entrepreneurial vision, knowledge transfer, random trials) observed historically, and (2) there is no correlation between the patterns of the system change paths and the changing systems themselves, the system in question is an outcome of multi-path system emergence. When the resulting system (i.e., set of routines) demonstrates stable and firm-specific competitive performance, the firm exhibits a certain evolutionary learning capability.

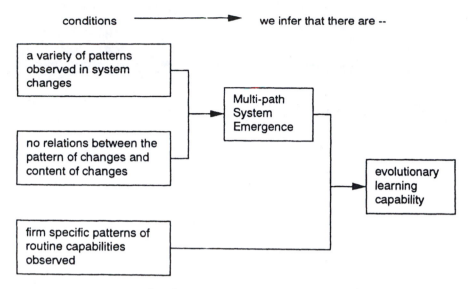

Figure 3.1 Operational Definition of System Emergence and Evolutionary
Capability

Step 3: The Evolutionary Paths of Toyota-style Subsystems

This section explores the evolution of various core elements of the
Toyota-style system. Just-in-time, mechanisms for productivity improvement, multitasking, flexible production, total quality control,
suppliers' design capability, and the heavyweight product manager
system (see chapter 4, appendix B, and chapter 6 for discussion of the
structures and functions of these core subsystems). By exploring as
many historical examples as possible at the element level, I present
further evidence that the process was, in fact, emergent—in that various paths of system changes were involved and in that Toyota had a
certain evolutionary learning capability, at least up to the 1980s.

Capability Building for Just-in-Time

The just-in-time (JIT) system originated through a complex combination of entrepreneurial vision, knowledge transfer from other firms
and industries, environmental constraints, and rational decision making on the part of Toyota managers.

Entrepreneurial Vision.   The idea and slogan of "just-in-time" was
created and advocated by Toyota's founder-entrepreneur Kiichiro Toyoda during the 1930s. Although concrete methods (e.g., "supermarket" system, *Kanban* system) did not exist, Kiichiro had strongly in-
sisted that the downstream should order just enough parts for what it

needed. When Kiichiro started the automobile business, he posted the phrase "just in time" (*jasuto-in-taimu*) on the wall and told his subordinates to receive just twenty engine blocks in the morning and nothing more if twenty were all that were needed day. Kiichiro frequently walked about the factory and threw away anything above what was needed.[1]

Transfer from Ford.   Toyota's just-in-time method and the Ford system of the early days (Henry Ford's era of Highland Park experiments in the 1910s) had much in common, in that both pursued synchronization of upstream and downstream processes.[2] The Ford system synchronized the workstations by physically linking them via continuous conveyers, whereas just-in-time created pressures for synchronization by reducing buffer stocks between the stations (i.e., an invisible conveyer line). It is thus quite natural to infer that the early production system architects at Toyota were influenced substantially by the Ford idea of synchronization. For example, When Eiji Toyoda and Shoichi Saito visited the Ford plants in 1950 for purposes of benchmarking and learning, the conveyer systems at its famous River Rouge plant impressed them. Eiji Toyoda wrote: What attracted my attention most at Rouge, the largest factory at Ford, was its materials handling. . . . That is, all the materials and parts for automobile production were connected by conveyer lines and merged into the final assembly lines without failure as the production made progress."[3]

Saito set up a materials handling committee (*unpan taisaku iinkai*) when he returned to Japan. He standardized pallet boxes, used more forklift trucks and small tractors-trailers inside the plant buildings, and made a wide use of conveyers. These measures became a foundation for subsequent Toyota production system changes, according to Toyota's company history.[4] Also, the strong influence that original Ford system concepts had is quite obvious in Taiichi Ohno's book on the Toyota production system.[5]

Note, however, that the *kanban* (supermarket) system can be characterized as "incomplete synchronization," in that the system needs inventories between workstations, as opposed to the Ford idea of seamless conveyer networks. There is an interesting contrast between the Ford and Toyota systems: What Ford and other American mass producers achieved in practice was essentially *partial adoption of complete synchronization*, while Toyota's efforts can be seen as *thorough adoption of incomplete synchronization*. That is, whereas Toyota diffused the *kanban* and JIT systems (i.e., incomplete synchronization) throughout the company and extended it to its supplier system, Ford and other major American makers created islands of complete synchronization (e.g., conveyers, transfer machines) in the middle of a sea of large-batch production. In the long run, Toyota's approach turned out to be more effective, as Taiichi Ohno points out in his book: "I guess that the real intention of Henry Ford was not understood accurately (by the American auto makers). . . . Despite the smooth flows in final assembly lines, other production processes failed to create flows; they rather established a method that made production lots as large as possible, which blocked the flow.[6]

Whereas single-model production of the original Ford system enabled Ford to achieve a high level of both synchronized *and* large-lot production, subsequent market pressures for product variety created a situation in which automakers could no longer pursue both at the same time. The major American automakers chose to emphasize large-lot production and deemphasize company-wide synchronization. Toyota's production architects, by contrast, emphasized semi-synchronization (e.g., *kanban*) with small-lot production throughout its production and supplier systems.[7] Thus, Toyota's knowledge transfer from the Ford system was rather selective.[8] The choice of small-lot semi-synchronization may have been a deliberate one, but the fact that Japanese automakers could not adopt a pure Ford system, owing to their fragmented small domestic market, may also have facilitated this critical choice.

Transfer from Textiles.   Another important source of the Toyota production system seems to have been the production experiences of Toyoda Spinning and Weaving, with knowledge transferred by Taiichi Ohno, the de facto inventor of JIT. When Ohno was a supervisor at the spinning factory, he realized through a benchmarking study that rival Nichibo (Japan Spinning) was outperforming Toyoda in productivity. Further studies revealed that Nichibo's production system was very different from that of Toyoda Spinning and Weaving. Toyoda had separate buildings by process steps; Nichibo had adopted a line layout along the process flow. Toyoda moved yarns in large lots; Nichibo conveyed them in small lots. Toyoda had emphasized the skills of rework (yarn tying) at the downstream step; Nichibo had emphasized making good yarns at the upstream and eliminating rework at the downstream. In this way, Ohno obtained some of the key ideas for the Toyota production system, including product-focused layout, small-lot production, and "doing things right the first time." When Ohno moved to Toyota Motor Manufacturing in 1943, his first impression was that it would be easy to raise productivity by three to five times, simply by introducing the production system adopted by Toyoda Spinning and Weaving.[9]

Historical Imperatives—The 1950 Crisis.   Although productivity increased rapidly, Toyota faced a crisis during the 1948–49 recession. With many inventories of finished goods piling up, Toyota was on the verge of bankruptcy. It also fired 2,000 employees, which triggered a series of strikes by the union.[10] Two lessons that Toyota was forced to

learn from this crisis, among others, regarded "limited volume production" (*genryo seisan*) and human resource management, with long-
term stabilization of employment. Taiichi Ohno noted in a 1984 interview: "We got a lesson from the crisis that productivity increase and
cost reduction had to be accompanied by 'limited volume production,' which meant that we had to produce just enough to sell and just
when we could sell. We learned that productivity increase for the sake
of itself was no good, and that we should not simply imitate the American style mass production."[11]

Diffusion of Kanban System.   Although the idea of just-in-time was
created by Kiichiro Toyoda in the 1930s, the *kanban* system, a formal
mechanism that materialized that idea, started in the late 1950s under
the leadership of Taiichi Ohno.[12] The system was originally called the
"supermarket system," in that the downstream station had to come to
upstream to pick up just enough part as needed, whereas the latter
had to produce just enough to replenish what was taken by the former (i.e., the "pull" system).[13] The system, which linked the upstream
and downstream stations by standardized returnable containers and
reusable slips called *kanban*, had already been articulated around
1949, according to Ohno, but the Japanese tax office did not allow this
arrangement until the mid-1950s, on the grounds that the system did
not document accurate accounting records for each transaction.

Unlike total quality control, diffusion of JIT was rather slow, starting as Ohno's informal experiment as opposed to a company-wide
movement. Initial experiments were made only where Ohno directly
supervised. He introduced the *kanban* system first in the body welding line, in which small-lot production was key. Ohno told the shop
floor people, "*kanban* is like money: if you take out parts without *kanban*, you are stealing the parts." The *kanban* system was then introduced to upstream press operations and to such components as engine oil pans and tappet covers. It was also installed at the Motomachi
assembly plant upon its completion in 1959. In the early 1960s, Ohno
became the main plant manager, when he introduced *kanban* to casting, forging, and heat treatment, the most difficult processes for small-
lot production.[14] In 1962, *kanban* was adopted on a company-wide
level, and in 1965, Toyota formally started extending the system to its
suppliers.[15]

Evolution of Body Buffer Policies.   The flow of car bodies at Toyota's
assembly plants has been controlled by a "push" system, as opposed to
assembly parts delivered mostly by a "pull" system. Plant engineers
and managers try to minimize buffer inventories of car bodies between
and within welding, painting, and final assembly processes based on
the just-in-time idea, but a certain level of body buffer inventories always remains for certain necessary functions (e.g., safety inventories

against upstream line stops and reworks, decoupling inventories for changing body sequences).

The main function of the body buffer inventories at Toyota has changed as the market and technological environment have changed, according to Kaneyoshi Kusunoki, a former manufacturing executive of Toyota.[16] In the case of painted body buffers between paint and assembly shops, for example, the functions changed as follows:

1950s: At first, there were large body inventories because the body, paint, and assembly shops were not synchronized. In the mid-1950s, higher synchronization was achieved, and body inventories were reduced accordingly.[17]

1960s: Some painted body buffers were used as safety inventories against upstream line stops. This was the time when mechanization of the upstream processes (press, welding, painting) made major progress, increasing the upstream down times. The company had to respond by adding body buffers between welding, painting, and assembly shops.

1970s: The main function of the painted body buffers changed from that of safety stocks to changing body sequences, thereby coping with increased product varieties and interversion differences in product content, caused mainly by the rapid the expansion of exports. Levelization (*heijunka*), or the even distribution of assembly workload over time, became a key constraint when determining the sequence of bodies on the final assembly line, and this meant that a random sequence of product variations, typically with a batch size of one, was necessary.[18] The upstream paint and body processes of those days, however, did not have enough process flexibility to handle such a random sequence; they needed a larger batch size (e.g., ten red bodies in a row before a color switch). To absorb this difference in optimal body sequence between the assembly shop and the paint shop, painted body buffers were increasingly used as decoupling inventories (i.e., for changing body sequences between the upstream and downstream processes). The upstream down time, on the other hand, became less of a problem as the firm's process and maintenance capabilities improved.

1980s–: The policy was basically kept unchanged, but efforts were made to reduce the painted buffer levels by improving manufacturing capabilities.

Thus, the body buffer policy is largely an example of long-term adaptation to changing environments based on rational calculation, taking into account the various functions of buffer inventories. In the short run, however, the company used trial and error to determine the actual level of body inventories. In any case, it should be noted that Toyota is not a "zero inventory" company, although it is sometimes referred to as such. The firm has tried to reduce inventories to the minimum, given its capability, but usually that does not mean zero inventory. The firm had had to search for optimal inventory levels partly using rational calculations based on inventory theories and partly through experimentation.

Capability Building for Productivity Improvement and Multitasking

Kiichiro's Vision and Benchmarking.   Soon after the end of the World War II, Allied General Headquarters approved Totota's production of trucks. Relying mostly on old equipment dating back to the 1930s, Toyota saw its production activity severely limited by financial and capacity constraints. Annual production finally surpassed the prewar peak (about 16,000 units) in 1953.[19] It is remarkable that, in this desperate situation, Kiichiro Toyoda already had future competition with the Western automakers in mind. According to Taiichi Ohno, as early as the fall of 1945, Kiichiro presented an ambitious vision of catching up with the productivity level of American automakers within three years.[20] Ohno estimated the productivity level of American makers to be ten times that of Toyota right after the war.[21] Although Kiichiro's goal was too ambitious, by 1955 Toyota had increased productivity by ten times in some of its core operations, according to Ohno. When Ohno visited Ford and GM engine plants in 1956, he found that the American plants had not improved their productivity since the 1930s, and that productivity at Toyota's engine plant was already higher in gross terms (i.e., unadjusted for product and process characteristics).

It is important to note that GM and Ford, having established their knock-down assembly plants in the mid-1920s, virtually dominated the Japanese motor vehicle market, with a combined market share of about 90 percent in the early 1930s until the Japanese government enforced its protectionistic law in 1936. It is likely that the memory of dominance by the American mass producers led Kiichiro and other Toyota managers to continue benchmarking and setting high operational targets, thus competing with their imaginary rivals in America even in the middle of a fully protected domestic market from the 1930s to '50s.[22]

Adoption and Modification of Taylorism.   The indigenous craft-type system persisted in Toyota's production processes during the 1930s and '40s.[23] Foremen-craftsmen led teams of workers as masters and were responsible for volume and quality. They told their subordinates, "Steal the way in which others are doing," "Learn for yourself by your skin feeling." Workers machined parts using general-purpose equipment, while sharpening their own cutting tools. Process flows were often disturbed, work-in-process inventories piled up, and there was a lack of balance in machine utilization.

This kind of craft-type production environment persisted even after World War II, but it was gradually replaced by standardization of operations, product-focused layout, and multiskilled workers handling more than one standard job. Taiichi Ohno, champion of just-in-time, recalled the situation when he was assigned as section head of Toyota's machine shop in 1946:

> The first thing that I did was standardization of jobs. The shop floor of those days was controlled by foremen-craftsmen. Division managers and section managers could not control the shop floor, and they were always making excuses for production delays. So we first made manuals of standard operation procedures and posted them above the work stations so that supervisors could see if the workers were following the standard operations at a glance. Also, I told the shop floor people to revise the standard operating procedures continuously, saying, "You are stealing money from the company if you do not change the standard for a month."[24]

In this way, the shift from craft-type production to Taylor-type standardization made progress in the late 1940s, at least in Toyota's machine shops, despite some resistance from traditional craftspeople. It should be noted, however, that the seemingly Taylor movement of work standardization at Toyota was accompanied by continuous improvements of the standards themselves. Thus, unlike the Ford system in America, in which work standardization tended to mean a freezing of standard operations and vertical separation between single-skilled workers and elite industrial engineers, standardization under Ohno's leadership emphasized continuous improvements on the shop floor.[25] Also, in Ohno's machine shops, work standardization and training of multiskilled workers were carried out in parallel. In other words, the decomposition of craft jobs into standardized tasks and the recombination of those tasks to multiskilled jobs occurred at the same time. Unlike the American Taylor-Ford approaches that essentially created single-skilled workers, Toyota in the late 1940s replaced traditional craft jobs with multiskilled jobs. Overall, Ohno claims that Toyota increased productivity by five or six times by 1950 while relying mostly on machines of the 1930s.[26]

Transfer from Textiles.   It is obvious that Ohno, with his experience in spinning operations, applied the concept of multimachine work assignment to the automobile industry. He noted:

> Improvement of productivity from 1945 to 1950 was relatively easy. For example, there were three or four workers around one machine, particularly when it was an important one, prior to the war. So simply assigning one worker to one machine increased productivity by three, four times. Workers with craftsmen's mentality resisted to such measures, but labor saving was relatively easy as turnover ratio was very high at that time.[27]

Historical Imperatives—Forced Growth.   The introduction of work standardization, centralization of tool maintenance, and productivity improvement with low production growth created tensions between management and the craft-type foremen or the machinists. Researchers point out that the militant craftsmen-foremen played a central role in Toyota's labor conflict in 1950.

Although Toyota increased its production capacity in response to special orders of trucks from the U.S. Army for the Korean War, it carefully avoided adding employees for this expansion, as the memory of its labor crisis was still fresh (see figure 3.2). Toyota also had to expand its capacity while using old machinery. So it is likely that Toyota was predicting a fluctuation in volume in accordance with business cycles and trying to minimize the size of a permanent workforce in order to avoid layoffs and strikes.

This prediction of fluctuating volume turned out to be generally wrong, however. Production started to grow rapidly in the 1950s, and continued to grow without deep recessions until 1990. Toyota maintained a rather conservative recruitment policy, however, particularly in the period between the first oil crisis and the early 1980s (i.e., slim management, or *genryo keiei*). Productivity increased almost naturally by expanding the production scale while restricting any increase in the number of workers (see figure 3.2). Thus, the pattern of production expansion without adding many employees, and reduction of finished goods inventory (i.e., limited volume production), was a reflection of Toyota's experiences of the crisis and subsequent growth. During the high-growth era of the 1960 and '70s, Toyota met the workload requirements for growth by hiring temporary workers, subcontracting out subassembly jobs, increasing overtime, and improving labor productivity—but it tended to maintain a conservative recruitment policy as far as permanent worker were concerned.

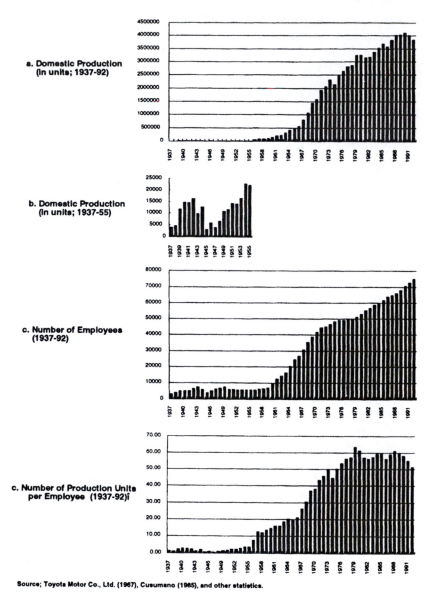

a. Domestic Production
(in units; 1937-92)

b. Domestic Production
(in units; 1937-55)

c. Number of Employees
(1937-92)

c. Number of Production Units
per Employee (1937-92)ï

Source; Toyota Motor Co., Ltd. (1967), Cusumano (1985), and other statistics.

Figure 3.2 Long-Term Trend in Toyota's Production, Employment, and
Productivity

Capability Building for Flexible Production Equipment

Visions for a Modified Ford System. When Kiichiro Toyoda of Toyoda Automatic Loom started his research and prototyping of automobiles and engines in 1931, his business concept at this early stage was
as follows:

1. Develop a 3000 cc class automobile and compete directly with the American models in both price and performance.
2. Although Toyota can learn from the American system of mass production, it must take into account characteristics of the Japanese market that limit production to several hundred units per month, and modify the system accordingly.[28]

Kiichiro's vision to compete directly with Ford and GM was a quite ambitious, even reckless one. (Note that this was five years *before* the Automobile Manufacturing Enterprise Law, which subsequently protected the three licensed domestic truck manufacturers, including Toyota.) His vision appeared to ignore the principle of economy of scale and cost curves. On the other hand, Kiichiro did not try to introduce the Ford system directly, but rather adapted it to Japanese conditions (small market, bad roads, etc.), in both product and process technology. Kiichiro's vision, although unrealistic at that time, functioned as a driving force for Toyota's dramatic productivity improvements in the late 1940s and early '50s. This seems to demonstrate Kiichiro's "capability of business conceptualization" (Okochi, 1979) at this early stage of business development.

Forced Flexibility of Machines. When Toyoda's Kariya assembly plant was completed in 1936, its capacity (150 units per month) was quite small compared to a standard American plant.[29] Based on Kiichiro's vision to "match our unit cost of producing 20,000 to 30,000 units per year with that of Americans producing several hundred units per year,"[30] the company had to modify the Ford system for small-volume production. For example, it replaced part of its body stamping processes with manual jobs in order to save fixed costs for tooling. The Koromo plant, established in 1938, was still much smaller than the average American factory (2,000 units per month, 5,000 employees). Thus, Toyota continued to select production technologies deliberately, considering its limited production scale.[31] For example, it purchased only several press machines for the door panel process, whereas American makers would have installed several dozen machines. Toyota also kept its machining operations somewhat flexible by introducing multispindle boring and horning machines that were adjustable to design changes, unlike the standard Detroit-type machines. It also made the shop floor flat so that its process layout could be changed easily. In this way, the small scale of Toyota's production forced the company to chose flexible production systems.

Transfer from Machinery Industry. A typical example of simple mechanization in the late 1940s is welding jigs.[32] While Toyota was consigning some of its body welding jobs to a heavy machinery maker, its inspectors found that the cabins made by the outside company were more accurate in dimensions than those made by Toyota, which commonly had deviations of 5 to 10 millimeters. A supervisor at Toyota's welding factory visited this company and found that it had been using jigs for dimensional accuracy. The Toyota of those days had neither welding jigs nor a production engineering department in charge of making them, so the supervisor collected the information and made body assembly jigs himself.

Learning from Ford.   Soon after the 1950 labor crisis ended, Eiji Toyoda and Shoichi Saito, who eventually became leaders of Toyota, visited Ford's River Rouge factory and other facilities. Their study of American automobile factories was intensive and lasted for three months. The visits were obviously motivated by Toyota's plan to modernize its production facilities. Soon after their return, Eiji and Saito launched a five-year plan for modernization of production equipment (1951–1955). The goal was to replace old equipment with new, to introduce conveyers and automation, and to expand monthly production to 3,000 units. Although Toyota was suffering a severe cash shortage, the company managed a 4.6 billion yen investment, with continuous casting lines for engine blocks, 2000-ton press machines, and multiple spot welders introduced. As mentioned earlier, Eiji was particularly impressed by the conveyer system at River Rouge factory, and told his staff to use conveyers extensively. He also ordered standardization of pallets and containers, which subsequently may have facilitated introduction of the *kanban* system.

The transfer machine, a typical Detroit-type automation that links a series of single-purpose machine tools by an automated transfer device, was introduced in the engine machining process in the late 1950s. The first machine, developed jointly by Toyota and Toyoda Machine Works, was installed in 1956. Although it is likely that Toyota studied transfer machines in Detroit, the machines themselves were developed and built by the Japanese, including Toyota itself.

Historical Imperatives—Shortage of Investment Funds.   In the first five years of postwar restoration, Toyota was forced to increase productivity and produce 1,000 trucks per month without sufficient funds and equipment to do so. Therefore, improvements in Toyota's production system during this period tended to involve "soft" methods such as work standardization, changes in layout and job assignment, and purchase of relatively inexpensive jigs.

Taiichi Ohno took charge of the Koromo assembly plant in 1945. He emphasized factors other than machines, because he had observed a large productivity gap between Toyota and the Western makers even though they were using similar equipment. Here we see the beginnings of subsequent Toyota production system philosophies, such as taking steps to reveal the true problems and making total system improvements rather than mechanization changes. This may be partly ascribed to insights on the part of Toyota's managers, but it is also likely that the historical imperatives of capital shortages forced the company to seek other than mechanization solutions. The concept of low-cost automation and semiautomation for cost effectiveness still prevails at Toyota.[33]

Product-Focused Layout.   Although the engine machining factory had already adopted a product-focused layout (i.e., installing machine tools according to process sequence for a particular product group), the transmission and suspension factories had been organized by type of machine (e.g., boring, lathe, milling, grinding).[34] The level of in-process inventories was high, and it took Ohno and his staff two years to convert the layout to a product-focused one. As the number of machines was increased, the machine utilization ratio decreased, but Ohno told his people to disregard this apparent loss.[35] The number of workers was not increased much, however, because Toyota trained multiskilled workers who could operate multiple machines, often in a U-shape layout, along the process flow (i.e., *takotei mochi*). It should be noted here that multiskilled workers are different from traditional craft-type workers: the former did a series of standardized tasks along the process flow; the latter were all-round players who did everything related to their trade regardless of process flow or work standards.

In a sense, the product-focused layout may be regarded as an incomplete version of Detroit-type automation, with fully automated material handling and a product-focused machine layout (e.g., transfer machines). While the use of transfer machines at Ford was rather limited to high-volume items, Toyota's application of the process-focused layout was widespread.[36] Simply speaking, the patterns of mechanization use at Ford and Toyota may be contrasted as *incomplete diffusion of complete automation* versus *complete diffusion of incomplete automation,* respectively—(similar to the contrast between partial adoption of complete synchronization at Ford and thorough adoption of incomplete synchronization at Toyota, as just-in-time. The latter approach tended to have more significant positive effects on cost reduction and productivity improvement.

Jidoka.   Machines that automatically detect defects and stop operations is the bases of *jidoka*. These were introduced in the late 1960s, according to Ohno.[37] Although the philosophy behind *jidoka* originated with Sakichi Toyoda earlier in the century, it was the sophistication of sensor technology that enabled automatic machine stop mechanisms.[38] The key feature of *jidoka* is that the machine simply stops responding to the defect, which dramatizes the problem and forces human intervention, which in turn triggers a problem-solving cycle by shop floor people resulting in a process improvement. Thus, *jidoka* is recognized as an important part of the Toyota production system for effective problem recognition and organizational learning.

With today's advanced automation technology, it is possible for a machine to not only detect errors but also automatically correct them. The proponents of *jidoka* oppose such high-tech solutions, however, arguing that automatic correction hides the problem and thus hampers root cause analysis and improvement by workers. An interesting question here is whether the *jidoka* concept was deliberately selected as a tool for problem recognition or it was designed because of a lack of advanced automation technologies (or for saving investment costs). Its problem-revealing effect might have been discovered only afterward—another positive but unforeseen consequence.

Capability Building for *Kaizen* and Total Quality Control

Adoption of the Suggestion System and TWI from the United States. When Eiji Toyoda and Shoichi Saito visited Ford in 1950, one practice that impressed them was the suggestion system (i.e., workers make suggestions for improvements on various technical and organizational issues). Soon after they came back to Japan, they started the "idea suggestion system" (*soi kufu teian seido*), which subsequently became a core element in Toyota's total quality control and *kaizen* (continuous improvement) systems. Toyota recognized the suggestion system as a competitive weapon from the beginning; Saito commented in 1951: "In order to survive in the competition with foreign automobiles in future, we have to reduce manufacturing cost by making use of our suggestions."[39]

Another important system that Toyota introduced from America was formal training in "scientific management" for supervisors, called training within industry (TWI).[40] Introduced at Toyota in 1951, TWI was offered to general foremen (*kakari-cho*) and the managers above them, and included training of improvement activities by supervisors. These supervisors subsequently played a leading role in *kaizen* activities at Toyota, whereas the role of supervisors was very limited at Ford after it had established its mass-production system. According to Nemoto (1992), *kaizen* activity was formally incorporated as a responsibility of shop floor supervisors (*shoku-cho* and *kumi-cho*) around 1955.[41]

The training of shop floor supervisors may be closely related to the replacement of traditional foremen-craftsmen with modern supervisors in the early postwar era. Facing a shortage of talent for the new jobs, Ohno had to transfer plant staff and engineers to supervising jobs as a temporary measure. Toyota thus needed a formal training program for those new supervising jobs, and it is likely that TWI was used.

From SQC to TQC.   The Japanese automobile industry did not play an active role when the idea of total quality control emerged in the 1950s. After both Nissan and Toyota dispatched their staff to seminars on the U.S.-born method of statistical quality control (SQC) in 1949, and then adopted it, both companies began emphasizing capability of inspection, but the concept of company-wide quality management still was not prevalent.[42] Then in 1960, Nissan moved one step ahead of Toyota and won the Deming Prize. The company outperformed Toyota in both its domestic car market and exports in the early 1960s. The APA criticized the insufficient quality level of some of Toyota's products.[43] Import liberalization was also forthcoming. So the focus was on how to improve the quality of Toyota's passenger cars.

Against this background, Toyota introduced total quality control (TQC) in 1961. Unlike JIT, TQC was diffused in a top-down manner, and quickly. Eiji Toyota explained the objectives of TQC as follows:

> Improvements in quality did not progress as fast as improvements in efficiency. Also, the problems of newly recruited workers, insufficient education programs, lack of managers' capabilities and skills, and poor coordination across functions surfaced. At the same time, competition of quality against the rival auto makers intensified.[44]

In 1963, a model changeover of the Corona (a small passenger car) was chosen as a company-wide theme for TQC. In 1965, Toyota received the Deming Implementation Prize. Unlike Nissan, whose top managers tended to regard TQC as merely a campaign slogan for winning the prize, Toyota's managers were committed to a continuation of TQC. In 1965, Toyota created its Purchasing Administration Division (*Kobai Kanri-bu*) and started to expand both JIT and TQC to its suppliers.[45] Toyota won the Japan Quality Control Award in 1970, when the company had outperformed Nissan in the rapidly growing domestic market.

Capability Building for Suppliers

In the early 1950s, the Japanese automobile supplier system was very different from what we see today. Many of the basic patterns of the Japanese supplier system, including long-terme relations, multilayer hierarchies, "Alps" structure, just-in-time delivery, subassembly of components by first-tier suppliers, involvement of first-tier suppliers in product development, competition by long-term capabilities, and close operational control and assistance by the automakers, were gradually formed from the 1950s to '70s (see appendix B3 and chapter 5).[46] The high growth in volume and the proliferation of models during the 1960s facilitated this multilayer hierarchy of control and assistance.

Technical Assistance to Suppliers.   According to Kazuo Wada (1991), a management diagnosis of Toyota and its twenty-one suppliers (*keiretsu shindan*), conducted by staff of the Aichi prefecture in the early 1950s, showed that Toyota had not provided enough technical support to its *keiretsu* suppliers, and that its purchasing department needed more people. Although Toyota initially took this diagnosis rather reluctantly, it quickly responded and strengthened its technical assistance, inspection, and data collection for suppliers. On the supplier side, the *kyoryoku-kai* (the suppliers association that an auto firm organizes) started to hold a series of joint seminars and plant visits. By the mid-1960s, the activities of Kyoho-kai (Toyota's suppliers association) had been coordinated with Toyota's annual management objectives, and *kanban* had been introduced to some of the suppliers.

Evolution of the Specialist Suppliers.   In the 1950s, the main focus of the automakers' purchasing policies was to acquire additional production capacity from suppliers in response to an increase in production. During the 1960s, however, automakers made significant efforts to grow specialist parts makers within their supplier networks, each of which specialized in a particular component in terms of technology, manufacturing, and subassembly. Instead of purchasing piece parts from many smaller suppliers, the assemblers bought subassembled functional parts from a smaller number of specialist suppliers. While the selection process of first-tier suppliers went on, multilayer hierarchies of suppliers were gradually developed. The assembler encouraged the specialist suppliers to sell components to other assemblers to pursue economies of scale.

Although this division of labor between assemblers and suppliers contributed to a competitive advantage for Japanese automakers in the 1980s, the assemblers' initial motivations might have been to relieve workload pressures, subcontracting out a larger fraction of their production-engineering activities to suppliers during the high-growth era of the 1960s.

Black Box Parts.   The "black box parts" system refers to a certain pattern of transactions in which a parts supplier conducts detailed engineering of a component that it makes for an automobile maker, based on the latter's specifications and basic design.[47] One of the origins of this practice is a transfer from either the locomotive or the aircraft industry of the prewar era, since the earliest adopters of this practice included prominent suppliers in these industries. (Chapter 5 details the evolution of the black box parts system.)

The American auto industry was not the source of this practice, however. Evidence indicates that the transaction between Toyota and Nippondenso (an electric-electronic component supplier of the Toyota group, which was separated from Toyota in 1949 in response to the latter's financial crisis now called Denso.) was probably another origin of the practice. Historical imperatives or technological constraints seem to have played an important role here: First, before the war, Toyota could not find decent electric parts suppliers in Japan, so it was almost forced to design and make such parts in-house; second, after the war, Toyota had to separate the electric parts factory for its own survival; third, when Nippondenso was created in 1949 as a result of the separation, Toyota found that it had to rely on the engineering capability of Nippondenso, as virtually all its electrical engineers had moved to the spunoff company. In this way, historical imperative forced Toyota to adapt the black box parts system.

The diffusion of the black box practice among the Japanese parts suppliers peaked much later—in the late 1960s, when the car makers faced market pressures for rapid model proliferation. This makes it easy to infer that another historical imperative—that of high growth with limited resource inputs in the product engineering area—created the pressure to subcontract detailed component engineering wherever possible.

From the supplier's point of view, the black box arrangement is a great opportunity to develop its own design capability, build up a technological entry barrier against the automakers' efforts to make the parts in-house, and survive as a first-tier parts supplier. Competitive pressures from rival suppliers also accelerate the efforts to build up a design and engineering capability.

It should be noted, however, that the black box parts practice was, in fact, very different at Toyota and Nissan, that the former exploited the potential benefits of the practice in terms of cost reduction and that Nissan adopted Toyota's system during the 1980s, only after it realized the benefits.[48] Although both companies had to respond to similar pressures from the environment, their evolutionary learning capabilities were significantly different.

Capability Building for the Heavyweight Product Manager (*Shusa*) System

Transfer from the Aircraft Industry.   The heavyweight product manager (or *shusa*, in the case of Toyota) system, is a core capability of an effective product development organization (Fujimoto, 1989; Clark and Fujimoto, 1991). The origin of this powerful project leader system is the "chief designer" organization of the prewar aircraft industry (Hasegawa, 1993; Maema, 1993). Because of the nature of the aircraft, which required a high system integrity, its development project inherently needed a strong product manager—an aircraft engineer—who acted as concept creator and project coordinator at the same time. When the Japanese aircraft industry disappeared after the war, a large number of talented aircraft engineers were forced to find jobs in other industries, including automobiles. The massive inflow of aircraft engineers dramatically enhanced the technological capability of postwar automakers.

Toyota as Pioneer.   Although all of the postwar automakers benefited from the technological capabilities that these ex-aircraft engineers brought with them, including body structural analysis and aerodynamics, Toyota was virtually the only company that directly adopted the institutional aspect of the aircraft development system: the heavyweight product managers (or what Toyota called *shusa*) system. Tatsuo Hasegawa, once a young chief designer of Tachikawa Aircraft, recalls that he had the clear intention of introducing the chief designer system to Toyota when he joined the company right after the World War II.[49]

> When I converted myself from an aircraft guy to an automobile guy, I considered the following technology transfer: aerodynamics, monocoque structure and other weight reduction technologies, and standards for structural strength. I also considered introducing the chief designer system and product planning methods into the automobile industry (Hasegawa, 1993).

Toyota formally adopted the product manager system in the 1950s, far ahead of the other Japanese automakers. Hasegawa led some projects as product manager during the 1960s, including the first generation of Corolla car.

Diffusion Process.   The diffusion of the heavyweight management system occurred much later. Honda introduced a strong project leader system in the early 1970s, after Soichiro Honda, the one-man chief engineer, retired. All the other auto firms moved toward heavyweight product manager organizations between the late 1970s and the 1980s (see figure 3.3). The sizable time lag between the origin of the system and its diffusion indicates that its real competitive advantage became obvious only when the market started to emphasize product integrity, or coherence of total vehicle design.[50] During the 1980s and the early 1990s, the heavyweight product manager system was also adopted by many of the Western automakers.

Step 4: System Emergence and Evolutionary Learning Capability

This final step of our analysis applies the operational definition of system emergence (see figure 3.1) to the foregoing historical evidence. For this analysis, Toyota's capability building can be classified according to the types of routines and types of paths shown in table 3.1. It is now clear that:

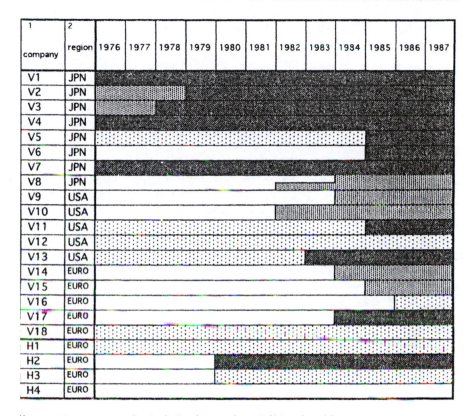

company	region	1976	1977	1978	1979	1980	1981	1982	1983	1984	1985	1986	1987
V1	JPN												
V2	JPN												
V3	JPN												
V4	JPN												
V5	JPN												
V6	JPN												
V7	JPN												
V8	JPN												
V9	USA												
V10	USA												
V11	USA												
V12	USA												
V13	USA												
V14	EURO												
V15	EURO												
V16	EURO												
V17	EURO												
V18	EURO												
H1	EURO												
H2	EURO												
H3	EURO												
H4	EURO												

Note: company names are disguised   V: volume producer H: high-end specialist

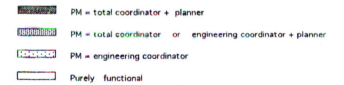

PM = total coordinator + planner

PM = total coordinator   or   engineering coordinator + planner

PM = engineering coordinator

Purely   functional

Source: Fujimoto (1989).

Figure 3.3 Trend in Product Development Organizations (1970s–1980s)

1. There were a variety of system change paths for each main component of the Toyota-style manufacturing system (see the variety of explanations at each column of table 3.1).
2. There was no clear correlation between the nature of the routines and the types of paths (compare the patterns of explanations across the columns).

Therefore, by applying the operational definition specified in figure 3.1, I argue that Toyota's routine capability building can be character-

Table 3.1   Summary of Evolution of Selected Production-Development Capabilities

	Just-in-Time	Multi Tasking with Product-Focus Layout	Jidoka and Flexible Equipment	Kaizen and TQC	Black Box Parts	Heavyweight Product Manager
Competitive effect (rationality)	creating pressure for productivity improvement throughput time inventory cost	productivity improvement	pressures for quality improvement flexibility	quality improvement productivity improvement	cost reduction by manufacturability development lead time and productivity	high product integrity development lead time and productivity
Entrepreneurial vision	Kichiro Toyoda, 1930s ("just in time" slogan) Taiichi Ohno, 1940s-50s (system building)	Kichiro Toyoda, 1945 (a vision of rapid productivity catch-up without economy of scale)	Kichiro Toyoda, 1931 (a vision of high productivity with small volume production)			
Transfer from other industry	textile (bench marking of Nichibo) prewar aircraft production	textile: multimachine operation in spinning (through Ohno)	textile: Sakichi Toyoda's automatic loom	TQC was established in other industries (e.g. process industry)	prewar locomotive or aircraft parts supplier	prewar aircraft industry (chief designer system) forced transfer (collapse of aircraft industry)
Transfer from Ford system	the synchronization idea from Ford (invisible conveyer line) kanban as "incomplete synchronization"	productivity bench marking with Ford modified Taylorism	adoption of Detroit-type automation where feasible U-shape layout as "incomplete transfer machine"	suggestion system from Ford Training Within Industry Statistical Quality Control		
Imperative of forced growth with resource shortage		limit of permanent work force after the 1950 strikes "forced" productivity increase in the 1960s	shortage of investment fund: low cost automation had to be pursued	shortage of supervisors replacing craftsmen-foremen = needs for TWI	high production growth and model proliferation created pressures for subcontracting subassembly and design	
Imperative of forced flexibility with small & fragmented market			"forced" flexibility of equipment due to small volume		product proliferation of the 1960s created pressures for subcontracting out design jobs	product proliferation with limited engineering resource created pressure for compact projects
Imperative of shortage of technology	lack of computer production control technology in the 1950s and 60s		lack of adaptive control automation; Jidoka needs human intervention		lack of electric parts technology at Toyota in 1949 (separation of Nippondenso)	
Ex-post capability of the firm		flexible task assignment and flexible revision of work standards to better exploit opportunities of productivity increase		Toyota maintained momentum for TQC by creating organizations for diffusing it to suppliers	Toyota institutionalized a version of black box parts system that could better exploit competitive advantages	Only Toyota adopted heavy weight product manager system from the aircraft industry as early as 1950s

ized as a *multi-path system emergence* and that Toyota, creating distinctively competitive routines though the emergent process, possessed an *evolutionary learning capability*.

Next, we need to examine how such a process of system emergence resulted in the pattern of manufacturing routines characterized as the "stylized facts" at the beginning of chapter 2—the coexistence of universally adopted routines, region-specific routines, and firm-specific routines. Let's reclassify the foregoing historical data into these three categories.

Factors Affecting Universally Adopted Routines

- *Pressures of international competition.* Toyota's routine capability building was consistently motivated, since the 1930s, by perceived competitive pressures from the U.S. mass producers, particularly Ford. Even with a strongly protected domestic market between the 1930s and '50s, Toyota's consciousness of imaginary competitive pressures persisted.
- *Direct and indirect adoption of the Ford system.* Motivated partly by the perception of international competition, Toyota

adopted many elements of the Ford system and American mass-production system mostly indirectly, including moving conveyers, transfer machines, product and component designs, the Taylor system, supervisor training program, and statistical quality control. A pure dichotomy between the Ford system and the Toyota system is therefore misleading.

Factors Affecting Region-specific Routines

- *Benefits of forced growth*: Some region-specific historical imperatives that all the Japanese firms faced during the postwar era almost forced them to make certain responses, some of which turned out to be competitive advantages. Many such responses were not recognized as competitive weapons when the firms first adopted them. For example, the imperative of forced growth, in both production and product development, with a limited supply of production inputs and fear of labor conflicts, turned out to facilitate capability building for productivity improvements through avoidance of intrafirm overspecialization, division of labor between assemblers and suppliers, and avoidance of excessive use of high-tech equipment on the shop floor.
- *Benefits of forced flexibility.* The imperative of forced flexibility in a fragmented market benefited the Japanese firms. This is partly because of the region-specific patterns of industrial growth: a *rapid production growth accompanied by rapid product proliferation* (see figure 3.4). The flexibility that the firms acquired tended to be recognized as a necessary evil to cope with the fragmented market, rather than a measure for international competition. It should also be noted that, as is obvious from the comparison of Japanese and U.K. production systems, fragmented markets do not automatically create effective flexibility.
- *Benefits of lack of technology.* While excessive use of high-tech automation equipment often became an obstacle to productivity improvement in many of the Western automakers of the 1980s, the effective Japanese automakers apparently avoided such problems. This may be partly because they consciously rejected the temptation of overspecialization; but it also seems to be partly because high technology was not there in the first place. To the extent that this was caused by certain region-specific technology gaps, the lack of technology may bring about unintended competitive benefits to firms of a region.
- *Benefits of intended knowledge transfer.* Region-specific patterns of capabilities may emerge when intraregional knowledge transfers are more dense and frequent than interregional ones. The supplier networks shared by the Japanese firms was

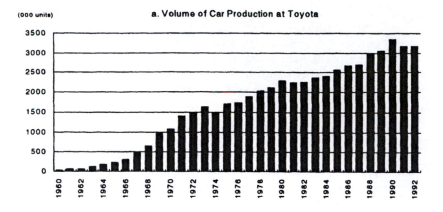

a. Volume of Car Production at Toyota

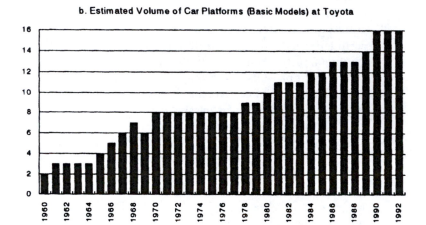

b. Estimated Volume of Car Platforms (Basic Models) at Toyota

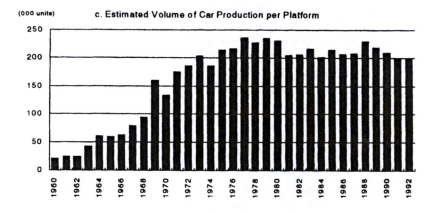

c. Estimated Volume of Car Production per Platform

Source: Toyota Motor Corporation, etc. The number of platforms was estimated by the author.

Figure 3.4 Rapid Production Growth with Rapid Product Proliferation at Toyota

one such transfer instrument. Intense competition among domestic makers during the 1960s and '70s may have also facilitated their efforts to learn from domestic competitors.

- *Benefits of unintended knowledge transfer.* As in the case of engineers from the prewar aircraft industry, the "push" type of knowledge transfer, which the receivers did not intend to make, brought about a rapid increase in automobile technologies and product development systems in the postwar automobile industry in Japan.
- *Benefits of incomplete knowledge transfer.* Although the Japanese auto firms tried to adopt many of the practices and techniques from U.S. mass producers, some of them were incomplete owing to the historical imperatives mentioned above and a lack of the firms' absorption capacities. In this sense, the *kanban* system may be regarded as an incomplete version of the conveyer system, the U-shape machine layout as an incomplete transfer machine, and *jidoka* as incomplete adaptive automation. The very incompleteness of the transfer may have facilitated its subsequent diffusion through the entire system.

Factors Affecting Firm-specific Routines

- *Benefits of self-fulfilling visions.* Firm-specific entrepreneurial visions sometimes played an important role in building distinctive manufacturing capability. This was particularly the case when an apparently unrealistic vision triggered self-fulfilling efforts to achieve bold objectives. Kiichiro Toyoda, in the 1930s and '40s, played a pivotal role in advocating cost reduction without economy of scale, catchup with Ford, and the just-in-time philosophy. Nissan of those days did not have his counterpart.
- *Benefits of linkage to other industries.* Toyota's inherent connection with the textile industry may have facilitated knowledge transfer from it (particularly through Taiichi Ohno) and helped create the automaker's competitive advantages in production control techniques.
- *Advantages of opportunistic (ex-post) learning capability.* Even when no firms recognized the potential competitive advantage of the new system when they first tried it, some could still create firm-specific advantages by exercising an *opportunistic (ex-post) learning capability:* by recognizing the potential competitive advantage of the new system, modifying it to exploit the potentials, institutionalizing it, and retaining it until the advantages are realized. For example, even though all Japanese automakers faced similar environmental pres-

sures for adopting the black box parts system in the 1960s, only Toyota appears to have created a system that could fully exploit the potential advantages of this practice. Although all the Japanese automakers accepted aircraft engineers after the war, Toyota was the only company that institutionalized the heavyweight product manager system that was prevalent in the aircraft industry. Thus, even when all the Japanese firms faced certain historical imperatives that facilitated new practices, only some of them materialized this potential luck through firm-specific evolutionary learning capability.

Refining Solutions into Capabilities: An Organizational Processes Model

In this and the previous chapter I have presented and analyzed historical evidence for *system emergence* and *evolutionary leaning capability* in the case of the Toyota-style manufacturing system. There is, however, another important question that remains to be answered: *what is a firm's evolutionary leaning capability?* To address this, what is needed ultimately is a systematic empirical study of the organizational processes and cultures that bring about evolutionary learning capability, but that is beyond the scope of this book. My goal instead is to provide some groundwork, to present a conceptual framework that may characterize the organizational process behind a firm's evolutionary learning capability: what I call dual-level problem solving.

I have so far argued that the manufacturing systems of successful Japanese automakers of the 1980s have a certain competitive rationality as total systems. At the same time, historical analysis indicates that the system of routine capabilities, even though they were observed to be ex-post rational in terms of competitiveness, were not created all at once by deliberate and intentionally strategic decisions, but evolved as a result of cumulative and emergent processes. Individual elements of routine capabilities tended to be tried, selected, and retained in the system at different times and for different reasons, while the total system gradually and steadily improved its total competitive capability until the 1980s. The logic of the origin, diffusion, and stability of a new system was sometimes divergent, as in the case of the black box parts practice. Routine capabilities were often adopted unintentionally, as Toyota was forced to respond to certain historical imperatives, or at least without knowing the potential competitive benefits. Solutions often existed prior to competitive problems.

Among organizational theories, a standard model of complete problem-solving cycles that flows smoothly from goal setting to problem recognition, alternative search, alternative evaluation, selection, and retention of the solution does not seem to explain this phenomenon well.[51] At the same time, we have to keep in mind that the pro-

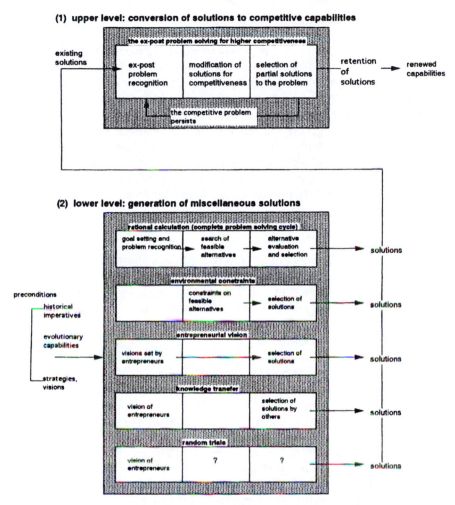

(1) upper level: conversion of solutions to competitive capabilities

the ex-post problem solving for higher competitiveness

existing solutions

| ex-post problem recognition | modification of solutions for competitiveness | selection of partial solutions to the problem |

retention of solutions → renewed capabilities

the competitive problem persists

(2) lower level: generation of miscellaneous solutions

rational calculation (complete problem solving cycle)

| goal setting and problem recognition | search of feasible alternatives | alternative evaluation and selection | → solutions

environmental constraints

| | constraints on feasible alternatives | selection of solutions | → solutions

preconditions

historical imperatives

evolutionary capabilities

entrepreneurial vision

| visions set by entrepreneurs | | selection of solutions | → solutions

strategies, visions

knowledge transfer

| vision of entrepreneurs | | selection of solutions by others | → solutions

random trials

| vision of entrepreneurs | ? | ? | → solutions

Figure 3.5 Dual-Layer Problem Solving: A Simplified Framework

cess eventually created a rational system at Toyota in terms of competitive advantage. Again, the process was neither totally chaotic nor irrational. It was a multi-path system emergence.

For a conceptual model that may help us understand this evolutionary process, I propose a *dual-level problem-solving* framework, one that consists of two levels of partial or incomplete problem-solving processes (see figure 3.5). The lower level mechanism, representing the process of system emergence, generates miscellaneous solutions for various purposes, while the upper level mechanism, reflecting a certain evolutionary learning capability of the firm, absorbs the solutions and converts them to manufacturing capabilities.

Lower Level—Generation of Solutions.   As figure 3.5 indicates, the lower level consists of various types of complete and incomplete problem-solving cycles that generate solutions (patterns of activities that the firm selects) of various kinds through multi-path system emergence. *Rational calculation* represents complete problem-solving cycles with explicit goal setting, problem recognition, deliberate examinations of constraints on the alternatives, evaluation, and selection of feasible alternatives. *Entrepreneurial visions*, on the other hand, tend to lack deliberate assessment of constraints: the solutions are chosen predominantly by the entrepreneurs' goals, regardless of their feasibility. In the case of *environmental constraints*, recognition of such constraints, rather than competitive goal setting, drives selection of solutions. And in *knowledge transfer*, solutions that other organizations selected are often replicated without deliberate analysis.

Upper Level—Refinement of Solutions.   The upper level of figure 3.5 is oriented toward refining existing "crude" solutions in light of the problem of competitiveness. This mechanism is a kind of problem solving or learning process in a broad sense, but it differs from regular problem-solving cycles in that the problem is never fully solved but persists in the long run, and the solutions are only partial solutions. After all, the process of competition is endless, and so is the problem of maintaining and enhancing the firm's competitiveness. In March and Olsen's term, the mechanism may resemble a huge "garbage can" that is never emptied while absorbing miscellaneous solutions from the lower level.[52] In the current model, however, I assume that solutions are generated by a complex system emergence process, unlike the formal "garbage can" model that assumes random generation of solutions.

For our purposes, the "garbage can" takes in the miscellaneous existing solutions, created originally for coping with other problems, as raw materials; gives them a competitive focus; and converts them to a system of competitive capabilities. In this sense, information processing at the upper level may be regarded as a solution refinement process rather than a full-scale problem-solving cycle. Various competitive and noncompetitive solutions arrive at this conversion process one after another, trigger ex-post problem recognition, and are retained for subsequent processing and modified to exploit their potentials as competitive weapons. Thus, the system evolves for higher competitiveness in the long run, but the problem of winning the competition itself never goes away.

The Questions that Remain

With the above model, I can now interpret a firm's evolutionary learning capability as its ability to perform this dual-level process better than rivals in the long run. Ex-ante (intentional) learning capability is linked to the lower level, ex-post (opportunistic) learning capability to the upper one. In this book, I pay a particular attention to the latter: a company with a high ex-post (opportunistic) learning capability, like Toyota, converts miscellaneous existing solutions, many of which are unpolished, to a set of distinctive routine capabilities in product development, production, and purchasing.

What are, then, the organizational properties that may facilitate the solution-refinement cycle? Again, systematic empirical research will be needed to detail this, but it is my impression that, after many contacts with Toyota employees, they view new situations in daily life—whether new problems, solutions elsewhere, partial solutions to the present problems, or chance events—as potential opportunities to improve competitiveness more often than those in other firms. The original trials may be pure luck or unintended consequences rather than intended and realized success, but a firm with many "prepared" people who associate everything with its competitive effects may be able to recognize the competitive value of such trials and exploit them more effectively than rivals (Cohen and Levinthal, 1990, 1994). We return to the organizational aspects of Toyota's evolutionary learning capability in chapter 7, where it will be reinterpreted as a certain effective pattern of "internal evolutionary mechanisms" built into the organization.

Other questions follow naturally from the above discussion: How was the evolutionary learning capability formed in the first place in a particular company? Where did such a company-wide "competition-consciousness" or "prepared mind" come from in Toyota? These are intriguing questions, but there are no clear answers. Some say that the spirit of Kiichiro Toyoda or even Sakichi Toyoda was long retained in the employees' attitudes; others claim a distinctive culture of eastern Aichi prefecture (traditionally called Mikawa) shaped their tenacity and concentration. Both are plausible, but neither is convincing alone. After all, the formation of the evolutionary learning capability itself is so rare that it is extremely difficult to analyze as a subject of social science. For now, suffice it to say that historical circumstantial evidence leads us to infer that Toyota had distinctive evolutionary learning capabilities, at least up to the 1980s.

One last question: If we agree that Toyota's manufacturing routine capabilities were formed through a system emergence, why were such manufacturing routines created this way (i e , multi-path system emergence) rather than through other patterns? The short answer is that manufacturing routines are too complex to be built by either a purely rational or a random process. How and why are they complex? The next chapter tackles this question.

4

THE ANATOMY OF MANUFACTURING ROUTINES
An Information View

Now that we have considered the history of manufacturing at Toyota and its overall evolutionary capability, we can focus on the routinized aspects of the system. In this chapter, I examine the "anatomy" and "physiology" of manufacturing routines—or a company's routinized manufacturing and learning capabilities. In other words, as shown in figure 4.1, what follows is an analysis of the structures of manufacturing routines and an explanation of how they generate functional consequence, or competitive performance.

Through the analysis in the previous chapters, we have already learned that Toyota-style manufacturing routines were formed through multi-path system emergence, enjoyed overall competitive advantages in the 1980s, and were rather difficult for rivals to grasp and imitate in their totality. So far my tentative answer as to why this happened has been that Toyota's total manufacturing system was very *complex*, yet this is not a full answer to such a fundamental question. In this chapter, I explain in what sense and why Toyota-style routine capabilities were complex.

Let's start the analysis by briefly discussing what we know and do not know about the Toyota-style system. My impression, as of the late 1990s, is that many, if not all, basic elements of the Toyota-style manufacturing system have already been explained by researchers and practitioners worldwide, and that the general notion that a total manufacturing system matters is also widespread. But our specific knowledge as to how these elements and subsystems complement one another in generating total system performance is not sufficient. Few companies have reached the level of total manufacturing performance that Toyota has reached, and the learning process is still going on at many companies more than ten years after Western catchup efforts

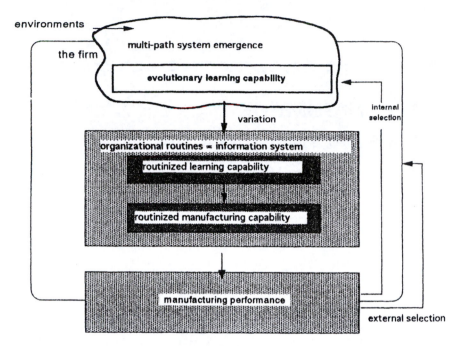

Figure 4.1 Routines as Information System: The Focus of Chapter 4

started in the early 1980s—and more than twenty years after the Japanese export surge of the 1970s.

Based on the research literature to date, it is easy enough to construct a laundry list of Toyota-style manufacturing practices (see appendix A); yet there have been few systematic and consistent explanations of how the *total manufacturing system* brings about performance advantages.[1] Even when a systematic explanation is given for the Toyota production system (TPS), how it interacts with other subsystems such as TQC to create competitive performance and improvements has not been clarified (a notable exception is Shonberger, 1982). Even if TPS and TQC are convincingly explained as an integral system, how they collaborated with other functions, such as product development and supplier management, to create competitive performance advantages is seldom explicitly discussed.[2]

This, of course, does not mean that we have learned everything about individual elements of the system. Even at the level of basic fact and evidence, there still seems to be many misunderstandings, myths, and ignorance about the Toyota-style manufacturing system, despite the extensive research in this field since the 1980s. Tacit knowledge, subtle know-how, and difficult-to-imitate skills exist even in seemingly well-understood areas like inventory control. We need, therefore, to continue empirical studies on many basics of production, product development, and supplier systems used by Toyota and other Japanese auto firms.

I nevertheless emphasize the importance of the total system perspective. Our knowledge of individual practices and subsystems will continue to grow rapidly, but without integrative knowledge, it will remain a fragmented collection of individual techniques. Indeed, the general idea that the Toyota-style manufacturing system should not be regarded as a simple collection of techniques or practices has prevailed for some time, but what we really need now are more *specifics* about the total system.

To fill this important gap, I apply an information system approach to a structural-functional analysis of manufacturing routines. I argue here that we can understand the totality of this manufacturing system only when we reinterpret its practices and performance consistently as patterns of information assets and their processing. The basic facts regarding practices and performance of the Toyota-style manufacturing system can then be mapped in this informational framework. In this way, the present chapter tries to clarify the relationship between routinized capabilities of the total manufacturing system and its competitive performance. This may be an overly ambitious task, but at least we can take an initial step toward explaining a total manufacturing system like Toyota's.

The Information-Knowledge Point of View

The basic building block of the present framework is *information*. Of course, "information is an imprecise term as commonly used."[3] Generally speaking, it is an elusive concept to which different researchers attach different meanings or nuances. But for our analytical purposes, information can be defined very broadly as patterns of material or energy that potentially represent some other events or objects. The representation may be based on causal relations or on social rules.[4] What is represented by information can be physical objects, physical events, other information, or concepts in human minds. As such, the current definition is broader, for example, than that in Shannon-Wiener-type theories of information, management of information literature, information-processing theories of organizations, and microeconomics.[5] In this book, computer data, human knowledge, symbols—as well as shapes of press dies—are all regarded as certain types of information. For example, *knowledge* is regarded as a kind of structured information stored in human memory; when retrieved or activated, it represents concepts or events.

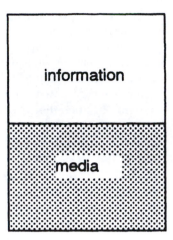

Figure 4.2 Information Asset
(Productive Resource)

Information Assets and Processing

Information cannot exist without the materials or energy in which it is embodied—its *medium*. Therefore, the basic unit of an information system is a combination of information and its medium—an *information asset* (see figure 4.2). Now consider the way information assets change and flow over time on a microscopic level. This book generally defines *information processing* as activities that change the state of an information asset, including information content, medium, and location, as well as combinations thereof. It includes the following three modes of change (figure 4.3):

1. *Transformation,* in which the content of information may change so that it represents something different, while staying in the same medium (e.g., individual learning or engineering design changes on the same blueprints).
2. *Transfer,* in which the same information, representing the same thing, may be transferred or copied to different media (e.g., copying body styling from a clay model to a line drawing or making a press die from CAD-CAM die data).
3. *Transportation,* in which the same information and its medium may be simply moved to another place (e.g., sending a blueprint from product engineering to process engineering).

Note that this definition of information processing includes not only what computers and telecommunication devices do but also human communication, knowledge creation, and even physical transformation. In other words, information processing as defined here is not limited to data processing in computers.

(i) transformation

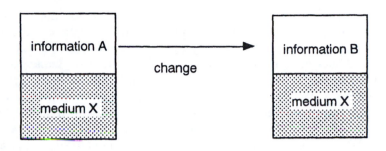

(ii) transfer

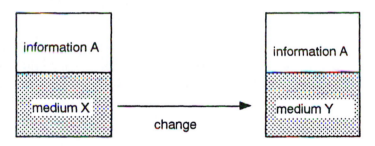

(iii) transportation

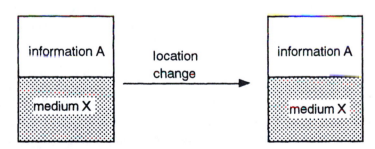

Figure 4.3 Types of Information Processing

The Information System and Change Processes

Let us move on to the next level. In this book, an *information system* refers to a set of information assets that are interconnected, in which certain information processing is performed. The concept of the information system is defined broadly, again, so that it covers not only computer-telecommunication systems but also human communication networks, bureaucratic flows of papers, and physical transformation processes. We can conceive of it as an open system, in which a firm takes in information through its boundary, processes it, and delivers new information (mainly in the form of products) to the outside.

We can conceive of a *steady state* of the system, in which the given information content is partitioned and deployed into separate information assets that are linked in a certain regular pattern to each other. Information may be duplicated and transferred from one asset to another through regular channels, but neither new information nor a new transmission pattern is created in the system as a whole. As described later, a repetitive production process in a stable environment can be described as a certain steady-state information system.

In addition, we need to examine the dynamic aspect of the information system. An information *system change* here refers to creation of new information content, new patterns of partitioning, deployment and linkages among the information assets, or new patterns of information transmission among them, which results in higher functionality of the open system (e.g., survival, growth, fit, competitiveness).

There are different conceptual models that may represent actual system change processes. At the one extreme, we may hypothesize that a purely random process brings about fluctuations in the information system (e.g., a neo-Darwinian concept of changes in genetic information system). At the other extreme, an omnipotent system controller changes the system to an optimal state based on perfect knowledge of the world. Neither model, in its pure form, however, is a reasonable representation of the actual system change process in most cases. It is hard to explain the system improvement process that we observe in the manufacturing systems by a simple random walk; it is not realistic to assume perfect information of the system builder, given the complexity and turbulence of the system and its environment.

Between the two extremes, there are at least two models that may explain the information system changes more realistically: problem-solving cycles and multi-path system emergence. *Problem solving* refers to a certain pattern of information processing that can enhance the functionality of the system in a more or less routine manner, even if the knowledge of the system builder is limited (i.e., bounded rationality). The multi-path system emergence is a more ill-structured process, in which the system builder can predict and control the change process only partially. Since I've already discussed system emergence

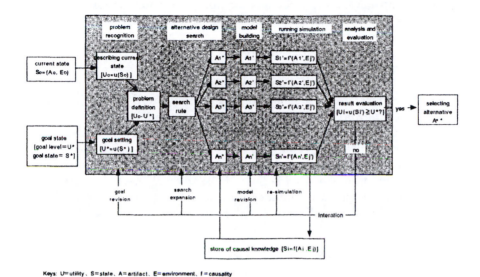

Keys: U=utility, S=state, A=artifact, E=environment, f=causality
Source: Adopted and modified from Fujimoto (1989).

Figure 4.4 A Generic Model of Problem-Solving Cycles (H. Simon Type)

in previous chapters, let's move on to a further elaboration of problem solving here.

The Problem-Solving Cycle

I have already introduced problem-solving cycles as part of an overall approach to manufacturing processes. In the literature of organizational behavior in general, it has been long argued that a certain heuristic pattern of information processing can create useful information in a consistent manner, even when causal knowledge of the information creator is imperfect (Simon, 1945/1976; March and Simon, 1958). Here a *problem-solving cycle* refers to a series of information processing in which goals or problems (i.e., input information) are converted to solutions to the problems (i.e., output information), using regular heuristics under the conditions of uncertainty and bounded rationality.

A generic model of a problem solving cycle with five steps (goal setting, alternative idea generation, model development, experiment, and selection) is illustrated in figure 4.4.[6] As the diagram indicates, a cycle of problem solving is typically initiated by recognition of certain problems (i.e., gaps between goals and current situations). Alternative ideas are then created or retrieved from the repertoire. Since knowledge of the causal relationship between the alternatives and their consequences is normally imperfect, the cycle typically develops simulation models and conducts experiments for various possible combinations. After the results are evaluated, an acceptable alternative may be selected or a new cycle of problem solving may begin. As a result of a problem-solving cycle, the solution set (i.e., information content) of the firm changes.

Although there may be alternative models that can explain the same phenomenon, classical problem-solving heuristics still seem to be one of the most powerful tools to analyze this type of incremental system change in human organizations, particularly in the case of the manufacturing organizations. After observing numerous examples of repetitive system improvements and recoveries from disruptions in products and production processes, I believe that the problem-solving model can explain the repetitive and incremental system changes in this field most effectively. We will come back to this issue later in this chapter.

Reinterpreting Manufacturing Activities as an Information System

Having defined basic concepts, we can now apply the information perspective to the manufacturing system. Since customer value, embodied in product and its price (and the costs behind it), is jointly created and delivered by product development and production (often involving suppliers in both cases), the two subsystems should be analyzed as a total system. Product development is essentially the cumulative creation of information assets for commercial production; commercial production is essentially repeated transmission of product design information from the process to the product. Thus, information is a common denominator that can be consistently used for the analysis of resource and routinized capability in product development and production.

Firms, Products, Consumers: The Overall System

The overall development-production-sales-consumption process involves interactions between a manufacturing firm and consumers, where the former tries to satisfy the latter. In this section, *consumers* means customers in general, including industrial users. This model assumes that information circulates through the system from development to production, to marketing, to consumption, and finally back to development (see figure 1.2). The information conveys value to the consumers while it changes its content, medium, and location.[7]

A *firm* can be seen as an open system in terms of value-carrying information. It faces the market environment (consumption process), which itself is another information system. The firm delivers a bundle of value-carrying information, which is interpreted and appreciated by customers. The information bundles are created cumulatively by development, production, and marketing on the producer side. The information on how consumers process the information and generate satisfaction (i.e., the consumption process) flows back to the producer as input. In this way, the firm and the consumer exchange information through their boundaries and jointly create customer satisfaction.

Products are primary outputs of manufacturing firms to the market. In the information view, the essential part of what manufacturing firms deliver to the customer is a bundle of information or messages that each product carries, rather than the product itself as a physical object. The information that the product delivers to the customers has two aspects: structure (i.e., form) and function. Structural information is stored in the product, while functional information is transmitted from the product to the customers as they interact with a certain user environment. Manufacturing firms absorb information from the outside, create potentially value-carrying information through product development and production activities, ultimately embody it in the physical product, and deliver it to the customers.[8]

Consumption is also regarded as information processing or information creation by the customers.[9] In other words, what customers ultimately consume is not the physical object but the bundles of structural and functional information that the product transmits to customers. They receive the information from the product, interpret it, compare it with their expectations, and generate satisfaction (or "value" in the marketing sense) for themselves. Therefore, customer satisfaction is created jointly by firms providing the product-embodied information and the consumers attaching meanings to it.

Productive Resources as Information Assets

The bundle of information that the products eventually embody is gradually developed through a network of what economist Edith T. Penrose, in her seminal work, *The Theory of the Growth of the Firm*, calls *productive resources* within manufacturing firms.[10] In the information view, each unit of productive resource (more precisely, developmental-productive resource) can be regarded as an information asset that consists of a combination of the value-carrying information and a medium

The information component of the developmental-productive resource represents certain functional or structural aspects of a product, and is deployed in the development-production system. As product development and production processes go on, the information becomes refined from product concepts to basic or functional product designs, finalized as detailed (structural) product designs, translated and deployed in production processes, and eventually transmitted to the products. We may call such value-carrying information product design information, since it is designed to represent a certain aspect of the final product. Thus, the information component of the resource tends to be product-specific and firm-specific.

Let me reemphasize that the product design information, an intangible pattern or form, does not exist without media. Physical materials, human brains, blank papers, and various computer memory devices are all media that can potentially embody the product design information within the firm. At each stage of the manufacturing process, the appropriate media that can receive, store, modify, and transmit the information are deliberately chosen. When a firm purchases the "blank" media without product design information (e.g., untrained workers, raw materials, general-purpose equipment), we can regard them as "undifferentiated production inputs" in the classical economic sense.[11]

The media mix of a firm's productive resources may change over time. For example, bureaucratization and Taylorism can be regarded as media switches from human-embodied resources (e.g., craft-type skills) to paper-embodied ones (e.g., manuals); hard automation usually is a switch from human-embodied to capital-embodied resources in the production process; programmable automation is a shift to computer-embodied resources. Generally speaking, the media mix of direct (if not indirect) productive resources in the auto industry has historically shifted from human memories to papers and mechanical hardware, and further to computer-related media.

Penrose's concept of productive resources can be reinterpreted as certain information assets, each of which consists of a pair of value-carrying information and a medium. A firm's manufacturing system, then, consists of interconnected productive resources. When using relatively undifferentiated media purchased from outside (i.e., production inputs in microeconomic terms), productive resources become firm-specific to the extent that the content of product design information and the patterns of interactions between the productive resources are different across firms. The product itself is an example of a productive resource, and so are dies, jigs, tools, standard operating procedures, product-specific skills of the workers, numerical control data for machine tools, prototypes, engineering drawings, computer-aided design files, clay models, technical papers, and market research reports.

Manufacturing Activity as Information Processing

The *activities* of product development and production (or what Penrose calls "productive service") can be regarded as information processing between productive resources that cause changes in their information content, media, or location (see figure 4.3). A series of activities (information processing) that are regularly linked together may be simply called a *process*.

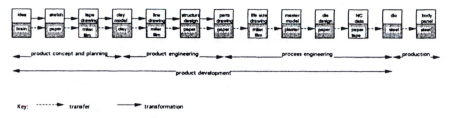

Figure 4.5 Development-Production Activities Between Productive
Resources: The Case of Body Panel (1980s)

An example of automobile body design and stamping is illustrated
in figure 4.5, in which the product design information for the body
panel is gradually created, transformed, and transferred though a series
of activities in product development and production. In this process (a
typical one in the 1980s), a new idea for a product's exterior design is
created in the mind of a designer; the idea is refined (transformed) and
transferred to three-dimensional clay models (or in computer-aided
styling models); it is further refined and transferred to line drawings,
detailed body parts drawings, and so on; the body design data are
translated into stamping die designs; and the die design data are transferred through numerical control machine tools on to "soft" dies for
trials, as well as steel dies for production. Finally, at the commercial
production stage, the body design information that the dies contain is
transferred to steel sheets one after another. In this way, product development and production can be described and analyzed as an intertwined system of information processing among various information
assets.

Product Development as Information Process

Product development activities can be described as a cumulative
process of information creation and transmission, which gradually develops information assets necessary for commercial production (figure
4.6).[12] In this process, information on market needs and technological
opportunities are combined and translated into a set of information assets, which in turn are converted to actual products through commercial production. In this sense, product development can be regarded as
an upstream function of production in terms of information flow.

As the figure shows, a typical car development project creates various kinds of information assets in a cumulative way; some become
input for the development of others. Such information assets include
product concept documents, product/project targets, layout drawings,
styling sketches, clay models, line drawings, engineering drawings, a
CAD data base, prototypes, pilot vehicles, prototype test results, CAE
simulation results, production process plans, process flow charts,

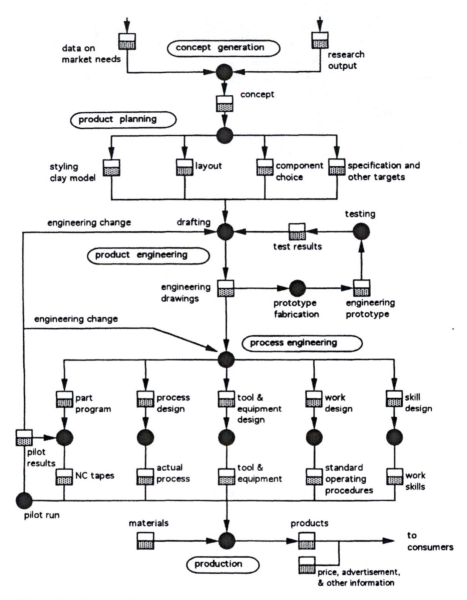

Figure 4.6 Product Development as Information Processing

work designs, tool/equipment designs, tools, jigs, dies, equipment, NC tapes, and work skills.[13] These information assets are embodied in various media such as papers, tangible materials, and magnetic disks.

In the case of automobiles, four distinctive stages can be identified in the standard product development process: product concept generation, product planning (i.e., functional and basic designs), product engineering (i.e., detailed and structural designs), and process engineering (i.e., production preparation).[14] First, *concept generation* combines information on potential market needs and technical possibilities and creates product concepts, which are the company's basic visions on how to satisfy target customers. Second, *product planning* translates the concepts into more specific plans such as project targets (performance, specification, sales, cost, investments, etc.), main component choice, layout drawings, and exterior/interior styling. These outputs become goals for the subsequent engineering stages. Third, *product engineering* translates the product plan into detailed parts drawings, and prototypes are built based on these drawings. Product performance is checked against the plan through a series of tests and reviews. Fourth, *process engineering*, or production preparation, translates product designs into process planning of production lines, as well as work designs, tool and die designs, equipment designs, and part programming for each production station. Actual production factors are then manufactured, developed, inspected, and deployed on the plant floors. Finally, the capability of the production process as a whole is checked through a series of pilot runs.[15] At the end of process engineering, elements of production processes are deployed for commercial production on the shop floor.

Note that a set of activities for developing a product, often called a project, consist of many problem-solving cycles connected to one another.[16] Each of the cycles includes the generation of alternative designs, as well as evaluation and selection of them in light of objectives of product development: customer satisfaction. Product development activities are also essentially a simulation of future production and consumption processes.[17] That is, performance of product development is affected by accuracy and efficiency of the simulation.

Production as Information Process

Production activity can also be regarded as transfers of the product design information from the production process to the product (see figure 4.7). At each station of the process, a fraction of the product design information—stored in the workers, tools, equipment, manuals, and so on—is transferred to material or work in process, which "absorbs" the information step by step and is transformed eventually to a product. In the field of production and operations management, the sequence of transformation in which the materials and work in process receive the information is often called *process flow*, while the transfer of the information from a given station is usually called *operation*.

For example, in the stamping process, a series of body dies contains information representing part of the body shell. As the sheet metal goes through the stamping machines, it receives the information from the dies and become a body panel (see figure 4.7). Similarly, spot-

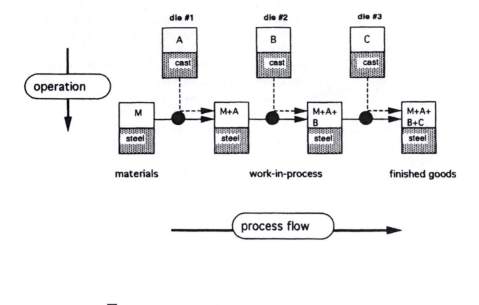

Figure 4.7 Production as Information Processing (The Case of Body Stamping)

welding robots transfer information on spot locations/conditions from computer memories to body shells. Transfer machines impose information about cutting routes/conditions, which is stored in electromechanical media, on engine blocks. Assembly workers apply information stored in their memories, or skills, to assemble parts in each operation.

Whereas a production process is usually described and analyzed as physical transformation of tangible materials, this book focuses instead on its intangible (i.e., informational) aspect because, again, I want to analyze production, product development, and consumption in an integrated manner. It is information, rather than material, that runs through these three stages. Also, as computer-integrated manufacturing has become one of the key issues in today's manufacturing engineering and production control, the entire production activity has become increasingly recognized as an integrated information-processing system.

As for the information-creation aspect of production activities, the emphasis on knowledge accumulation and continuous improvement in manufacturing since the 1980s implies the importance of the information (including knowledge)-creation capability of workers, supervisors, and plant engineers.[18] For example, it became obvious in the 1980s that productivity and quality in the long run depend greatly on

management's perception of the worker: rather than a simple trans-
mitter of given information (i.e., the traditional Tayloristic view), he or
she can be seen as an information creator who continuously accumulates and reorganizes production knowledge and skills (i.e., the JIT-
TQC view typically found at some Japanese manufacturers of the
1980s).

Sales and Marketing as Information Process

Although sales and marketing are generally outside the scope of this
book, it is obvious that they are also critical components in the overall
system of information creation and transmission between the firms and
consumers.[19] Significant parts of marketing and selling activities can
also be regarded as an information-processing system, in which companies transmit a bundle of product-related information to potential
customers. First, as indicated earlier, the product itself can be viewed as
a bundle of information embodied in materials, which may potentially
satisfy the customer. This is, in fact, a core marketing concept.[20] Thus,
physical distribution of the products to the customers is in itself a kind
of information transmission. Second, product-related information that
is embodied in nonproduct media—for example, advertisements, cat-
alogs, sales talks, and showroom displays—can also be created and
transmitted to target customers. In this way, marketing attempts to develop a package of consistent information around a product and then
deliver it to potential buyers in order to influence them.

Supplier Systems as Information Process

Finally, let's consider the issue of supplier management from the information point of view, since this is an important source of competitiveness and customer satisfaction in the automobile industry. Generally speaking, both product development (wherever it exists) and
production activities of parts and material suppliers can be described
in exactly the same manner as they are for the automobile producers.
Automakers and their suppliers are connected through various informational linkages, by which they jointly create value-carrying information to the customers. Therefore, the overall information-processing
system of production and development is divided among automobile
producers and various suppliers, and informational interfaces are
thereby created among these firms.

   Supplier management—defined here as management of the informational interface between the firms—can be analyzed along three dimensions:[21] interfirm task partitioning, supplier competition, individual transactions. Note that these three dimensions are highly
complementary. Later in this chapter, and in appendix B3, I analyze
the functions of the Toyota-style supplier system, showing that its

three corresponding system properties (bundled outsourcing, dynamic small number competition, and long-term relational transactions) complement one another in creating its performance advantage.

Patterns of Interfirm Task Partitioning. This means decisions about where to draw the line for make-or-buy decisions in terms of both production and product development (i.e., defining a firm's boundary in the network of interconnected information assets for manufacturing).[22] To the extent that an assembly product such as the automobile has a hierarchical architecture in which a product can be decomposed into subassembly modules, components, and piece parts, the task partitioning results also in hierarchical linkages of assembly firms, first-tier suppliers, second-tier firms, and so on, for a given product (see figure 4.8). As is clear in the figure, opportunities for interfirm transactions take place where the boundary cuts across the hierarchy of productive resources. Because an assembly firm with high vertical integration (a high in-house production ratio) would have a boundary that cuts across the lower part of the productive resource hierarchy, it is natural to predict that the higher the in-house ratio, the more suppliers a company has to deal with, other things being equal. This was one of the reasons a highly integrated firm such as GM had a much larger number of suppliers to deal with than Toyota, which had much lower in-house production ratio.

Note that make-or-buy decisions have to be made for multiple stages of the manufacturing process, including not only for production activities but also for production process (equipment, tools, jigs, dies, etc.), process designs, detailed product designs (engineering drawings), and basic product designs. In other words, the boundaries may be drawn differently for different development-production activities, which would result in an overlaid pattern of boundaries for a firm defined upon multiple hierarchies of productive resources (see figure 4.9). For example, a given component may be detail-designed in house but manufactured by outside suppliers (e.g., detail-controlled parts), or both may be done by the suppliers (e.g., black box parts). In any case, such decisions influence the division of contractual responsibility (e.g., responsibility for quantity and quality assurance) and eventually the patterns of distribution of manufacturing capabilities between assemblers and suppliers.

Patterns of Supplier Competitions. When a buying firm selects more than one supplier for a single transaction opportunity (e.g., dual or multiple sourcing), or nominates more than one potential supplier prior to the selection (e.g., bidding, development competition), it results in competition between suppliers. The buying firm may alternatively nominate or select only one supplier for each transaction opportunity. Such selection of competitive structure would affect be-

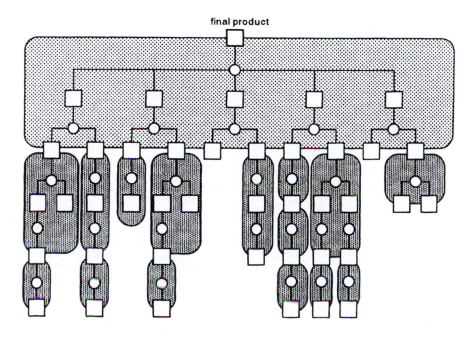

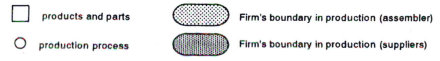

Figure 4.8 Hierarchy of Products, Processes, and Suppliers

havioral patterns, organizational structures, capabilities, and performance of both suppliers and assemblers.

Conversely, a supplier chooses a set of its transaction partners for
each parts item. It may choose to be a dedicated supplier for a given
component, or it may decide to be more independent by selling to multiple firms. The combination of the single-multiple suppliers and single-
multiple buyers results in four typical cases, shown in figure 4.10.

Patterns of Individual Transactions.   When the make-buy boundaries
and transaction partners are decided on the network of productive resources and activities, details of each individual transaction have to
be designed and implemented. As each transaction consists of a bundle of information flows defined upon the interface between the two
firms, this means detailed design of information flows in terms of content, timing, media, and so on. For each transaction, the pair of firms
may choose between long-term and short-term contracts, frequent and

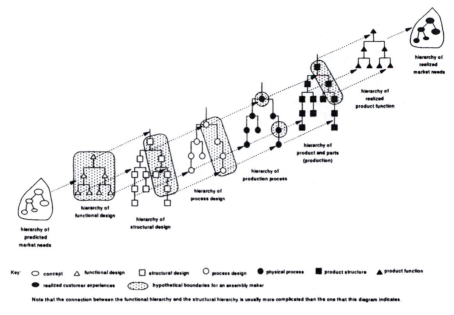

Key: ○ concept   △ functional design   ☐ structural design   ○ process design   ● physical process   ■ product structure   ▲ product function
● realized customer experiences   ⬭ hypothetical boundaries for an assembly maker

Note that the connection between the functional hierarchy and the structural hierarchy is usually more complicated than the one that this diagram indicates.

Figure 4.9 Multiple Hierarchies and Overlaid Boundaries

infrequent contacts, early or late contacts, formal and face-to-face communications, and so on. Also, to the extent that there are multiple organizational units on the boundary that handle different aspects of the transactions, these boundary spanning units also need to be coordinated internally.[23]

Manufacturing Routines Reinterpreted

Having gone through the production, product development, and supplier systems consistently from the information point of view, we can now give the organizational routine for manufacturing a clearer definition: the manufacturing routines this book describes are nothing but stable and/or repetitive patterns of the information system I've just presented, as well as its changes. Accordingly, a company's routinized manufacturing capability and routinized learning capabilities can be consistently analyzed as a certain pattern of routines that contributes to firm-specific competitive advantages.

Reinterpreting Competitive Performance

Let's turn to performance. Only after we describe both the routines and the performance of manufacturing systems in informational terms can we move on to a thorough definition of a company's manufacturing capabilities. In the present framework, *competitiveness* (or the competitive performance) of a product is defined as the influence a

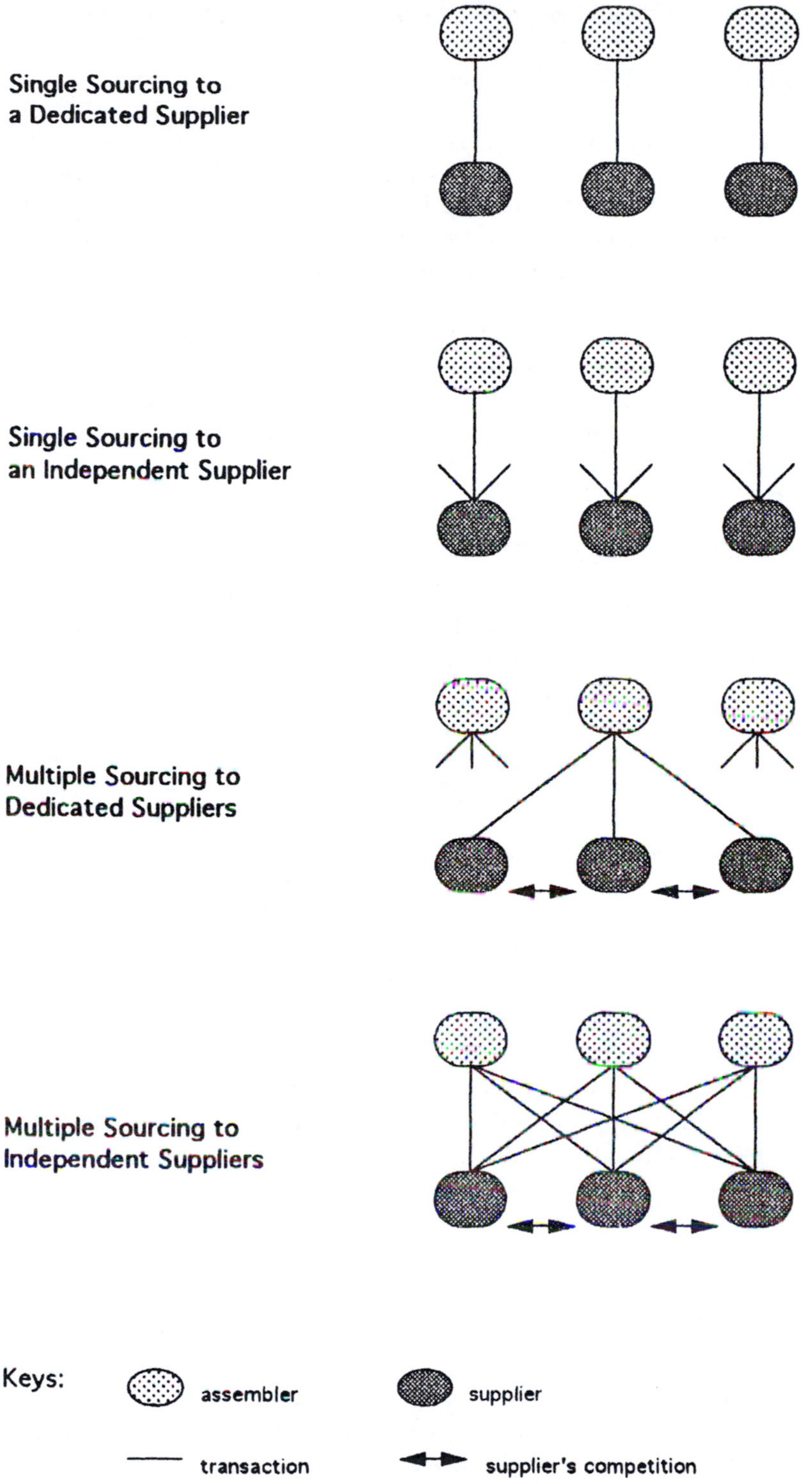

Single Sourcing to
a Dedicated Supplier

Single Sourcing to
an Independent Supplier

Multiple Sourcing to
Dedicated Suppliers

Multiple Sourcing to
Independent Suppliers

Keys: assembler   supplier

transaction   supplier's competition

Figure 4.10 Types of Transaction Networks and Competition

product-embodied information bundle has in attracting and satisfying potential and existing customers. As such, product competitiveness is a joint result of the manufacturer's ability to provide a distinctive product (information bundle) and the customer's ability of discerning and interpreting the information. A firm's system of resources and activities in product development and production can contribute to its product competitiveness through at least four dimensions: *productivity, throughput time, product quality,* and *flexibility.* Productivity and throughput time measure efficiency of information transmission between productive resources; product quality is related to fitness of the information content or accuracy of information transmission; and flexibility means information redundancy for coping with variety and change.

Productivity as Efficiency of Information Transmission

By viewing production activities as the transmission of value-carrying information from the production processes to materials or work-in-process, one can reinterpret productivity and throughput time as efficiency of information transmission and information reception respectively.

Factor productivity in manufacturing (at a given process step for a given product) can be regarded as efficiency of information transmission from a factor in production processes, such as worker and equipment, to work in process or materials. It affects product competitiveness through unit product cost, given the unit factor price. For example, labor productivity at a certain workstation, measured by work hours per unit, can be seen as efficiency in the transfer of value-carrying information from the worker to the work-in-process (see figure 4.11). A high level of labor productivity for this process can be achieved by either of two methods—the "density" approach or the "speed" approach:[24]

- Increasing *density* of information transmission (the fraction of the time when value-carrying information is being transmitted from the production process) by reducing such non-value-adding time as waiting, walking, and setup.[25]
- Increasing *speed* of the information transmission itself (the time needed for transmitting a given chunk of value-carrying information) by performing each individual value-adding task more quickly, or introducing new production technologies for faster processing.[26]

Interestingly enough, in various automobile production processes (e.g., stamping, machining, assembly), U.S. firms of the 1970s and early '80s tended to emphasize the speed approach, while Japanese makers, operating with a Toyota production system philosophy that emphasized reducing "muda," or non-value-adding-time, tended to

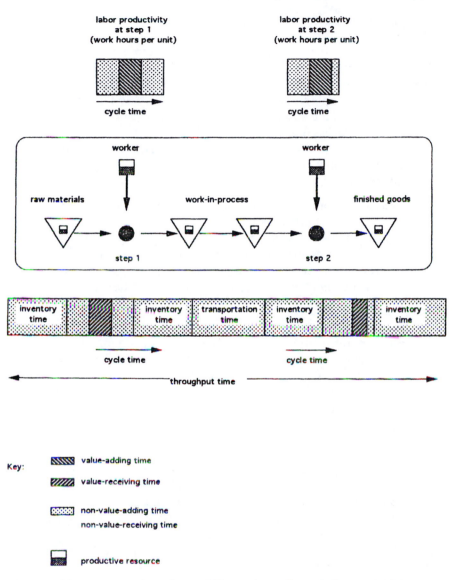

Figure 4 11 Factor Productivity and Throughput Time: A Conceptual Case

emphasize the density approach. This latter approach—increasing Information transmission density—is the heart of the Toyota-style manufacturing system and the source of its productivity advantage.

Throughput Time as Efficiency of Information Reception

Throughput time is elapsed time from reception of a given material to
shipping of the product. It affects delivery time to the customers in

the case of production to order; in the case of production to stock, shorter throughput time may improve the accuracy of demand forecast and thus reduce both finished goods inventory and stockouts. While factor productivity in volume production means efficiency of information transmission on the sender's side (i.e., workers and equipment in a given operation), throughput time refers to efficiency and speed of information absorption on the receiver's side (i.e., materials and work-in-process in a given process flow).[27]

As shown in figure 4.11, as in the case of productivity (assuming a simple process flow with a linear sequence of production steps), one can reduce throughput time by:

1. Reducing non-value-receiving time such as inventory time (including materials, work-in-process, and finished goods), transportation time between the steps, waiting time of the work-in-process within each process step, and so on;[28] or
2. Speeding up the value-receiving process itself at each step (including parallel operations of value-adding tasks).

Once again, the *density* approach (i.e., reducing the fraction of non-value-receiving time, or "muda") turned out to be the more competitive solution during the 1980s, as inventory reduction under the just-in-time system demonstrated.[29] Reducing throughput time through the density approach meant that the process flow was more efficient in making the materials absorb information from the production steps and transforming them into final products.

Quality as Accuracy of Information Transmission

The concept of product quality, in the present framework, is related to fitness of information content or accuracy of information processing along a chain of productive resources that link customer needs, product concepts, product designs, process designs, process, and products (i.e., the chain of quality; see figure 4.12).[30]

Total product quality ("fitness for use," in the definition of J. M. Juran) measures how the information content embodied in the actual product matches customer needs and expectations. It can be decomposed, along this chain, into design quality and conformance quality.

Conformance quality (also called manufacturing quality) measures how well the information embodied in the actual products corresponds to that in the product design. Once the complete set of detailed product design information is developed at the product engineering stage, it is transferred to process design, to the actual processes deployed on the shop floor, and eventually to the final product. However, product design information is subject to deterioration through this chain of quality. To the extent that transmission errors accumulate between product designs and actual products, the informa-

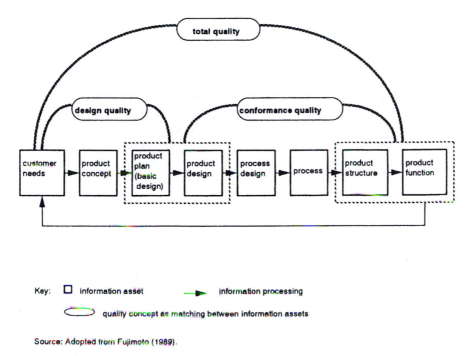

Key: ☐ information asset   ➤ information processing

⬭ quality concept as matching between information assets

Source: Adopted from Fujimoto (1989).

Figure 4.12 Quality Chain and Quality as Accuracy of Information Processing

tion that the products ultimately carry can deviate from what the company intended at the product design stage and conformance quality goes down.

Design quality, on the other hand, means fitness of the product design with target customer expectations, or intended product quality at the design stage. It measures how well the customer expectations are translated into product concepts and then into detailed product designs. As the chain of quality indicates, a high level of total product quality is achieved only when both design quality and conformance quality are high. Even when design quality is very high, its value does not reach the customers if conformance quality is low; when conformance quality is high, customers are not satisfied when the product design does not fit what they expected in the first place.

Flexibility as Information Redundancy

Generally speaking, a system's flexibility refers to its ability to respond to a given environmental change or variety with less deterioration in performance. As such, the concept of flexibility in the manufacturing system has various aspects, depending upon which change and which performance we are talking about. For now, let's focus on the case of flexibility in cost against product variety.[31]

Functionally, flexibility absorbs the cost impact of product variety. In modern mass production, it costs manufacturing firms significantly to develop and maintain such productive resources as machines, workers, and blueprints. When single-model mass production is prevalent (e.g., Ford Model T), firms pursue a simple economy of scale, in which each productive resource transmits the same information to as many products with identical design as possible, multiplying the information and spreading the cost over them. When the market is diversified and firms produce different products, however, some of the productive resources need flexibility to enjoy an economy of scope. The cost impact of product variety is absorbed through two steps: first, *parts flexibility*, with a common component design shared by multiple products, reduces the overall variety of parts designs while maintaining the product variety; second, *process flexibility* further reduces the variety of production processes for making a given set of products and components (see figure 13.a). The two types of flexibility jointly reduce the cost impact of offering a variety of products.

Structurally, flexibility against variety means redundancy of information assets in a given productive resource. When a unit of productive resource is flexible, it contains both general-purpose information subassets and product-specific information subassets (figure 13.b). For example, a flexible stamping process consists of general-purpose press machines and product-specific (or product-family-specific) dies; a flexible machining system has general-purpose numerical control (NC) machines and product-specific NC programs; flexible assembly workers master both general and product-specific skills; flexible product design consists of common parts and product-specific parts. In this way, the cost for general-purpose elements is spread over different products. At the same time, each productive resource carries redundant information in that all of its information is not activated when a particular product is made. Similar logic holds in the case of flexibility against changes in production volume and product designs.

Application: Routinized Capabilities for Toyota-style Production

Now that we have reinterpreted manufacturing routines—a firm's routinized manufacturing and learning capabilities—and competitive performance consistently from the information point of view, let's look specifically at the Toyota-style manufacturing system—first production, then product development and supplier management.[32] For a start, the production capability of the most effective Japanese automakers, illustrated above, can be summarized as *dense and accurate information transmission between flexible (information-redundant) productive resources*. The density of information transmission from

a Function of Flexibility to Variety

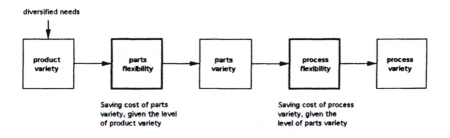

diversified needs

| product variety | → | parts flexibility | → | parts variety | → | process flexibility | → | process variety |

Saving cost of parts
variety, given the level
of product variety

Saving cost of process
variety, given the
level of parts variety

b Structure of Flexibility to Variety

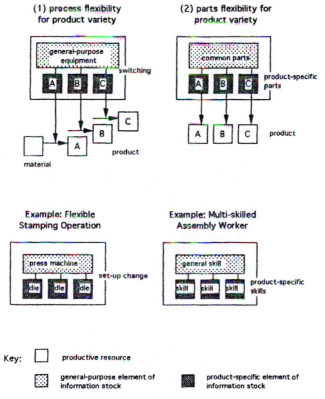

(1) process flexibility for product variety

(2) parts flexibility for product variety

Example: Flexible Stamping Operation

Example: Multi-skilled Assembly Worker

Key: □ productive resource

▨ general-purpose element of information stock

▩ product-specific element of information stock

Figure 4.13 Flexibility as Redundancy of Information Stock

the process to the materials leads to high productivity and short throughput time at the same time, with accurate information transmission from product design to the product.

Capabilities for Higher Productivity and Shorter Throughput Time

The Toyota-style production system focuses on reduction of "muda," or the time when information transmission is *not* happening (i.e., nontransmission time) on both the sender and receiver side. For example, take a labor-intensive process in which trained workers are the senders and works-in-process are the receivers of the value-carrying information. The system aims at low levels of non-value-adding time on the worker side (e.g., waiting time) on the one hand, and non-value-receiving time on the work-in-process side (e.g., inventory) on the other. Elimination of unnecessary nontransmission time is particularly emphasized. In essence, what the Toyota production system defines as "muda" is unnecessary nontransmission time, which includes inventory, overproduction, transportation, and defects on the information receiver side, and waiting and unnecessary motions on the sender side.[33]

Thus, the ideal system for Toyota-style production resembles a network in which information continues to be transmitted and received between the nodes without much intermission. Such a system, with a high-density of information transfer between productive resources, is called lean by some authors, as it has a low level of the "fat" called nontransmission time.[34]

In order to approach to the lean situation, some principles of information handling need to be applied to the system—those of "receiver first," transmission density, information redundancy, and regularity. Figure 4.14 maps productivity-delivery-related practices identified in appendix A into a coherent informational diagram. The Toyota-style production system incorporates the following:[35]

Design the System from the Information Receiver Side First. The production system is designed from the information receiver side, or downstream of the information flow. First, the pace of the entire production process (i.e., cycle time) is set based on the demand of the ultimate information receiver: final customers or dealers. This means minimizing the finished goods inventories. Second, the pace of production (i.e., information transfer) upstream is determined by the pace of the downstream process: the principle of just-in-time and *kanban*. Third, efforts for rationalizing the process flow (i.e., the information receiver side) precede those for rationalizing the operations at each process step (i.e., the information source side).[36] For example, reduction of throughput time by process synchronization, reduction of in-process inventory, product-focused layout along the material flows,

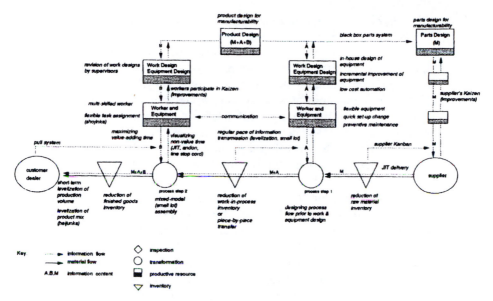

Figure 4.14 Capabilities in Productivity and Throughput Time: The Dense Information Network

piece-by-piece transfer of work-in-process, and so on precede improvements in factor productivity. In other words, the effort to reduce non-value-receiving time on the process flow side tend to precede efforts to reduce non-value-sending time on the operation side at each process step.

Give Priority to Density of Transmission Rather than Speed of Information.   I've already noted that factor productivity can be enhanced either by increasing the density of information transmission or by speeding up the transmission itself. The Toyota-style production system has given a clear priority to the former. In the TPS, taking out non-value-adding time ("muda") is much more important than speeding up individual value-adding operations. For example, Toyota's plant managers would emphasize reduction of setup time in the press shop rather than increase the number of stamping strokes per hour; reduce air-cutting time in machining operations rather than increase cutting and feeding speed; reduce waiting time by giving multiple tasks to each assembly worker rather than speed up the line and the assembly motions.[37] Traditional American auto factories of the 1970s tended to emphasize the "speedup" (i.e., compression of value-adding time itself) approach and thus the technology-driven approach of mass production. The Toyota-style approach, on the other hand, often brings about significant productivity increases without introducing new production technologies.

Allow Information Redundancy as Long as it Enhances Transmission Density. Redundancy of information stored in a given productive resource may mean flexibility, but additional or duplicated investment on equipment or human resources can result (e.g., overlapped multiple-job training for permanent workforce). However, the Toyota-style system allows, or even facilitates, such redundancy if it contributes to a higher density of information transfer in the operation. Multiskilled workers, job rotation, flexible stamping processes with quick die changes, and flexible welding jigs and robots are all examples of information redundancy or duplication in the productive resources.

Emphasize a Regular Pace of Information Transfer. When the information system is designed by the "receiver first" principle, the production pace is determined by customer demand and process flow is rationalized first (e.g., inventory reduction). This, however, can become a constraint against improving productivity at each station because it tells the information senders (e.g., workers and machines) precisely when they have to transmit the information. Sender flexibility (information redundancy) may alleviate the constraints, but another measure is to make the transmission timing as regular as possible, like pulses. At Toyota, this levelization is called *heijunka*.

Capabilities for Higher Conformance Quality

In seeing production as information transmission from the process to the materials, we may illustrate the typical pattern of capability for high conformance quality. (Figure 4.15 maps quality-related practices identified in appendix A into a coherent informational diagram.) The Toyota-style production system emphasizes:

1. *The information source side.* Contrary to the case of productivity and throughput time, a conformance quality control system is designed from the information sender side. That is, the system is designed so that the information sources (e.g., workers and equipment) do not make transmission errors in the first place. This notion of "do right transfer the first time" (*tsukurikomi*) contrasts with traditional quality control systems that emphasize optimal design of inspection on the information receiver side. Many of the techniques and practices that are prevalent in the effective Japanese automakers are consistent with this "information source first" concept: making the transmission of error messages physically impossible by certain foolproof mechanisms built into equipment (e.g., *poka-yoke, jidoka*); eliminating sources of "noise" in the production process by giving the shop floor order, clarity, and cleanliness (e.g., 5-S campaign); preventive maintenance of

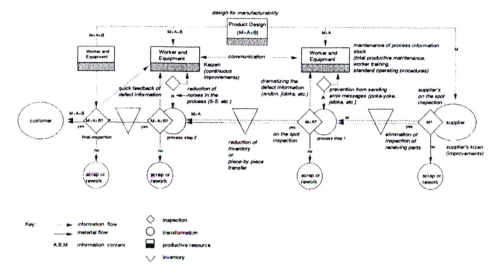

Figure 4.15 Capabilities in Quality: The Accurate Information Transmission

information stored in equipment and workers (e.g., total productive maintenance, training of workers); improvement of equipment and work methods in the information source (e.g., root-cause analysis, 5-why approach to action plans); product designs that are robust (e.g., design for manufacturing, Taguchi method).

2. *Quick feedback of defect information.* Once the transmission errors happen, they have to be detected and proper remedies have to be implemented. Effective automakers tend to reduce the lead time between fabrication and inspection, and thereby make information feedback cycles quick. On-the-spot inspection, in which direct workers (including team leaders) inspect what they just made before transferring it to the downstream step, is a typical example. Another application of this concept is to let parts suppliers inspect their own parts and to eliminate inspection of incoming parts. Reduction of cycle inventory and piece-by-piece transfer of work-in-process between process steps also reduce lead time between fabrication and inspection.

The Improvement Capability in Production

Continuous improvement of productivity and quality (*kaizen*) is often seen as a core capability of effective Japanese production systems.[38] The idea of a factory as a "learning laboratory" applies here.[39] The elements of both just-in-time and total quality control appear to contribute jointly to a Toyota-style capability of routinized learning (i.e., repetitive problem solving), although the two systems tend to be separate in the textbooks.[40] In any case, *kaizen* activities in the Toyota-style production system emphasize:

1. *Revealing the production problems on the spot.* There are various practices that reveal, visualize, and dramatize potential problems to organizational members. Reduction of inventories in JIT reveals non-value-adding time of worker and equipment; *jidoka* (automatic machine stop against defects) and the line-stop cord visualize and dramatize defect problems; neatness and cleanliness of the shop floor (5-S) make disorders visible. Above all, "*kaizen* mind," or problem consciousness of workers, supervisors, and plant engineers, facilitates quick detection of problems on the shop floor.

2. *Quick problem solving at all levels of the plant.* Once the problems are identified, the people who have daily experience with the causal networks on the shop floor are empowered and equipped with tools for identifying root causes, finding alternatives, and solving the problems. In effective auto factories, such as Toyota's, supervisors keep on making and revising standard operating procedures, workers are involved in the suggestion system and small *kaizen* groups, and maintenance workers and plant engineers constantly patrol the shop floor. Although the supervisors tend to play a pivotal role, all players jointly create and evaluate alternative plans for improvements.[41]

3. *Standardization of problem-solving tools.* It is important to note that the tools for improvement and problem solving are highly standardized in the effective TQC adopter, although standards for operations themselves are frequently revised. So-called QC stories and the "seven tools for quality control" (standard problem-solving routines and supporting statistical tools, respectively; see appendix B1) have prevailed among the TQC participants. This kind of standardization facilitated diffusion and retention of improvement skills and experiences to the employees. The diffusion of standard problem-solving tools is particularly important because actual manufacturing problems on the shop floor tend to be ill-structured and ambiguous. Thus, artificially imposing a standardized problem-solving model on real problems in the plant facilitates organizational learning and improvements.

4. *Quick Experimentation and Implementation.* At Toyota, implementation of revised production methods often precedes proposals or suggestions. Changes are experimented with and implemented first, *then* they are proposed through the suggestion system or regular improvement programs. (This may explain why there are so many suggestions and why their ac-

ceptance ratio is high at Toyota.) Thus, experimentation and implementation are often inseparable.

5. *Routinized Retention Through Knowledge-manual Interactions.* The retention mechanism of effective automakers depends on *both* manuals and human resources. At a given point in time, Toyota's factories may look quite Tayloristic, in that they have a massive accumulation of standard operating procedures. Over time, however, the standards are frequently revised; the revisions are done not by expert industrial engineers but by shop floor supervisors. At the same time, stability of the workforce helps the retention of new methods stored in collective human memories. Therefore, whether a Toyota-style system depends on manuals or tacit knowledge does not seem to be a relevant question; it depends on both. What matters seems to be a rapid and two-way conversion of information between tacit knowledge and formal written procedures.[42]

Application: Routinized Capabilities for Toyota-style Product Development

Let's move on to product development capabilities. Today's major auto producers are multimodel firms that conduct many product development projects at the same time, to add new models or to replace old ones. The same routines and standard schedules tend to be used repeatedly across these projects, each of which creates a new set of information assets for the production of a new model. Therefore, product development capability is basically a routinized learning capability, which consists of various individual routines that bring about better management of problem-solving cycles, as well as information flows between them.

Empirical evidence supports the above view. For example, Harvard Professor Kim Clark and I conducted an international comparison of product development performance (lead times, development productivity, and total product quality) involving about twenty major auto companies and thirty projects in America, Europe, and Japan in the 1980s (Clark and Fujimoto, 1991). Through data analysis and field studies, we identified some routines that better performers of product development tended to adopt (see chapter 6). These high-performance routines can be reinterpreted in an information map, such as in figure 4.16, as a capability to manage interconnected problem-solving cycles.[43] This pattern of problem solving and information transmission can be summarized as follows:

1. Direct and continual flow of information from market to concept generation units, which creates product concepts proactively, rather than reactively.

2. Continual and cumulative elaboration of product concept information throughout the project period for flexible adaptation of the concepts to changing market needs.
3. Direct and continual internal flows of information among the concept generation units, product planning units, and product engineering units throughout product development. Since the product concepts cannot be fully articulated by product plans or other documents, direct interaction between concepts and designs is of particular importance.
4. Early information exchange to bring downstream experience upstream effectively and to reveal conflicts during the early stages. This is expected to lower the subsequent information-processing workload owing to design changes and to shorten overall lead time.
5. Early information exchange between the automakers and suppliers. Many of the first-tier suppliers, with detailed engineering capabilities, work closely with the automakers by maintaining frequent communications of component design information (see also chapter 5).
6. Overlapping problem solving. Downstream problem-solving cycles start before upstream cycles are completed in order to shorten lead time. To do this effectively, upstream and downstream have to be integrated through the early release of preliminary information in both directions.
7. Fast problem-solving cycles within each stage in order to respond quickly to continuously changing inputs. This includes speeding up individual activities such as searching and simulation, as well as reducing iterations of cycles needed for reaching the final solution.

Toyota-style product development can be therefore characterized as fast, efficient, and high-fidelity problem-solving cycles, as well as accurate, early, frequent, and high-band-width transmission of information between appropriate cycles at the right time. Such a pattern of information creation and transmission leads to a higher success ratio of new products, which many observers believe was the case at Toyota during the 1980s.

The above routines can be seen as the factors that enhance success ratio of individual projects. Another important factor to increase the number of successful new products is simply the number of projects per period, given the R&D resources available. The former helps the firm raise its batting average, while the latter increases the number of batting opportunities. The two elements are obviously complementary in increasing the number of hits, or the successful projects.

Given the R&D inputs available (e.g., R&D budget per year), the key parameter for increasing the number of new product projects per pe-

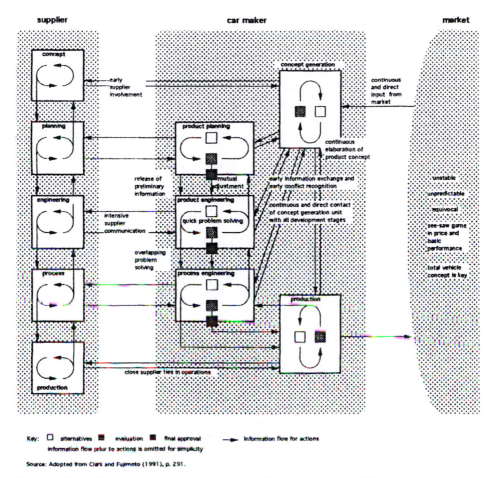

Key: ▢ alternatives   ▤ evaluation   ▨ final approval   ━▶ information flow for actions
Information flow prior to actions is omitted for simplicity

Source: Adopted from Clark and Fujimoto (1991), p. 291.

Figure 4.16 Information Patterns of Product Development at Effective Japanese Automakers

riod (i.e., frequency of major product design improvements) is development productivity.[44] Kim Clark and I, for example, pointed out that the main source of interfirm difference in the frequency of new product introductions was not the difference in R&D resource inputs but how efficiently given R&D inputs were used (R&D expenses to sales ratios were not significantly different among the auto firms).[45] Conversely, the capability of high development productivity tended not to be used directly for cost reduction, but to increase the pace of product changes while matching the unit R&D cost with competitors.

In short, the above-mentioned data seem to indicate that a firm with the capability of fast-cycle information processing tends to achieve a high development productivity, a short development lead time, and a high level of total product quality at the same time. Such a company is likely to enjoy more frequent opportunities for new product development, as well as a higher probability of success per each opportunity.[46]

Also note that, as shown in table 4.1, there are some striking similarities between the basic pattern of routinized capabilities in production and product development at the effective Japanese automakers. They are characterized as dense information networks, in which value-carrying information is continually transmitted, absorbed, and renewed in each developmental-productive resource. Cycles of information processing and problem solving are short in both cases. Information assets are incrementally revised as the resources receive new information inputs and the revised information is immediately transferred to other resources. From the information point of view, the basic patterns and principles of production capability and development capability have much in common.[47]

Application: Routinized Capabilities for Toyota-style Supplier Management

Finally, let's apply the information view to Japanese supplier systems. Many of these supplier management capabilities are shared among a group of Japanese automakers, although distinctive purchasing capabilities are also identified at Toyota specifically (see chapter 5 and appendix B3 for details). The patterns observed for Japanese parts supplier relations in the 1980s seem to complement each other in jointly contributing to their competitive advantages. The three aspects may be summarized as follows: (1) long-term relational transactions, (2) bundled outsourcing, and (3) dynamic competition for capability building among a small number of suppliers.

Long-term Relational Transactions

Much existing research has recognized the stable and long-term contractual relationship between buyers and sellers as one of the main characteristics of the Japanese supplier system, analyzing how it contributes to competitive advantage of the end products, as well as why such a pattern persists for a long time. But what explains such relationships between firms? The concept of *relational transaction* has often been used by economists to describe this phenomenon.[48]

Explaining the Stability. One hypothesis, typically made by theorists of transaction cost economics, assumes that people are selfish and opportunistic, but will voluntarily maintain long-term contractual relations under certain economic conditions.[49] Some economists argue that a relational transaction is stable when both parties know that the costs (both actual cost and opportunity cost) incurred from terminating the transaction are high enough (Miwa, 1989). Such costs of transaction ter-

Table 4.1   Similarity of Patterns of Production and Product Development
Capabilities

Production	Product Development
frequent setup changes	frequent product renewals
short production throughput time	short development lead time
reduction of work-in-process inventory between production steps	reduction of informational inventory between product development steps
piece-by-piece transfer (not in batch) of parts from upstream to downstream	frequent transmission (not in batch) of preliminary information from upstream to downstream
quick feedback of information on downstream problems	early feedback of information on potential downstream problems
quick problem solving in manufacturing	quick problem-solving cycle in engineering
upstream activities are triggered by real-time demand of downstream (pull system)	upstream activities are motivated by market introduction date in downstream
simultaneous improvement in quality, delivery, and productivity	simultaneous improvement in quality, lead time, and development productivity
capability of upstream process to produce saleable products in the first place	capability of development (i.e., upstream) to produce manufacturable products in the first place
flexibility to changes in volume, product mix, product design, etc.	flexibility to changes in product design, schedule, cost target, etc.
broad task assignment of workers for higher productivity	broad task assignment of engineers for higher productivity
attitude and capability for continuous improvement and quick problem solving	attitude and capability for frequent incremental innovations
reduction of inventory (slack resources) forces more information flows for problem solving and improvements	reduction of lead time (slack resources) forces more information flows across stages for integrated problem solving

Source: Adopted and modified from Clark and Fujimoto (1991): p. 172.

mination would include retaliation from the other firm, deterioration of
their reputation with other transaction partners, lost growth opportunity, lost opportunity for joint cost reduction, and loss of the value
of transaction-specific assets (Williamson, 1979, 1985). The last hypothesis has been the most prevalent one (Asanuma, 1989; Ito, 1989;
Nishiguchi, 1994). That is, by mutually holding the transaction-specific
assets, whose value will be lost when the transaction is terminated, the

two parties find themselves in a mutual "hostage-holding" situation. The relationship stabilizes as a result. This hypothesis, however, does not itself explain why various firms made transaction-specific investments in the first place, as Toshihiro Nishiguchi argues.[50]

Other, more sociologically oriented researchers (Dore, 1987; Sako, 1992) assume that interfirm relationships are "embedded" (Granovetter, 1985) in the social structure, and argue that there tend to be certain country-specific cultures that nurture mutual trust, reduce opportunism, and thereby save transaction costs, which in turn makes relational transactions more feasible than in other cultures. Although we should avoid tautology (e.g., "a relational-transaction-oriented cultures result in relational transactions"), this may partly explain why long-term relations were more often observed in Japan than in the West during the 1980s.

However, cultural theory does not explain dynamic changes to supplier systems on an international scale, which have actually been observed since the late 1980s (Nishiguchi, 1994). As this book argues, we need to introduce an evolutionary perspective to supplement the above theories on comparative supplier systems—a topic that will be explored in more depth in the next chapter.[51]

Contribution to Competitiveness.   The next question is why relational transactions contribute to overall competitiveness. Stable relationships would facilitate information sharing between the firms (Ito, 1989) and thereby promote "inter-firm problem solving mechanisms" (Nishiguchi, 1994), which may in turn result in incremental improvements of productivity and quality (Miwa, 1989). The benefits of manufacturing cost reduction owing to long-term contractual relationships is often called *relational quasi-rents* (Aoki, 1988; Asanuma, 1989).[52] Mari Sako (1992) argues that the long-term relations (the obligational contractual relations in her framework) facilitate not only reductions in product cost (i.e., relational quasi-rents) but also reductions in transaction cost.

However, it should be noted that the same system may bring about negative competitive effects when suppliers take advantage of the assemblers' commitment to the relations, exercise sellers' monopoly power, and thereby raise component prices. Helper and Levine (1994) clearly point out this tradeoff. They compare two purchasing policies, the "exit" strategy (low commitment and low information sharing between assemblers and suppliers) and the "voice" strategy (high commitment and high information sharing), and conclude that the former strategy (typical of U.S. auto firms up to the 1970s) brings about short-term benefits, since buyers can exercise negotiation power vis-à-vis suppliers—but may sacrifice long-term benefits of cost reduction. The latter strategy (common in the postwar Japanese auto industry) may yield long-term benefits, but can bring short-term disadvantages, since automakers are more vulnerable to suppliers' monopoly-rent-seeking behaviors.

And yet, in the 1980s, the Japanese automobile makers did *not* suffer from supplier price increases; actually there was a continuous reduction in parts prices.[53] While such economic concepts as asset specificity, relational quasi-rent, and relational transactions are powerful tools for explaining the advantages of the Japanese supplier systems of the 1980s, they alone do not fully explain the phenomenon. We have to look at other aspects of the system.

Bundled Outsourcing

As already noted, one of the important characteristics of the Japanese supplier system in terms of interfirm task partitioning is that the outsourcing ratio is high not only in manufacturing but also in product development, and that the same company tends to get the two jobs at the same time. Note that, with the same outsourcing ratio, a firm can assign the product development and production jobs of a given component to one company (e.g., a technologically capable supplier) or to two or more separate companies (e.g., a production subcontractor, a prototype parts specialist, and an engineering house). The former pattern may be called *bundled outsourcing*, in that a bundle of functionally related tasks is subcontracted out to one company as a package.[54] The Japanese auto firms of the 1980s tended to choose bundled outsourcing. For example, they outsourced machining and assembly (subassembly delivery), detailed engineering and manufacturing (black box parts), or production and inspection (elimination of receiving inspection) of a given component to one supplier.

The suppliers, in turn, can build a certain integrative capability in the long run by repeatedly conducting the bundles of related tasks, which may enable them to reduce costs or improve quality. Thus, bundled outsourcing may result in higher component performance, at least potentially. Nishiguchi (1994), for example, points out that the establishment of system suppliers (i.e., suppliers with this integrative capability) in Japan contributed to their competitive performance. Kim Clark and I (1991) also reported that the black box parts system tended to contribute to higher product development performance.[55] It is also generally known that the black box parts system facilitates design for manufacturing (i.e., designing easy-to-make components) and thereby reduces component manufacturing costs.

It should be noted, here, that bundled outsourcing tends to create transaction-specific assets. Toshihiro Nishiguchi (1994) argues that the Japanese system suppliers accumulated transaction specific assets and thereby facilitated the stable relational transactions mentioned earlier. Banri Asanuma (1989) also points out that transaction-specific skills in product development and production are accumulated most in the case of black box parts transactions. Generally speaking, when a product is made by assembling relatively generic parts in a product-specific way, we can predict that the purchased component will become more product-specific as it turns into a larger subassembly module (e.g., a complete seat). Relational transactions and bundled outsourcing, then, may be correlated with each other to the extent that bundled outsourcing results in asset specificity, which in turn facilitates long-term relational transactions.

The remaining question is why system suppliers do not take advantage of their integrative capabilities, seeking monopoly rents vis-à-vis assemblers and so possibly wiping out potential competitive advantages for the latter. We have to explain why bundled outsourcing actually tended to contribute to competitive advantages of the Japanese auto industry in the 1980s.

Capability-Building Competition Among a Small Number of Firms

At the level of parts categories, there can be more than one supplier competing for contracts. Indeed, competition among a small number of suppliers tends to be so-called *development competition*, particularly in the case of black box parts. But what are the impacts of such competition on the performance of the supplier system? A standard economic theory, based on the assumption of price-based competition, would argue that this is an oligopolistic situation, which will result in monopoly rents on the side of suppliers (i.e., a relatively high parts price). Motoshige Ito (1989), however, describes the supplier competition in Japan as "face-to-face competition" and argues that competition in this condition may become more intense than usual price competition, even though the number of competitors is small.[56] Hiroyuki Itami (1988) proposes a similar concept, "competition by visible hands," and also argues that such competition can be more intense than classic perfect competition under certain conditions and that it will facilitate dynamic improvements of technologies through information sharing between suppliers and assemblers (i.e., relational quasi-rent).[57]

Thus, these researchers argue that the competition among a small number of suppliers, under certain conditions, can result in intense competition, rather than their monopoly rent seeking, in terms of not only pricing but also long-term capability building. These hypotheses seem reasonably realistic in describing how most Japanese first-tier suppliers operate. When a small number of suppliers face each other and compete for long-term contracts—and when the firms are evaluated by buyers in terms of not only price but also dynamic improvement capabilities in cost, quality, and technology—intense and dynamic competition based on capability is likely.

On the empirical side, a number of researchers have observed that suppliers' long-term ability to build manufacturing capabilities, rather than their short-term performance, has been much emphasized by the most successful automakers, like Toyota. As a result, the Japanese suppliers' capability for subassembly, detailed component design, quality control, short throughput time, and continuous improvements were developed as a package mainly in the 1960s and '70s.[58] With or without intention, each of the first-tier suppliers replicated the capabilities of effective car makers and developed its own intrafirm network of information assets, which boosted the competitive performance of Japanese automakers.

Overall, I argue that these three dimensions—long-term transactions, bundled outsourcing, and capability-based competition—complement each other in creating superior performance. Although further investigation is needed both theoretically and empirically, my tentative proposition is that the coexistence of the three system dimensions was necessary for the high performance of the Toyota-style supplier system, and that this is why it has been so difficult for Western automakers to replicate.

A Total Information View of Manufacturing: Implication and Summary

Complex Structure, Simple Function

Let's return to the basic question I posed at the beginning of this chapter: In what sense are the Toyota-style manufacturing routine capabilities complex and thus difficult to grasp and imitate? The foregoing analysis indicates that the system of Toyota-style routines includes numerous elements that are physically and organizationally dispersed— from design rooms to factories to suppliers to marketing office—and that these elements are interconnected by intangible links—information flows. But for employees working in highly specialized units of large companies, such an invisible network connecting each routine ultimately to the customer interface may not be that obvious. Therefore, even if all individual elements of the system are fully articulated, the core nature of the total manufacturing system may still be far from self-evident to its practitioners. In addition, what makes this total system even more difficult to grasp is the fact that it consists of long chains of information. Such a system, be it a telephone game or the genetic mechanism of the human body, is vulnerable to even a slight malfunction of a single piece; yet such impacts tend to be underestimated by employees dealing with routines inside specialized units.

Thus, a set of routines can be difficult to create and difficult to imitate, even without invoking the notion of tacit knowledge. Again, I fully agree with the idea that even the most mechanistic version of today's mass production involves many pieces of tacit knowledge, but

I also argue that the most organic version of it, such as Toyota's, is to a large extent standardized, articulated, and functionally transparent. Tacit knowledge is an attractive way of explaining the firm-specificity of manufacturing systems because obviously it does exist on real-life shop floors. But we should not rely entirely on this logic when analyzing manufacturing routines of a modern mass-production system, be it Toyota's or Ford's.

Another conclusion to be drawn here is that the functional principle behind effective manufacturing routines is quite simple and straightforward. The *structure* of the manufacturing routines may be quite entangled, but their ultimate *function* is almost always clear—to outperform rivals in attracting and satisfying customers. Once this principle is explicitly or intuitively understood, it is not difficult to explain the competitive function or dysfunction of an existing manufacturing routine. No matter how remote the routine-holding units are from the customer interface, they are connected to customers by the information web. No matter how remote two organizational units are (e.g., a stamping shop and a dealer's showroom), they share one informational node—the customer. And *all* the information held by effective routines eventually flows into this node, like all the little streams that eventually join the river.

This is why the concept of "customer orientation by all employees" is crucial—not only because it is good for customers but also because it maintains the overall integrity of manufacturing routines. Even though Toyota's employees may never call their practices an information system, they are virtually and intuitively referring to the informational nature of their system's routine capabilities when they emphasize customers (ultimate note of information), "muda" (noninformation-processing state), "the downstream station is the customer" (accurate transmission of information to the next step), and so on. In this sense, I argue that the information network is the deep structure that governs Toyota's manufacturing activities.

Therefore, Toyota-style manufacturing routines, as a total system, are complex in the sense that they were not created by any prior grand design and have been difficult to imitate, even if the system's elements are well known. But the system is also simple in the sense that the ultimate function of individual routines can be clearly explained by a simple principle of customer satisfaction, whether they were created to achieve this intentionally or unintentionally. This is why companies like Toyota, which have applied such a principle throughout the firm, could consistently outperform others by cumulatively building routines that turn out to create high performances through a combination of system emergence and evolutionary capability; for such companies, the system of manufacturing routines is too complex to design ex-ante, but simple enough to grasp ex-post.

Manufacturing Success as an Informational Pattern

The present chapter explored the routinized capabilities of the Toyota-style manufacturing system and its performance. By using mostly secondary materials as empirical evidence, I tried to demonstrate that the total system perspective and information creation-transmission view of manufacturing, presented in chapter 1, can be applied to the case of the Toyota-style system. Both routinized manufacturing and routinized learning capabilities in production, development, and supplier management were discussed as a coherent pair that contributes to higher manufacturing performance. Through this informational analysis, I tried to strengthen a link between the resource-capability theories of the firm at the strategic level and detailed process-performance analyses of manufacturing systems at the operational level. The main findings are as follows:

- *Total system view and information system approach.* Such concepts as firm; resource; activity; product; consumption; competitive performance; and routinized capability in production, product development, and supplier management can be consistently described as an integrated system of information assets and their creation and transmission. Both aspects, knowledge creation and information transmission, are crucial for understanding the development-production capability of a manufacturing firm.

- *Routinized production capabilities reinterpreted.* The production capability of the effective Japanese automakers of the 1980s can be characterized as dense, regular, and accurate transmission of value-carrying information between flexible information assets. The system for higher productivity and shorter throughput time is designed from the information receiver side, while the system for higher conformance quality is designed from the information source side.

- *Routinized learning capabilities in production reinterpreted.* There are a variety of mechanisms that facilitate repetitive problem finding, problem solving, and solution retention for consistent and rapid improvements for competitive performance. The core part of the Toyota-style system (e.g., Toyota Production System, JIT, and TQC) is this organizational learning process.

- *Routinized product development capabilities reinterpreted.* The product development capability of the effective Japanese automakers can be illustrated as dense information processing with frequent and high band-width transmission of information that is created and elaborated incrementally by short problem-solving cycles.

- *Routinized supplier management capabilities reinterpreted.*
  The Toyota-style supplier management capabilities can be
  characterized as a combination of at least three systems traits:
  long-term relational transactions, bundled outsourcing, and
  capability-building competition among a small number of
  suppliers. The three patterns are complementary with one another in jointly contributing to a higher overall performance.

Overall, I tried to show how a highly complex system of organizational routines, the Toyota-style system, can consistently bring about
a simple function: product competitiveness and customer satisfaction. In this sense, information seems to be a critical linchpin between
structural complexity and functional simplicity of the effective manufacturing system.

In these first three chapters, I have attempted to fill in three missing
pieces in the story of how a total manufacturing system evolves: the
evolutionary perspective for detailed manufacturing analysis; the information approach to manufacturing routines at the total system
level; and the three-layer framework of organizational capabilities—
routinized manufacturing, routinized learning, and evolutionary learning. However, the foregoing general discussions were mostly based on
secondary data. There are still many unexplained phenomena and
unanswered questions remaining, and my evolutionary arguments
can be enriched and strengthened. For this purpose, the following
chapters discuss further details of the evolutionary process in specific subsystems—supplier management, product development, and
production—using more original materials. The next chapter revisits
the black box parts practice of Japanese supplier systems, presenting
original data.

EMERGENCE AND FUNCTIONS
OF THE THREE SUBSYSTEMS:
SUPPLIER, DEVELOPMENT,
AND PRODUCTION

5

EVOLUTION OF THE BLACK BOX
PARTS SUPPLIER SYSTEM

In this chapter, one of the main elements of the Japanese automobile supplier system, the black box parts transaction, is analyzed in detail, based on first-hand data. This case backs up the argument that distinctive organizational routines were created through the process of multi-path system emergence, and that Toyota demonstrated its ability to exploit such an emergent process to build up more competitive routines than other firms. It will also highlight a new aspect of capability building: an ability to help other firms (e.g., suppliers) build their own capabilities.[1]

Structure and Function of the Black Box Parts System

As already introduced briefly in previous chapters, the *black box parts system* refers to a certain pattern of transactions in which a parts supplier conducts detailed engineering of a component that it makes for an automobile maker on the basis of the latter's specifications and basic designs. In a sense, this is a kind of joint product development between a system maker and a component supplier, in that the latter is involved in the former's new product development process. In the framework discussed in the previous chapter, the black box parts system means a particular pattern of interfirm task partitioning that can be characterized as *bundled outsourcing*.

Although the system is referred to variously as "black box parts," "gray box parts," "design-in," and "approved drawings (*shoninzu*)," it has been known to be a prevalent practice in the Japanese automobile industry and one of the sources of its competitive advantages revealed in the 1980s. It was also one element of the Japanese supplier system that many of the U.S. auto suppliers tried to adopt in order to narrow the competitive gaps between them and the leading Japanese automakers since the late 1980s (Ellison et al., 1995).

Thus, the black box parts practice has attracted the attention of both researchers and practitioners internationally. Its historical origins and patterns of evolution, however, have not been studied much by business historians in the past. The published company histories of the major Japanese automakers do not seem to have touched upon this aspect of supplier management, either.[2] Thus, research on the historical evolution of the black box parts system seems to be by itself important for those who wish to understand, transfer, or adopt the practice.

In the broader context of this book, the empirical and historical study of the black box parts transaction may provide us with additional insights and evidence on the structure, function, and evolution of manufacturing systems. By focusing on one element of the total· manufacturing system and by collecting first-hand data tailored to this particular topic, we can make a more coherent analysis as to whether the process that built up capability for the black box parts system was multi-path system emergence. That is, if the current analysis reveals that the ex-post competitive functions of this routine were not always recognized by the system builders in advance, we infer from this fact that the process was evolutionary; the ex-post function of the system (system stability) and ex-ante reasons the system was made that way (system change) are explained separately. And if the current analysis reveals that the process in which the company acquired the black box routine was a complex and interrelated combination of historical imperatives, entrepreneurial visions, learning from other firms, and so on, we can infer from this fact that the process was a system emergence.

First, I describe structure and function of the supplier involvement in product development in the major Japanese automakers, such as Toyota and Honda, and present a brief literature survey. Then I examine the origin and historical evolution of the black box parts practice mainly at Toyota and Nissan.[3] The last section focuses on the supplier side by analyzing some preliminary results of a questionnaire and field surveys.

Basic Concepts of Black Box Parts

Let us first define some key concepts. Kim Clark and I classified transactions between automobile makers and their suppliers into three broad categories, depending on the supplier's level of involvement and capability in product development.[4] Figure 5.1 illustrates typical examples of supplier involvement in product development by using a simplified information asset map.

Three basic categories were identified here: supplier proprietary

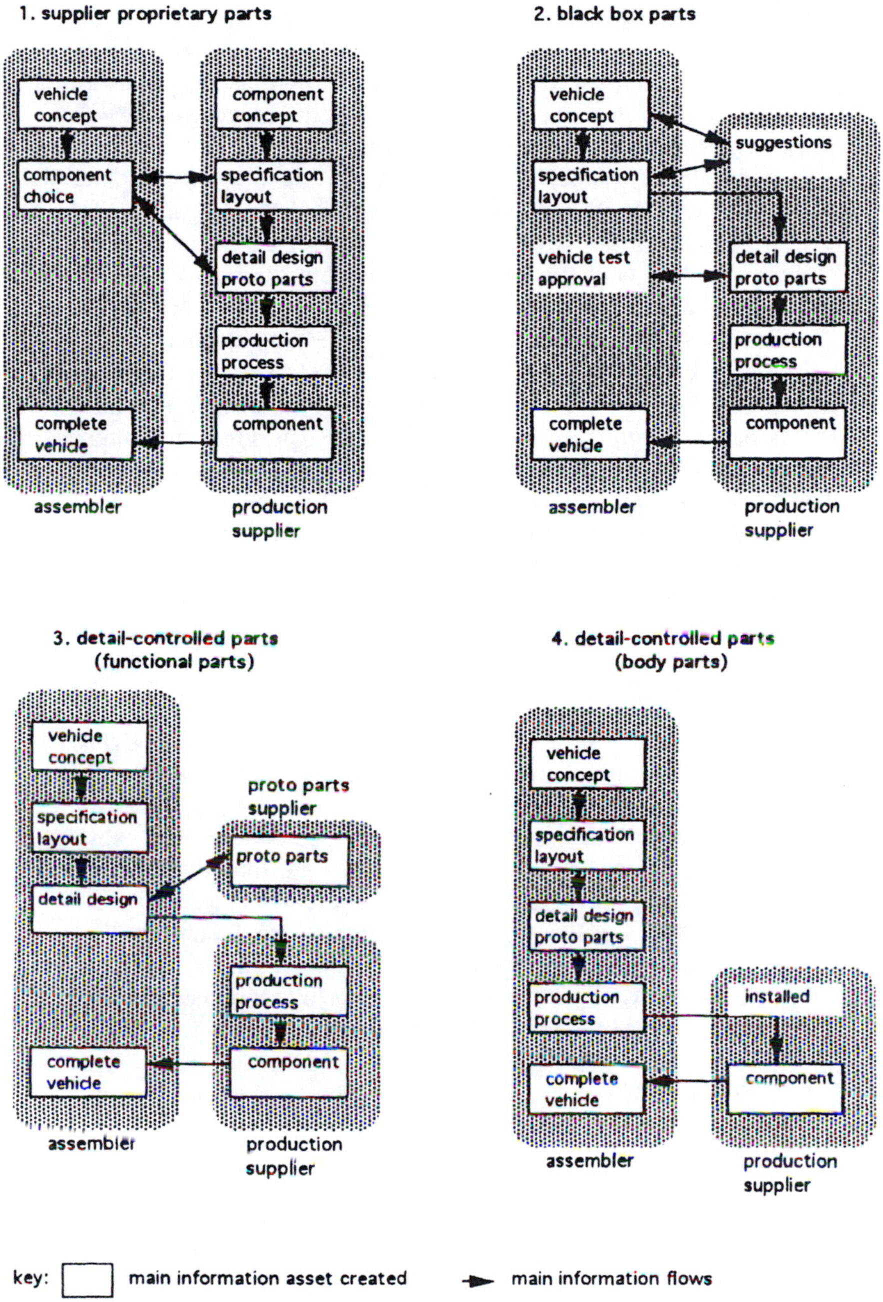

1. supplier proprietary parts

vehicle concept → component choice → specification layout → detail design proto parts → production process → component → complete vehicle

assembler / production supplier

2. black box parts

vehicle concept → suggestions → specification layout → vehicle test approval → detail design proto parts → production process → component → complete vehicle

assembler / production supplier

3. detail-controlled parts (functional parts)

vehicle concept → specification layout → detail design → proto parts → production process → component → complete vehicle

proto parts supplier

assembler / production supplier

4. detail-controlled parts (body parts)

vehicle concept → specification layout → detail design proto parts → production process → complete vehicle → installed → component

assembler / production supplier

key: ▢ main information asset created   ➤ main information flows

Source: Clark and Fujimoto (1991), p. 141.

Figure 5.1 Typical Information Flows with Parts Suppliers

parts, black box parts, and detail-controlled parts. This classification is basically the same as that by Asanuma (1984, 1989): marketed goods, drawings approved (*shoninzu*), and drawings supplied (*taiyozu*). The magnitude of supplier involvement in engineering is higher in the former classification and lower in the latter.[5]

1. *Supplier Proprietary parts.* The supplier develops a component entirely from concept to manufacturing as its standard product (*shihanhin*); the assembler simply orders the item from the supplier's catalogue. In this way, the supplier carries out almost all of the developmental work for the component. Some highly standardized components, such as batteries, may belong to this category.

2. *Black box parts.* Developmental work for the component is split between the assembler and the supplier. In a typical case, the former creates basic design information such as cost/performance requirements, exterior shapes, and interface details based on the total vehicle planning and layout, while the parts supplier does the detailed engineering. It is not clear what fraction of the total work is done by the supplier, but a general consensus in our study seems to be roughly 70 percent. In general, many of the functional parts and subassembly systems belong to this category. As shown in figure 5.2, there are two subcategories of black box parts: approved drawings (*shoninzu*) and consigned drawings (*itakuzu*).

- *Approved drawings.* After the supplier is selected, it carries out detailed engineering, such as drafting of parts and subassembly drawings, prototyping, and unit testing. The car maker then reviews the parts drawings, tests prototype vehicles using the parts, makes sure that the requirements are met, and approves the design.[6] In this case, the drawings are eventually owned by the supplier, which assures design quality and patent rights over the parts in question. That is, the supplier has to make engineering actions in response to field claims related to the parts. In exchange for this responsibility for quality, the supplier enjoys a greater degree of design discretion for better manufacturability and cost reduction. Switching suppliers between the engineering stage and manufacturing stage is rather rare in this case.
- *Consigned drawings.* Unlike approved drawings, final drawings are owned by the car maker, but detail engineering work is subcontracted out to the supplier. The former pays the design fee to the latter as a separate contract, and is free to switch suppliers at the manufacturing stage. It is the car maker that takes responsibility for quality assurance, though. Many so-called design-in arrangements in the United States in recent years are based on this system.[7] Overall, the consigned drawings system comes between approved drawings and detail-controlled draw-

Detail-Controlled Parts (Provided Drawings)

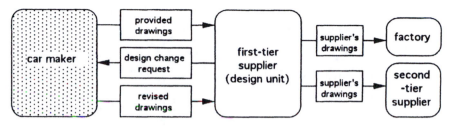

Black Box Parts (Consigned Drawings)

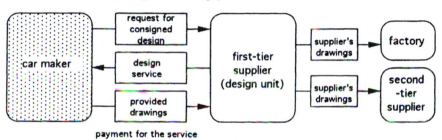

Black Box Parts (Approved Drawings)

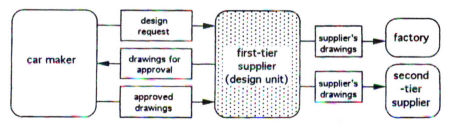

: owner of the drawings

Source; Company A (revised and translated by Fujimoto).

Figure 5.2 Basic Paper Flows for Each Mode of Transaction

ings in terms of the degree of supplier involvement in product engineering. While approved drawings tend to be applied to functional parts, the consigned drawing system is found more often when dealing with press and plastic parts.

As already suggested in chapter 4, patterns of interfirm task partitioning, such as the black box parts system, tend to affect patterns of

Table 5.1   Design Involvement and Competition of Suppliers

(1) Model Renewal (N=201)

Design \ Competition	Detail-Control	Black Box	Supplier Proprietary
Bidding	(45%)	9%	8%
Development competition	5%	(49%)	33%
No competition	48%	48%	42%
Others	10%	5%	25%
Total	* (100%)	* (100%)	* (100%)

Note: * The numbers do not add up to 100%, as multiple responses are possible.

(2) New Model (N=201)

Design \ Competition	Detail-Control	Black Box	Supplier Proprietary
Bidding	(53%)	11%	0%
Development competition	7%	(64%)	50%
No competition	38%	31%	33%
Others	10%	6%	25%
Total	* (100%)	* (100%)	* (100%)

Note: * The numbers do not add up to 100% as multiple responses are possible.

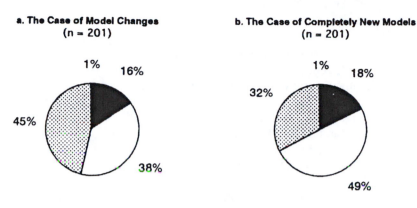

a. The Case of Model Changes
(n = 201)

b. The Case of Completely New Models
(n = 201)

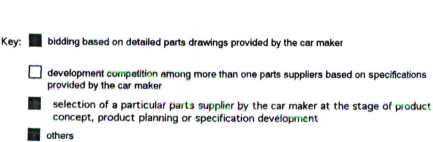

Key: ■ bidding based on detailed parts drawings provided by the car maker

☐ development competition among more than one parts suppliers based on specifications provided by the car maker

▓ selection of a particular parts supplier by the car maker at the stage of product concept, product planning or specification development

▓ others

Source: A Questionnaire survey by the author in 1993. Almost all of the respondents are first-tier suppliers belonging to Japan Auto Parts Industries Association.

Figure 5.3 Types of Competition Among Japanese Parts Suppliers

competition among suppliers. In the current case, for example, information on requirements may be provided to two or three potential suppliers, who compete for the job based on their component development capabilities.[8] This selection process is called *development competition*, which normally takes a half to one year.[9] Table 5.1 clearly shows that there is, in fact, a strong correlation between the occurrence of black box parts transactions and development competition.

The intensity of development competition among suppliers differs depending upon the parts categories: in conventional parts, the supplier for an old model tends to get a new contract for the new model; for technology-intensive items such as plastic resins for bumpers, switching of suppliers takes place more often and development competition is more severe.[10] The suppliers may initiate developmental actions and suggestions without waiting for inquiries from the car makers. Also, as shown in figure 5.3, development competition occurs more frequently for parts for completely new models than for model replacement (i.e., major model changes).[11] In any case, development competition is more prevalent than bidding among Japanese first-tier suppliers (i.e., the prevalent pattern of competition in the traditional supplier relationships in the United States), and this reflects the prevalence there of the black box practice.

3. *Detail-controlled parts.* The third category is the case in which most of the component engineering work, including parts drawing, is done in-house. In this way, not only basic engineering but also detailed engineering are concentrated in the hands of the car maker, although the suppliers can make requests for design changes for better manufacturability and cost reduction. In the typical case of a functional component in the United States, the suppliers, selected through inquiries and bids, take responsibility for process engineering and production on the basis of blueprints provided by the car maker. For this reason, it is called the *provided drawings* (*taiyozu* or *shikyuzu*) system in Japan.[12] Fabrication of prototype parts may be carried out by a different supplier specializing in prototypes. In the case of some body parts, the car maker may also carry out process engineering, build and own tools and equipment, and lend them to a supplier. In this case, the supplier is regarded as nothing more than a provider of production capacity.

There are some other ways for suppliers to get involved in new car development projects, including an arrangement called *guest engineer,* or *resident engineer,* in which component engineers are dispatched from the supplier to the car maker to work jointly with the latter's engineers.

Overall, each company or project chooses the degree of supplier involvement component by component, which in turn determines the overall division of engineering work between assembler and suppliers (see figure 5.4). It is important to note here that the decisions regarding manufacturing vertical integration and engineering vertical integration are two separate issues: for a given production in-house ratio, the engineering in-house ratio could range widely. In any case, the decision on the mix of parts types depends upon the company's strategy, the nature of the component, and the capabilities of suppliers and characteristics of supplier networks.

The Case of Toyota's Black Box Parts System

Toyota is the company that established the intracompany procedures for the black box parts system (approved drawings in particular) earliest in the industry. Although the black box parts system is supported not only by formal procedures but also by skills, attitudes, and other factors of organizational culture, the system of formal documents is the backbone of the system.

Figure 5.5 describes the system of formal documents at Toyota (reconstructed from an interview at Toyota) as of the early 1990s. First, a parts design request form is issued by Toyota's product engineering

	interfirm task partitioning			responsibility and authority		basic type*
	parts production	detail design	basic design	drawings ownership	quality respons- ibility	
in-house production	C	C	C	C	C	organi- zation
outsourcing — detail-controlled parts	S	C	C	C	C	relat- ional contr- acts
outsourcing — black box parts — consigned drawings	S	S	C	C	C	
outsourcing — black box parts — approved drawings	S	S	C	S	S	
outsourcing — supplier proprietary parts	S	S	S	S	S	market

Note: C = car maker; S = supplier. * = based on classification by Asanuma (1997).
For simplicity, interfirm task partitioning for tools, dies and jigs was omitted.

Figure 5.4 Types of Parts Transactions

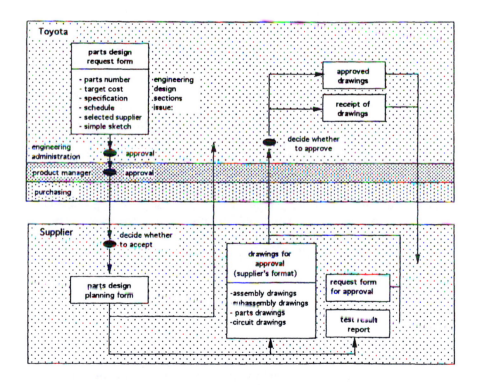

Source : Internal documents of Toyota Motor Corporation.

Figure 5.5 Flow of Documents for Approved Drawing System at Toyota

design section, which gets the approvals of product managers (chief engineers) and the Engineering Administration Division (*Gijutsu Kanri-bu*). It is then released to the potential supplier through the Purchasing Planning Division (*Kobai Kikaku-bu*). After examining Toyota's request and deciding whether to accept it, the supplier completes a parts design planning form by adding necessary information to the design request form and sends it back to Toyota.

The supplier then conducts detailed engineering, completes a set of drawings, makes component prototypes, and tests them. The format of the drawings is based on each supplier's format, although it has to be approved by Toyota's engineering administration department. The drawings for approval include assembly drawings (detailed), subassembly drawings, circuit drawings, critical parts drawings, and print circuit board drawings.

The supplier then sends the package of the drawings, a request form for approval, and a test result report back to Toyota to get the latter's approval. Toyota checks the documents to decide whether to approve the drawings. Once it gets the approval, the supplier owns the drawings and has to take full responsibility for quality assurance of the parts.

Toyota also established in the early 1990s formal procedures for shifting a particular component transaction from a detail-controlled approach to the black box parts system (or starting a new transaction with the black box arrangement) in order to clarify basic principles and criteria for such decisions. According to this system, Toyota's product engineering sections can submit a request form for changing a transaction from the detail-controlled system to the black box parts system to the purchasing department, which negotiates with the engineering section to coordinate engineering and cost requirements. If the purchasing department approves the change, the transaction is shifted to the black box parts system. If not, product engineers still have a second chance for further discussions with the purchasing people on future change. Although the purchasing department is formally in charge of negotiations with suppliers for any shift, product engineers informally talk to the suppliers in advance, asking them, "Are you ready for taking quality assurance responsibility?" Becoming an approved drawing supplier is a kind of tough experience, to which they might answer, "Yes, we are ready now."

The procedure also specifies the following criteria for a shift:

1. The shift to black box parts should not result in erosion of Toyota's technological potentials or leaking of its basic know-how. Toyota should refrain from subcontracting an engineering design just for saving in-house engineering resources.
2. The shift should save engineering person-hours, which can be used elsewhere.
3. The supplier should be capable of testing and evaluating the

component as a unit based on Toyota's specification requirements.

4. The shift should result in total cost advantage. That is, the
   cost saving in Toyota's engineering hours must be compared
   with the increase in the parts cost.
5. For certain parts, the suppliers should be capable of handling
   computer-aided design (CAD).

The above procedure indicates that Toyota is continually making decisions on whether to subcontract design engineering to parts suppliers by evaluating marginal costs and marginal benefits of the shift.

Results of the Supplier Survey

In order to further investigate current practices and historical origins of
the black box parts system, in September and October 1993 I conducted a mail survey among member companies of the Japan Auto
Parts Industries Association (JAPIA), most of which are first-tier parts
suppliers making direct transactions with the Japanese auto assemblers.[13] Figure 5.6 shows some of the results related to the current practice of design activities by Japanese first-tier auto parts suppliers. The
results are generally consistent: about three-fourths of the respondents
answered that their main type of transaction was black box parts, with
either specifications (55 percent) or rough drawings (19 percent) provided by the automakers. Detail-controlled parts (20 percent) and supplier proprietary parts (6 percent) were decided minorities.[14]

Specification documents, layout drawings, details of interface design, and exterior design were the information inputs that the automakers provided most frequently, which is also consistent with the
general description of the black box parts system in Japan. Also, the
most frequently conducted engineering activities among the sample
firms included parts prototype building, parts testing, and parts detailed engineering, followed by tool designs, parts specifications, and
parts concept proposals.

The survey also showed that average R&D spending per sales of the
sample companies was 2.6% (sample size 185) and capital spending
per sales was 0.1 percent. They employed on average about 170 product engineers and 280 manufacturing engineers.

Existing Literature on Black Box Parts

Generally speaking, although there have been many studies on manufacturing practices and subcontracting systems in the Japanese auto
industry, studies of the product development side of the supplier system have been relatively scarce. One of the important exceptions has
been a series of systematic studies by Banri Asanuma (1984, 1989),

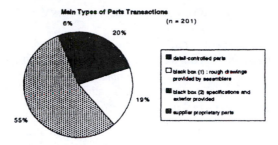

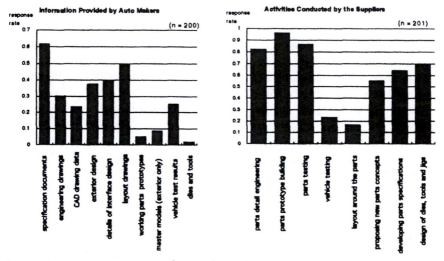

Source: Questionnaire survey to the members of Japan Auto Parts Industries Association in 1993.

Figure 5.6 Some Results of the Supplier Survey

which described and analyzed the interfirm flow of design information between assemblers and suppliers. He defined various categories of suppliers in terms of a combination of suppliers' relation-specific skills (a capability that is useful only for transactions between two specific firms), and made some predictions on how the level of relational quasi-rent would differ among the categories.[15] In this way, Asanuma gave a clear economic interpretation of the effectiveness and stability of the black box parts system. Asanuma also pointed out that the approved parts system may have originated either from marketed goods or from provided drawing parts in different ways, and that black box parts (approved drawings) are found more often in the Japanese automobile industry than in the electric machinery industry.

Nishiguchi (1994) thoroughly studied the practice of the Japanese-style subcontracting system and described it as "strategic dualism," a new form of contractual relations that was based on "problem-solving-oriented collaborative manufacturing." He also argued that the system was the evolutionary product of a complex historical interaction. Nishiguchi suggested that the black box design concept evolved from "bilateral design" in the late 1950s and early 1960s, in which suppliers made value analysis (VA) and value engineering (VE) proposals, as well as supplier-driven innovations, for the automakers.

Kim Clark and I, by collecting data from twenty-nine product development projects from Europe, United States, and Japan in the late 1980s, found that the average Japanese project in our sample relied much more on black box parts than the average American project, which relies heavily upon detail-controlled parts (figure 5.7).[16] Europeans are positioned in the middle. Together with supplier proprietary parts, the average Japanese project of the 1980s relied on supplier's engineering in roughly 70 percent of purchased parts, as compared to 20 percent in the United States and 50 percent in Europe. Note that the average fraction of procurement cost in total production cost was about 70 percent in Japan, 70 percent in the United States (this includes parts from component divisions of each company), and 60 percent in Europe in the same sample.[17] We also estimated that the lower in-house development ratio of the Japanese makers contributed to their lower engineering hours per project (i.e., higher development productivity). In our second-round survey conducted in 1993, we found that the U.S. car makers increased the ratio of black box parts significantly to about the 30 percent level. This is considered to be part of their catchup efforts to narrow the competitive gap with better Japanese makers.[18]

In another study with Sei and Takeishi, I collected data from about 120 parts suppliers in Kanagawa Prefecture of Japan, which included not only first-tier but also second-, third-, and fourth-tier parts suppliers.[19] This research showed that a majority of first-tier suppliers in the sample (59 percent) made either black box or supplier proprietary parts, while the fraction was much smaller (23 percent) among the second-tier suppliers and zero among the third- and fourth-tier suppliers. This implies that the black box parts practice is concentrated heavily among the first-tier suppliers.

The Black Box Parts System as an Effective Routine

Let's summarize what we have learned at this point on structure and function of the black box parts system.

Structure.   We have identified several types of parts transactions that have different patterns of interfirm task partitioning, as well as distribution of responsibility and authority (figure 5.4). In this context, the

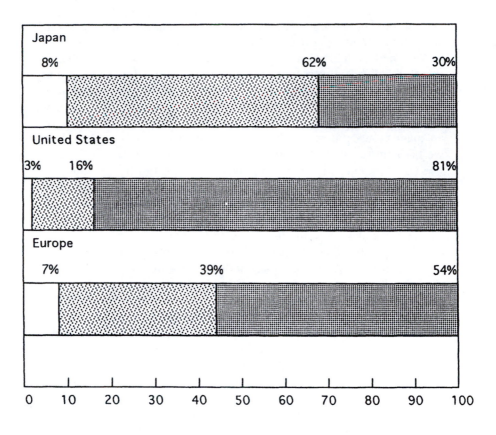

Note: Percentages shown represent fractions of total procurement cost.

 Supplier Proprietary Parts

Black Box Parts

Detail-Controlled Parts

Source: Clark and Fujimoto (1991), p. 145.

Figure 5.7 Types of Parts Procured by Suppliers

black box parts system can be seen as an example of bundled outsourcing, in which functionally related tasks (detailed engineering and production) are outsourced to the same supplier as a package.[20]

Also, we found that patterns of information flow differ depending upon the types of transactions, and that the assembler-supplier communication tends to be the most complicated in the case of the black box parts system, apparently because the make-or-buy boundary is drawn in the middle of the product development process (i.e., between basic and detailed engineering).[21]

Function. Research in the 1980s tended to identify certain competitive advantages of the black box parts system in terms of product development performance (Clark and Fujimoto, 1991). Although no systematic research has been done on the impact of black box parts on parts manufacturing cost, it is well known to practitioners that there is greater potential for parts cost reduction in the case of black box transactions than in the other types, to the extent that the suppliers have capability and incentive to do design for manufacturing (i.e., designing easy-to-manufacture parts) for themselves. The fact that the U.S. automakers increased their reliance on black box parts between the 1980s and the early 1990s (Ellison et al., 1995, see chap. 6) is additional circumstantial evidence indicating its potential competitive advantage.

Having analyzed the structure and function of the black box parts system in the 1980s and thereafter, let's now shift our focus to its historical origins and evolutionary paths.

History and Analysis of the Black Box Parts System

Hypotheses on the Origin and Evolution of Black Box Parts

As with any manufacturing system component, there are variety of paths through which the black box parts system might have emerged: random trials, rational calculation, environmental constraints, entrepreneurial vision, and knowledge transfer.

Let's also accept some "stylized facts" regarding this phenomenon. 1. the black box parts system is basically a postwar phenomenon; 2. the practice gradually spread to Japanese suppliers; 3. one of the early adopters of the system was Toyota. Applying the above generic framework and starting with these stylized facts, I consider the following hypotheses and provide a preliminary evaluation of whether they fit the historical facts.

The black box parts system emerged because:

Hypothesis 1. The automakers made deliberate choices based on cost-effectiveness analyses (rational calculation). Although this is a popular explanation after the fact, the cost-effectiveness of the black box parts practice is not that obvious. One may argue that the Japanese automakers knew that long-term advantages of joint development would more than compensate for the short-term disadvantage of early selection of suppliers. However, there is some evidence that the automakers, particularly purchasing departments, emphasizing cost reduction through competitive pressure among the suppliers, tended to insist that they would lose negotiating power if they chose the black box parts suppliers too early. The hypotheses that the Japanese makers knew the long-term benefit of the system while the Americans did not may be plausible, but we should not rely too much on this type of after the fact explanation.

Hypothesis 2.   The automakers did not have component technology in-house (environmental constraints). This hypothesis assumes that early Japanese automakers did not have sufficient component technology capabilities and had to rely on design activities by the parts manufacturers. While it was true that early auto assemblers in Japan tended to lack sufficient component engineering capability, so did the early component manufacturers. Prior to the 1930s, automobile mass production did not exist in Japan: the domestic auto assemblers were little more than low-volume prototype makers. Design drawings for mass production did not exist. Ford and GM dominated the Japanese market in the late 1920s and early 1930s, but their assembly operations in Japan relied mostly on imported knock-down parts. Finally, when the protectionist regulations of . 1936 ousted Ford and GM and helped Toyota and Nissan to start up, these Japanese assemblers had a hard time finding reliable parts suppliers in Japan. Toyota was almost forced to rely more, not less, on in-house engineering and manufacturing of its components. Thus, the early history of the Japanese auto industry does not seem to support the hypothesis that a lack of component engineering capabilities among the assemblers created the black box parts arrangements.

Hypothesis 3.   The automakers did not have a sufficient amount of resources (environmental constraints). The Japanese auto industry grew rapidly in terms of both production volume and number of models between the 1950s and 1980s. There is a possibility that Japanese car makers could not expand their production and engineering capacities rapidly enough to match the pace of market growth. One of the ways to respond to this "forced growth" problem might have been to subcontract out a significant portion of both production and engineering activities to suppliers. In other words, this hypothesis simply says that the car makers created the black box parts system because they were too busy to handle all of the rapidly expanding workload. While this hypothesis may explain why the black box parts system prevailed in a high-growth period, it may not explain why the system was initiated before high growth started, as discussed later.

Hypothesis 4. The practice already existed in other industries (knowledge transfer). Another possibility is that the practice of black box parts already existed in other industries, and the automobile industry adopted the system from them. Some other machinery industries, such as ship building, locomotives, and aircraft, have to be examined on this point.[22] However, so far researchers have not found any clear evidence that the concept of black box parts was transferred from such industries.

Hypothesis 5. The practice already existed in other firms in the industry (knowledge transfer). Since the early automakers, including Toyota and Nissan before the war, adopted many of the elements of Ford and GM production systems, one may wonder if this was the case with the black box parts system.[23] However, GM and Ford, while they were making motor vehicles in Japan during the 1920s and '30s, did not use the black box parts practice: their operations were essentially knock-down assembly. Back in America, black box parts was not a prevalent practice, either. In America, car makers prior to the mass-production era relied heavily on marketed goods (supplier proprietary parts), while the contemporary U.S. producers tended to rely on detail-controlled parts.[24] Thus, it is not likely that the black box parts system was originally imported from the Western automakers.

However, the transfer mechanism inside Japan will, of course, explain why the system subsequently spread rapidly among the Japanese automakers and suppliers. That is, the diffusion of the black box parts system may have been the result of either direct or indirect transfer of knowledge among automakers, among parts suppliers, from assemblers to suppliers, or from suppliers to assemblers.

Hypothesis 6. Founders/entrepreneurs of the automakers had foresight about this practice (entrepreneurial vision). Kiichiro Toyoda, the de facto founder-entrepreneur of Toyota Motor Corporation, deserves special attention. It is known that Kiichiro Toyoda made many visionary statements in the early days of Toyota.[25] Some of the visions were unrealistic in the short run (e.g., catching up with the U.S. makers in productivity within three years, after 1945), but many of them still have a long-term impact on Toyota's corporate culture. The question is, did Kiichiro have entrepreneurial intuition in the area of supplier management? Since, generally speaking, his discourses about Toyota's early supplier system are not widely known, we need to examine historical materials more carefully.

Hypothesis 7. It occurred through pure chance (random trials). Any historical evolution of a new system is likely to be influenced at least partly by pure chance. The case of black box parts does not seem to be an exception. From a researcher's point of view, though, explanation of system formation by a sequence of chance events should be the last, not first, recourse. In other words, while I don't deny the possibility of pure chance, I didn't explicitly ascribe the system emergence to chance.

In system emergence terms, the foregoing preliminary analysis of each hypothesis indicates that hypotheses 2 (technological constraints), 3 (growth with resource constraints), 4 (interindustrial transfer), 5 (intraindustrial transfer in Japan), and 6 (entrepreneurial vision of Toyota's founders) deserve further investigation. Let me emphasize that the origin and diffusion of the system may be separate in logic and timing from each other, and thus require separate explanations. On the basis of the above preliminary assumptions, subsequent sections explore these hypotheses more in detail.

Origin of the Black Box Parts System

Toyota in the Prewar Era: In-house Parts Production. Only two Japanese auto companies had the possibility of initiating the black box parts practice on a mass-production basis: Toyota and Nissan. The two companies, established in the 1930s after Ford and GM were virtually ousted from Japan by the 1936 Automobile Manufacturing Enterprise Law, were obviously the first large-scale automobile manufacturers in Japan. Of the two companies, however, some historical evidence indicates that Toyota introduced the black box parts system in a more systematic manner, if not earlier, than Nissan. For this reason, I will focus mainly on the early history of Toyota.

As already discussed in chapter 2, Toyota's automobile production, led by Kiichiro Toyoda, began in the early 1930s. After getting top-management approval to start an automobile division in Toyoda Automatic Loom Works, Kiichiro and his staff ordered machine tools for prototype building from Germany and the United States, purchased a Chevrolet car, reverse-engineered it, sketched the disassembled parts, and estimated materials used. They then started making prototypes by using idle time on the loom production line, while selecting a site for a new automobile plant.

After visiting some imitation parts makers in Tokyo and Osaka, they found that the quality of the parts from those potential suppliers was quite low, and that Toyota would have to make most of the parts in-house at the initial stage, relying heavily on parts designs by Ford and GM. Toyota decided to design the first prototype by combining designs of the Chevrolet engine, which was regarded as fuel efficient, and the Ford chassis, robust enough for Japan's bumpy roads. When the Kariya plant started in 1936, Toyota could not obtain appropriate sheet steel from Japanese makers and had to import it from Armco of the United States. Electric parts made up the largest portion of the imported parts, and this led Toyota to make them in-house.[26] They were based, however, on sketches of American parts that had been reverse-engineered.

Thus, it was difficult for Toyota to purchase appropriate parts and materials from domestic suppliers in the initial stage of automobile production. Despite this difficulty, 55 percent of the unit manufacturing cost was for that of parts purchased from outside companies in 1936; only 12 percent were imported parts, the rest (43 percent) being from domestic sources.

In 1939, after World War II started in Europe, Toyota changed its management policy to expand production. As part of the new policy, Toyota emphasized in-house production of parts. The number of purchased parts per vehicle (excluding bolts and nuts) was about 700 in 1939. The number was reduced to 570 (about 3,000 yen per vehicle) by 1940, when a new target, 380 items (1,000 yen per vehicle), was set.[27]

In the long run, however, Kiichiro Toyoda wanted to form a group of component specialist companies outside Toyota. In the case of electric parts, for example, Toyota had to make the parts in-house at its Kariya plant, but Kiichiro wrote in a 1940 memo that he planned to farm out electric parts production to specialist companies as soon as production volume expanded.[28] Although Toyota had to emphasize in-house production for the time being, Kiichiro had a long-term vision of creating specialist parts vendors.

Prewar Categories of Toyota Suppliers.   In the 1940 order to switch to in-house parts production, Toyota classified purchased parts into three categories:[29]

1. Ordinary outsourcing (*ippan gaichu*). Parts that are made by general-purpose equipment. Toyota can therefore switch suppliers when necessary. Inspection of in-coming parts is necessary
2. Special outsourcing (*tokushu gaichu*). Parts that require certain equipment and technical assistance from Toyota, as well as close capital or financial ties with the automaker. Toyota has to let the suppliers make development prototypes as much as possible. Inspection is conducted at suppliers' premises.
3. Specialist factory outsourcing (*senmon kojo gaichu*). Specific types of parts that require special-purpose equipment. Close capital and financial ties with Toyota would be needed in the future. Inspection is conducted at suppliers' premises.

It is obvious that category 1 resembles the Western-style supplier contracts, with supplier switching and inspection. Categories 2 and 3, however, involve long-term contracts and close capital or financial ties. Toyota had to have long-term relations with the suppliers of these categories apparently because they needed technical assistance in manufacturing, and because such suppliers used transaction-specific equipment. Toyota also expected the category 2 suppliers to have prototyping capability. But there were no descriptions of suppliers' design capability. Overall, Toyota intended almost from the start to establish long-term ties with a group of suppliers, mainly because of transaction-specific equipment and know-how in manufacturing. In actuality, however, design capability on the part of suppliers was not explicitly considered as a condition of long-term supplier relations during the prewar era.[30]

The Change in Procurement Policy at Toyota after the War.   Soon after World War II ended, Toyota changed its procurement policy again, this time emphasizing outsourcing. In an early Toyota history, Kiichiro described it thus:

> I want to change the parts manufacturing policy drastically. In the past, for various reasons, Toyota made many parts in-house and thus could not concentrate on parts procurement. From now on, we should encourage specialization among our suppliers, have them do research in their specialty, and nurture their capability as specialist factories. We will ask such specialist manufacturers to make our specialist parts.[31]

Although there are some signs that Kiichiro had this vision of creating a group of specialist vendors in the prewar era, it was only after the war that he declared it an official policy.

The Birth of Nippondenso (1949).   In 1949, Nippondenso separated from Toyota and became an independent company, in accordance with a restoration plan (*saiken seibi keikaku*) that Toyota submitted to the government. The electric parts factory of Toyota was suffering a deficit.[32]

The new company, Nippondenso, had design and engineering capability from the beginning; virtually all of Toyota's electric component engineers, who were making parts drawings based on sketches of parts in the U.S. cars (e.g., Delco and Lucas), were transferred to the new company to form an engineering department there.[33] It naturally followed that the transactions between Toyota and Nippondenso were based on a black box parts system from the beginning. Engineers of Nippondenso made their parts drawings on the basis of specification drawings (rough assembly drawings) provided by Toyota, which in turn gave approval of the former's drawings. In other words, an approved parts (*shoninzu*) system has existed at Nippondenso since 1949.[34] In 1951, a post was created to handle approved drawings when the number of such drawings increased. In 1952, Nippondenso expanded transactions with non-Toyota makers such as Mazda (Toyo Kogyo), Mitsubishi, and Honda, which virtually meant diffusion of the black box parts practice outside the Toyota group.

In 1953, Nippondenso made a big decision on the choice of its technological base: it forged a technical tie-up with Bosch of Germany to switch virtually all the parts drawings to those made by Bosch under a license agreement. Initially, Nippondenso copied the Bosch drawings, which were then modified according to customer specifications. Production of Bosch-based parts started around 1955. In 1956, formal rules for handling approved drawings were established. Drawings with direct Bosch influence continued until the late 1960s.

Toyota's Procedures on Approved Drawing. Assuming that Toyota is the first mass-producing automaker that systematically used the black box parts system, it is necessary to identify when Toyota formally started this practice. According to a survey of Toyota's purchasing and engineering procedures, the oldest documents available that use the phrase "approved drawings" at Toyota are Approved Drawings Rule (*shoninzu kitei*) and Approved Drawings Handling Rule (*shoninzu shori kitei*) from 1953.[35] These internal rules of the design office, in turn, mention that they replaced similar rules from 1949. The 1949 documents themselves no longer exist at Toyota, according to our survey. It is not clear whether any internal rules existed prior to 1949, but given the fact that systematic formats for Toyota's documents were established in 1948, it is likely that the 1949 rule was the first formal rule to define the approved drawings.[36]

The coincidence in timing makes us suspect that the separation of Nippondenso from Toyota (also in 1949) might have been closely related to the origin of the black box parts (approved drawings) system. It is not clear if this separation itself forced Toyota to establish the black box parts rule, however.[37]

In any case, Toyota's 1953 approved parts rule was rather simple: only one page of a few sentences. The rules specified that the approved drawings be submitted to Toyota's engineering department via the purchasing department, that the engineering department is to process the drawings according to the Approved Drawings Handling Rules, and that approved drawings be sent back to the supplier via the purchasing department. The rules have remained essentially unchanged since then.

Possibility of Knowledge Transfer in the Prewar Era. Although the transaction between Toyota and Nippondenso is likely to be the origin of the Toyota-style approved drawing system, it does not necessarily mean that it was the origin for the Japanese auto industry in general. In fact, according to the survey that I conducted in 1993, six of the sample firms (i.e., 3 percent of the 177 respondents) answered that they had established the approved drawing system in the prewar era (before 1945). The six companies were three Nissan group suppliers and three independent parts makers (i.e., supplying parts to both Toyota and Nissan).

Looking at these early adoptions of the approved drawing system more closely, one may hypothesize that the approved drawing system was in fact imported from other industries, such as the prewar locomotive and/or aircraft industries. In fact, three of the above six companies had close connections with one or other of those two industries: a brake parts maker (established in the early 1920s; initially making locomotive brakes under a license from an American manufacturer), a piston parts maker (established in the early 1930s; making piston parts for aircraft, automobiles, ships, etc.), and a shock absorber maker (established in the late 1930s as a subsidiary company of a locomotive parts supplier). The other two[38] were suppliers of rather generic parts (textile and oil sealing, respectively), so they were probably supplier proprietary parts makers rather than black box parts makers. Also, according to the same survey, early adopters of the approved parts system in the postwar era (1946 to 1955; eighteen companies) included companies closely related to the prewar aircraft industry, such as two bearing makers, a shock absorber maker, a magneto maker, a carburetor maker, and a former aircraft fuselage maker. Many of the other companies supplied relatively generic parts (i.e., merchandise goods), such as tires, paint, oil filters, cables, and gaskets.

The black box practice may have been transferred from the locomotive and aircraft industries because they were more advanced than the auto industry.[39] For example, Sawai (1985) argues that some locomotive and component suppliers accumulated technological capabilities and started joint engineering with the customer, the Ministry of Railroad, during the 1920s. The aircraft industry might have started the black box parts practice later (1930s), but its influence on the postwar auto industry might also have been more direct. As some of major aircraft parts suppliers were located in the eastern part of Japan, Nissan, with most of its plants located in the same area, might have learned this practice more directly than Toyota at this initial stage.

The above survey results also indicate the possibility that there is another path to the black box parts system: suppliers of relatively generic parts (e.g., tires, paint, etc.), or supplier proprietary parts, converted themselves to black box parts suppliers when automakers decided to make such parts or materials more product-specific for some technical or commercial reasons.[40]

It would be reasonable to infer from these findings that the Toyota-Nippondenso partnership in 1949 was not the pioneer of the approved drawing system. It is nevertheless important to note that Toyota's approved parts system turned out to be significantly more systematic and effective than that of the other automakers, including Nissan's. Thus, the Toyota-Nippondenso transactions might not have been the earliest of the black box parts practice in general, but it is likely that they originated the relatively effective version of the system.

Diffusion of the Black Box Parts System

Postwar Development of the Japanese Supplier System. Let's now turn to the diffusion phase of the system's evolution. Before discussing the issue, though, we need to take a brief look at the background in the 1950s and thereafter.

Back in the early 1950s, the Japanese automobile supplier system was very different from today's. Many of the basic patterns of the so-called Japanese supplier system—including long-term relations, multilayer hierarchies, the "Alps" structure, just-in-time delivery, subassembly of components by first-tier suppliers, involvement of first-tier suppliers in product development, competition by long-term capabilities, close operational control and assistance by the automakers, and so on—were gradually formed from the 1950s to 1970s. The high growth in production volume and proliferation of models during the 1960s facilitated the formation of a multilayer hierarchy of control and assistance.

According to Kazuo Wada (1991), for example, a management diagnosis for Toyota and its twenty-one suppliers (*keiretsu shindan*), conducted by staff of Aichi Prefecture in the early 1950s, pointed out that Toyota had not provided enough technical support to its *keiretsu* suppliers, and that its purchasing department needed more people. Toyota quickly responded to this diagnosis and strengthened its technical assistance, inspection, and data collection for its suppliers. On the supplier side, the Kyoryoku-kai (suppliers association) started to hold a series of joint seminars and plant visits. By the mid-1960s, activities of the Kyoho-kai (Toyota's supplier association) had been coordinated with Toyota's annual management objectives, and *kanban* had been introduced to some of the suppliers. By the end of 1970s, most of what we see today as the Japanese supplier system had been installed. The question is, whether the black box parts system followed this pattern.

Toyota and Nissan in the 1960s: Model Proliferation If the Japanese auto companies could not recruit sufficient engineers and workers to deal with the rapid expansion of production in 1960s, it would be reasonable to predict that pressures to subcontract out a larger fraction of their operational tasks to the parts suppliers increased during that time. In fact, literature on the Japanese subcontracting system generally points out that it was during the 1960s that the automakers started to purchase subassembly components, rather than piece parts, from their first-tier suppliers, and that they emphasized "specialist"

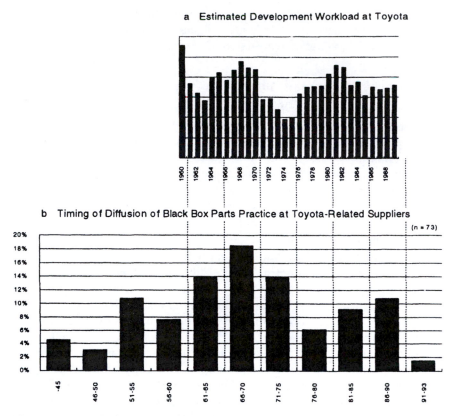

Figure 5.8 Toyota's Estimated Development Workload and the Shift to Black Box Parts

parts suppliers.[41] Thus, it would be reasonable to infer that the Japanese automakers actually subcontracted out a larger fraction of the production tasks to the suppliers under pressure to grow rapidly while constrained by in-house production resources.

A similar logic may hold in the case of product development and black box parts, although the pattern of model proliferation may have been somewhat different from that of production volume expansion. The number of Japanese basic models in 1960 (excluding foreign models produced by license agreements) was eight in 1960 (two from Toyota), twenty-four in 1965 (four from Toyota), thirty-seven in 1970 (eight from Toyota), and forty-six in 1980 (ten from Toyota).[42] Thus, proliferation of basic models occurred mostly in the 1960s (the latter half in particular), but it slowed down in the 1970s.

Figure 5.8 shows a rough estimate of the product development workload for Toyota and its suppliers since the 1960s. There were a few waves of development workloads: the late 1960s (Japan's motorization period), around 1980 (between the two oil crises), and the late

1980s (the bubble era).[43] Although the results are very preliminary, the figure seems to indicate that there may have been significant pressures for Toyota and other major Japanese automakers to alleviate the problem of growing development workload by asking the parts suppliers to do a part of the product development tasks.

In the area of product development, very few researchers have pointed out that the black box parts system (i.e., subcontracting of engineering tasks) was diffused rapidly during the 1960s. However, my 1993 survey clearly shows that the late 1960s was, in fact, the peak period for adoption of the approved drawing system among the Japanese first-tier suppliers.

An interview conducted by the author with a purchasing manager at Nissan also indicates that the black box parts system prevailed during the late 1960s at this company.[44] The diffusion process is said to have been quite informal, though. While an informal process of spreading the black box parts system was going on at Nissan, Toyota was already refining its formal process for the system. In 1961, the internal rules on approved parts became company-wide rules (*sekkei kenkyu kitei*) seven pages in length. By the late 1970s, the rules had evolved into a very detailed procedure of nearly fifty pages. As is discussed later, Nissan lagged behind Toyota in formalizing and systematizing the black box parts practice.

The Case of Company A (1972–1992).   The data for company A, a supplier of interior and other plastic parts, provide an intriguing illustration of how the black box parts system spread within a supplier, as the company supplied a wide variety of parts. The data show how the company has accumulated design capability in the past twenty years.[45] As figure 5.9 indicates, the company almost quadrupled the number of parts drawings based on either approved drawings (*shoninzu*) or consigned drawings (*itakuzu*) between 1972 and 1992. The share of black box parts in the total number of drawings grew from 24 to 55 percent in twenty years. Interestingly, the fraction of consigned drawings increased very rapidly during the 1980s. This seems to coincide with the period when product variations (particularly those of auto interiors) proliferated, partly because of the bubble economy. In view of a comment by a former executive of company A, that the main reason car makers adopt the practice of consigned drawings is a shortage of their own in-house engineers, the rapid expansion of this category in the 1980s was very likely caused by the increased workload imposed on car makers by the proliferation of product variations.

Breaking down the data by items provides even more intriguing facts: the patterns of design capability building differ widely across the types of the components (figure 5.10). In the case of functional parts, such as steering wheels and antivibration rubber, approved drawings increased. This is essentially because their functional tar-

new drawings per
year (disguised)

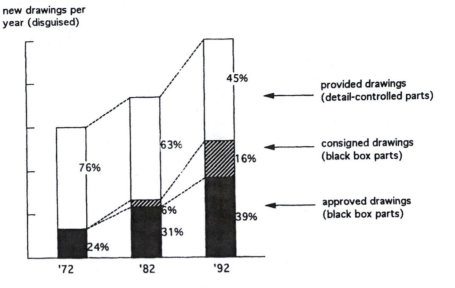

Source: Company A

Figure 5.9 Number of Parts Drawings by Type of Transaction (Company A)

gets can be unequivocally defined, and responsibility for quality assurance can be assigned. In the case of weather strips (bands of rubber
connecting window glass and bodies), consigned drawings, in which
automakers own designs and take responsibility for quality, have become a dominant mode; that's partly because responsibility for quality assurance is difficult to assign among the car maker (body), glass
supplier, and weather strip supplier. On the other hand, the detail-
controlled system (provided drawings) still covers a majority of interior trim parts, apparently because such parts are integrated with the
car makers' total vehicle (interior) design.

Indeed, types of parts transactions may differ, depending upon the
characteristics of parts: when the parts are inseparable from the total
vehicle design (e.g., body stamping parts), they tend to be detail-controlled with provided drawings; when the parts can be functionally
defined independently from the total vehicle design, they tend to be
approved drawing parts (or supplier proprietary parts in an extreme
case); when responsibility for the parts' functions cannot be clearly
assigned between the car maker and the supplier, consigned drawings
tend to be chosen.

*Toyota in the 1980s: Continued Diffusion of the Black Box Parts Prac-
tice.*   Diffusion of approved drawings continued at Toyota during the
1980s. According to company data, the proportion of approved draw-

Steering Wheel

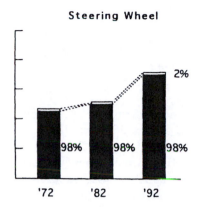

Weather Strip

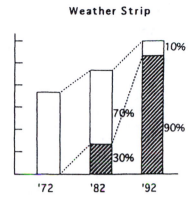

Anti-Vibration Rubber

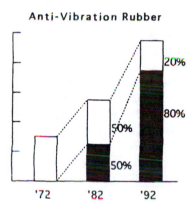

Interior Parts

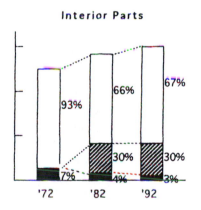

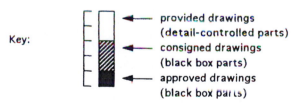

Key:

← provided drawings
(detail-controlled parts)

← consigned drawings
(black box parts)

← approved drawings
(black box parts)

Figure 5.10 Number of New Drawings Per Year by Type of Transaction and Item (Company A)

ings in total number of engineering drawings increased from 30 percent in 1980 to 37 percent in 1992 (in the case of the Mark II model).[46] Proliferation of product variations after the mid-1980s is likely to have created pressures to rely more on the engineering resources of the suppliers (see figure 5.8 again).[47]

Nissan in 1980s: Benchmarking and Institutionalization. Although Nissan's black box parts system may have originated before the war and was diffused in the 1960s, as was the case at Toyota, the system is said to have lacked coherent and effective formal procedures. It wasn't until 1986–87 that Nissan finally established a system of formal procedures for black box parts, which Nissan called the New Approved Drawing System.[48] This was apparently part of Nissan's efforts to renovate its organization in the late 1980s.

Preparation for this shift started in the early 1980s, when the Japanese auto industry was recovering from the second oil crisis. This was when Nissan switched from restrictive to expansive strategies in production and product mix. Thus, Nissan was predicting a rapid increase in product development workload. At the same time, Nissan's managers were concerned about the fact that its approved drawing system was not as developed as that of Toyota. After a benchmarking study of Toyota's practice, for example, it was revealed that Toyota's inputs to black box parts suppliers (a few pages of specification documents with rough sketches) were much simpler than those of Nissan (a roll of fairly detailed specification drawings). This implied that Nissan's black box parts system consumed more in-house engineering resources and that it put more restrictions on supplier efforts to make the parts design easier. It was also pointed out that the timing when the component specifications are frozen at Nissan was late compared with Toyota.

After a series of analyses, Nissan's engineering administration department proposed the following revision of the black box parts system in the mid-1980s (figure 5.11):

- The old approved drawing system used specification drawings or *shiyozu* (incomplete drawings that the suppliers were expected to complete) as inputs to the suppliers.[49] The new system abolished specification drawings and introduced a specification instruction form (*shiyo teiansho*), which was closer to Toyota's design request form. In this way, suppliers could enjoy more design discretion to apply their technological expertise to the designs.
- Division of responsibility for development tasks between Nissan and the suppliers was not clear in the old system. In the new system, Nissan proposed that a Design Task Assignment Table and a Check Sheet clarify the responsibility of each

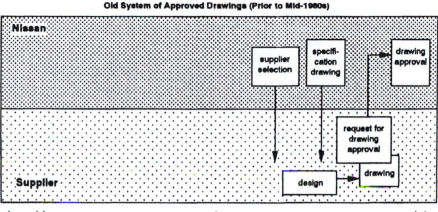

Old System of Approved Drawings (Prior to Mid-1980s)

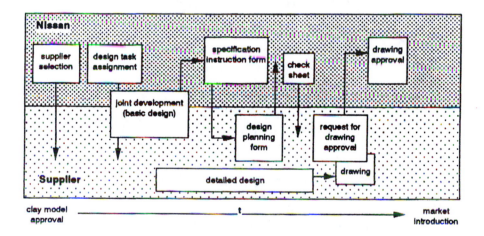

Source: Nissan Motor Co., Ltd.

Figure 5.11 Nissan's Adoption of New Approved Drawing System (Mid-1980s)

party. This measure was expected to eliminate duplication of development work between Nissan and the suppliers.

- Responsibility for quality assurance was not clear in the old system, either. In the new system, Nissan proposed that the approved drawing suppliers take full responsibility for the functionality of the component as a unit.
- In the old system, supplier selection occurred relatively late in product development. In the new system, supplier selec-

tion was made much earlier (around the end of the product planning phase); this gave the supplier a longer lead time for component design.

- Specification drawings were unilaterally submitted to the suppliers in the old system. The new system added a period during which Nissan and the supplier jointly develop specifications.

Overall, the new approved drawing system adopted some of the practices that Toyota already had: a relatively simple specification form, clear division of responsibility for quality assurance, early supplier selection, and joint development of specifications. At the same time, Nissan managers expected that the new system would save engineering person-hours for its in-house engineers.

There was some controversy inside Nissan over the shift to the new system. Some argued that technological hollows might be created in the new system, in that Nissan's engineers would cease to be real engineers if they stopped making engineering drawings. (Japanese design engineers tend to believe that drafting capability is a prerequisite for a good engineer.) However, the argument that Nissan would have needed thousands of additional engineers to maintain the old system when it had to expand its product line overshadowed such concerns, according to one Nissan manager.[50]

It might be that Nissan was among the last of the Japanese automakers to adopt the Toyota-style approved drawing system because there had been a tacit agreement that Toyota group suppliers (e.g., Nippondenso) could supply parts to any Japanese automaker except Nissan group assemblers, while Nissan group suppliers took the opposite step of excluding the Toyota suppliers (see type 1 and type 2 in figure 5.12). Although independent and neutral suppliers (type 3 in figure 5.12) might have acted as intermediaries that transferred the essence of the Toyota-style system to Nissan, it is likely that the separation of Toyota and Nissan supplier groups was at least partially responsible for Nissan's lateness in adopting a more effective black box parts system.

According to the data analysis by Kim Clark and I, the fraction of black box parts in total procurement cost was consistently high among the Japanese automakers.[51] Thus, the diffusion of the approved drawing system among the Japanese automakers appeared to end by the late 1980s.

A Survey Result. In my 1993 survey, I asked approximately when the companies started various activities related to black box parts practices. The results are generally consistent with the above description of the diffusion process (figure 5.13):

1. The peak period of institutionalization of the approved drawing system, as well as actual diffusion of the system within

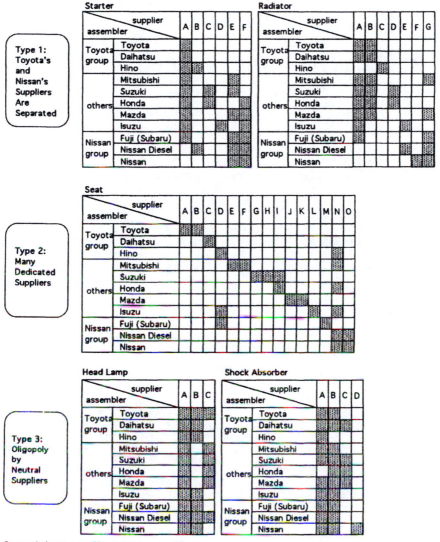

Type 1: Toyota's and Nissan's Suppliers Are Separated

Type 2: Many Dedicated Suppliers

Type 3: Oligopoly by Neutral Suppliers

Source: Industry experts.

Transactions exist as of 1990.

Note : In-house production is omitted for simplicity.

Figure 5.12 Patterns of Assembler and Supplier Relationships (1990)

each supplier, was the late 1960s. The next wave came in the 1980s (diagrams 2 and 3 of figure 5.13).
2. The peak time for the start of informal requests from the automakers was the early 1960s. The pattern of informal requests tended to precede that of formal institutionalization (diagram 1).

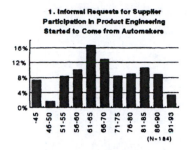

1. Informal Requests for Supplier Participation in Product Engineering Started to Come from Automakers

(N=184)

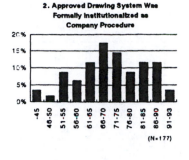

2. Approved Drawing System Was Formally Institutionalized as Company Procedure

(N=177)

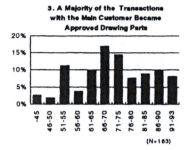

3. A Majority of the Transactions with the Main Customer Became Approved Drawing Parts

(N=163)

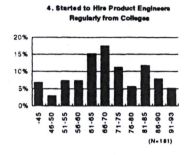

4. Started to Hire Product Engineers Regularly from Colleges

(N=181)

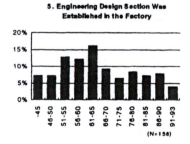

5. Engineering Design Section Was Established in the Factory

(N=156)

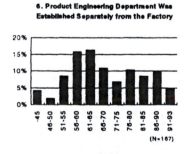

6. Product Engineering Department Was Established Separately from the Factory

(N=167)

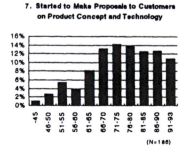

7. Started to Make Proposals to Customers on Product Concept and Technology

(N=186)

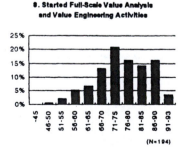

8. Started Full-Scale Value Analysis and Value Engineering Activities

(N=194)

Source: A questionnaire survey by the author in 1993.

Figure 5.13 The First Timing of Supplier's Engineering Activities

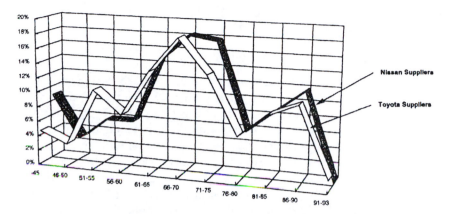

Note: Toyota-related suppliers include those which supply both Toyota and Nissan.

Source: A questionnaire survey by the author in 1993.

Figure 5.14 Comparison of Toyota-Related Suppliers and Nissan Suppliers in the Timing of Institutionalization of Approved Drawing System

3. Many of the first-tier suppliers started to regularly hire college graduates for engineering jobs during the 1960s. Establishment of formal engineering sections or divisions in and outside the factories tended to precede full-scale activities in product engineering (diagrams 4, 5, and 6).

4. The suppliers started to make engineering proposals and conduct VA-VE (value analysis and value engineering) activities mostly after the 1970s (diagrams 7 and 8).

These results seem to be consistent with the foregoing argument that the adoption of the approved parts system on the supplier side was influenced by the rapid increase in engineering workload on the side of the automakers (see figure 5.8), and that the formal establishment of the system may have been preceded by informal participation of suppliers in automobile product development.

What about the difference between Toyota and Nissan? Figure 5.14 compares the timing of institutionalization of the approved parts system between Toyota-related suppliers (including the independent type supplying both Toyota and Nissan) and Nissan group suppliers. Apart from the difference in the content of the black box parts system between the two groups, discussed earlier, the timing in introducing some kind of approved drawing system is fairly similar, although the Toyota-related suppliers tended to be slightly earlier.[52] Also, there is a small spike in the early 1950s in the case of Toyota-related suppliers. This, however, does not seem to be a diffusion effect related to the creation of Nippondenso.[53] Again, the origin of the black box parts system (Toyota version) and its diffusion seem to be generally separate both in logic and timing.

The Case of Company B: Evolution of Black Box Parts

In order to examine more closely how each supplier's design capability evolved over time, company B, a supplier of interior parts, was chosen as a case.[54] This company maintains a close tie with Toyota in terms of capital participation and transaction.[55] Established in the early 1960s, the company itself is fairly new, and it started with virtually no design capability. In addition, interior parts are relatively difficult to fit into the black box parts system because of their close interdependence with total vehicle design. Thus, the case indicates how a "latecomer" to the black box parts system accumulated design capability step by step.

There are two dimensions to design capabilities: width and depth. By width of design capability we mean the number of transactions that adopt the black box parts practice. In fact, the width of company B's design capability increased when the number of Toyota's models for which it supplied certain parts on the basis of the black box parts arrangement increased. Company B also expanded the types of parts adopting the black box parts system from parts category X to category Y.[56]

By depth of design capability we mean the level of the knowledge base. In this regard, company B gradually added capabilities in detailed parts design, subassembly design, testing, styling, and basic design and planning. The case indicates that the process of design capability building takes a significant amount of time and requires careful management and a long-term perspective.

Width of Design Capability. Figure 5.15 shows the product line of Toyota for which company B adopted the black box parts system in parts X and/or Y.

- Starting from parts X for the first-generation Publica, Toyota's entry-class model, company B expanded its width of business as Toyota expanded its product line.
- Company B's business with Toyota continued, but the automaker switched suppliers at the level of individual transactions, for various reasons.[57]
- Company B started its black box parts arrangement with a single product, the Crown, and gradually expanded the range of Toyota models that adopted this arrangement.
- The company also expanded those of its products that adopted the black box parts system from parts X to parts Y.

Another milestone is that in the mid-1960s, prior to beginning black box parts transactions with Toyota, company B started to supply parts X for forklift trucks to Toyoda Automatic Loom Works, Ltd., a Toyota group company, on the basis of the approved drawings system.

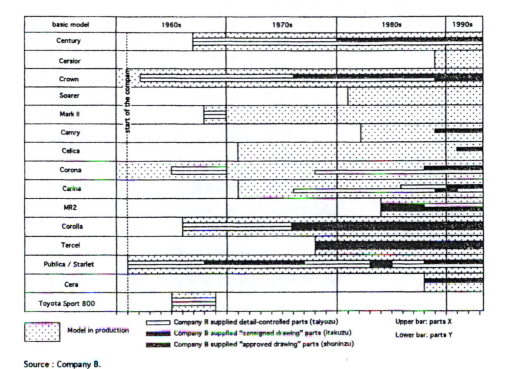

basic model	1960s	1970s	1980s	1990s
Century				
Cersior				
Crown				
Soarer				
Mark II				
Camry				
Celica				
Corona				
Carina				
MR2				
Corolla				
Tercel				
Publica / Starlet				
Cera				
Toyota Sport 800				

Model in production

Company B supplied detail-controlled parts (taiyozu) — Upper bar: parts X
Company B supplied "consigned drawing" parts (itakuzu) — Lower bar: parts Y
Company B supplied "approved drawing" parts (shoninzu)

Source : Company B.

Figure 5.15 Company B's Transactions with Toyota (Passenger Car)

The parts for the forklifts were simpler and technically easier, but this case taught company B an important lesson: shifting from a detail-controlled to an approved drawing system is not easy, as it means taking on responsibility for design quality assurance. Although the original motivation for this move was to reduce company B's dependence on the automobile business, it served company B, after the fact, as a rehearsal for entering the approved drawing business with Toyota, which was more demanding than in the case of the forklifts.

Depth of Design Capability.   The depth of company B's design capability increased over a period of thirty years. Figures 5.16 and 5.17 explain how the company acquired skills necessary for black box parts, such as detailed parts design, prototyping, detailed assembly design, testing, industrial design, basic design, and product planning. Here is a brief history:

- In the early 1960s, company B started its business with a small engineering department of three or four people. The unit had the capability for engineering administration (i.e., handling given drawings), basic production engineering (i.e., making bills of materials based on Toyota's parts drawings),

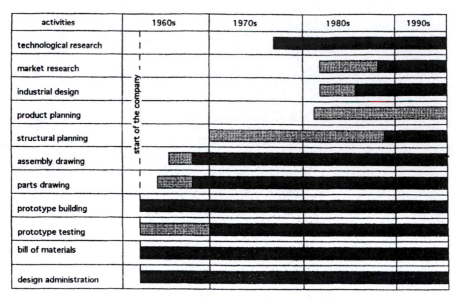

activities	1960s	1970s	1980s	1990s
technological research				
market research				
industrial design				
product planning				
structural planning				
assembly drawing				
parts drawing				
prototype building				
prototype testing				
bill of materials				
design administration				

start of the company

■ Independent capability ▦ Capability of working with car makers

Note: The forklift business was omitted for simplicity.

Source: Company B.

Figure 5.16 Step-by-Step Acquisition of Engineering Capability at Company B

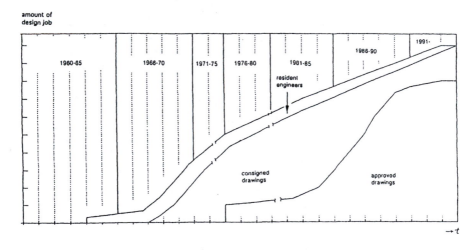

amount of design job

1960-65 1966-70 1971-75 1976-80 1981-85 1986-90 1991-

resident engineers

consigned drawings

approved drawings

→ t

Note: This diagram represents an image held by the company staff rather than actual data.
Source: Company B.

Figure 5.17 Workload of Product Design at Company B by Type of Drawing

and prototyping, but it had virtually no capability for designing and drafting its products. The company was fully dependent on detailed drawings provided by Toyota.

- In the mid-1960s, three years after the establishment of company B, it started to send its young engineers to Toyota's interior engineering department for one or two years each. They worked on Toyota premises, learning not only product technologies but also Toyota's engineering process itself. The young engineers from company B at first did miscellaneous jobs assisting Toyota's interior engineers, but Toyota soon started to give them a set of jobs related to company B's target product. They acquired the capability to make assembly drawings of parts X around that time.

- In the mid-1960s, company B started a job for Toyoda Automatic Loom Works on an approved drawing basis.

- In the late 1960s, company B started to get some jobs from Toyota on a consigned drawing basis. Toyota still took final responsibility for quality assurance, but the arrangement was more like a joint development, in that the engineers from both companies often worked on Toyota premises. The amount of work under this arrangement grew rapidly in the early 1970s.

- In the 1970s, company B established a system to test and evaluate prototypes, following Toyota's testing standards. As Toyota still took quality assurance responsibility, however, the testing conducted by company B was consigned testing.

- In the same period, company B's engineers started to participate in setting detailed specifications, basic designs, and test standards.[58] Thus, company B gradually acquired the capability of not only detailed design but also basic design (i.e., specification setting).

- Also in the early 1970s, company B's engineers became capable of making assembly drawings for parts Y, ten years later than the case of parts X.

- In the mid-1970s, fifteen years after the establishment of the company and eight years after it started consigned drawings, company B finally began doing business with Toyota on an approved drawings basis. It started this system in one model. The switch from consigned to approved drawings meant that company B had to take a risk as to quality assurance, but it acquired more discretion to design manufacturable parts. For Toyota, this also meant further reduction of its own engineering workload.

- During the same period, company B's engineers working on Toyota premises started to be treated as full-fledged engineers, which seems to reflect improvements in the former's engineering capabilities.

- In the late 1970s, company B won the Toyota Quality Control Prize (Toyota's version of the Deming Prize), which implied that company B was now ready to move to the approved drawings system and become a specialist parts supplier. The prize thus triggered rapid growth in company B's design jobs. Also, the company started its own research activities around this time. Its initial research efforts were concentrated on claims regarding the functionality of parts X.
- Also in the late 1970s, the company created a quality assurance department, which included test engineers, separate from its engineering department. It started to dispatch test engineers to Toyota.
- In the early 1980s, company B extended its engineering capability further upstream, participating in some of Toyota's product planning. It also started market studies on the durability and functionality of parts X independently or jointly with Toyota.
- In the early 1980s, company B started to hire industrial designers. A few years later, it started dispatching designers to Toyota, as well as design engineers and test engineers.
- In the mid-1980s, jobs based on approved drawings started to grow rapidly. This was partly because the approved drawing system was adopted for the company's two major products: parts X for Toyota Corolla and Crown. The shift was completed in the early 1990s.
- In the late 1980s, company B started to do structural planning for Toyota on a consigned drawing basis. This virtually meant working jointly with Toyota's engineers to make basic designs, from which company B made detailed drawings on an approved drawing basis. The number of resident engineers was reduced during the same period.

In this way, it took company B over twenty years to acquire full capability for black box parts with dozens of engineers and designers. Interactions between Toyota and company B were carefully managed with a long-term perspective. For example, resident engineers meant that the engineers of company B had access to the engineering rooms of Toyota (i.e., beyond the reception area). Of about two hundred suppliers that Toyota dealt with, less than one hundred had the privilege of dispatching resident engineers.

It should be also noted that consigned drawing (*itakuzu*) parts functioned as a kind of rehearsal that paved the way to company B's transformation to an approved drawing (*shoninzu*) parts supplier. In other words, whereas in the first case, company A chose either consigned or approved drawings depending upon the nature of the components, over time company B shifted its emphasis from the former to the latter.

The Multi-Path Emergence of Black Box Parts: Why and How

The case of the black box parts practice among Japanese automakers provides a good example of how a group of manufacturing firms build new capabilities over time. The foregoing discussions indicate that the system emerged and evolved over time by a complicated combination of driving forces surrounding the industry. As the case of company B suggests, the process of developing a black box design system requires step-by-step collaboration and tenacious capability building by both the assembler and the supplier. Also, as shown in table 5.2, the present case seems to indicate multi-path system emergence, based on the variety of evolutionary paths. In any case, it should be noted that the black box parts system was not a practice that the Japanese automakers adopted from the Ford system in America, unlike many other elements of the Toyota-style system.[59]

Origins

The foregoing story implies that the black box parts practice emerged, not because of rational calculation by the automobile companies (at least before the fact), but because of a set of constraints or historical imperatives imposed on the automakers. The auto companies apparently realized the benefit of this practice much later, when their engineering workloads started to soar as a result of product proliferation in the 1960s.

Technological constraints seem to have played an important role here. First, before the war, Toyota could not find decent electric parts suppliers in Japan, so it was almost forced to design and make such parts in-house. Second, after the war, Toyota had to spin off the electric parts factory for its own survival. Third, when Nippondenso was created in 1949 as a result of the separation, Toyota found that it had to rely on the engineering capability of Nippondenso, as virtually all the electric engineers had moved to the new company. Because Toyota lacked the technological capability for electric parts, it was then forced to apply the approved drawing (i.e., black box parts) system to its transactions with Nippondenso from the beginning.

Interindustrial transfer of the practices in the prewar locomotive and/or aircraft industries may also partly explain the origin of the black box parts system. Transformation of supplier proprietary parts (e.g., tires and paints) to black box parts may be another passage to the new system. Further investigation is needed to examine theses hypotheses, though.

But entrepreneurial visions apparently did not play a decisive role. There is some evidence that the founder of Toyota Motor Manufacturing had a vision of nurturing parts specialist suppliers even prior to the war, when Toyota had to make many parts in house. Although Ki-

Table 5.2 Summary of the Emergence Logic for Black Box Parts System

Logic	Empirical Evidence
Rational Calculation	● Before the trial: Benefits of black box parts are not well predicted. ○ After the fact: Toyota was quick in institutionalizing what it inadvertently tried and found to be effective.
Environmental Constraints (Technological Dependence)	● Few suppliers had engineering capability in the 1930s and '40s. ○ Toyota - Nippondenso case: Toyota lacked electric parts engineering capability as it spun off Nippondenso in 1949.
Environmental Constraints (Insufficient Number of Engineers)	● Black box parts practice originated before the model proliferation period. ○ Survey result: The peak time of diffusion of the black box parts system coincided with model proliferation period in the late 1960s. ○ Respondents of the survey tended to agree that high engineering workload of the automakers triggered the shift to black box parts. Interviewees at Nissan, company A and company B at least partially agreed with this hypothesis.
Knowledge Transfer	● Ford and other U.S. mass producers did not have black box parts, and thus they were not the source of the practice. ⊖ Prewar aircraft industry in Japan may have been a source of the back box practice. ○ Indirect knowledge transfer (benchmarking) from Toyota to Nissan in the 1980s. ○ Rapid diffusion of black box parts practice among the Japanese first-tier suppliers (survey results).
Entrepreneurial Vision	● No clearly stated comments on the black box parts system by Toyota's executives were found in the formal company history ○ Kiichiro Toyoda's vision of growing specialist parts vendors after the war might have facilitated the development of black box practice.

Note: ○ = evidences consistent with the hypothesis

● = evidences contradicting the hypothesis

⊖ = inconclusive

"Random trials' was omitted from the table.

ichiro's remarks did not refer to a black box parts system, it is possible that what he meant by "specialist" was a parts maker that also had research and development capability for designing a certain type of parts. To the extent that Kiichiro's specialist concept implied capabilities for parts design, it is possible that his vision of the supplier system served as a catalyst, if not a driving force, for subsequent development of the black box parts practice. However, in the case of black box parts, entrepreneurial visions were not unequivocally and explicitly put into words by the executives and managers, unlike the case of just-in-time and total quality management.

Diffusions

The foregoing cases also indicate that the historical imperative of high growth with limited resource inputs in the product engineering area of the auto companies (i.e., shortage of in-house engineers at model proliferation time) created constant pressures to subcontract detailed component engineering wherever possible.

From the supplier's point of view, the black box parts arrangement meant a great opportunity to develop design capability, build up a technological entry barrier against the automaker's efforts to make the parts in house, gain some quasi-rent, and survive as a first-tier parts supplier, although it was accompanied by the risk of taking full responsibility for quality assurance. Competitive pressures from rival suppliers also accelerated the efforts to build up design and engineering capability in order to match competitors' efforts. Thus, once the automakers started to offer the opportunities of shifting to the black box parts arrangement, the suppliers tended to have rational reasons to accept the offers, as long as they had enough managerial capability to do so.

Transfer of knowledge and managerial resources between suppliers (e.g., from Nippondenso to other suppliers), between assemblers (e.g., from Toyota to Nissan), as well as between an assembler and a supplier (e.g., from Toyota to company B), was a key engine for diffusion of the black box parts practice. Originating presumably from the transactions between Toyota and Nippondenso in the late 1940s, the black box parts practice grew rapidly during the high-growth era of the 1960s; the diffusion process tapered off within Japan in the 1980s, but diffusion has been in progress across national borders thereafter — from Japan to the United States, for example.

The diffusion of the black box parts system in general, in terms of timing, did not differ much between Toyota and Nissan. However, it was in the content and effectiveness of the system that the two companies differed for a long time. Thus, it was only in the 1980s that Nissan modified its black box parts system to make it more like the Toyota version.

To sum up, the origin and evolution of the black box parts practice, which is one of the sources of competitive advantages for the Japanese auto industry of the 1980s, may be explained by a combination of historical imperatives and interfirm/interindustrial knowledge transfers, rather than through rational calculation or deliberate strategic choices prior to the events. While the system, after it was established, might have turned out to contribute to competitive advantage, the benefits were not clearly recognized by the firms when it was emerging. After the companies learned from their unplanned trials, however, some of the firms started to adopt the new system more intentionally, deliberately, and institutionally.

To the extent that an ex-post rational system emerged out of unintended imperatives or constraints, it may be meaningful to explore and analyze the logic of multi-path system emergence. More important, it was this capability of systematizing the new elements after the trials, rather than that of rational calculation, that seems to explain the difference in the content and effectiveness of the black box parts systems of Toyota and Nissan up to the mid-1980s. This leads to our last question: what is the source of interfirm differences in performance and capabilities?

Patterns of Capability Building

The evolution of the black box parts system provides some additional insights and empirical foundation for the propositions made in the earlier chapters of this book. In short, the analyses in this chapter are generally consistent with the argument in a broader context that the Toyota-style manufacturing system evolved through a process of multi-path system emergence, and that Toyota's evolutionary learning capability created distinctive manufacturing routines for its competitive advantage in the long run. Specifically, we can summarize the black box parts case from an evolutionary point of view:

- *Long-term evolution of suppliers' capabilities.* The suppliers accumulate the capability of component engineering through long-term collaboration between assemblers and suppliers. The process needs step-by-step enhancement of design and engineering capabilities both in width and depth.
- *Competition based on capability building.* As the case of company B indicates, suppliers making similar components competed with each other in terms of gaining component design capability. Thus, short-term price competition (i.e., bidding) is not the only mode of competition. In the long run, competition in building engineering capabilities becomes crucial.
- *The limits of rational calculation.* Toyota was more effective than some other makers in designing and implementing the black box parts system. But is this because Toyota was more capable than others in predicting the effectiveness of the system? It seems unlikely. Even Toyota could not predict the effectiveness of the black box parts system prior to its trials, and this automaker, forced by historical imperatives and environmental constraints in many cases, tended to make initial trials in an unplanned manner. Thus, the interfirm difference in re-

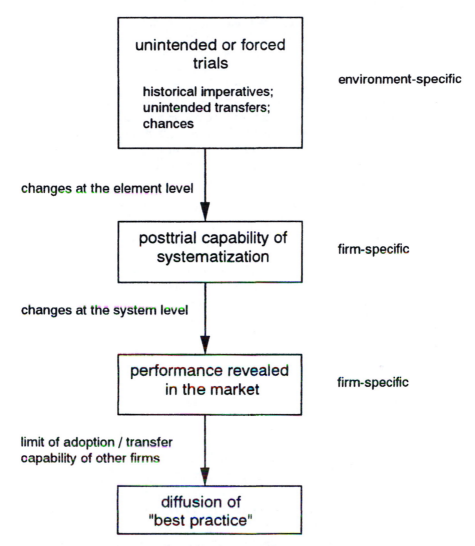

Figure 5.18 A Typical Pattern Observed in the Case of Black Box Parts Evolution

sults does not seem to be caused principally by interfirm differences in rational calculation. That is, the process was *emergent* to a certain extent.

- *Interfirm gaps in capability of systematizing successful trials.* What Toyota could do better than its rivals seems to be not so much rational calculation before the trials as systematization and institutionalization *after* the trials. Opportunities for making certain trials for new systems came to other companies as well. For example, Toyota and Nissan faced the same historical imperatives by which they were virtually forced to rely partially on suppliers' engineering resources. They both made trials in this direction. However, as Nissan itself found in the mid-1980s, the effectiveness of the resulting systems differed significantly. This seems to be because Toyota had the capability to learn quickly from what it inadvertently tried, understanding the core benefit of the trials, institutionalizing them as a set of formal procedures, and diffusing them within the company and throughout the supplier network better than its rivals.

There are various ways in which a company changes and differentiates its routine capability for competitive performance in a dynamic way. In some cases, differences in entrepreneurial visions may create the competitive advantage of a particular firm (Okouchi, 1979). Rational calculation may be critical in other cases. In still other cases, pure luck may give some firms certain advantages. In the current case of the black box parts practice, though, it seems to be the ex-post learning capability in systematizing unplanned trials that created Toyota's advantages over its rivals (figure 5.18). And differences in such an *opportunistic (ex-post) learning capability* seem to have played a primary role in creating competitive differences among the automakers in terms of utilizing supplier potentials in component engineering.

Thus, the present chapter reconfirmed the emergent nature of the manufacturing system formation and the central role of the evolutionary learning capability, which we have already identified in previous chapters, this time by using the detailed first-hand data on the black box parts practice in particular. Through in-depth field researches and historical studies at Toyota, Nissan, and a few Japanese first-tier suppliers, as well as questionnaire surveys for about two hundred Japanese suppliers, both functions and emergence of this supplier management practice were systematically investigated. Throughout this evolutionary analysis, Toyota's distinctive capability of evolutionary learning, in addition to its routinized capabilities, was once again quite obvious.

In the next chapter, we turn to the second major element of Toyota-style manufacturing system—product development—to gain further insights into the dynamics of capability-building competition among the auto firms worldwide.

6

EVOLUTION OF PRODUCT
DEVELOPMENT ROUTINES

As with the black box parts practice of Japanese suppliers, a second major component of the total manufacturing system—product development—offers specific examples of system evolution in the automobile industry. This chapter enriches and extends my evolutionary arguments by presenting both statistical and clinical-historical data on product development.[1] Regardless of what official company histories indicate, the Japanese firms like Toyota that ended up with effective product development routines in the 1980s did so through system emergence—that is, through a combination of intended and unintended consequences.

Here, I approach product development from four different research angles. The first section of this chapter presents a functional analysis of routine capabilities to show how they contributed to advantages in product development performance, based on an international comparative study of automobile product development in the 1980s led by Kim B. Clark of Harvard University (and in which I was a participant).[2] Five main product development routines this study identified —supplier capabilities; in-house manufacturing capabilities; overlapping product and process engineering; wide task assignment for engineers; and the heavyweight product manager system—and their functional consequences are briefly discussed. Second, I examine the same set of routine capabilities from a historical or genetic point of view to show that each was essentially created through the multi-path system emergence. The third and fourth sections of this chapter extend the research scope to the 1990s by looking at (1) international diffusion of product development routines, as exemplified by the catchup of U.S. automakers; and (2) overshooting or overbuilding of capabilities, which resulted in what I call fat product design at Japanese automakers—a problem that indicates how the very strength of a firm may have dysfunctional effects.

Through these four angles, I aim to reinforce the evolutionary/total system arguments made in earlier chapters while also expanding the analyses geographically and conceptually. I supply several missing pieces of this evolutionary story by describing how some of the Japanese automakers built a set of distinctive product development routines by the 1980s; how Western automakers started catching up with the Japanese by systematically adopting some of the latter's routines; and how the Japanese automakers overused these capabilities and thereby created a problem of high-cost products—and how they then responded to such new competitive challenges in the first half of the 1990s.[3] In this chapter, we explore the evolutionary processes of creating, maintaining, transferring, overusing, and renewing capabilities in product development. Once again, think of such routine capabilities as the equivalent of a company's "genes": the new set of effective product development routines emerged in a small number of auto firms by the 1980s; they were selected and retained as the "fittest" in the competitive environment of the 1980s; they started to be diffused to other firms since then; they were overdeveloped in some cases, but overall these routines continued to be basically effective in the long run. In this chapter, I make such evolutionary analyses, focusing consistently on the same set of product development routines.

A Brief History of Japanese Automobile R&D

Before focusing on product development in the 1980s, let's recap the relevant historical facts about Japanese R&D in this sector. Product development in the Japanese auto industry started in 1910s and 1920s with sporadic trial production based on rather primitive vehicle designs, many of which were foreign imitation or patchwork, by small venture businesses. In the 1930s, Toyota (then Toyoda Automatic Loom), under Kiichiro Toyoda's leadership, started with a simple product development unit that reverse-engineered foreign models and made prototypes, while Nissan decided to buy a set of engineering drawings from an American company. Both production and process technologies during the prewar era were far behind internationally competitive levels, though.

After World War II, particularly after the 1960s, Japanese R&D organizations increased in size and became gradually structured. Toyota's product development organization, for example, started from a very small group in the 1930s but had become a specialized organization with many functional units by the 1970s (see figure 6.1). Many of the first-tier parts suppliers also established formal product engineering departments or sections during the 1950s and 1960s (see figure 5.13). Some of the Japanese automakers introduced packages of car designs

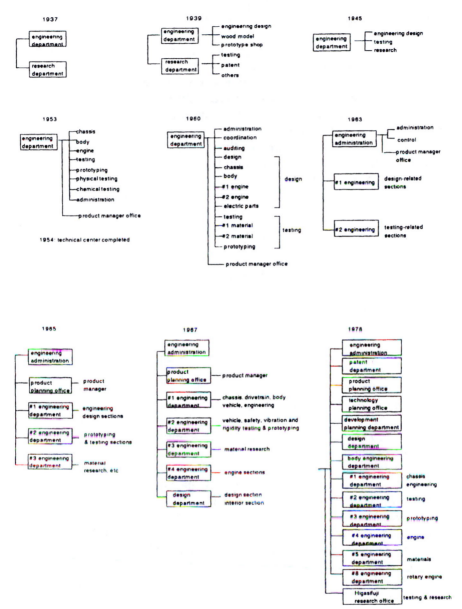

Source: Reconstructed from Toyota Motor Co., Ltd. (1967), Toyota Motor Co., Ltd (1978), and Ikari, Yoshiro (1985).

Figure 6.1 History of Toyota's Product Development Organizations

and technologies mostly from European makers under licensing agreements (Nissan-Austin, Hino-Renault, Isuzu-Roots, Mitsubishi-Willys), although Toyota decided not to do so. Imports of component technologies from U.S. and European makers to first-tier Japanese suppliers also increased in the late 1950s and thereafter.

New product development activities for Japanese passenger cars were dramatically accelerated in the 1960s, when so-called motorization (a sharp increase of household car ownership) happened in Japan. The automakers increased the number of basic models rapidly to capture this market opportunity. Note, also, that the four-year model change cycles that are most common today had already been established in the early 1960s in Japan, primarily because the main Toyota and Nissan models of the time were competing against each other in the domestic market. This practice prevailed in other companies subsequently (see figure 6.2). Thus, intense domestic competition apparently forced Japanese companies to introduce new products frequently, and thereby to build product development routines that facilitated rapid model renewals. As a result, in the 1980s the Japanese overwhelmed the Western automakers in the number of new model introductions per period or per sales, which contributed to a freshness of models and an expansion of model varieties.[4]

By the mid-1970s, the Japanese were wrestling with strict domestic emission regulations and the first oil crisis. Such external pressures forced Japanese automakers to improve their product technologies dramatically—for small internal combustion engines in particular. This was a turning point for a Japanese automobile technology. For instance, the engineering workload for developing new technologies for better emission control and fuel economy was so enormous that they had to shift resources from new model development projects to engine research, which led to delays of the former activity. R&D expenses to sales ratios increased accordingly from about 2 percent in 1970 to about 3 percent in 1980 (see table 6.1). Indeed, Japanese automakers were arguably the leaders in the technological advancement of small combustion engines during this period and thereafter.

Throughout the 1980s, the advancement of Japanese product technology accelerated via the application of electronic controls and new materials, but without radical changes in the product itself (that is, alternative engines or drastic changes in material composition didn't occur). The patterns of automotive innovations during this period may be characterized as "rapid incrementalism" rather than "reinvention" or "dematurity."[5] This, however, did not mean deceleration of technological advancement—R&D expenses to sales ratio increased further to about 4 percent level by the early 1990s, accordingly (see table 6.1). In other words, Japanese cars during the 1980s became more sophisticated in terms of total vehicle technologies and product integrity without breakthrough innovations in component technologies.

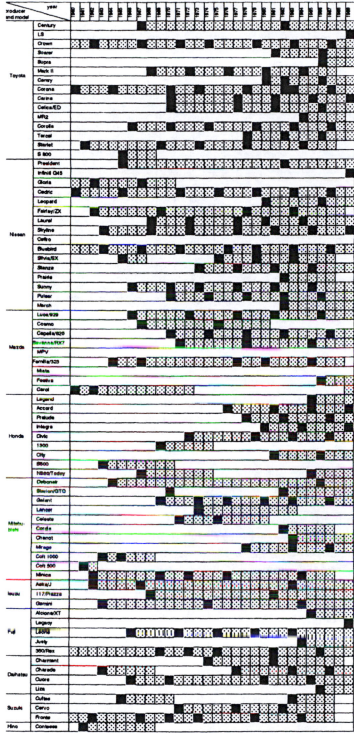

Figure 6.2
Model Change
History of
Japanese Auto
Industry

Note: Models with extremely small volume and short life are excluded. Jeep-type models and cab-over vans are also excluded. Only the most common name plates are shown.

■ New model or major model change   ⊞ In production

Source: Adopted from Clark and Fujimoto (1992).

Table 6.1   R&D Resource Inputs of the Automobile and Parts Makers with more than 10,000 Employees

year	company	total number of employees (A)	number of person engaged in R&D (B)	regular researchers (C)	B/A (%)	C/A (%)	C/B (%)	sales (bil yen) (D)	Intramual R&D Expenditure disbursement (E)	cost (F)	R&D/sales E/D (%)	F/D (%)
1970	6	159,076	13,695	2,709	9%	2%	20%	2,151	43,082	39,384	2.00%	1.83%
1971	7	175,895	15,197	3,090	9%	2%	20%	2,658	56,972	50,616	2.14%	1.90%
1972	7	179,927	16,874	3,384	9%	2%	20%	3,102	70,846	64,838	2.28%	2.09%
1973	7	186,814	19,407	3,707	10%	2%	19%	3,524	89,684	77,115	2.54%	2.19%
1974	6	181,207	21,410	4,894	12%	3%	23%	3,889	123,213	105,852	3.17%	2.72%
1975	7	204,443	24,837	5,160	12%	3%	21%	4,843	148,053	141,419	3.06%	2.92%
1976	7	200,505	24,622	5,571	12%	3%	23%	5,830	142,524	143,008	2.44%	2.45%
1977	7	204,298	23,651	5,372	12%	3%	23%	6,675	170,322	168,971	2.55%	2.53%
1978	7	202,863	24,323	5,478	12%	3%	23%	7,732	209,833	202,622	2.71%	2.62%
1979	7	207,229	25,480	6,283	12%	3%	25%	8,426	258,744	231,543	3.07%	2.75%
1980	7	217,591	27,082	6,976	12%	3%	26%	9,625	291,608	262,811	3.03%	2.73%
1981	8	230,876	26,414	7,358	11%	3%	28%	11,503	330,343	303,596	2.87%	2.64%
1982	10	259,780	30,723	8,594	12%	3%	28%	13,416	440,811	395,121	3.29%	2.95%
1983	10	269,172	32,150	8,660	12%	3%	27%	14,198	485,656	471,157	3.42%	3.32%
1984	10	265,881	34,568	9,991	13%	4%	29%	15,571	496,355	491,303	3.19%	3.16%
1985	9	264,795	34,632	10,152	13%	4%	29%	16,654	546,817	532,452	3.28%	3.20%
1986	9	268,389	35,831	10,858	13%	4%	30%	18,521	622,227	604,548	3.36%	3.26%
1987	9	264,678	36,698	11,468	14%	4%	31%	18,118	659,842	615,071	3.64%	3.39%
1988	11	259,578	36,452	12,397	14%	5%	34%	18,250	628,565	604,727	3.44%	3.31%
1989	11	294,498	38,434	13,515	13%	5%	35%	20,352	732,839	711,679	3.60%	3.50%
1990	11	295,630	41,920	15,000	14%	5%	36%	22,402	875,505	849,219	3.91%	3.79%
1991	11	304,839	43,429	15,901	14%	5%	37%	24,445	1,017,238	976,399	4.16%	3.99%
1992	11	300,711	44,787	17,643	15%	6%	39%	25,594	1,031,368	1,000,287	4.03%	3.91%

Source: Statistics Bureau (Tokei-kyoku), Management and Coordination Agency (Somu-cho), Report on the Survey of Research and Development (Kagaku Gijutsu Kenkyu Chosa Hokoku)

Product Development Performance and Routines in the 1980s: Functional Analysis

Product development has always been an important aspect of interfirm competition in the world automobile industry, but its significance has increased since the 1980s. The question is, why? Consider the following factors.

- *Diversity.* As the lifestyles of car-owning households diversified, and as cars became closely linked with lifestyles, consumers as a whole requested more varieties of cars at the fundamental (i.e., basic model) level. This means that competing firms needed to achieve a high productivity of product development, other things being equal, in order to match the required model variety.
- *Changes.* As both state-of-the-art technologies and market needs changed rapidly, and as competing products were also renewed frequently, the Japanese auto firms had to make major changes to their products frequently. Other things being equal, this meant an environmental pressure toward high productivity of product development.
- *Uncertainty.* Market needs and product technology trends are not only fast-changing but also difficult to forecast, as customer expectations for cars have become complex, equivocal, and holistic. In this situation, shorter lead time for product development becomes more important for better forecasting of future customer needs.

- *Sophistication.* Customers' capabilities of evaluating products have evolved over time and become sophisticated. The customers, as they accumulate product experiences, have shifted their attention from catalogue performance and individual component technologies to overall balance and total vehicle integrity of the cars. Since the process of product development mirrors the nature of the products, total product quality and organizational integration have become keys to product success.
- *Global convergence.* Prior to the 1980s, the basic product concepts of automobiles significantly differed between American and European (and the Japanese to a lesser extent) manufacturers. Typical American cars were large, general-purpose cruisers that emphasized comfort, while the typical European cars were compact driving machines that emphasized handling. The Japanese cars were more or less eclectic. After the second oil crisis, however, the American, European, and Japanese models started to converge in size, packaging concept, styling, drive feel, and so on. As a result, international competition became more direct; individual models from different firms and regions competed against each other within the same global segment of the market. International convergence in basic product concepts caused direct competition among individual products during the 1980s.

To the extent that the international mass market of the 1980s was characterized by diversity, change, uncertainty, sophistication, and convergence, three performance criteria became critical for product success in the market: productivity of development, lead time, and total product quality. The successful volume producers of this era needed to outperform the others in all three at the same time. In fact, a small number of Japanese automakers enjoyed world-class status in all three criteria during the 1980s.[6]

Product Development Performance in the 1980s

In order to examine the relationships between patterns of product development management and its performance, Kim B. Clark and I conducted an international comparative study of twenty-nine product development projects at twenty auto manufacturers in Europe, America, and Japan in the late 1980s. Our key findings in product development performance were as follows:[7]

- In *development productivity* (measured by hours worked per project, adjusted for project content), the Japanese projects were on average nearly twice as efficient as the U.S. and the European projects (figure 6.3).

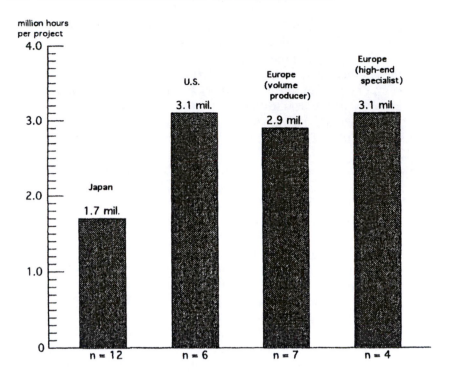

Note: Unadjusted engineering hours is hours spent on product planning and product engineering.
Adjusted engineering hours was calculated from the following ordinary least square regression model

UNADJEH= -3993+0.061* PRICE+7500*NH+729*BODY+1420*USA+1211*EUROVOL+1331*HIGH
(1008)(0.033)   (1357)   (208)   (541)   (518)   (916)

R = 0.76,   Standard error = 987;   Degree of Freedom = 22 ; Standard errors in parenthesis.

Average of PRICE is 14032. Average of NH is 0.44. Average of BODY is 2.14.
Adjusted average was calculated by applying the average PRICE, BODY and NH to the above regression

For definition of the variables, see Clark and Fujimoto (1991).

Source: Fujimoto (1989).

Figure 6.3 Adjusted Engineering Hours by Regional-Strategic Group

- In *development lead time* (measured by the time elapsed from concept study to start of sales, adjusted for project content), the Japanese projects were also on average about a year ahead of the Western cases (figure 6.4).
- But in *product integrity* (measured by total product quality index, or TPQ, which is a composite of such indicators as total quality, manufacturing quality, design quality, and long-term market share), no regional pattern was detected. The

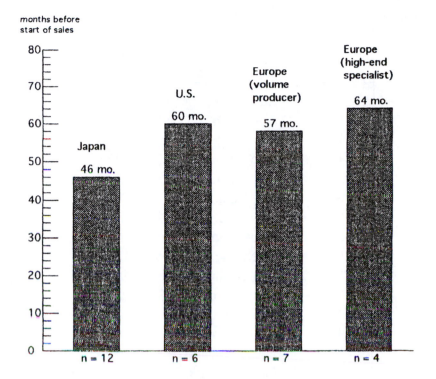

months before
start of sales

Note: Unadjusted lead time is time between start of concept study / product engineering and market
introduction (start of selling) of the first version.
Adjusted lead time was calculated from the following ordinary least square regression model

UNADJLT = 23.9+0.00048*PRICE+29.3*NH+1.23*BODY+14.2*USA+11.1*EUROVOL+18.2*HIGH
(9.1)(0.00030)   (12.3)   (1.88)   (4.9)   (4.7)   (8.3)

R^2 = 0.69,   Standard error = 8.9 ;   Degree of Freedom = 22;   Standard errors in parenthesis.

Average of PRICE is 14032. Average of NH is 0.44. Average of BODY is 2.14
Adjusted average was calculated by applying the average PRICE, BODY and NH to the above regression.

For definition of the variables, see Clark and Fujimoto (1991).

Source: Fujimoto (1989).

Figure 6.4 Adjusted Lead Time by Regional-Strategic Groups (1980s)

Japanese companies included both top-rank players and
bottom-rank ones, as did the European and American group.
The top-rank Europeans turned out to be high-end specialists
(table 6.2).

The above findings imply that the more efficient projects (mainly
Japanese) tended also to be faster. In other words, there was apparently no tradeoff relation between development speed and develop-

Table 6.2   Ranking of Organizations in TPQ Index

Ranking	Regional Origin	Score
1	Europe (high-end)	100
1	Japan	100
1	Japan	100
4	Europe (high-end)	93
5	Japan	80
6	U.S.	75
6	U.S.	75
8	Europe (high-end)	73
9	Europe (high-end)	70
10	Japan	58
11	Europe (volume)	55
12	Europe (volume)	47
13	Japan	40
14	Europe (volume)	39
15	Europe (volume)	35
15	Japan	35
17	Europe (volume)	30
18	Japan	25
19	U.S.	24
20	Japan	23
21	U.S.	15
22	U.S.	14

Note: Based on ranking in Table 3.X.
  Weghts = 0.3 for total quality; 0.1 for conformance quality
  0.4 for design quality; 0.2 for customer share.
  Scores = 100 for top 1/3; 50 for middle 1/3;
  0 for bottom 1/3; 100 for share gain; 50 for share loss;
  75 for border case.

Source: Clark and Fujimoto (1991).

ment efficiency (figure 6.5). And there were a few Japanese companies whose product development achieved speed, efficiency, and integrity at the same time—the all-round high performers. Our subsequent study of organization and management of product development naturally focused on these few Japanese firms (Clark and Fujimoto, 1991). But note that, while some Japanese companies had short lead times

A. Unadjusted

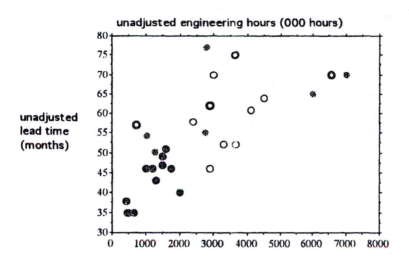

unadjusted engineering hours (000 hours)

unadjusted
lead time
(months)

B. Adjusted for Project Content

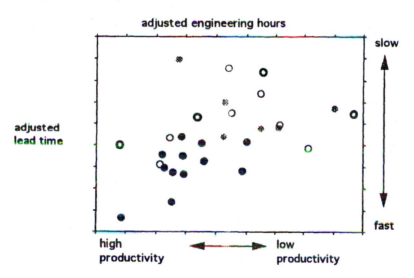

adjusted engineering hours

slow

adjusted
lead time

fast

high
productivity

low
productivity

Note: 1 segment in panel B stands for 0.5 million hours (horizontal) and 5 months (vertical) respectively.

● Japan   ✹ U.S.   ○ Europe (volume)   ◉ high-end specialist

Source: Fujimoto (1997e), "The Dynamic Aspect of Product Development Capabilities: An International Comparison in the Automobile Industry," in Goto, A. and Odagiri, H., ed., *Innovation in Japan*. New York: Oxford University Press: 57–99.

Figure 6.5 Lead Time and Engineering Hours—Unadjusted and Adjusted

and were high in development productivity, they weren't effective in product integrity (i.e., TPQ scores). Thus, to be fast and efficient—or to be Japanese—did not guarantee product integrity and market success. The pattern of product development performance of the 1980s that we identified was a combination of both region-specific and firm-specific advantages. And a few European high-end specialists achieved high product integrity without being fast and efficient in product development. This indicates that, at least during the 1980s, high-end specialists were playing a quite different competitive game in a segment well isolated from the volatile mass market.

Product Development Routines: Region-Specific and Firm-Specific

Kim Clark and I also found that region-specific and firm-specific patterns of product development routines or capabilities often coexisted, contributing to the performance advantages based on statistical analysis and field studies.[8]

Our basic research question was as follows: What are the characteristics of the development organizations that achieve speed, efficiency, and integrity at the same time? We investigated this question in two steps. First, we explored patterns for fast and efficient (but not necessarily successful in the market) product development by focusing on certain Japanese practices that apparently contributed to a shorter lead time and higher development productivity. (Note again that the Japanese development projects in general tended to be both fast and efficient.) Second, we tried to identify certain organizational patterns that may achieve speed, efficiency, *and* product integrity simultaneously by focusing only on the all-round high performers mentioned above.

Suppliers' Engineering Capabilities. As already discussed in detail in the last chapter, the Japanese companies tended to keep the size of their development projects compact by letting parts suppliers do a significant part of the engineering jobs (figure 6.6). The compactness of the projects, in turn, contributed to a shorter lead time and higher development efficiency by simplifying the task of project coordination to a manageable level. For example, Kim Clark and I identified statistically significant positive effects between the degree of supplier's participation and the overall speed or efficiency of the projects.[9] The Japanese makers also enjoyed a lower component cost by letting the suppliers pursue "design for manufacturing" (i.e., designing components that are easy to produce in the first place).

The U.S. automakers, by contrast, often tried to keep the project compact by using existing component designs developed by other projects, but excessive use of common parts tended to deteriorate product

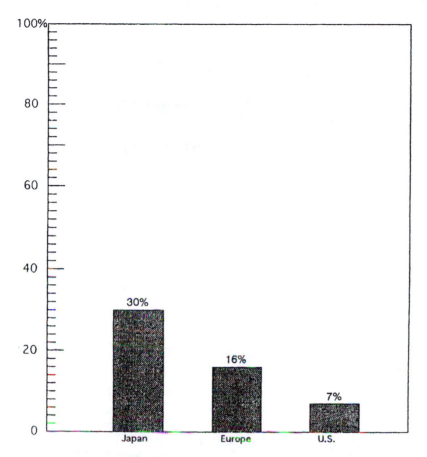

Note: Percentages represent the ratio of supplier parts engineering effort to total engineering effort. This is calculated as the product of the fraction of supplier engineering in total parts engineering and the ratio of parts engineering to total engineering effort.
Source: Adopted from Clark and Fujimoto

Figure 6.6 Supplier's Contribution to Product Development

integrity and distinctiveness. While depending upon traditional bidding, the U.S. makers apparently failed to exploit the potential of cost reduction by letting the suppliers design the parts they make.

Production Capability for Product Development. There are many "hidden" production activities in product development processes, such as prototyping, die making, pilot run, and production ramp-up. Unless a firm does such production-related jobs speedily and efficiently, it cannot achieve high performance in product development. Thus, effective firms in product development have also to be good at production.

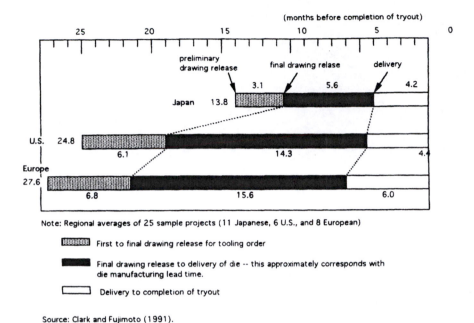

Note: Regional averages of 25 sample projects (11 Japanese, 6 U.S., and 8 European)

▓▓▓▓ First to final drawing release for tooling order

▊▊▊▊ Final drawing release to delivery of die -- this approximately corresponds with die manufacturing lead time.

☐ Delivery to completion of tryout

Source: Clark and Fujimoto (1991).

Figure 6.7 Lead Time for a Set of Dies for a Major Body Panel

The Japanese automakers tended to apply their capabilities in production to critical activities in product development, such as prototype fabrication, die development, pilot run, and production startup, which, in turn, contributed to improvement in the overall performance of product development. For example, application of the just-in-time philosophy to body die shops at least partly explains why the die development lead time of the average Japanese project was much shorter than that of a Western project (figure 6.7). Their capabilities of managing prototype parts procurement, mixed model assembly, and quick shop-floor improvements also helped the Japanese makers carry out fast and effective prototyping, pilot run, and production startup.

Overlapping Product and Process Engineering. The Japanese projects tended to overlap upstream stages (e.g., product engineering) and downstream stages (e.g., process engineering) more boldly than the American and European projects in order to shorten overall lead time (figure 6.8). The Japanese practices indicate that the overlapping approach can effectively shorten lead time only when it is combined with intensive communications between upstream and downstream. Effective overlapping also requires upstream and downstream people to cope with preliminary information, as well as flexibility, mutual trust, and goal sharing between the two stages. Without such condi-

A. Definition   simultaneity ratio = (X + Y) / Z   where,

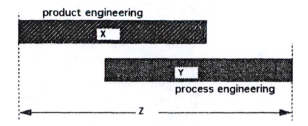

B. Regional Averages of Simultaneity Ratio

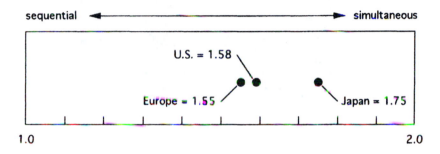

c. Simultaneity Ratio and Engineering Lead Time

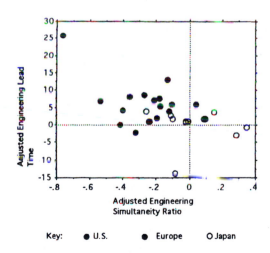

Source: Modified and adopted from Clark and Fujimoto (1991).

Figure 6.8 Definition and Result of Simultaneity Ratio

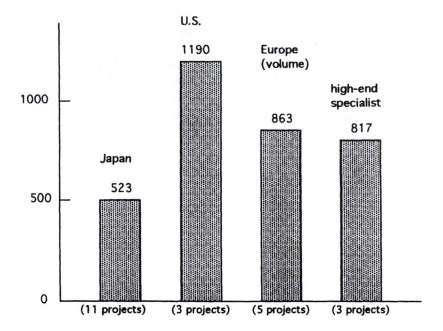

Note: The number of participants is adjusted for project content
(price, body types, and project scope). It is assumed
that all the producers carry out a standard project with
average project content (retail price = 14032 dollars,
body types = 2.13, project scope = 0.612).
There was no significant difference between Europe
and the U.S.
Source: Adopted from Clark and Fujimoto (1991).

Figure 6.9 Average Number of Long-Term Project Participants

tions, stage overlapping often results in confusion, conflict, and deterioration in product development.

Wide Task Assignment.   The Japanese projects also tended to be relatively compact: the average number of long-term participants per
project, adjusted for project complexity, was about half of their Western counterparts (figure 6.9; see also column 1 of figure 6.10). This, in
the field of product development, meant that task assignment for each
individual engineer tended to be wider in the average Japanese projects than in the U.S. and European ones. This statistical finding was
consistent with the observations of many engineers themselves that
Western projects up to the 1980s often suffered from overspecialization by engineers, which could result in parochialism and coordination difficulties.

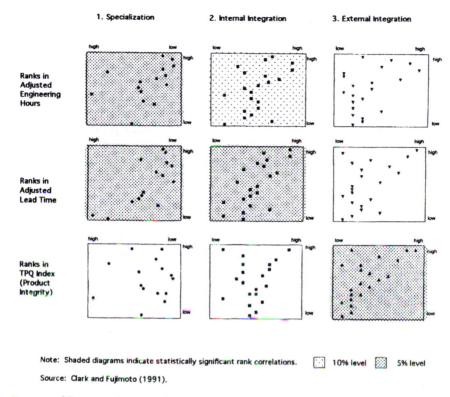

Note: Shaded diagrams indicate statistically significant rank correlations.　☐ 10% level　☐ 5% level

Source: Clark and Fujimoto (1991).

Figure 6.10 Specialization, Integration, and Development Performance

Heavyweight Product Managers. The above four routines were more or less region-specific, which we tend to find in the Japanese product development organizations in general. The last routine—what we call *heavyweight product managers*—demonstrated a rather firm-specific pattern: we found organizations of this type in *only a few* of the Japanese automakers during the 1980s. In fact, this was the capability in which the high performers in all three performance indicators mentioned above distinguished themselves from their Japanese, as well as from their Western, rivals. Let's focus on the structure and function of this last routine next.

Focus on Heavyweight Product Managers:
What Makes Specific Firms Succeed?

Looking at Japanese practices in general no longer provides the answer to why some specific development organizations managed efficiency, speed, and integrity all at the same time. Only a few Japanese automakers could achieve all three in the 1980s. To investigate this question, we focused on three aspects of organizational design:

internal integration (i.e., cross-functional coordination or mutual adjustment inside the production firm), *external integration* (i.e., coordination or mutual adjustment between the firm and the future target customers), and *functional specialization*.[10] We developed indicators for these three accordingly: specialization of engineers, strength of internal integrators (i.e., project coordinators), and strength of external integrators (i.e., concept champions). We then examined the relationship between the three organizational dimensions and the three performance dimensions. Without getting into details of definitions and measurement, the 3 X 3 results are shown in figure 6.10. The results indicate the following relations:

- The lower the specialization (i.e., the broader the task assignment of each engineer), the faster and more efficient the projects tend to be. Many development organizations (mostly Western) seemed to suffer from overspecialization syndrome, while some others (mainly Japanese) appeared to benefit from lower levels of specialization without losing technological expertise. Note, however, that specialization does not seem to be related to product integrity.
- The stronger the internal integrator (project coordinator), the faster (and somewhat more efficient) the project tends to be. Reduction of lead time would call for stage overlapping with intensive communication between the stages, which, in turn, would have to be facilitated by powerful project coordinators. Again, however, internal integration was not correlated with product integrity.
- The stronger the external integrator, the higher the product integrity. This correlation indicates that powerful champions who create and realize the distinctive product concepts that might be keys to product integrity and market success.

In the 1980s, therefore, the development organizations that achieved high performance in lead time, productivity, and product integrity simultaneously were those that combined powerful internal and external integrators in one role. As already mentioned in chapter 3, we called this role the *heavyweight product manager*—a combination of strong project coordinator and strong concept leader (see the bottom two cases of figure 6.11).[11]

To examine whether a heavyweight product manager system could actually achieve high performance in all three dimensions, we then developed an indicator to measure how close a given organization is to the ideal profile of the heavyweight system. The result (figure 6.12) indicates that the heavyweight product manager system often results in high scores in all three dimensions of product development performance. (This did not apply to the high-end special-

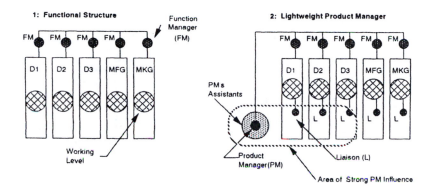

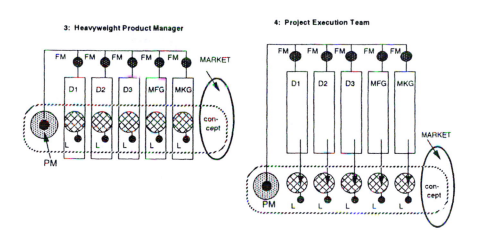

Note: D1,D2, and D3 stand for functional units in development. MFG stands for manufacturing; MKG for marketing.

Source: Fujimoto (1989), Clark and Fujimoto (1991).

Figure 6.11 Four Modes of Development Organization

ists, though, in which high product integrity was achieved with rather insignificant internal/external integrators.) Based on our clinical field surveys, we characterized the best product manager as someone who:

- Coordinates responsibility in wide areas, not only engineering but also production and sales.
- Coordinates responsibility for the entire project period from concept to market.
- Takes responsibility not only for cross-functional coordination but also for concept creation and concept championing.

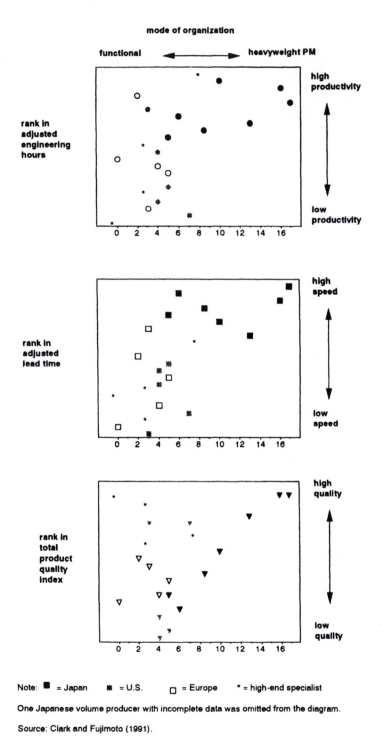

Figure 6.12 Mode of Organization and Development Performance

- Maintains responsibility for specification, cost target, layout, and major component choice, making sure that product concept is accurately translated into technical details of the vehicle.
- Builds direct and frequent communication with designers and engineers at the work level, in addition to indirect ties through liaisons.
- Establishes direct contact with customers. (The product manager office conducts its own market research besides the regular market surveys done by the marketing group.)
- Is multilingual and multidisciplined so that he can effectively communicate with designers, engineers, testers, plant managers, controllers, and so on.
- Is not just a neutral referee or passive conflict manager. He may initiate conflicts in order to prevent product designs/plans from deviating from the original product concept.
- Has market imagination, or the ability to forecast future customer expectations based on ambiguous and equivocal clues in the present market.
- Walks around and advocates the product concept, rather than doing paper work and conducting formal meetings.
- Is mostly an engineer by training. He has broad, if not deep, knowledge of total vehicle engineering and process engineering.

Although most of the automobile product development organizations of the world already had some kind of product manager or project coordinator in place by the 1980s, most of them were lightweight; their actual behaviors, attitudes, and skills were very different from those of the heavyweight product manager. Only a small number of the Japanese makers had a system close to this ideal type in the 1980s, and those were also the firms that achieved a high level of product development performance in all three dimensions during the same period.

It should be noted, however, that each of the Japanese product development teams of the 1980s was not brought together into one large room (except in the case of some special urgent projects).[12] Desks of the engineers were normally located in the rooms for functional units (e.g., body design department, chassis design department, etc.), although these units themselves were usually located fairly close to each other. Functional managers held their authority on personnel issues of the working engineers, although product managers could informally influence their appraisal and promotion processes in many cases. Also, product engineers were usually assigned to more than one project, rather than dedicating themselves to one project at a time. In other words, the Japanese product development projects were neither "co-located" nor "dedicated" on a regular basis. Even the firms with heavyweight product managers emphasized functional specialization as well. What we observed at these companies tended to be a coexistence of strong functionalism and strong project orientation, rather than unilateral project organization.

Historical Evolution of Product Development Routines: Genetic Analysis

Given that the routinized product development capabilities of the 1980s were partly region-specific and partly firm-specific, what is the explanation for why these patterns coexist? The evolutionary perspective suggests two separate explanations: system stability or functionality (explaining why the phenomenon is observed as a stable pattern), and system changes or variations (explaining why the phenomenon took place in the first place).

So far I've presented a functional analysis of the system. Based mainly on the Harvard study, it appears there was a certain correlation between region-specific capabilities (e.g., supplier involvement, manufacturing capability, overlapping problem solving) and region-specific performance indicators (development productivity and lead time), as well as that between firm-specific capabilities (e.g., heavyweight product managers) and all three performance indicators. This is consistent with the proposition that these routines existed in a stable form once they were built because they were functional in terms of competitive performance. It is likely that the Japanese firms of the 1980s in general possessed at least partial capabilities and enjoyed partial performance advantages accordingly; only a few of them possessed the full range of capabilities and thus all-round performance advantages.

But how was this coexisting pattern of region-specific and firm-specific capabilities built in the first place? The main proposition of this book is that an ex-post rational system does not have to be explained solely by ex-ante rational decision-making processes with clear objectives and an accurate understanding of environmental constraints. An ex-post rational system may be created through a process of system emergence, and certain firms may possess evolutionary learning capabilities by which they build firm-specific routine capabilities out of such emergent processes. Focusing now on multi-path system emergence, let us reexamine the historical process of capability building for the five patterns of product development routines identified earlier.

Suppliers and Black Box Parts. As already detailed in chapter 5, the process by which the black box parts system was built could be characterized as multi-path system emergence. The most important driving force behind the diffusion of this practice appears to be the engineering workload for creating wide product variety. The Japanese automakers were almost forced to rely on black box parts regardless of their international competitive strategies, and the system's subsequent competitive advantage was not clearly recognized by decision makers of the time.

Production Capabilities for Product Development. Up to now, there has been virtually no historical analysis that directly deals with the evolution of manufacturing capabilities in product development, such as prototype making, die making, and production startups. What we can do at best in this situation is to make some conjectures based on certain circumstantial evidence. First, we know that major model change intervals back in the 1960s were on average almost as short as those in the 1980s. Second, the stamping process with dies had been extensively used by the 1960s as the Japanese firms moved toward mass production of passenger cars. Third, die making, prototype making, and production startup had all been recognized among the engineers as activities on the critical path for a long time. Fourth, at least a part of the manufacturing capabilities in die making and production startup appear to have adopted just-in-time principles. Fifth, no description has been found so far in company histories and other documents in the public domain that explicitly discusses capabilities of rapid die making, prototyping, and startup as effective means for international competition in and before the 1970s.

By combining the above circumstantial evidences, we can infer system emergence in the case of Toyota: (1) part of the manufacturing capabilities in product development were built in the 1960s at the latest; (2) the firm was more or less forced by the competitive reality of frequent model changes to shorten their critical path activities, including die making, prototyping, and startups; (3) JIT principles, which had prevailed at Toyota by the 1960s, were applied to such manufacturing activities in product development; (4) while the efforts for short-cycle die making, prototyping, and startup may have been motivated initially by the pressures of domestic competition, these capabilities were not recognized as weapons for international competition until the late 1970s at least.

Overlapping Problem Solving. With regard to this topic, there are also not sufficient historical data that directly describe how the product development schedules of Japanese firms changed from the 1950s to 1970s. Still, we can infer the following based on the circumstantial evidence available. First, as indicated in figure 6.2, the four-year model change cycles for the main Japanese car models started as early as the early 1960s—between the Crown and Cedric, Corona and Bluebird, as well as Corolla and Sunny (Sentra). The four-year cycle virtually became a tacit industry norm by the mid-1970s. Second, one of Toyota's

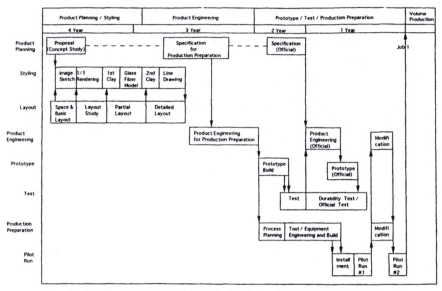

Source: Seki, T., ed. (1980) _Jidosha no kihon keikaku to design_ [Basic planning and designing of the automobile]. Tokyo: Sankaido.

Figure 6.13 Typical Product Development Schedule

internal documents suggests that, by the mid-1970s, the development lead time had become constrained by the four-year model change intervals (Note that automakers usually try to keep the development lead time within the major model change interval in order to make the product planning reasonably accurate.) This was also the time when Toyota established a standard product development schedule that specified when to start and when to finish the main development activities. Third, the same document pointed out that Toyota needed to enrich the content of its products, which was likely to prolong the time needed for product and process engineering respectively, in the mid-1970s. According to some sources, body exterior designs, body detail engineering, and press die development were critical-path activities then.

The relatively short model change cycle that was needed for the intense domestic competition since the 1960s apparently set the upper limit of the lead time, and overlapping of developmental activities on the critical path (e.g., body engineering and die engineering) became imperative at least in the 1970s, when the product complexity required by the market increased. Figure 6.13, which shows a development time chart for an anonymous Japanese auto firm of the 1970s, matches this story. It is obvious from the figure that this company was then aiming at the four-year lead times partly by overlapping product and process engineering stages.

In any case, it is likely that the reality of domestic competition forced the Japanese automakers to build the capability of simultaneous engineering and intense interstage communications, and that they did not fully recognize its potential as a weapon for international competition when the practice emerged. Its secondary effect on interstage communication and coordination (e.g., design for manufacturing), for example, does not seem to have been fully anticipated by these firms when the practice was first implemented. The overlapping practices may have been recognized as imperatives rather than capabilities by the Japanese makers of those day.

Another finding that is consistent with the above view is that this practice did not have a particular name among the Japanese firms until the late 1980s, when American practitioners and researchers started to call this practice *simultaneous engineering* or *concurrent engineering*, which were translated back into Japanese. Considering that previous Japanese practices intended to be tools for competition (e.g., JIT, TQC, TPM) got names almost without exception, the fact that overlapping product and process engineering did not have a particular name makes me strongly suspect that the practice was first implemented as a means to enable the four-year model-change cycles for domestic, not international, competition.

Small Team and Wide Task Assignment.   We do not have sufficient direct evidence for this either, but it seems likely that a chronic shortage of engineers during the continuous-growth era virtually forced the Japanese makers to keep project teams compact, which forced individual engineers to keep their skill ranges wide. In other words, historical imperatives appear to have played a significant role in keeping the project compact, but its potential as a competitive tool was not recognized at least until the 1970s. The Japanese firms of those days might have regarded it even as a disadvantage because it meant less specialization.[13] The broad task assignment appears to have been recognized as a source of productivity and lead time advantage only later, in the 1980s.

Other indirect evidence for system emergence here comes in the case of product development for the niche-oriented Mazda Miata of the late 1980s, in which the company lacked sufficient resources for this "minor" model, forcing Mazda to make the project extremely slim and compact.[11] The inadvertent result was an unusually small project team, wide task assignment for each engineer, shorter lead time, and high development productivity compared to the regular projects of the company. Again, this was not a strategically intended result. In fact, I regard this case as a dramatic replication of the dynamics that Japanese firms in general were going through during the continuous-growth era.

Heavyweight Product Managers.   There is historical evidence that the origin of the heavyweight product manager system was the prewar aircraft industry, which attracted the best and brightest college graduate engineers of those days (see also chapter 3). After World War II, the aircraft industry, essentially a big military goods sector, was forced to disappear by the occupation authority. Many young and talented engineers in this industry had no choice but to seek jobs in related. civilian industries, including locomotives and automobiles.

Interestingly enough, it was much later, in the late 1970s and early 1980s, that the advantages of the heavyweight product manager system became apparent. Toyota was the only Japanese auto firm that systematized the heavyweight product manager system, known as *shusa* at the company, as early as the 1950s—much earlier than the other firms. There were also ex-aircraft engineers who came to the other automakers and acted much like heavyweight product managers (e.g., Shin-ichiro Sakurai of Prince-Nissan), but their informal style of project management was not institutionalized as a company-wide system until the 1980s.

Origins of Regional and Firm-Specific Patterns: Adaptation and Diffusion

Overall, the above analysis identifies several patterns through which the product development routines evolved over time. Some are region-specific, others are more firm-specific. There were obviously some cases where the Japanese firms since the 1960s tried to adapt their capabilities to the domestic situation, in which rapid model changes and product proliferation were the imperatives. In a sense, on the side of the producers, you could call this a rational approach with a clear goal of surviving the competition. Other factors, however, like luck or unintended positive consequences, also played a part. For instance, some of those routine capabilities of the Japanese were formed with an intention to cope with the domestic competition, which was already intense in the 1960s, but the Japanese, at this point, do not appear to have anticipated a subsequent contribution of such routines to their international competitiveness after the 1970s.

To the extent that the Japanese and Western markets and domestic competitive environments were different prior to the 1980s, each firm adapted its organizational capabilities mainly to its "home ground," which shaped certain region-specific patterns. But when the world auto markets more or less converged, Japanese firms in general enjoyed certain advantages, at least temporarily, because their past domestic environment (many rivals, many products, rapidly changing market needs) had forced them to preempt certain routines that turned out to be quite effective in the new international competition. In other words, the companies that could adapt themselves to the Japanese competitive environment in the 1960s and 1970s tended to perform well in the global market of the 1980s as well—a combination of rational behavior and historical luck.

In other cases, the competitive consequences of an organizational routine were not fully recognized when they were first adopted. The heavyweight product managers system came from the aircraft industry after the war because out-of-work engineers needed jobs; the black box parts system was diffused in the 1960s apparently in order to absorb the mounting workload for in-house engineers. When overlapping problem solving was adopted, the main intention was probably to maintain new product launch schedules, not specifically to achieve world class lead-time performance.

It's also clear that differences among individual firms matter, and that significant interfirm differences in capabilities do exist among the Japanese firms. One source of interfirm differences may be entrepreneurial vision (such as Soichiro Honda's), but the historical cases indicate that *opportunistic learning capabilities* — or the firm-specific ability to make the most of unintended trials or luck — may be even more important in this particular area. We have already seen that some Japanese firms such as Toyota, facing similar historical imperatives, eventually created a more effective black box parts system and heavyweight product manager system than its competitors. These seem to be obvious examples of an evolutionary learning capability.

Once the competitive advantage of an organizational routine becomes clear to competitors, they will try to imitate it. This tendency can be observed in the long run, but diffusion is slow in many cases, as the resource-capability view of the firm predicts. When it comes to product development, diffusion of certain practices has been rather slow even between the Japanese firms.

Generally speaking, tacit knowledge is difficult to imitate. More important, from an evolutionary perspective, a routine created by a process of system emergence and evolutionary learning capabilities may be more difficult to transfer. It is more likely that its purposes and functions are not clearly known even to insiders; its content is not systematically described and publicized in the company's official documents, histories, or textbooks by consultants; it may not even have a name. Thus, an organizational routine created by an emergent process may have another unintended advantage: it's difficult to imitate. Such a process of system emergence appears to have played an even more significant role in the evolution of product development capabilities than in production.

Having explained how system emergence led to the combination of region-specific and firm-specific patterns of product development routines in the 1980s, let's turn to the next topic: how Western automakers tried to reduce the gap in product development performance through international diffusion of such routines.

Adopting Japanese Practice: The U.S. Catchup

Once the competitive advantages of the product development capabilities of better Japanese firms became obvious, Western automakers started to transfer certain modified versions of the Japanese product development systems. U.S. makers, facing stronger pressure from international competition, moved to catch up with the Japanese.

This catchup process—which is still occurring as of the mid-1990s—is in itself remarkable to both practitioners and researchers as a valuable example of long-term organizational learning.[15] It provides an insightful case of companies deliberately adopting routines that were mostly created through the multi-path system emergence. Thus, the adopter may have to refine, purify, or systematize the emergent routines before it accepts them. This kind of purification process may result in interesting dynamics that can affect adopters favorably or unfavorably.

Adopting and Creating Routines: A Top-Down
Approach and Purification

First, let's look at how U.S. auto firms changed their product development routines to catch up with the target Japanese firms from the late 1980s to early 1990s. Our update of the Harvard study (Ellison et al., 1995) identified convergence in product development routines in such areas as supplier involvement, die making lead times, prototype making lead times, product-process overlapping ratio, "heaviness" of product managers, and so on (see table 6.3). Thus, in most cases of the effective routines that Clark and Fujimoto (1991) identified, we observed partial adoption by the Western automakers by 1993.[16]

Higher Supplier Involvement. U.S. automakers adopted Japanese-style supplier management systems beginning in the 1980s. Chrysler's senior manager, for example, says it has thoroughly changed its supplier management system, increased both production outsourcing and the component design outsourcing ratio, reduced the number of first-tier suppliers (consolidated supply base), let them become system suppliers (specialist makers of subassembled components), built a multilayer procurement network, involved the suppliers in the product development process (black-box parts), shifted from competitive bidding to collaborative cost reduction, introduced a market-driven cost planning method, and strengthened ties with the suppliers in terms of knowledge sharing and technical assistance.[17] Many of the purchasing practices that Chrysler adopted in recent years were similar to what some of the Japanese makers acquired gradually between the 1950s and 1970s. Reflecting this trend, the updated Harvard study (Ellison et al., 1995) shows that the ratio of black box parts in total

Table 6.3 Regional Comparison of Product Development Performance, 1980s versus 1990s

		Japan	U.S.	Europe	total
number of sample projects	1980s	12	6	11	29
	1990s	8	5	12	25
unadjusted total lead time (mo.)	1980s	43	62	61	53
	1990s	51	52	59	55
unadjusted engineering hours	1980s	1.2 mil.	3.5 mil.	3.4 mil.	2.5 mil.
	1990s	1.3 mil.	2.3 mil.	3.2 mil.	2.5 mil.
adjusted total lead time (mo.)	1980s	45	61	59	53
	1990s	55	52	56	55
adjusted engineering hours	1980s	1.7 mil.	3.4 mil.	2.9 mil.	2.5 mil.
	1990s	2.1 mil.	2.3 mil.	2.8 mil.	2.5 mil.
% of supplier proprietary parts	1980s	8	3	6	6
	1990s	6	12	12	10
% of black box parts	1980s	62	16	29	40
	1990s	55	30	24	35
% of detail -control parts	1980s	30	81	65	54
	1990s	39	58	64	55
prototype lead time (mo.)	1980s	7	12	11	9
	1990s	6	12	9	9
die lead time (mo.)	1980s	14	25	28	22
	1990s	15	20	23	20
% of heavy weight PM projects	1980s	17	0	0	7
	1990s	25	20	0	12
% of mid to heavy PM projects	1980s	83	17	36	52
	1990s	100	100	83	92
% of common parts	1980s	19	38	30	27
	1990s	28	25	32	29
product complexity index	1980s	95	92	83	90
	1990s	68	76	100	85

Source: Ellison, Clark, Fujimoto, and Hyun (1995).
Note: For the methods of adjustment for product complexity and definition of product complexity index, devised by Ellison, see appendix of the above paper.
For other definitions, see also Clark and Fujimoto (1991).

procurement cost at the sample U.S. projects jumped from 16 percent on average in the 1980s to 30 percent in the early 1990s. (The equivalent number in Japan is about 50 to 60 percent; see table 6.3.)

Higher Production Capabilities for Product Development. Japanese projects on average maintained their advantages in lead times for core engineering activities such as prototype building and die development (table 6.3). The lead time for developing first engineering prototypes did not change much in both Japanese and American cases: about half a year in the former, about a year in the latter. European averages improved, but the U.S. average did not. The Japanese also maintained significant advantages in die development lead times: the Japanese die lead time on average became slightly longer, to fifteen months, while the U.S. average was reduced to twenty months and Europeans to twenty-three months in the 1990s, but the difference still remained (Ellison et al., 1995).

More Overlapping. U.S. makers on average increased their degree of overlap between product and process engineering by involving the latter earlier in their projects. The average schedule data of the Harvard project, for example, show that the start of process engineering (average of the U.S. projects; unadjusted) shifted from about thirty months before the start of sales in the 1980s to about forty months before in the 1990s.[18] U.S. managers' discourses during this period that they were introducing simultaneous engineering, were generally consistent with this trend. (See also figure 6.14.)

Heavier Product Managers. Ford, for instance, has introduced a system of stronger product managers and coherent cross-functional project teams, following mainly Mazda's and Toyota's practice since the early 1980s. The period of change in Ford's product development organization roughly coincides with the period of its new product success, including Taurus (Clark and Fujimoto, 1994). Chrysler, on the other hand, is said to have mainly followed the product development organization of Honda, as well as Jeep which it merged with in the mid-1980s. This is consistent with the data that Clark, Ellison, and I collected in 1993 as an update of the earlier Harvard study, which clearly indicated that U.S. automakers changed their product development structures from mostly lightweight product manager types in the 1980s to mid- to heavyweight ones in the 1990s (table 6.3).

In this way, American automakers started to adopt the effective routines that the previous Harvard study had identified, but they did not follow the evolutionary path of the Japanese makers—or system emergence. They tended, instead, to introduce the new system deliberately as a package from the top down. Thus, some of the Japanese emergent practices, which they were using partly as tacit knowledge, had to be systematized, articulated, and given names by the American practitioners. For example, as mentioned earlier, the practice of overlapping problem solving evolved through a more or less emergent process in Japan, and it did not even have a name. In the late 1980s, American practitioners (SAE in particular) focused on this practice as a key to shorten development lead times, described it as an explicit process, and gave a name to it: simultaneous engineering. This term was exported back to Japan and is widely referred to now, together with the concurrent engineering concept.

Many of the emergent routine capabilities that the Japanese automakers gradually built up during the postwar era were introduced into the American firms in the 1980s to '90s explicitly as rational systems, after a certain "purification." One potential problem here may be that some critical factors for success still remain tacit and might be overlooked by the adopting firms. At the same time, this approach may have an advantage to the extent that an adopter can rationalize the practices and roll them out quickly—a "late comers' advantage," which was originally enjoyed by the Japanese manufacturers when they adopted Western technologies in the past.

In addition to the fact that the U.S. makers adopted part of the Japanese-style practices through a different path, they introduced what even Japanese makers did not do regularly. In other words, the U.S. firms may have created something new as more or less an unintended result of their imitation efforts.

For example, some U.S. makers (e.g., Chrysler) have organized so-called dedicated-co-located product development teams for each of the basic models, which helps them dramatically reduce product development lead times. Some of the Japanese makers did use this organizational structure in the past (e.g., Mazda for its Miata), but the regular project teams of typical Japanese makers have consisted of product engineers who are mostly assigned to multiple projects and work at the functional departments geographically while they belong to the projects organizationally. Some Japanese practitioners, on the other hand, argue that, although the co-location approach would shorten lead time, using this approach regularly results in a duplication of engineering resources, insufficient accumulation of component technologies, and lack of interproject knowledge transfers. In this case, the U.S. makers leapfrogged the Japanese as they departed from the traditional functional approach and shifted to a purer project team organization, which apparently enabled some Western automakers to accelerate their catchup with the Japanese in such important performance indicators as overall (concept-to-market) lead times in the early 1990s.

While U.S. makers identified and adopted Japanese-style practices, this process was more than a simple imitation of best practices; they articulated and systematized what the Japanese themselves did not explicitly recognize as a coherent system—and U.S. automakers sometimes adopted even more radical approaches than the Japanese. To the extent that there is a growing opportunity for the Japanese firms to counter-learn from the new American and European practices, the dynamic process of catchup may open a road to the era of mutual learning between the Japanese and Western auto firms.

Narrowing Performance Differences

The Japan-U.S. difference in product development performance started to narrow after the late 1980s, partly as a result of the adoption of Japanese-style practices by U.S. firms. In order to examine this dynamic process of the Western catchup, Kim Clark, David Ellison, and I replicated the survey of product development performance discussed above. The samples (as of 1994) consist of twenty-eight major product development projects (eight Japanese, five U.S., twelve European, and three Korean) from twenty-three manufacturers (eight Japanese, three U.S., nine European, and three Korean). The results, compared with those in the 1980s, indicate that the average Western projects (U.S. in particular) significantly reduced or virtually eliminated the performance differences against the Japanese in development lead time and productivity.[19]

Product Development Lead Time. The adjusted lead time of product development from the beginning of concept generation to market introduction indicates that U.S. makers reduced their lead time from about five years in the 1980s to about four years in the early 1990s (table 6.3; figure 6.14).[20] The Japanese average lead time, on the other hand, became longer, apparently as the automakers emphasized more deliberate product planning in response to changes in competitive environments. The European average has also been reduced, but to a lesser extent than the U.S. case so far. Thus, the lead time difference between the Japanese and the U.S. projects was totally eliminated by 1993, with the average adjusted lead time of fifty-six months in Europe, fifty-two months in America, and fifty-five months in Japan. (The equivalent unadjusted figures were fifty-nine months in Europe, fifty-two months in America, and fifty-one months in Japan, respectively.)

Breaking down the lead time into its components, however, we found that the reduction of lead time by the U.S. makers came mostly from shortening the planning lead time (from the beginning of concept creation to the approval of the product plans) rather than shortening the engineering lead time (from the beginning of product engineering to the beginning of sales). That is, as shown in figure 6.14, the U.S. average planning lead time was reduced by about half a year between the 1980s and the early 1990s, while the engineering lead time was almost unchanged (about forty months both in the 1980s and in the 1990s). In addition, the U.S. automakers increased the overlap pe-

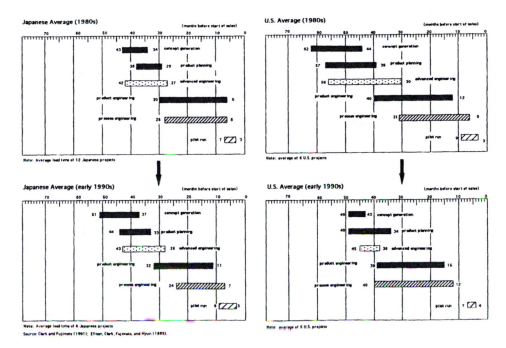

Figure 6.14 Average Project Schedule (Unadjusted)—1980s versus early 1990s

riod between planning and engineering from almost none to about a half a year between the two periods. As a combined result of shorter planning lead time and more planning-engineering overlapping, the U.S. average lead time was reduced by almost a year without a significant reduction in engineering lead time.

The average Japanese performance during the same period presents quite a contrast. First, the engineering lead time (unadjusted) increased slightly (around thirty months in both the 1980s and the '90s). Second, the planning lead time was prolonged more significantly by about a half year. Third, unlike the U.S. case, the average Japanese projects did not overlap planning and engineering periods. In short, the U.S. catchup in total lead time so far has been caused mainly by a combination of shorter planning lead time for the average U.S. projects and longer planning time for the Japanese. This may be partly because many of the Japanese models needed fundamental conceptual changes (e.g., conversion to luxury models, niche-oriented models, or simple product designs). The difference between the U.S. and Japanese average engineering lead times persisted, however; the U.S. catchup in lead time has been partial as of the early 1990s.

Development Productivity.   The U.S. makers also caught up with the Japanese in development productivity measured by adjusted person-hours per project. Average adjusted engineering hours in the 1993 survey was estimated to be 2.8 million in Europe, 2.3 million in America, and 2.1 million in Japan (Average unadjusted engineering hours per project was 3.2 million in Europe, 2.3 million in America, and 1.3 million in Japan).[21] In short, product development productivity was essentially unchanged between the 1980s and the early 1990s in Europe and slightly increased in Japan, while the U.S. average was dramatically reduced. As a result, the estimated development productivity of the average U.S. projects became almost the same as that of the Japanese. The catchup of the U.S. makers was indeed remarkable here.

The fact that changes in product development practices in the U.S. firms (e.g., more supplier participation in product development, faster die development, more simultaneous engineering, heavier product manager organizations) and their improvements in product development performance coincided seems to be consistent with the proposition of the previous Harvard study on effective product development routines. Further empirical studies would be needed, however, to understand what exactly happened in the organizations and with performance of product development in the world auto industry of the 1990s.

Overbuilding Capabilities: The Japanese in the Early 1990s

The last topic in this chapter involves another dynamic phenomenon: an unintended negative consequence called overshooting or overbuilding capabilities. This is closely related to a problem observed in product development at the Japanese firms of the early 1990s: *fat product design*. Let us now look at this problem. Such high-cost designs included excessive product varieties, fast model change cycles, too few common parts, unnecessary options, overspecification, and overquality. Fat product designs have been blamed by many industry observers for overworking engineers before the postbubble recession started, as well as general competitive weakness of Japanese cars after the 1993 appreciation of the yen.

But these problems didn't emerge because the Japanese makers built a wrong set of capabilities in the first place. To the contrary, based on the evolutionary perspective adopted in this book, I argue that "overbuilding" of the same capability that created competitive advantages in the 1980s has been the source of new problems in the 1990s. Overall, the dilemma of fat product designs provides us with new insights about the subtle nature of the capability-building dynamics: effective manufacturing routines are difficult for a firm to acquire, but once it gains momentum to build them, it is also difficult avoid overrun—a side effect of capability-building competitions that we have often observed in industrial histories.

The Problem of Fat Product Designs

It is difficult to define *fat design* based on objective data. In theory, fat (or excessive) product design occurs where the marginal cost of adding one element of product design exceeds the marginal increase in revenue owing to improved customer satisfaction (i.e., higher reservation price, more sales). In practice, however, there is no operational criterion that can tell us if a given product design is fat. Thus, we accumulate circumstantial evidence, collect opinions of practitioners, and make an overall judgment about whether fat design exists in a given set of products. Consider the following.

Product Variety. It is important here to distinguish peripheral product proliferation at the level of variations within a model and fundamental product proliferation at the level of basic models offered by one company. In the latter case, product variety may still be important as long as market needs continue to become diversified. In fact, there has been no indication of variety reduction in the early 1990s at this level. When additional models are needed for growing overseas markets and domestic nonsedan markets, it's not reasonable for an automobile mass producer to advocate unilateral reduction of basic model varieties.

At the level of peripheral product proliferation, however, a general consensus existed among practitioners of the Japanese auto industry by the early 1990s: the number of product variations per model was excessive in some way or another. For example, around 1990, when Toyota's total output was about 300,000 per month, it was making about 60,000 product variations per month, of which 25,000 were assembled only one per month. A less-selling half of these variations occupied only 5 percent of the total sales. This level of product variations could have been justified if they had resulted from an equally diversified customer demand, but much less than half of the vehicles on the assembly line had been linked to firm orders by final users then. Thus, it was likely that many of the variations were contributing little to customer satisfaction, while they incurred additional cost owing to unnecessary product engineering, small-volume production, more complexity in assembly, increased risk of mistakes in production, and so on.

Parts Variety. Given the level of product variety, parts variety may be excessive if firms do not use common parts across their models when they could do it without sacrificing customer satisfaction. On the other hand, according to the Harvard study, the average ratio of parts common with other existing models within a firm (and/or carried over parts from previous models) was lower in Japanese new car projects of the 1980s (about 20 percent) than in their European (about 30 percent) and the U.S. (about 40 percent) counterparts.[22] The question is whether this Japanese average was too low, but it is hard to tell by these data alone. Lower common parts (i.e., more unique design parts) would certainly improve product integrity and product differentiation from other models, but this could also result in cost increase owing to the parts variety.

In retrospect, however, there may have been excessive parts variety because of a lower common parts ratio in many cases. For example, Honda's 1993 Accord and 1994 Odyssey both used over 50 percent common parts, unusually high rates for Honda historically, but it successfully created effectively differentiated products in both cases. Overall, there was a general consensus among the Japanese managers that they could increase common parts ratios in many products without sacrificing product integrity or total product quality.

Model Changes. The Japanese automakers on average have maintained about 4.5-year model change intervals between the 1960s and 1980s, with regular 4-year cycles for their main products in the sedan category, which has been much shorter than the U.S. and European counterparts (see figure 6.2 again).[23] Renewing models frequently could certainly have positive effects on customer satisfaction and competitiveness by keeping the models fresh in customers' minds and by integrating the latest technologies into the products. However, the model change cycles may be excessively fast for certain products when the marginal costs of product development and capital investments in both car makers and suppliers, extra work load of engineers, and damages to existing customers owing to reduced resale value of past models exceeds the marginal benefits mentioned above. This balance would be different depending upon the market segments, but there was a tendency for the Japanese automakers in the first half of the 1990s to prolong the model change cycle in selected products, if not their mainstream models.[24] It is important, however, not to confuse model change cycles with development lead times. As for the latter, there's been a clear tendency to shorten them further in the mid-1990s, not only in Western but also in Japanese car makers.

Overspecification and Overquality. It has been pointed out by many practitioners and researchers that the Japanese cars in the late 1980s and early 1990s suffered from high cost owing to overspecifications (i.e., unnecessary functions and equipment) and overquality (i.e., excessively sophisticated structures and/or materials for a given function). Whether excessive or not, Japanese cars were certainly increasing their product contents and size. The share of Japanese cars equipped with automatic transmission in the domestic market, for example, increased from 28 percent in 1980 to 73 percent in 1990; as for power steering, figures went from 24 percent in 1980 to over 90 percent in 1990. The share of Japanese cars with engines larger than 2000 cc also increased from 3 percent in 1980 to 9 percent in 1990. Note that it is virtually impossible to distinguish the factor of overspecification from that of normal product evolution in the above cases, however.

It is even more difficult to measure the degree of overquality, as this involves the cumulative effects of many small design decisions, such as whether to use two bolts or three bolts to tie a certain component, whether to use sheet steel that is 0.1 mm thinner in certain body parts, and so on. But the following anecdote is typical of the time. When I interviewed a product engineer at a German car maker in the late 1980s, he commented that one of the leading Japanese models was about $500 more expensive than the equivalent German model owing to overquality and excessive designs, other things being equal.[25]

Let me emphasize that, on the basis of such data, it is difficult to judge objectively if the level of product complexity was in fact excessive. But many practitioners clearly thought fat product design was a problem for the Japanese by the end of the 1980s. Accordingly, Japanese automakers started to make massive efforts to simplify their products. In the 1993 fiscal year alone, for example, Toyota cut its product cost by 160 billion yen in order to make up for its equally huge loss owing to the yen's appreciation, and as much as 100 billion yen of this reduction was ascribed to simplification of product designs (e.g., variety reduction, common parts, value engineering), apparently without much sacrifice in customer satisfaction. Judging from such enormous cost effect owing to product simplification, it would be reasonable to conclude, in retrospect, that fat product designs in fact existed in the late 1980s to the early 1990s.

Three Explanations for Fat Product Design. Having described the nature of the fat design problem, let's now explore some alternative ways of interpreting this phenomenon. I compare three hypotheses that may explain the fat design syndrome: (1) adaptation to the abnormal (bubble) environment, (2) misadaptation to long-term environmental changes, and (3) overadaptation to market variety and sophistication (table 6.4). Also, behind the three hypotheses lie three different views of the firm, respectively: (1) the *equilibrium* perspective, (2) the *paradigm change* (revolutionary) perspective, and (3) the *resource-capability-evolution* perspective. This comparison enables us to spotlight some of essential characteristics of the evolutionary framework proposed in this book.

Hypothesis 1: Adaptation to an Abnormal Bubble Environment (Equilibrium Perspective). The first interpretation, the adaptation hypothesis, regards Japan's so-called bubble economy in the late 1980s as a temporary and abnormal market environment, and argues that the

Table 6.4   Three Hypotheses and Perspectives on Fat Product Design

Hypothesis	Perspective	Assumptions on the Firm	Interpretation on the Environment
Adaptation to the bubble environment	Equilibrium	Firms can readapt resources / capabilities instantly / constantly	Late 1980s = abnormal (bubbly demand) Mid-1990s = back to normal
Misadaptation to the postgrowth environment	Paradigm change (Revolution)	Firms cannot readapt resources / capabilities. -- can only replace them altogether	Late 1980s = end of growth-proliferation era Early 1990s = start of post-growth era (variety is no longer emphasized)
Overadaptation to variety and integrity	Resource-capability (Evolution)	Firms can readapt resources / capabilities, but only in the long run	Late 1980s = variety and integrity emphasized Early 1990s = still emphasized (customers' evolution continues)

Japanese automakers accurately responded to this market need; they made a series of "bubbly" products with excessive variety and excessive design. In other words, fat product designs were created, not because the firms failed to adapt their products to the market, but because they adapted correctly to abnormal market needs. Thus, the fat design problem resulted from the very fact that the automakers were accurately responding to the market: the firms' adaptive capabilities were functioning, but they were responding to the "wrong" demands. So the prescription for these companies is simple: as market needs get back to the normal pattern of the postbubble era, auto firms have only to adjust their products once again to the new market environment and thereby cut the fat from their product designs.

This hypothesis fits the standard equilibrium view in neoclassical microeconomic theory. According to this perspective, firms can adjust their resources and capability instantly to the changes in market environments to reach an equilibrium, partly because of the assumption that firms' resources are malleable and that executives always make accurate decisions to maximize profits or present value based on perfect information. As the surviving firms are always found in the equilibrium point in the activity space, neither misadaptation nor overadaptation exists—in theory. From the equilibrium perspective, it is quite natural to conclude that the auto firms developed fat designs simply in accurate response to fat demand in the market.

Hypothesis 2: Misadaptation to Long-Term Environmental Change (Paradigm Change Perspective).   By contrast, the second interpretation, the misadaptation hypothesis, regards the fat design problem as a result of the firms' failure to adapt their productive systems to a fundamental change in the environment—the end of continuous growth.

According to this hypothesis, the problem was caused by an inability of the firms to adjust their resources to long-term structural changes in market conditions. As the long period of Japan's continuous growth finally ended around 1990, a set of manufacturing capabilities that had been built during that period no longer fit the postgrowth era. This hypothesis assumes that the nature of market needs changed when the growth period ended. That is, the level of product-market variety and sophistication, which was supported by the economy of scale and growth, could no longer be sustained in the postgrowth era.

Consequently, there persisted a significant gap between the requirements of the postgrowth environment and the capabilities built throughout the growth era. Japanese firms would have to change the existing system as a whole by prolonging their model change cycles, reducing the number of basic models, reducing variations, using more common parts across the models, emphasizing an economy of scale, simplifying product designs, deemphasizing product quality, and so on—all at the same time—in order to remain cost-competitive. The prescription that the misadaptation hypothesis proposes is virtual replacement of the old system with an entirely new system, rather than incremental adjustment of the existing system. This means total rejection of the growth with variety model of the postwar Japanese auto industry. It may even imply a return to the American-style mass-production system that emphasizes economy of scale. Such emphasis on a whole new system is connected with the *paradigm change* view of the firm. The perspective has its roots in Thomas Kuhn's theory of scientific revolution or even classic Marxist theories of economic system changes.[26] What is common among such revolutionary views is the assumption that a stable system exists not because it is adapted to external environments but simply because it is internally consistent. Even when a gap between the system capability and environmental requirements widens, that old system is unable to readapt itself to the new environment. Thus, system change occurs only in the form of replacement of the old regime by a new one.

Hypothesis 3: Overadaptation to Variety and Integrity (Evolution Perspective). The third interpretation, the *overadaptation* hypothesis, falls between the extremes of the first two: it does not deny a firm's basic ability to adapt its routines to a new environment, but it does not assume the system can always adapt to a changing environment smoothly and instantly, either.

Unlike the adaptation hypothesis, which see the fat design syndrome as a short-term problem specific to the bubble economy, the overadaptation hypothesis analyzes it as a long-term issue related to the limit of the growth-oriented system. Unlike the misadaptation hypothesis, however, this one does not reject all the capabilities developed by the 1980s as totally obsolete. Instead, it argues that the product development capabilities that Japanese automakers accumulated (e.g., variety expansion, frequent model changes, unique parts designs, a high level of quality and flexibility) are still contributing to their competitive advantage in the 1990s, because the market needs that emphasize fundamental product variety and product integrity continue despite the end of continuous growth. Whereas the misadaptation hypothesis emphasizes discontinuity between the 1980s and the 1990s, the overadaptation hypothesis recognizes their continuity in terms of diversity, uncertainty, change, and sophistication of customer needs. The real problem, according to this view, is that some firms excessively accumulated and utilized the very routines and capabilities that had contributed to their competitive advantages.

Why does such overshooting happen? For one thing, firms with relatively high evolutionary learning capabilities tend to overaccumulate or overuse their routine capabilities.[27] Generally speaking, business firms compete not only by price setting in the short run but also by capability building in the long run. Under intense pressures of such *capability-building competition*, a firm accelerates its efforts to outperform its rivals in the pace of capability building. But this firm does not know in advance the level of competitors' capabilities, nor the optimal level of capabilities the market will call for. As a result, firms that outpace the others in the capability-building competition also tend to suffer from overadaptation. By this logic, we can predict that *a firm with a high evolutionary learning capability tends to overshoot more often.*

It should now be obvious that this view of the firm reflects the evolutionary perspective of this book: in the long run, business firms are able to adapt their organizational capabilities to the direction that the competitive environments require; but in the short run, such adaptations tend to be incomplete owing to the "sticky" nature of resource capability, "bounded rationality" of the firms, and so on. In this way, the evolutionary perceptive disagrees with the notion that firms are totally unable to adapt their systems to the environment (the paradigm change perspective), as well as the assumption that firms can perfectly and continuously adapt their systems to the environments (the equilibrium perspective).

The evolution view of the firm also emphasizes the notion that "history matters." When a firm readapts its productive resources and capabilities to the changing environment, it does so by retaining and utilizing most of the existing systems, adding new elements of functions and structures, subtracting what is obsolete, and regaining the total balance. However, the firm's ability to move, speed up, slow down, and redirect such evolutionary processes is limited; the pattern of resource and capability at one point in time is constrained by that of the previous period, at least partially. This perspective is an especially good match for those industries in which the pace of technological changes and/or industrial transformation is neither very fast nor very slow, and the product's basic architecture is relatively stable—such as the automobile industry.

The Cause of Fat Product Design

The adaptation-to-the-bubble-economy hypothesis certainly explains part of the fat product design story, but it fails to distinguish long-term market evolution toward higher variety and sophistication of customer needs, on the one hand, and short-term deviation from the regular evolutionary path (i.e., the bubble economy), on the other. As a result, this view tends to over-emphasize the negative impact of the "bubble" market and simply rejects fat design as something abnormal. It cannot explain why the tendency of the Japanese firms toward higher variety and frequent model changes existed prior to the bubble era, either.

The misadaptation hypothesis is also persuasive in some ways, particularly in that it interprets the fat design syndrome in the broader and longer term context of the limit of the growth-oriented system. But such a revolutionary view may be too extreme and simplistic to explain the complexity of the phenomenon in question. A call for paradigm changes, for example, cannot explain why the Western auto firms are still trying to catch up with Japanese firms in both performance and capability, even in the mid-1990s. Thus, the rest of this discussion focuses on the overadaptation hypothesis, which seems to be most relevant in explaining the apparently complex process through which fat product design emerged.

I argue here that overuse or overbuilding of the same capability that created competitive advantages for the Japanese in the 1980s was a main source of their problems in the 1990s. To clarify this logic, let's reinterpret the recent history of automobile product design and technology. Specifically, the following stage model may help us understand the dynamics of the fat design syndrome:

1960s–'70s:	Pursuit of better functions and technologies at the individual component level. Organizational capabilities built around element technologies. Element-focused strategy for product development.[28] Functional organization best fits this stage.
Late 1970s to early 1980s:	The element-focused strategy reaches its limit. Firms find they cannot differentiate their products by superiority in component technolo-

gies alone.[29] The companies with superior component technology tend to fail in the market at this stage.

1980s: Companies start focusing on *product integrity* as a key differentiater at the system (total product) level. System-focused strategy for individual product development is chosen. Tight project teams and heavyweight project managers are better structures for this stage.[30]

Early 1990s: Companies pursuing customer satisfaction through total product quality face overquality and increasing cost as side effects of their efforts toward higher product integrity and variety. Companies with superior project management at the individual product level tend to fail in the market at this stage. Heavyweight product manager system and strong cross-functional teams, designed for higher product integrity, often lead to a lack of cross-project coordination.

Mid-1990s: Companies start to cut product cost dramatically by applying lean product design. Shifting focus from individual products to company-wide product line may be a key for this stage, as the problem of fat design tends to happen in lower-end products. Reorganization for multiple project management often becomes the issue (e.g., Nobeoka, 1993). Strong multiproduct planners who have a clear sense of product positioning or individual product managers who have a clear sense of priority and orientation to lean design often become essential people.

Also note that consumers' abilities to evaluate products tend co-evolve with a firm's capabilities to develop and produce products. For example, the shift from an element (component) focus to a system (product integrity) focus is likely to be accompanied by improvements in customers' abilities to discern subtle product differences in the total product.

Essentially, the above hypothetical framework implies that the *focus of competition* shifts over time, and the focus of capability building also shifts accordingly (Clark and Fujimoto, 1991). It also argues that capability building tends not to be a smooth and balanced process, but an unbalanced process of overshooting and rebalancing. A firm may focus on one dimension (or level) of product development capability, accumulate organizational capability along one dimension, do it too much, face problems in other dimensions or levels, and try to regain balance by shifting attention to other dimensions.

Of course, we should not impose one deterministic stage model on all cases in the real world. The actual processes would also be much more complicated than such a simple linear model implies. However, this kind of conceptual framework may still help researchers better understand the basic dynamics of the firms' capability building and adaptation, partly because it is linked to one of the main perspectives in the theories of the firm, and partly because there appear to be various cases where manufacturing firms in some Japanese fabrication-assembly industries of the 1980s–'90s (e.g., motor vehicles, single lens reflex cameras, men's suits, certain consumer electronics) have followed this basic pattern.

With the above general framework and historical context in mind, let's now examine the mechanism of overshooting. Although it is difficult to show systematic and quantitative evidence that supports this hypothesis, plenty of circumstantial evidence is interpreted consistently with the overshooting theory. Several examples are illustrated below:

Overuse of High Development Productivity.   Given that the amount of R&D resource inputs (budget, human resources) and other things are equal, a company with higher development productivity (less inputs per project) can develop a larger number of new models for wider model variety and/or more frequent model changes, which in turn can enhance its chance of having a successful product.[31] However, the same capability can become a cause of excessive product proliferation. If the Japanese automakers had not had relatively high levels of development productivity, it would have been impossible for them to develop too many variations too frequently in the first place. Again, those firms with a higher capability tend also to have a higher risk of overshooting when competitive pressures for the capability building race are intense.

Short Lead Times That Hamper Design Simplification.   When lead time is short, auto engineers tend not to have enough time to check the relevance of their engineering standards, even when they represent overquality from the customer's point of view. Today's automaker possesses engineering standards that as a whole are as thick as dozens of phone books. This huge accumulation of design rules facilitates quick and efficient execution of product engineering, but it can become a bureaucratic procedure that creates fat design. For example, when only two bolts are enough to hold a particular component in today's technology, an old standard that requires three bolts may remain unquestioned. When engineering lead time is short, there is a greater chance that old standards will remain unquestioned for generations of models.

Overemphasis on Product Integrity.   When product integrity is recognized as key to market success, designers and engineers tend to start insisting that high price can be justified by improvements in product integrity. When this period coincides with an economic boom, such as Japan's bubble economy, the notion that product integrity is sacred prevails, cost planning becomes less rigorous, and product cost increases. In other words, the period of reckless pursuit of product integrity may contribute to the long-term evolution of the firm's capability, but it is likely to result in cost increases in the short run. In fact, such a phenomenon was observed at Toyota and other Japanese makers in the late 1980s.

Overuse of the Customer Satisfaction Method.   The Japanese makers have historically emphasized customer satisfaction (CS), which, as a basic philosophy, has been always crucial. But this has often resulted in a pursuit of high scores on the Customer Satisfaction Index (CSI), which is often based on a long laundry list of "things to be done." (It is important here to distinguish CS *philosophy* and CS *method*.) If the engineers and designers emphasize such a list too much and try to fill it in without a sense of priority, the result tends to be a fat design. Besides, such a list often consists of customer dissatisfaction elements to be eliminated rather than customer satisfaction factors to be created, because dissatisfaction is easier to measure than satisfaction. Unfortunately, however, elimination of customer dissatisfaction does not automatically mean high customer satisfaction, as the two are often different dimensions. As a result, the pursuit of the CS technique based on the dissatisfaction list may create high-cost products that have no problems—but no fun built in, either.

Abuse of Supplier and Production Capabilities.   As discussed in chapter 5, flexibility and design capabilities of parts suppliers, as well as high manufacturing capabilities of in-house production units, contributed to the relatively high performance of the Japanese car development projects in terms of speed and efficiency throughout the 1980s. This, however, also meant that suppliers and manufacturing units could respond to a product development unit's requests for more and more product variety and/or for product-specific component designs. If they had not been flexible and responsive, such requests for fatter designs would have been difficult to realize in the first place.

Side Effects of a Heavyweight Product Manager. The heavyweight product manager system was a main source of product integrity and competitive advantage for some Japanese automakers in the 1980s, but this can also become a source of fat designs when excessively emphasized. When each product manager is powerful, cross-project coordination may become difficult, as individual managers tend to behave too autonomously. For example, product managers need a sense of ownership to enhance product integrity, but if this ownership is too strong, they start to insist that their products be unique down to every component for design optimization. In other cases, they may insist that their new products get novel technologies and equipment that were successfully introduced in the upper models in the past. Thus, the very existence of heavyweight product managers, particularly when competing for internal promotion, may contribute to excessive parts variety and product complexity.

Variety as Self-Fulfilling Prophecy. As Edith Penrose (1959) points out, firms tend to adapt themselves to perceived environments as opposed to real ones. When automakers increase product variety, they are reacting to the perception that consumers need variety, rather than the real variety in actual demands. When engineers plan and develop variety of product design, there is no way they can calculate an optimal level of product variety. In such a situation, they tend to create more varieties for insurance—a shotgun approach. When they manage to sell the variations in some way or other, including heavy discounts, the planned variety becomes a "self-fulfilling prophesy" (Merton, 1968). There is virtually no effective way to control this process of design multiplication. Thus, variety of product design tends to proliferate.

It should be clear from the above evidence that the main cause of the fat product design problem is nothing but the effective product development routines and capabilities identified earlier in this chapter. This problem is caused not so much by mischoice or rigidity in organizational routines, but overdevelopment of routines. Such a diagnosis makes the remedy for the fat design problem a lot more complicated; it is more than a simple matter of switching the routines to new ones. Let's examine the Japanese firms' responses next.

The 1990s Response: Lean Product Designs

In the early 1990s, the problem of the high-cost structure of the Japanese automobile designs surfaced as the era of continuous growth finally ended, customers in the postbubble era became much more price sensitive, and further appreciation of the yen wiped out Japanese cost competitiveness. Cost reduction was given the first priority, and cost planning (target costing) became critical in product development projects. While it was difficult for the companies that already had pursued efficient production systems through *kaizen* (continuous improvements) for many years to further reduce costs dramatically by shop floor efforts alone, product design simplification was recognized as the most effective means for massive cost reduction. After all, lean production systems needed "lean product designs."

The Japanese firms of the mid-1990s moved in this direction. A survey by the Japanese auto worker union, for example, indicated that a majority of cost reductions achieved at Toyota and other Japanese automakers in 1993–94 was due to design simplification (reduction of product varieties, using more components, value engineering), rather than reduction of overhead, reduction of capital investment, or *kaizen* activities. In these two years, when Toyota estimated a loss of about 100 billion yen per year by exchange rate alone, the company cut costs by roughly the same amount by design simplification alone. The situation was similar in other Japanese auto firms.

What made this challenge of design simplification more difficult was the fact that consumer expectations for product integrity (i.e., total product quality) and fundamental (not superficial) variety continued, as the evolutionary view predicts. Once consumers experience a product of high product integrity and design quality, for example, they tend to set their reference points based on these products. Thus, consumers' expectations on price tend to fluctuate as their budget constraints change between booms and recessions, but their expectations on total product quality tend to stay at the high level even after the boom period is over.

Achieving product integrity and product simplicity at the same time is not an easy job. As of the mid-1990s, there have been some cases in which excessive simplification of the Japanese new models, which apparently resulted in a loss in product integrity, lack of product differentiation, and perceived deterioration of design quality, have created customer dissatisfaction and loss in market share, despite their competitive prices. This seems to indicate that lean designs actually involve a subtle balancing and that there is always a risk of overshooting—or oversimplifying product design.

Although it is too early at this point to draw any conclusions about changes in management and organization of product development in response to this trend toward lead product design, the firms effective in this job are likely to need new or improved capabilities in such areas as leadership through cost planning by product managers; stronger cross-project coordination mechanisms for component sharing without losing product differentiation; early value engineering that starts from the concept creation stages; further simultaneous engineering between and within product and process engineering groups, and so on.

In retrospect, the automobile markets in many industrialized countries apparently started to emphasize product variety and product integrity by the end of the 1970s. This seems to be a long-term evolutionary process created by dynamic interactions between the firms and the customers on an international scale, which extends beyond the bubble era and Japan's high-growth era. Even after Japan's bubble economy and continuous growth ended around 1990, the international automobile markets—at least in major car-producing countries in Europe, America, and Japan—continued to emphasize product variety and product integrity. Thus, the fundamental pattern of co-evolution between producers and consumers in the worldwide industry did not change much between the 1980s and 1990s.

Thus, one of the most powerful prescriptions for the Japanese automakers to overcome their problems of the mid-1990s was lean design, which was neither a simple matter of "going back to normal" as the adaptation-to-the-bubble hypothesis would prescribe, nor "changing everything" as the misadaptation-to-the-postgrowth hypothesis would propose. *Lean design* means achieving a more subtle balance: firms have to simplify their product designs without sacrificing fundamental product differentiation and product integrity.[32]

The Capability-Building Competition Continues

Since international differences in product development performance at the individual project level have narrowed in the early 1990s, the patterns of competition in the world auto industry have changed as well—and they will continue to change. First, superior product development capabilities in individual firms, regardless of their geographical origins, will matter even more. Seeing industrial competition as battles between "national teams" will thus become somewhat obsolete. Second, multilevel management of product development (Clark and Fujimoto, 1991) will become more important, to the extent that a firm's capabilities beyond individual product development projects (e.g., management of company-wide product mix or component technology development) becomes a key to success in the market.

This is not the end of the story, though. As we enter the late 1990s, the international and interfirm competition of capability building still continues like an endless "industrial marathon."[33] In the mid-1990s, for example, some Japanese automakers started to shorten lead time again, setting the next stage of capability-building competition in this area.

Preliminary data in certain selected firms indicate that they cut lead time between exterior design approval and start of sales from about thirty months (the Japanese average of the 1980s and early 1990s) to twenty months or less.[34] The effective firms tended to emphasize the principle of *early problem solving* by a combination of further cross-functional integration, supplier involvement, effective use of prior knowledge from previous projects (i.e., knowledge front loading), preprototype design reviews, and selective and wise use of new technologies (e.g., three-dimensional CAD-CAM, early simulations by computer-aided engineering, rapid prototyping techniques) at earlier stages of product development (i.e., activity front loading).[35] In this way, problems are detected much earlier in the process, prototypes and engineering drawings are much more complete the first time, the number of subsequent design changes is dramatically reduced, the number of prototype iterations decreases, lead time for die development gets shorter, and overall engineering lead time gets shorter. New technologies are used for these improvements, but the old themes such as early problem solving and cross-functional integration continue to be the guiding principles.

This chapter examined the dynamic aspects of product development capabilities in Japanese automakers. The main messages may be summarized as follows:

1. The pattern of *product development performance* in the 1980s was partly region-specific and partly firm-specific. The Japanese makers in general tended to outperform the others in development productivity and lead times, but there were interfirm differences among the Japanese in total product quality. Only a few Japanese makers achieved high performance in all three criteria.

2. The pattern of *routinized product development capabilities* of the 1980s (e.g., suppliers' design capability, manufacturing capability in product development, capabilities in simultaneous engineering, wide-range skills of engineers, strength of product managers, etc.) was also partly region-specific and partly firm-specific, reflecting that of product development performance. The pattern consistence of the capabilities as a system contributed to overall success of some of the Japanese volume producers in the 1980s.

3. The product development capabilities of the effective Japanese firms of the 1980s evolved gradually as a result of *multi-path system emergence*. Although the system was ex-post rational from international competition's point of view, the advantages of the emerging systems were not always recognized by the firms when they were first tried. Historical imperatives and unintended technology transfers played an important role in this capability building process. At the same time, firm-specific abilities of converting unintended trials to

carefully designed systems was also important. Thus, the dynamic process of capability building itself was both region-specific and firm-specific at the same time.

4. Whereas the product development capabilities of the effective Japanese firms were gradually built as a result of an system emergence, the U.S. and European firms, facing the competitive challenges from the Japanese, attempted a *reverse catchup* with the Japanese best practice in product development. Unlike the Japanese, Western firms recognized the product development capabilities explicitly as a rational system and introduced them mostly in a top-down approach. Some modifications were made by them through this rationalization process. Partly as a result of this knowledge transfer, product development performance of the U.S. makers in lead time and productivity improved rapidly, and the average performance differences narrowed in many criteria.

5. The Japanese automakers, on the other hand, faced a problem of fat design, in terms of product varieties, model change frequency, model-specific parts, overspecifications, and over-quality. This phenomenon may be explained by *overshooting*, or overbuilding of capabilities by the Japanese firms. In other words, the problem in the 1990s may have been created, not because the Japanese firms deviated from their success pattern in the 1980s, but because they pushed the very capabilities to an extreme.

6. Some of the Japanese automakers and projects are already making efforts to solve the fat product problem by *design simplification* without sacrificing product integrity. This indicates that the dynamic process of capability building may not be a smooth and balanced one, but a zigzag path of overshooting and rebalancing of different aspects of capabilities and performance. The pace of capability building will be uneven over time.

Thus, intense competition based on product development performance, routinized capability, and capability building continues where mutual organizational learning between competing firms is the key. The foci of competition shift over time, and effective auto firms like Toyota have made, and will continue to make, tonacious efforts to respond to the moving targets by constantly reshaping their product development routines and capabilities. The process of capability building has often been emergent, where evolutionary learning capability is the key for long-term success.

And yet, despite such changes, some of the fundamental competitive themes seem to remain unchanged. Early and integrated problem solving through such measures as supplier involvement, effective prototyping and die making, overlapping of developmental stages, and strong project leadership has been, and will continue to be, a source of superior project performance at least partially toward the next century. As in other aspects of the manufacturing system, coexistence of constant change and remarkable continuity is quite obvious in the evolution of product development capabilities.

Having analyzed some details of the supplier management and product development routines of the Toyota-style manufacturing system, I shift my focus to the third, and the last, main subsystem to be investigated: production. In the next chapter, I highlight a recent evolutionary process in one of the core elements of Toyota-style production—final assembly lines—to examine internal organizational processes that lie behind Toyota's evolutionary learning capability.

7

EVOLUTION OF TOYOTA'S NEW
ASSEMBLY SYSTEM

This chapter explores a change that occurred in Toyota's production routines—the last of the three basic components of the total manufacturing system—between the late 1980s and the mid-1990s, particularly in its final assembly process.[1] In this last empirical analysis, I investigate some detailed aspects of the evolutionary learning capability itself at Toyota Motor Corporation. Up to now, the internal structure of this overall dynamic capability has not been analyzed systematically, but treated as a rather mysterious entity. But here I start by defining some of the internal evolutionary mechanisms that appear to matter most at Toyota.

As I've already argued, the Toyota-style manufacturing system evolved gradually through a multi-path system emergence process, and Toyota itself exploited this emergent process more effectively than other firms, thereby creating a distinctively competitive set of organizational routines (i.e., its routinized manufacturing and learning capabilities). This book has presented and reinterpreted a number of historical, clinical, and statistical data consistent with this view.

However, even if we can reasonably infer from this historical evidence that Toyota had an evolutionary learning capability, such data do not tell us much about the internal content of the evolutionary learning capability itself. A dual-level problem-solving model of solution emergence and refinement was proposed at the end of chapter 3, but it so far remains a hypothesis without much rigorous testing. This seems to be a problem inherent in a method that relies mostly on existing historical data: such data usually do not tell us about the details of the organizational process behind the revealed capability.

One way to fill this gap is to conduct statistical comparative studies across automobile firms. By collecting and comparing data systematically on various aspects of the organizations and their members, we may be able to identify a certain stable pattern behind the evolutionary learning capability. Such an organizational study with a large sample size is beyond the scope of this book. But the second way to reduce this gap is a detailed case study of a historical process that has emerged relatively recently. By focusing on recent events, we can systematically collect both clinical and statistical data that are better tailored to our research purposes, compared to a study using secondhand historical materials. The internal organizational processes behind the evolutionary learning capability may be easier to identify in this way.

This chapter takes this second approach, exploring an evolutionary process by which Toyota reorganized its assembly operations in response to changes in product and labor markets in the early 1990s. Through this case analysis, I aim to back up the evolutionary argument of this book in two ways: by examining if Toyota's evolutionary learning capability identified prior to the 1980s still existed in the early 1990s, and thereby checking the robustness of the organizational capability at this company; and by conducting an in-depth case analysis of a recent system change to provide a deeper understanding of the internal organizational process behind the evolutionary learning capability.

Outline of the Case

Toyota's assembly process designs have been significantly modified since the late 1980s, while maintaining much of its core manufacturing capabilities. The new system has tried to improve its attractiveness to a new generation of workers in Japan, where the number of youthful employees has been decreasing since the early 1990s, while trying to save its cash flow and lower the product cost by making the plant and equipment design simpler and by avoiding excessive automation and capital investment.[2] I call this a *lean-on-balance system*, as firms in this mode try, among other things, to improve the balance between employee satisfaction (attractiveness of their work processes in the labor market) and customer satisfaction (attractiveness of their outputs in the product markets) at the same time.[3]

Most of the Japanese automobile makers, facing the labor shortage and expansion of domestic demand around 1990, built a new generation of "human-friendly" assembly plants, such as the Honda Suzuka #3 line (1989), Mazda Hofu #2 plant (1990), Toyota Tahara #4 line (1991), Nissan Kyushu #2 plant (1992), with relatively high assembly automation ratios mainly for ergonomic purposes.[4] These assembly plants, however, suffered from high fixed cost owing in part to assembly automation when Japanese domestic production started to decline because of the postbubble recession and further appreciation of the yen in the early 1990s. It became clear that the Japanese auto companies had to readjust their basic designs of assembly factories, automation, and work organizations.

In this situation, Toyota appears to be the only Japanese company that could articulate and implement a new concept of final assembly that explicitly aimed at improving not only customer satisfaction but also employee satisfaction by the mid-1990s. The Miyata Plant of Toyota Motor Kyushu Inc., Toyota's new subsidiary on Kyushu Island (called Toyota Kyushu henceforth for simplicity), established in late 1992, was the first factory that materialized Toyota's new assembly process design as a coherent total system. The new assembly concept was then diffused to subsequent plant constructions and renovations, such as Motomachi #2 assembly line (renovated, 1994) and Toyota Motor Manufacturing USA's #2 line in Georgetown, Kentucky (TMM II, new construction, 1994). Thus, one research question is why Toyota could establish a coherent assembly process prior to its competitors in Japan. Although Toyota's market power and abundant financial resources could explain part of the story, a certain firm-specific organizational capability might also be behind this fact.

As for the process of system change, like the other chapters of this book, it is hypothesized here that the new system was created, not simply by a rational and monolithic process of strategic planning, but by a more complicated process of system emergence, which may involve not only ex-ante rational decision making but also trial and error, unintended changes, conflicts and coordination between different organizational units, and so on. As an example of such emergent processes, I focus here on recent constructions of Toyota's domestic assembly factories, including Tahara #4 and the Toyota Kyushu plant.

To the extent that Toyota preceded the other Japanese firms in reaching a balanced solution to the problems of the postgrowth era, we may infer that Toyota still maintained a certain evolutionary learning capability, by which a firm can handle a complex process of multipath system emergence better than the others, even in the early 1990s. In this way, the present chapter reinforces the argument of this book that Toyota's distinctive competence in manufacturing included not only its routinized manufacturing capability and routinized learning capability but also an evolutionary learning capability. It also challenges a rather stereotypical notion that Toyota is a monolithic organization in which changes are made by one-shot and ex-ante rational decision making. I instead describe the company as a rather dynamic and sometimes diversified organization, one that somehow "knows" how to handle complex emergent processes.[5]

Toyota's New Assembly Factories: Structures and Functions

Toyota's Conventional Assembly Process

Let us start with describing the traditional system. Because the structures and functions of the Toyota-style production system in general have already been discussed in chapter 4 (also see appendix B1), this section focuses only on the final assembly process at Toyota's conventional factories of the 1980s. It can be characterized as follows:

1. Toyota's volume factories adopted the Ford-style moving assembly lines (typically chain conveyers). Thus, there is nothing unique in the body transfer mechanisms and basic layouts of Toyota's conventional assembly lines, except that Toyota's main assembly lines (typically about 1 km) tended to be shorter than traditional lines of U.S. makers.

2. The conveyer lines tended to be separated into three line segments: trim, chassis, and final. Different conveyer systems tended to be used among them. However, no buffer body was allowed between the line segments, so the assembly process was operated as if there had been one long and continuous line.

3. Unlike machining or welding, there have been few robots and automated equipment on traditional final assembly lines at Toyota. In fact, Toyota's assembly automation ratio tended to be lower than some European makers that adopted advanced assembly automation systems (Volkswagen, FIAT, etc.). In other words, Toyota has achieved the world-class productivity in final assembly without relying on high-tech automation (Womack et al., 1990; Fujimoto, 1997a).

4. In order to achieve a high level of line balancing, Toyota's assembly lines trained multiskilled workers, assigned a set of multiple tasks per cycle, and thereby reduced "muda" (non-value-adding time) owing to line imbalance. While such multiple task assignments raised productivity without increasing work speed, meaningfulness of the assembly jobs tended to be sacrificed: a mutually unrelated set of tasks tended to be assigned to each worker in the name of line balancing.

5. One unique mechanisms of Toyota's assembly line was the so-called andon cord (or switch), which workers activate when troubles happen on the line. If the worker and/or team leader cannot fix the problem within that cycle time, the entire assembly line stops. This is said to be an example of Toyota's *kaizen* mechanisms, which reveal and dramatize the manufacturing problems and thereby facilitate shop floor problem-solving activities.

6. The performance of Toyota's assembly lines has been traditionally evaluated internally in terms of efficiency and product quality, as well as safety. The quality of work environment
   had not been equally emphasized, though. There was an evaluation system that identified tasks that are potentially harm-
   ful to workers' health, but evaluation criteria for measuring
   work fatigue had not been developed in the past.

Changes in Product and Labor Environments in the 1990s

The basic system of Toyota's manufacturing capabilities (routines) had
been established by the early 1980s. However, the labor and product
environments—to name just two—had changed significantly by the
early to mid-1990s. Toyota's assembly system (as well as others) had to
adjust to the new environments accordingly.

Labor Market.   By a combination of structural and cyclical changes
in Japan's labor market, it became increasingly difficult to hire and
keep a sufficient workforce for automobile production. As the population structure changed, the average age of automobile workers increased. It was expected that the population of eighteen-year-old
youth would shrink by about 40 percent from the mid-1990s to 2010.
Young people became less willing to work in certain manufacturing
factories, which they recognized as "3-D" (dirty, demanding, and
dangerous), including final assembly. One measure to alleviate this
problem was to reduce work hours per year, but this meant a further
decrease in labor supply. On the demand side, expansion of domestic
automobile production peaked in 1990 (about 13.5 million units),
and created additional labor demands for the automobile industry. As
a result, the Japanese auto industry suffered from severe labor shortage problems in 1990 and 1991, which forced the automakers to emphasize employee satisfaction, assembly in particular. Although the
subsequent recession and appreciation of the yen significantly reduced domestic production volume and wiped out the labor shortage
problem by the mid-1990s, companies like Toyota still regarded the
lack of job attractiveness as a long-term problem to be solved, because the labor supply was predicted to decrease as mentioned above
and because difficulty in recruiting people for the "3-D" workplaces
was expected to continue, regardless of macroeconomic labor market
situations.

Product Market.   The bubble economy of the late 1980s was the final
stage of forty years of continuous growth in Japan's domestic automobile production. In the early 1990s, domestic production started to decline from 13.5 million units (1990) to 10.2 million (1995), which cre-

ated financial burdens of high depreciation costs for those companies that had built new and highly automated assembly factories during the bubble era. Although the period of continuous production shrinkage in the early 1990s was apparently replaced by that of fluctuation (i.e., a typical pattern in matured auto markets) in the long run, it was clear, as of the early 1990s, that the era of continuous growth, through which the traditional Toyota system was established, was over.

Financial Environment. The Japanese automakers enjoyed relatively abundant cash flow in the late 1980s, thanks to the bubble era. The companies also expected that, by issuing convertible bonds when stock prices were soaring, they could finance capital investments with negligible cost. Such an atmosphere allowed auto manufacturers to make capital spending decisions without deliberate assessments. The situation changed completely in the early 1990s: the stock market collapsed, the problem of cash flow shortage surfaced, and companies were forced to evaluate capital spending much more conservatively.

International Competition and Conflicts. Appreciation of the yen and reverse catchup by Western automakers since the mid-1980s had virtually eliminated the cost-competitive advantages of automobiles built in Japan, if not overall advantages including other factors, by the mid-1990s. In addition, trade friction with the United States and Europe virtually restricted exports of completely built vehicles to such countries. The Japanese makers, in response to these problems, made adjustments in two main areas. First, they have expanded local assembly and manufacturing of cars and components in the United States, Europe, and Asia since the 1980s. Toyota, for example, was assembling cars at NUMMI in Fremont, California (a joint venture with General Motors), TMM I and II (Georgetown, Kentucky), and TMMC (Canada) in North America as of the late 1990s. Second, they made major cost-cutting efforts for products made in Japan. While a big jump in manufacturing productivity had become difficult by the 1980s, the main contributor to the cost cutting in the 1990s turned out to be simplification of product design itself, including product variety reduction, parts commonalty, and value engineering, because Japanese products at the beginning of the 1990s were by no means lean (see chapter 6).

Production Technology. While final assembly has been known as the last area to be automated in automobile manufacturing, the 1980s witnessed significant progress in robotization of final assembly lines in some Western assembly plants, including Volkswagen's Hall 54, FIAT's Cassino plant, and GM's Hamtramk plant.[6] Although such high-tech assembly plants demonstrated progress in automobile process technologies, their overall productivity turned out to be lower than the best-practice assembly plants in Japan, where the assembly automation ratio was much lower (Womack et al., 1990).

In the situation described above, it soon became obvious that the Japanese automobile makers needed to change their manufacturing systems (assembly in particular) to a more or less balanced one that could improve customer satisfaction and employee satisfaction simultaneously, as well as making both the production process and products lean.[7]

Toyota's New Assembly Concept

In response to the challenges of these postgrowth environments, Toyota modified its production system between the late 1980s and the early 1990s. Final assembly was where the change was most visible and significant. The new assembly concepts aimed at improvements in morale and motivation of the employees, as well as elimination of physically demanding jobs, with minimum capital expenditure (i.e., minimum cost increase). The new process also continued to focus on continuous company-wide improvements (*kaizen*) in quality and productivity. To sum up, the new system attempted to preserve the strength of the conventional Toyota (or lean) system in quality, cost, and delivery (QCD), while improving the attractiveness of its assembly work, both physically and psychologically.

The new system, as Toyota itself recognized, consisted of several subsystems, which are summarized in table 7.1: (1) a *functionally autonomous and complete process*; (2) *in-line mechanical assembly automation*; (3) an ergonomics evaluation system called Toyota Verification of Assembly Line (TVAL); (4) low-cost equipment for a better work environment and work posture; and (5) supporting human resource management (HRM) policies.[8] Let us now examine the main content and functions of the above subsystems.

A Functionally Autonomous and Complete Process of Assembly. The autonomous and complete line was implemented at Toyota Kyushu plant (1992), as well as at Toyota's subsequent plant constructions and renovations. It consisted of various elements, both physical and organizational, including the following (figure 7.1):

- The main assembly line has been broken down into five to twelve line segments, each of which is typically 100 meters or twenty workstations long.
- The shape of the assembly area is roughly square, so that the building can accommodate many short lines running back and forth.
- The line segments are linked by buffer zones, where up to about five bodies can be temporarily stored.[9]

Table 7.1 Conventional versus New Assembly System at Toyota

Conventional	New	
Continuously moving conveyer line; about 1000 m	→ Unchanged	Autonomous-complete assembly process
Sort cycle time (1 - 3 minutes)	→ Unchanged	
Decomposed into three line segments (trim, chassis, final)	→ Decomposed into 5 to 12 line segments (trim, chassis, final)	
No buffer zones between segments	→ Buffer zones between segments	
A few work groups per segment	→ One work group per one segment	
Functionally unrelated tasks may be packed into jobs for a worker or a group	→ Functionally related tasks are combined for a worker or a group	
Group leaders play key roles in Kaizen and line management	→ Group leaders function was strengthened	
Automation for workload reduction	→ Unchanged	In-line mechanical assembly automation
Off-line automation: bodies stop*	→ In-line automation: bodies move	
High-tech vision sensing for alignment*	→ Mechanical devices or alignment	
NC (numerical control)*	→ Simple sequence control	
Many industrial robots are used*	→ Compact and simple equipment for assembly automation	
Process evaluation by quality, efficiency, and delivery (QCD)	→ Unchanged	TVAL for assembly process evaluation
Posture & weight score to avoid illness	→ Unchanged	
-	→ TVAL for quantitative assessment of work load	
Emphasis on low-cost jigs and power-assist equipment	→ Unchanged	Low-cost equipment for better Ergonomics
-	→ A new generation of ergonomic devices: raku-raku seat, wagon carts, body lifting mechanisms, etc.	
Basic human resource management policies at Toyota	→ Unchanged	Supporting HRM policies
Complete day and night shift	→ Continuous day and night shift	
Informal career plan for multiskilling	→ Formal career plan for multiskilling	
-	→ Other new HRM policies	

Note: * stands for a rather recent and temporary pattern in the late 1980s to early 1990s.

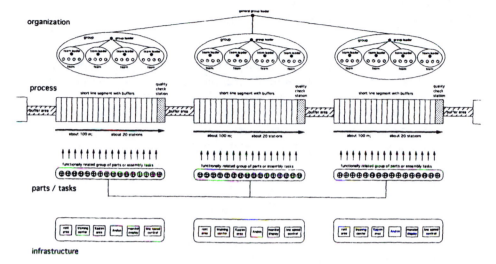

Figure 7.1 Autonomous and Complete Assembly-Line Concept

- A group of functionally related assembly tasks (e.g., piping) are assigned to one segment. Toyota defined 108 subcategories of assembly tasks, and changed the task assignment so that each subcategory was completed within a group of workers. Also, one assembly task for a given component is completed as one person's job, which is called "parts-complete" (*buhin-kanketsu*).[10]
- A quality check station is located at the end of each line segment. Criteria for quality assurance were defined for each of the 108 task subcategories.
- Each line segment corresponds to a group (*kumi*) of about twenty workers, within which job rotation and training are conducted.
- The function and responsibility of group leaders are strengthened. Each group leader, now in charge of a semi-independent line segment, enjoys more discretion in managing the group's operations. For example, each segment can fine-tune its line speed within a certain limit.
- Other supporting equipment for line control (line speed controllers, switches for planned line stops), information sharing (monitoring displays, andon boards), and self-actualization (*kaizen* shops, training centers, rest areas) is set up for each line segment.

Overall, the autonomous and complete line differed from Toyota's conventional assembly line in that the main line (typically about 1,000 meters) consisted of semi-independent segments, each of which was functionally, physically, and organizationally decoupled from the others. (Each line segment was a short version of a Ford assembly line equipped with continuously moving conveyers, however.)

Both quantitative and qualitative results, reported in terms of initial performance of autonomous complete lines, were generally consistent with what the process designers had aimed for:[11]

• *Quality and productivity.* As each set of assembly jobs assigned to a work group became more meaningful and easy to understand, and since each group could self-inspect quality more effectively, the productivity and quality of the autonomous complete line was generally higher than the conventional assembly line, particularly during the startup period.[12] In other words, productivity and quality learning curves at the startup period were significantly improved. The lead time for mastering a job was shortened to about a half. According to a survey of Toyota Kyushu assembly workers, over 70 percent of the respondents said they became more quality conscious and that their jobs became easier to understand, compared to previous assembly lines. Also, because the body buffer areas absorbed the impact of line stops at other segments, overall down time decreased.[13]

Another impact of the body buffers, according to a Toyota executive, was that the buffers lower psychological pressures for the workers to stop the line, as they do not have to stop the entire line (typically 1 kilometer) but stop their line segment only (typically twenty stations, 100 meters). A plant engineer at TMCA (Toyota's Australian subsidiary) witnessed that the number of line stops actually increased after the buffered assembly line was introduced there in 1994, apparently because of the reduction in psychological pressure. This means revealing more problems and facilitating more *kaizen.*

• *Morale.* As the assembly job became more meaningful, the morale of the assembly workers increased. In the survey mentioned above, about 70 percent of the respondents found their job more worth doing than before. According to our interview with group leaders and team leaders, they tended to become more proud of their job as instructor and *kaizen* leader as their tasks shifted from day-to-day troubleshooting (i.e., helping the workers in trouble) to more constructive work such as *kaizen,* supervising, and training. In the past, the workers tended to be swamped by the complexity and confusion on the line, partly owing to the unrelatedness of tasks assigned to them.

One caveat, however: some first-line supervisors did feel more psychological pressures because of their increased responsibility.

It should be noted, however, that the autonomous-complete line concept had to carry over both the strength and the weaknesses of the Ford-style conveyer lines with short cycle times.[14]

In-line Mechanical Assembly Automation. Toyota's new assembly lines adopted the concept of *in-line mechanical automation,* which

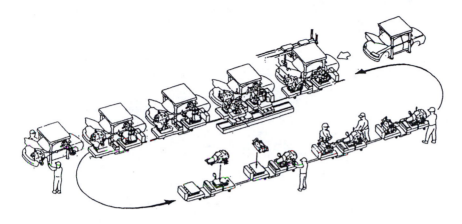

· Source: Toyota Motor Corporation (1994).

Figure 7.2 Process for Engine and Chassis Mounting

consisted of several elements (see figure 7.2 for an example of engine-transmission-suspension decking):

- Both automation equipment and component jig-pallets are synchronized with bodies that move on the conventional continuous conveyers, as opposed to stopping the bodies for automated assembly.
- The automation zone and the manual assembly zone coexist on the same assembly line. This contrasts with the idea of separate automated and manual zones. A group of assembly workers on the line, rather than off-line maintenance staff, are in charge of operating the equipment.
- Mechanical methods of alignment among bodies, jigs, equipment, and components, which tend to be inexpensive, simpler, easier to monitor and easier to fix, are used as much as possible. This contrasts with highly sophisticated and expensive ways of alignment that use electronic-vision sensing technologies.
- Automation equipment, including robots, tend also to be simple, compact, low power, and easy to maintain, so that it can coexist with assembly workers on the continuous conveyers. Jigs are also designed to be compact and inexpensive.
- Automated equipment is adopted selectively by taking cost, performance, and ergonomics into account, rather than by aiming at the highest assembly automation ratios that are technically possible.

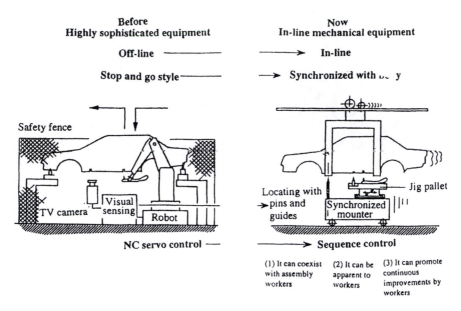

Figure 7.3 In-Line Mechanical Assembly Automation Concept

In-line automation was applied to such assembly tasks as engine-trans-mission-suspension installation and tire installation (setting and bolt-ing in both cases), which were physically demanding because of the weight of the components, high torque for bolting, and awkward work posture. This concept of assembly automation was significantly differ-ent from another type—off-line automation with visual sensing—that many Western and Japanese automakers adopted in the late 1980s and early 1990s (figure 7.3). In the latter cases (e.g., FIAT Cassino plant, Volkswagen Hall 54, Nissan Kyushu #2 plant, Toyota Tahara #4 line), automation zones equipped with large jigs, sophisticated robots, and electronic-vision sensing devices, are installed separately from con-veyer lines, and bodies are stopped for accurate alignment.

Compared with the off-line type, the in-line mechanical automa-tion tried to reduce negative impacts or side effects of assembly au-tomation, rather than making the operations more sophisticated. The negative side of existing off-line automation includes the following:[15]

- Large automation equipment tends to interfere with the man-ual assembly area and disrupt the teamwork there.
- Assembly automation in separate areas tends to create "resid-ual work," which is monotonous and meaningless to workers in such areas.[16]
- Highly sophisticated equipment tends to become a black box from the direct workers' point of view. The job of teaching,

operation, and maintenance of such equipment is usually done by maintenance workers and engineers.

- As complete automation tends to alienate human employees, continuous improvements in the process become difficult to attain.
- Off-line automation usually needs a large extra space for jigs and robots, as well as buffer stations before and after the process.
- Large automation equipment tends not to be flexible enough to model changes.

But by alleviating such side effects, in-line mechanical automation for assembly lines reduced manufacturing cost by saving depreciation cost, decreased machine down time, and promoted continuous improvements (*kaizen*) by workers. It also tried to improve employee satisfaction by letting workers control and maintain the equipment as much as possible, promoting a sense of ownership among them and keeping the assembly process visible from the workers' point of view. In short, in-line mechanical automation, just like the autonomous complete line concept mentioned above, attempted to balance employee satisfaction and customer satisfaction.

An Ergonomics Evaluation System: Toyota Verification of Assembly Line. TVAL is an indicator that measures the workload of each assembly job quantitatively. Based on existing physiological studies, the TVAL score was initially defined as follows:[17]

$$TVAL = 25.51 \log (t) + 117.6 \log \{f(K, W)\} - 162.0$$
$$\text{where} \qquad t = \text{task duration time}$$
$$K = \text{work posture}$$
$$W = \text{weight of parts/tools}$$

Based on some experiments, Toyota developed a table for calculation of $f(K, W)$. Using this table, Toyota measured the TVAL score of all final assembly jobs at the company.

TVAL was developed by the Assembly Process Engineering Division to help the company make the assembly work friendly to all kinds of people regardless of age, sex, and other differences. By using TVAL, assembly process planners could identify physically demanding jobs in an objective manner, prioritize the workstations to be improved, and concentrate efforts for improvements (e.g., automation, power assist devices, work design changes) on the workstations with high TVAL scores. Thus, TVAL was developed as a tool for improving physiological aspects of employee satisfaction, with the goal of making assembly jobs less demanding.

Low-Cost Equipment for Better Work Environment and Work Posture. In order to improve work environments in final assembly areas, Toyota introduced not only automation systems but also other means, usually less expensive ones. There were such tools and equipment designed for making manual assembly jobs physically less demanding and less dangerous. This category included the following examples:

- Height-adjustable conveyers or platforms with variable body lifting mechanisms for achieving the best work posture for assembly task.
- Wide floor conveyers that are synchronized with car bodies, so that workers do not have to walk while performing assembly tasks.
- Comfortable (*raku-raku*) seats that eliminate crouching work posture for assembly tasks inside cabins, which is physically demanding. Each in-cabin job is conducted by a worker sitting on a seat attached to an arm that can be reached inside the car body. An alternative way to reduce crouching work posture is certain work design changes that shift in-cabin tasks to those performed outside the car bodies.
- Wagon carts synchronized with car bodies, which carry parts and tools. This reduces walking distance for each worker. Another way of reducing walking distance is the doorless assembly method, in which doors are detached at the beginning of the final assembly line and reattached at the end of the line.
- Simple power-assist equipment that reduces the weight of the tools and components that workers carry.
- Easy-to-see job instruction sheets attached to the hoods of the car bodies. The instructions are printed out for each segment of the process, so that each sheet is simpler and easier to understand.
- Better lighting, air conditioning, low-noise power tools, low-noise roller-friction conveyers, and other equipment for improving the work environment.

Functionally, these devices and changes were mostly aimed at making assembly work physically less demanding (i.e., achieving low TVAL scores) rather than increasing productivity. Some of them needed basic process design changes (e.g., choice of conveyer types, doorless methods), while others could be implemented through regular *kaizen* activities (e.g., *raku-raku* seats, wagon carts, power assist). Generally speaking, they were aimed at improving work conditions with reasonably low equipment cost.

Support for HRM Policies. While various modifications of this company's human resource management were observed during this period, let's focus on two relatively major ones:

- *Continuous two-shift.* This new shift pattern, in which a day shift and a night shift are conducted back to back so that the second shift ends at midnight, was introduced in Toyota's assembly plants in 1995.[18] Compared to the complete day and night shift that Toyota had used previously, continuous two-shift enabled female workers to work on two shift assembly lines on a rotation basis (midnight work by female workers was still banned by the Japanese labor law, as of the mid-1990s, with the original intention of protecting them), and made assembly work more friendly to aged workers. But it also reduced flexibility in production expansion through overtime and made maintenance work more challenging.

• *Formal career planning for skill formation.* Although multiskilled workers were at the core of Toyota's manufacturing capability, there had been no formal system of career planning for individual employees in the manufacturing area. In order to give employees a better sense of individual growth and clearer goals for individual skill building, Toyota introduced a formal system for certifying skill levels in the early 1990s: an expert skill certificate system for team leaders (EX), group leaders (SX) and assistant managers (CX); and "work life plans" for production employees in general. The latter awards workers and leaders certain certificates starting from C and moving up to B, A, and S, according to the variety of skills that have been acquired.[19]

The Historical Process Behind Toyota's New Assembly System

The foregoing functional analysis of Toyota's new assembly system specifically makes it appear to be a rational response to changes in various environments. However, such ex-post rational explanations of a given system do not necessarily mean that the entire system was built by ex-ante rational decision making. It may be a result of certain trial-and-error processes, pure luck, or, most important, the learning capability of the firm. In order to assess whether Toyota's evolutionary learning capability still remained in the early 1990s, we have to analyze how the new assembly system has emerged since the late 1980s. That means looking into historical and dynamic aspects of Toyota's assembly organization.

The Production Organization at Toyota

First, let us briefly describe various organizational subunits that are related to Toyota's decision making in manufacturing process designs as of the mid-1990s (figure 7.4). As mentioned above, I do not regard Toyota as a monolithic decision-making unit, but analyze it as a collection of subunits with different skills, missions, and cultures, whose perceptions of the environment and evaluations of alternatives need to be coordinated.

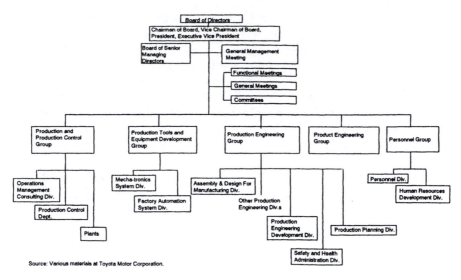

Source: Various materials at Toyota Motor Corporation.

Figure 7.4 Production Organization at Toyota Motor Corporation (1994)

Assembly and Design for Manufacturing Engineering Division (Sharyo Seigi-bu). At the time of this study, the production engineering (*seisan gijutsu*) group consisted of about ten process-specific engineering divisions, each of which specialized in a certain process, including assembly, welding, stamping, machining, and foundry, as well as the Production Engineering Development Division (which is in charge of advanced production engineering), and Safety & Health Administration Division. Assembly process engineers used to be organized as the Assembly Process Engineering Division. They tended to be regarded as "conveyer specialists" but had not taken enough initiative for assembly process designs. As one assembly engineer admits, final assembly was a process in which shop floor experiences were recognized as more important inputs than engineering expertise in process designs, unlike machining or forming. Managers and leaders on the shop floor tended to dominate assembly process design as a cumulative result of day-to-day *kaizen*.

In the early 1990s, however, an effort was begun to make the final assembly process design "real engineering." Accordingly, the Assembly Process Engineering Division was strengthened both quantitatively and qualitatively. The number of assembly engineers in this division was doubled; process engineers from other production divisions (e.g., equipment development, die development, machining, welding, and electronics process engineering), as well as plant general managers, were added.

In 1994, the Assembly Process Engineering Division was restructured, becoming the Assembly and Design for Manufacturing Engineering Division, or Sharyo Seigi-bu (literally Vehicle Production Engineering Division; since the latter name better represents its activity, I call it VPE division henceforth). With this reorganization, the mission of the division was also changed from that of simple assembly process engineering to integration of all production engineering divisions from the total vehicle's point of view. Also, a new position, vehicle production engineering (VPE) manager (*shusa*), was set up. Each of the VPE managers was in charge of a particular model and worked closely with the product manager of the model on the product engineering side, coordinating requests from various production engineering divisions. Each VPE manager, as a representative from the process engineering group, proposed a VPE manager vision to the product manager. In the past, each production engineering division coordinated with the corresponding product engineering division (e.g., body production engineering division versus body product engineering division), but the product-process coordination from the total vehicle point of view was not as active as expected. The new VPE division tried to improve this interface by assuming dual roles of specialist in assembly process engineering and integrator of the process engineering divisions.

As assembly process specialists, some managers in the VPE division insist that they are committed to process optimization rather than equipment technologies. That is, in planning and designing assembly lines, the VPE engineers tend to start by optimizing process designs and then move on to selecting and designing automated equipment. Equipment is regarded simply as a means to achieve process optimization. They evaluate the assembly lines in terms of the efficiency of the entire process, as opposed to the advancement of equipment technologies or automation ratios per se.

Mechatronics Systems Division (formerly #1 Machine Making Division). Separate from production engineering divisions (since 1990), there is a production tools and equipment development group, which consists of a Mechatronics Systems Division and Factory Automation (FA) System Division. They are in charge of developing and constructing production equipment and FA systems. As discussed later, the Mechatronics Systems Division (formerly called #1 Machine Making Division) played an important role in designing and developing in-house equipment in Toyota's early assembly automation experiments. Reflecting its central mission as an in-house equipment supplier, the Mechatronics Systems Division is more equipment-oriented than the VPE division, which is more process-oriented. In other words, the approach of the Mechatronics Systems Division to assembly automation was "technology push" rather than "demand pull."

Operations Management Consulting Division (Seisan Chosa-bu). This division is an organizational unit unique to Toyota. Established in

1970 by Taiichi Ohno as a staff office in the Production Control Division, the Operations Management Consulting Office (Seisan Chosashitsu) has been in charge of maintaining, diffusing, and educating employees about the Toyota production system (TPS) both inside Toyota and at Toyota Group parts suppliers. It became an independent division subsequently. Whereas members of the process engineering divisions, as well as plant engineers, are specialists in each process technology, the Operations Management Consulting Division is in charge of generic TPS principles that are commonly applied across different processes and plants. Also, while production engineers take charge of the planning and construction of new or renovated plants, this division is in charge of practical improvements after production starts.

Its current mission can be broken down as follows: educating people about the Toyota production system; implementing TPS principles on the shop floor in collaboration with TPS instructors (*shusa*) who belong to each plant; participating in "voluntary problem-solving studies" (*jishu-ken*) by the plants; and helping factories and suppliers solve problems when the division is requested and/or approved by Toyota's production executives to do so. As for education, there is a rotation arrangement by which plant engineers and production engineers are dispatched to the Operations Management Consulting Division for a few years. The division is strengthening TPS education to production engineers in recent years.

Because of its history, members of this division are generally thought of as Ohno's disciples, guardians of the TPS concept, or auditors of production processes from the TPS point of view, although they do not have official line authority over the plants. In any case, in accordance with the TPS concept, the Operations Management Consulting Division staff tend to be customer oriented and emphasize cost reduction for the purpose of customer satisfaction.

Production Control Division (Seisan Kanri-bu). This division is in charge of product allocation among the plants, as well as making production plans for levelization (*heijun-ka*) and assuring logistics to achieve such plans. Production Control, Production (plants), and Operations Management Consulting have been grouped together in Toyota's organizational charts since 1991, indicating their close relationships. The Production Control Division does not have direct influence on the design and construction process of assembly plants, though.

Assembly Plant. There are several domestic assembly plants at Toyota. Toyota's assembly plants are headed by plant general managers, who are often directors in manufacturing. There is an assembly division head for each plant, below whom are section heads (*ka-cho*), assistant managers (general group leaders; *ko-cho*), a group leader (*kumi-cho*), a team leader (*han-cho*), and team members (workers), as figure 7.5 shows. The first-line supervisors up to assistant manager are union

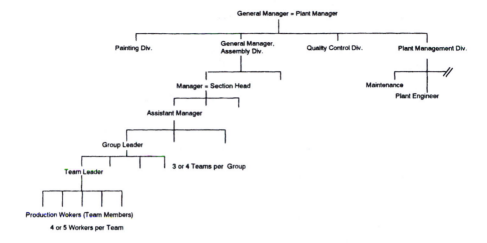

Figure 7.5 Plant Organization at Toyota Motor Corporation

members. The Maintenance Section and Quality Control Division, as well as the Plant Engineer Office and other administrative staff functions, are separate from the line organization. Consider the following selected functions and positions related to final assembly lines:

• *Production worker (team member).* There are typically several hundred workers in one assembly line, who rotate between day and night shifts. In the two-shift rotation process, workers at Toyota have been almost exclusively male, partly because of the labor law constraints prohibiting female midnight work. The average age of assembly workers (at Toyota's Motomachi Plant) is about thirty-six, or two to six years younger than that of other production processes. Before the labor shortage around 1990, annual turnover ratios for production workers were generally low (around 5 percent), but those for first-year rookies (mostly high school graduates) tended to be much higher (often over 10 percent). The ratio of temporary workers has been at most about 10 percent in recent years. Both turnover ratios and temporary worker ratio increased significantly at the peak of the bubble economy, reflecting the labor shortage and changes in young people's expectations about work. Permanent employees are trained (both on the job and off the job) to become part of a multiskilled workforce.

• *Team leader.* In assembly lines, the team leader (*han-cho*) is normally the head of a team of about five members. They are union members and essentially "playing managers" as on a baseball team, who function as relief workers who can replace absent team members, deal with line stops and other troubles, take initiative in *kaizen* activities, and do certain administrative jobs.

- *Group leader and assistant manager.* Called *kumi-cho* or *shoku-cho*, a group leader in final assembly is typically head of a group of twenty workers, or four teams. Group leaders are the lowest ranked as full-time supervisors and don't do direct assembly work. They report to assistant managers (*ko-cho*), each of whom is in charge of a few groups. Group leaders and assistant managers are regarded as playing pivotal roles on the shop floor in day-to-day supervision, troubleshooting, revisions of standard operating procedures, coordinating *kaizen* activities, and so on. Their performance is evaluated in terms of the efficiency, quality, and other records of their respective groups.[20]

- *Maintenance.* The maintenance organization has been centralized as a separate section at each plant, but there is a tendency (e.g., at the Toyota Kyushu plant) to decentralize it at the process level (e.g., press, welding, assembly). Maintenance people used to be in charge of maintenance and operation of automated equipment, but now direct line workers are trained to handle minor fixes and preventive maintenance on their own equipment under the total productive maintenance (TPM) arrangement. In this way, the maintenance function and direct workers have become increasingly integrated in recent years.

- *Plant engineer.* There is a Plant Engineer Office (*gijutsu-in shitu*) at each plant. Plant engineers are in charge of major improvements and major maintenance of production equipment.

- *TPS shusa.* TPS instructors (*shusa*) are stationed at each plant. They make sure that the principles of the Toyota production system are implemented properly, in close collaboration with the Operations Management Consulting Division.

Personnel Division/Human Resource Development Division.   There are two personnel-related divisions at Toyota: the Human Resource Division (Jinji-bu) and Human Resource Development Division (Jinzai Kaihatsu-bu). The latter is in charge of recruitment, education, and performance appraisal, whereas the former deals with labor relations and other communications inside the company, including that between management and employees, management and the union, employees and the union, as well as supervisors and subordinates. Communication is regarded as critical for maintaining and improving employee satisfaction, as well as active organizational cultures.

Labor Union.   Toyota's labor union (*Toyota roso*) has developed and maintained cooperative relationships with management since the 1950s, when there was a series of large strikes.[21] The union maintains regular communication with its members and management. It tries to listen to the many voices of its members, including team leaders and group leaders, articulate them, and make concrete requests through quarterly labor-management meetings (*roshi kyogi*), as well as other submeetings. Such meetings are held at not only the company level but also at the plant level.

Once an agreement is reached on new policies or systems (e.g., introduction of the continuous two-shift), union and management, through their respective channels, try to persuade shop floor people to accept the new proposal. The key people in this situation are first-line supervisors (team leaders, group leaders, and assistant managers), who are at the bottom of the management hierarchy, members of the union, and opinion leaders of the shop floor organizations at the same time. At Toyota, a new policy is generally not implemented until a consensus is built in the shop floor organizations, even when union leaders and management both agree with it.

Product Engineering. Product engineers are not directly involved in the production process design, but they coordinate with production functions through simultaneous engineering and design for manufacturability. In recent years, product engineers and production engineers have also conducted joint reverse engineering of competing products, which serves as an important opportunity for mutual understanding between both groups.

Directors from Production Engineering. Finally, there are the executives in the production area. Toyota in recent years has appointed a disproportionate number of top executives (director level or above) from the production engineering area, which indicates that the company recognizes production engineering as a key function. Those directors are often nominated to be heads of assembly plants at the same time.

In addition to the top-level executives in charge of production (e.g., Toshimi Onishi, executive vice president as of 1995), several people at the director (*torishimari-yaku*) to senior managing director level (*jomu or senmu torishimari-yaku*), as of the mid-1990s, have significantly influenced the evolution of Toyota's new assembly system, including Akira Takahashi (former Motomachi and Tahara plant general manager), Tadaaki Jagawa (Tahara plant general manager), Mikio Kitano (former Motomachi plant general manager, currently heading TMM), and Kosuke Shiramizu (former Tahara Assembly Division head). They all came from the production engineering area and were appointed as head of one or more of Toyota's newer (or renovated) assembly plants. Overall, over half of the recent assembly plant general managers came from the production engineering group (the rest being from plant operations) in recent years (figure 7.6). As for the Toyota Kyushu plant, Kiyotoshi Kato, head of the plant as of 1995, was former head of the Assembly Division at the Motomachi plant.

When I interviewed these executives, I found that they tended to have unique individual characters and ideas, but still shared a basic

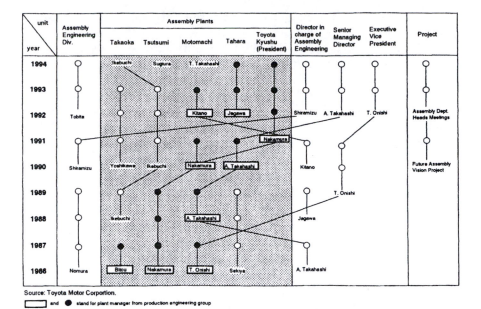

Source: Toyota Motor Corportion.

☐ and ● stand for plant manager from production engineering group

Figure 7.6 The Heads of Assembly Plants from Production Engineering

understanding of Toyota's core capabilities and philosophies in manufacturing (*mono-zukiri*). I will return to this point later.

A History of Toyota's Assembly Process Concept

Having described the main actors in this evolutionary process, I turn
to a history of Toyota's assembly system in the late 1980s and the early
1990s (see figure 7.7). The main opportunity for experimenting with
and adopting new assembly concepts comes, naturally, with the new
construction or renovation of assembly plants. Most of Toyota's assembly plants were built in the 1960s to 1970s.[22] In the 1980s, most
new construction and renovation of major assembly plants occurred
outside Japan: NUMMI (U.S.; joint venture with GM; renovation,
1984), TMM (U.S.; new, 1988), and TMMC (Canada; new, 1988),
reflecting trade frictions and the yen's appreciation. The construction
of domestic assembly plants during the 1980s occurred only at
Tahara—the #2 plant (1981) and #3 plant (1985).

In the 1990s, though, another wave of assembly plant constructions and renovations began, both in Japan and overseas. This generation includes new domestic plants with new assembly concepts
(Tahara #4, 1991; Toyota Kyushu, 1992), new overseas plants (TMUK
in the U.K., 1992; TMM #2 in the U.S., 1994; TMCA in Australia,
1994), and renovations of domestic plants (new Motomachi #2,

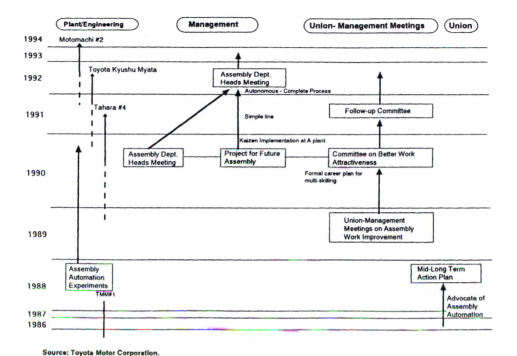

Source: Toyota Motor Corporation.

Figure 7.7 Steps Toward the New Assembly Concept (Toyota and Toyota Union)

1994). There were further plans for new overseas plants and domestic renovations as of the late 1990s. It is said inside Toyota that, as the number of assembly plant constructions and renovations has increased, so has the relative power and influence of the production engineering group.

In the case of new construction, it normally takes Toyota a few years from basic plant planning (e.g., layout) to conveyer design, conveyer installation, equipment installation, overall tryout, pilot runs 1 and 2, and plant startup.[23] Basic plant planning takes roughly half a year. The lead time is significantly shorter in the case of major model changes at existing plants. Note also that conveyer installation always precedes equipment installation.

Plan and construction of an overseas plant takes a half to a whole year longer than a domestic plant, on the other hand. The planning and fabrication of major equipment are done in Japan up to the first pilot run, then the equipment is shipped to the overseas construction site, where equipment installation, a second pilot run, quality confirmation, and startup are conducted. Because of this time lag, for example, basic plans for the Tahara #4 plant (1991) and TMUK (Toyota's British manufacturing subsidiary; 1992) were in fact made almost at the same time, as were those for Toyota Kyushu (1992) and U.S. TMM #2 (1994).

TMM: Transplants in America (1988).   Toyota Motor Manufacturing USA Inc. (TMM) is Toyota's first full-scale, wholly owned assembly plant in the United States. Plant construction in Kentucky was announced in 1985, and production of the Camry started in July 1988. The basic plant design of TMM replicated that of Tsutsumi, its mother. plant in Japan that also produced the Camry, in order to make the training process of TMM's maintenance and assembly workers efficient. Since Toyota's new assembly concept discussed earlier began to emerge only after 1988, it is clear that the basic design of TMM #1 plant was still along the lines of traditional Toyota plants. Toyota's tradition of combining paint and final assembly areas in one building was also replicated.[24]

But there was something new in TMM's plant layout, because the plant was located in the United States. Since both U.S. parts and Japanese parts were purchased, the final assembly building was designed such that U.S. parts came from the north end, while Japanese parts came from south end of the building. The interface between the two receiving docks and the assembly line was designed to be long for better logistics of in-coming parts from the docks to the line side. As a result, the shape of the final assembly area became closer to a square, compared to Toyota's traditional layout. Accordingly, the main assembly line was broken down into eight segments running back and forth (three trim, three chassis, and two final line segments, excluding the inspection line and the door subline). It was 1.3 times as long as that of Tsutsumi.

These eight segments were linked by buffer zones. Thus, the physical aspect of the autonomous complete line (i.e., many short segments with buffer zones) was already there. Unlike the subsequent assembly lines, however, this physical layout was not linked to the spirit of the autonomous complete assembly process. TMM's final assembly layout was driven mainly by the parts logistics mentioned above. Also, buffer zones were used subsequently for reducing overall down time, but the autonomy of each group was not recognized as a benefit of such buffers.

Experiments of Off-Line High-Tech Assembly Automation (1989–92).
It was 1988 when Toyota started to consider experiments of advanced assembly automation technologies. One of the major motivations was completion of Volkswagen's new Hall 54 assembly plant, which soon became famous for its ambitious assembly automation concept.[25] Stimulated by the new wave of assembly automation in Europe, some of the Japanese news media launched campaigns advocating the future potential of assembly automation technologies. Encouraged also by

the bubble economy, some other Japanese automakers announced construction of highly automated assembly plants (Nissan Kyushu #2, Mazda Hofu #2, Honda Suzuka #3).

Facing such pressures from outside for promoting assembly automation technologies, in 1989 Toyota's managers decided to start experimental development of assembly automation equipment. The #1 Machine Making Division (now called the Mechatronics Systems Division) took charge of developing an experimental assembly automation line, which eventually consisted of about thirty automated stations, in a research building of the production engineering group. The experiments alone cost Toyota millions of dollars. If realized fully at a commercial plant, the line would have achieved a higher assembly automation ratio than Volkswagen's Hall 54, one of the world's highest.

The equipment development engineers at #1 Machine Making Division predicted that the effective assembly technologies would need corresponding changes in vehicle architecture (e.g., modularization of the product design) and assembly process configuration, which was the case with Volkswagen and FIAT. They approached the product engineers and assembly process engineers and asked about this possibility, but no clear answers came back. Therefore, the equipment engineers at #1 Machine Making Division decided not to wait for the architectural changes on the product-process side and went ahead and developed experimental automation equipment, in the hope that such changes would occur in the future. Thus, the motivation for the experiment was essentially a technology push. With this policy, various element technologies for assembly automation, including installation or bolting of the engine/transmission, tires, front window, and instrument panel, as well as detachment of doors, were developed during the first phase of the experiment and received rather favorable feedback from Toyota's management.

The second phase of the experiment, which got another management review in 1991, targeted the practical application of the equipment to a commercial-scale assembly line at plant A's assembly line in 1992.[26] However, the engineers of the automation experiments could not persuade the product engineers of the Corona model to design the vehicle structures for effective assembly automation: only one-tenth of the design change proposals by the former were approved by the latter. In addition, the process layout of plant A, designed for manual assembly only, did not fit assembly automation. After all, part of the automated equipment developed in this experiment was installed at plant A's assembly line in 1992, but was subsequently modified based on Toyota's new assembly automation concept by the mid-1990s.[27]

The second experiment revealed some problems with the assembly automation concept of those days. The equipment tended to be too large to install on existing assembly lines; assembly automation had to be done off-line, or outside the manual conveyer line; workers tended to be alienated from the off-line automation processes, making their *kaizen* activities impossible; the automation system tended to be too expensive to be cost-competitive; and product costs were expected to increase if the product architecture was modified to facilitate this type of assembly automation. Nevertheless, refined versions of the equipment developed in this experiment were selectively incorporated into the subsequent plant construction and renovation, such as the Toyota Kyushu and Motomachi plants.

Tahara #4 Assembly Line: Implementation of Assembly Automation (1991). The basic layout of the Tahara #4 plant was developed at the end of 1989, and production started in 1991. Because of the timing of plant planning (the peak of the bubble economy, with labor shortages in Japan, and assembly automation in Europe), Tahara #4 line aimed at (1) reduction in the number of workers necessary for a given production process through automation, (2) increase in work attractiveness by reducing workload, and (3) exploration of technological frontiers in assembly automation. As for the third point, some production engineers admit that there was a desire to show off the capabilities of Toyota's production engineering by building a showcase factory; budget constraints were not emphasized there. Considering the timing, it is also likely that its plant design was influenced at least partially by the assembly automation experiments Toyota conducted between 1988 and 1991.

Tahara #4 adopted a main assembly-line layout that consisted of eight segments (excluding subassembly lines and inspection lines).[28] There were already buffer zones between the segments at Tahara #4. This is physically similar to the layout of TMM (Kentucky), which also has eight segments, but the motivation for the multiple-segment layout was different: While TMM's multiple-segment layout was based mainly on component logistics, the off-line assembly automation drove Tahara's assembly-line segmentation, as manual assembly segments and automated segments had to be physically separated with buffers for off-line automation.[29] At the same time, it should be noted that early and partial trials of the autonomous complete assembly at Tahara #4 had already been conducted. The concept was not fully articulated at this point, however.

It is true that automated equipment following the concept of the experimental line was introduced in engine-transmission-suspension installation (so-called decking) and tire bolting. But the Tahara #4 line adopted the results of the automation experiment line rather selectively: Tahara decided not to automate door disassembly, for example, which the experimental line had automated. The plant did automate air conditioner units, batteries, instrument panels, and windshields, but its method of automation was different from that adopted in the off-line assembly automation experiments.

In any case, the Tahara #4 plant became a symbol of Toyota's new-generation factories, emphasizing employee satisfaction and advanced automation technologies when it started production in 1991. After the bubble era ended, however, the plant was criticized for its high capital investment cost, which was a high fixed-cost burden for Toyota.

Labor Union Initiatives and the Committee for Improving Attractiveness of Production Work (1988–1992). The union side had already recognized the assembly problems by the time when it announced its Mid-Long-Term Action Plan (Chu-choki Katsudo Hoshin) in October 1988. The action plan endorsed the following policies: (1) reducing annual labor hours; (2) strengthening functions of various union-management meetings; (3) promoting stable shop floor units that can respond flexibly to demand fluctuation; (4) programs that address the issue of aging labor force; (5) programs in response to the introduction of microelectronics technologies on the shop floor; (6) programs in response to internationalization of business; (7) other programs that address the mental health care problems, improvement of work environments, and so on. Although policies 3, 4, and 5 were all potentially related to the assembly problem, it was not featured as a central issue in the plan.[30]

At the level of detailed programs, however, the union had already been an advocate (not an opponent) of assembly automation. Under policy 3, assembly automation was recognized as a means to alleviate the labor shortage problem, which the union had already predicted then, and thus to respond to the upswing of production volume. The union had aimed at 20 percent assembly automaton ratio by 1993 (which was not realized) and 30 percent ultimately (which is unlikely throughout the 1990s).

Following this plan, a union-management meeting (*roshi kondankai*) on manufacturing issues was held in April 1989. The main agenda items were: (1) short-term measures to cope with production expansion (hiring and subcontracting); (2) long-term mission of making the workplace more attractive; (3) improvement of the assembly process in terms of workload, work posture, job attractiveness, and aged workers; (4) interplant transfer of workers. At this point, the assembly problem emerged as one of the central issues.

Between December 1989 and May 1990, three additional meetings on assembly work improvement were held between the union and management. The agendas proposed by the union included setting appropriate standard time and evaluation criteria; the possibility of assembly automation; interplant transfer of workers which destabilizes shop organizations; the demanding nature of assembly work; and pressures on team leaders and group leaders owing to "firefighting" on the shop floor. Management promised to improve on the above issues.

Management became more actively involved in the job attractiveness issue by the spring of 1990. Toyota chose "Creating an Attractive

Workplace" as an annual slogan for the company in 1990, and proposed a joint union-management Committee for Improving Attractiveness of Production Work in May 1990. The committee held seven meetings (June 1990–June 1991) and five follow-up meetings (July 1991–August 1992). Improvements in the production work environment, as well as desirable assembly process design, were discussed. In 1991, Toyota articulated an implementation plan for improving direct production work, including air conditioning, dirty jobs, dust, noise, and physically demanding jobs.

Project for Future Assembly Plants and Plant A's Experiments (1990– 1991). Parallel with the union-management discussions, plant managers and production engineers started to articulate their visions and action plans for better assembly processes. In the summer of 1990, the Project for Future Assembly Plants was initiated, under supervision of a high-level executive in manufacturing. One of plant A's trim lines was chosen as a model process, where certain experiments were made. Plant A's Assembly Division, Assembly Process Engineering Division, Operations Management Consulting Office, Production Control Division, and Human Resource Division were involved in the project.

Reflecting the environment of the bubble economy, the project addressed three background problems: labor shortages, stricter quality requirements, and the impact of product proliferation (complexity) on assembly lines. The proposed solutions included improvements in shop floor organizations (e.g., strengthening functions of team leaders, group leaders, and assistant managers), as well as improvements in assembly processes and work designs (e.g., simplification of job instructions, human friendly-work design).

The project continued until the end of 1991. Experiments at plant A's assembly line resulted in proposals on the new assembly concept aimed at simpler and more rhythmic job designs, and better work environment (lighting, noise, ergonomics, and so on). The concept of an autonomous complete assembly line was not the main issue in this experiment at plant A, though. It was discussed in another subgroup of the Project for Future Assembly Plants.

Overall, the Project for Future Assembly Plants was led mainly by the plant staff and plant engineers; the Assembly Process Engineering Division had not yet played an active role. And the results of plant A's experiments did not lead directly to the core concepts of the new assembly system at Kyushu (e.g., autonomous complete assembly and in-line mechanical automation).

Assembly Division Head Meetings (1992). Assembly-related division head meetings (*kumitate bucho kaigi*) were also being held in close collaboration with the Project for Future Assembly Plants. By 1992, these division head meetings, which continued after the Project for

Future Assembly Plants was over, were the main arena in which the autonomous complete assembly concept (*jiritsu kanketsu kotei*) was finally articulated at the company-wide level. At this stage, unlike the previous project, the Assembly Process Engineering Division, which had been significantly strengthened by then, played a leading role in developing the new assembly concept.

The Motomachi plant also played a key role in shaping this concept. There is some evidence that Motomachi, under supervision of Director Akira Takahashi, had already tried a partial prototype of complete process designs on one of its assembly lines in the late 1980s, where the line was not separated into short line segments, but job assignments and process sequence were oriented to parts-complete jobs for each worker, if not functionally complete ones at the group level.

Toyota Kyushu: Establishment of the New Assembly Concept (1992). The Toyota Kyushu plant, which started production of the Mark II series in December 1992, introduced as a package (1) the autonomous complete assembly process; (2) in-line mechanical automation for assembly; (3) TVAL (systematic measurement of work load); and (4) various tools and equipment for better work conditions.

In a sense, the lessons from the Tahara #4 plant fully reflected the design of the Kyushu plant by assembly process engineers.[31] There was obviously knowledge transfer from Tahara to Kyushu. Also, considering the timing of the plant startup, and the fact that Motomachi (the former assembler of Mark II) was the mother plant of Toyota Kyushu, it is likely that the idea of parts-complete job designs, an element of the subsequent autonomous complete assembly concept, was transferred from the Motomachi plant.[32]

As for physical plant layout, Toyota Kyushu succeeded the recent trend since TMM and Tahara #4, with eleven line segments (three trim, two chassis, and six final and assembly inspection, excluding final inspection and subassembly lines) and buffer areas in between.[33] The building was separated from the paint shop, and its shape became closer to square, so that parts from the Tokai area (the central part of Japan's main island) and those from Kyushu are received from opposite sides of the building (the TMM method). A functionally related set of tasks was concentrated in each line segment, and one group (about twenty workers) and one group leader corresponded to each segment for each shift. The continuous two-shift was introduced for the first time at Toyota group factories (October 1993).

As for automation, the experiences at the Tahara #4 line, both positive and negative, helped the assembly process engineers establish the in-line automation concept, which is also consistent with the philosophy behind the autonomous complete process (see table 7.2 for a comparison of the assembly automation equipment of Tahara #4 and

Table 7.2 Comparison of Automation at Tahara #4 and Toyota Kyushu

Process	Tahara #4	Kyushu Miyata
Engine mount	Robot	In-line mechanical automation
Fuel tank	Robot	Robot
Tire	Robot	In-line mechanical automation
Windshield	Robot	Robot
Rearshield	Robot	Robot
Front seat	Robot	Robot
Battery	Robot	In-line mechanical automation
Air conditioner	Robot	Robot

Source: Toyota Motor Corporation.

Toyota Kyushu). Experiments for in-line assembly automation were conducted at the same facility as used for the off-line assembly automation experiment mentioned before. Unlike the previous experiment, which was assigned to the #1 Machine Making Division as more or less a showcase model line, the in-line mechanical automation experiments were conducted by the Assembly Process Engineering Division in a piecemeal manner. The equipment pieces tested experimentally was introduced to Kyushu one after another.

Overall, the final assembly process design at the Toyota Kyushu plant can be seen as a synthesis of previous plants and experiments. Although Toyota Kyushu does not represent the ultimate form of Toyota's new assembly lines, it is certainly the first systematic outcome of its evolution.

Another important feature of the Kyushu plant is that the system introduced there took into account its transferability for plant renovations, as well as new plant constructions. As Toyota's domestic plants needed renovations, adaptability for such cases was much emphasized in the plant design of Toyota Kyushu.

TMM #2: Transferring the Concept Overseas (1994).   The Kyushu assembly concept was also partially transferred overseas, including the TMM's #2 line in Kentucky (1994) and TMCA's new plant in Australia (1994). TMM #2, whose basic planning started at almost the same time as Kyushu's, adopted the same new assembly system, but only selectively.[34] As for plant layout, TMM #2 was very similar to that of Kyushu: near square assembly building separate from paint shop; twelve line segments (three trim, five chassis, four final) with buffer areas in between. It did not adopt most of the in-line automation equipment that Kyushu introduced, although space for future automation has already been prepared. The major reason for this decision, according to TMM's plant coordinators, besides the constraints of capital equipment spending, was insufficient capability of TMM's maintenance people, which would result in more down time than in the case of Toyota's assembly plants in Japan. When their capability increases to a sufficient level, it would consider the introduction of more assembly automation.

The function of the assembly-line layout was also different from Kyushu's. First, although the line segments corresponded to work groups, the capabilities of TMM's group leaders had not fully developed as of the mid-1990s, so that TMM could not exploit the full potential of the multisegment layout for higher group autonomy, according to Mikio Kitano, president of TMM as of 1995. Thus, the first thing to do was to develop the capabilities and attitudes of the leaders for self-management of their groups.

Motomachi #2 Assembly Line: Application to Existing Plants (1994).
Toyota Motomachi #2 plant (producing the RAV4), renovated in 1994, is the first case of Toyota's new assembly concept applied to a renovation of the existing assembly plant.[35] As for the autonomous complete concept, the Motomachi layout was less drastic than Kyushu's because the former had to use the existing building, which is long and attached to the paint shop: Toyota's traditional plant layout. Motomachi #2 line was separated into five segments (one trim, two chassis, and two final), each of which is longer and corresponds to two work groups, not one.

As for in-line mechanical automation, on the other hand, the new Motomachi line shows some incremental improvements compared to Kyushu. For example, jigs, pallets, and automated equipment for engine installation have become even simpler and more compact at Motomachi. There have also been some new applications of automation for better work posture (e.g., automated detachment of guide caps for tire installation).

Overall, the case of Motomachi shows an interesting combination of realistic approaches to cope with the constraints of renovations, as well as the continued evolution of the assembly technologies.

This pattern is likely to be observed repeatedly in Toyota's other as-sembly plants, which will be renovated one after another after the late 1990s.[36]

Analysis: Multi-Path Emergence of the New Assembly System

Having illustrated the historical events in chronological order, let's now analyze Toyota's patterns of organizational problem solving and learning. First we examine the process of problem recognition with re-gard to the labor issue, then move on to problem solving in terms of the generation and evaluation of alternative action plans in several components of the new system.

Gradual Recognition of the Assembly Problem

Because the changes in Toyota's labor environment during the late 1980s and early 1990s were rather subtle and equivocal, the company as a whole could recognize the assembly-line problem only gradually, and there were significant perception gaps among different parts of the organization during the transition period. As already described, the problem had been addressed initially by the union between 1988 and 1989; it became a central issue to be discussed between union and management by 1990; management started to increase its initia-tives on this issue by spring of 1990. Let's now reinterpret the forego-ing historical case as a process of gradual problem finding.

Problems related to job attractiveness and employee satisfaction in manufacturing, particularly on the assembly lines, seems to have been recognized first by the labor union in the late 1980s.[37] When the Toy-ota Motor Worker's Union announced its action plan in 1988, the re-duction of labor hours, new policies for aging workers, and absorption of excess labor demand were clearly depicted, but "attractiveness of work" was not explicitly pointed out. The quantitative aspect of the labor shortage was much emphasized, but the concept of assembly automation for better quality of the work environment had not been articulated.

The attractiveness of the company and its shop floor, particularly in the assembly process, was chosen as an agenda at the union-manage-ment meeting (roshi kondan-kai) on manufacturing issues in April 1989, which was presumably the first official meeting where the assembly-line problem (its attractiveness, work posture, and work-load) was explicitly addressed. In the subsequent union-management meetings on assembly work improvement, the main issue was still the quantitative labor shortage, but qualitative aspects of job attractive-ness became an increasingly important agenda item as their discus-sion deepened.

Toyota's management became actively involved in the job attractiveness issue by the spring of 1990, when it took the initiative in creating the joint Committee for Improving Attractiveness of Production Work. Then, it keenly recognized assembly problems between 1990 and 1991 because of the alarming results of opinion surveys the Human Resource Division had conducted biannually since the 1970s, as well as the turnover record. The job turnover rate jumped (particularly at the final assembly lines), and workers' subjective evaluations of job satisfaction and self-esteem dropped sharply.

Some plant managers were apparently recognizing the problem earlier. A former assembly division head, for example, says he recognized the problem when the number of temporary workers increased in the late 1980s. The relatively low morale of the young temporary workers at that time made him realize that the mind-set of the younger generation was changing and that the assembly process had to be changed accordingly. However, such concerns were not addressed as a critical company-wide issue at this point.

The early and qualitative information from the union, as well as subsequent quantitative data that the Human Resource Division collected, finally triggered a consensus-building process on the work attractiveness issue. Also, the Project for Future Assembly Plants may have functioned as the mechanism through which awareness of the assembly problem was diffused among different divisions. The assembly-related division head meeting was another means for coordinating and exchanging information among different divisions.[38]

Communication between the shop floor organization and the assembly process engineers was also strengthened in the early 1990s, facilitating diffusion of the knowledge from the shop floor to the engineering departments. In 1992, for example, core members (section heads) from the Assembly Process Engineering Division were dispatched to work on the assembly lines to gain direct experiences about workload and fatigue. This helped the process engineers acquire "gut" knowledge of the nature of assembly work, which was used subsequently for development of TVAL.

In summary, Toyota was by no means monolithic in this process of problem recognition. There were significant differences in the levels of problem awareness between the union and management, among the different organizational units, and among individuals throughout this transition period.

Diversified Evolutionary Paths to the Solutions

Let's move on to the stage at which solutions to the assembly problem were formed. As explained earlier in this chapter, Toyota eventually reached several solutions, or new production routines, all of which contributed to balanced improvements in employee satisfaction and customer satisfaction (*lean-on-balance system*), but patterns of the

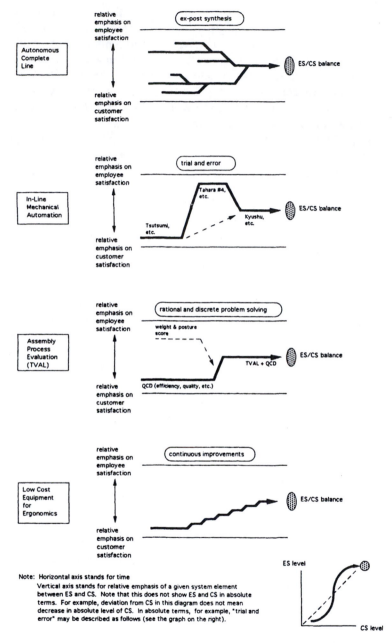

Figure 7.8 Types of Evolutionary Paths Toward ES/CS Balance

paths to such solutions were strikingly diversified. Figure 7.8 summarizes the different evolutionary paths for each element of Toyota's new assembly system: autonomous complete process, in-line automation, TVAL, and ergonomic devices.[39]

Autonomous Complete Process: Ex-post Synthesis. In the case of the autonomous process, the system concept emerged as the synthesis of various elements, each of which was developed for various reasons. Some of the elements were not developed as components of the autonomous system, but were reinterpreted and adopted after they were developed. In this sense, the evolution of the autonomous complete line appears to be ex-post synthesis (see figure 7.8). For example, TMM in Kentucky already had multisegment and buffered assembly lines, but they were developed apparently for logistical reasons, not as elements of the autonomous process. The Tahara #4 line was also multisegment with buffer areas, but the concept of an autonomous and complete assembly process was not linked to this layout (see figure 7.9).

In the Project for Future Assembly Plants, the short assembly-line concept had already been discussed and reported in the summer of 1990. The discussion was headed by Kosuke Shiramizu, head of the Assembly Process Engineering Division then. By the end of 1991, the "vision" project was completed. The complete assembly process had already been examined by that time, but it was not the main concept. Simplification of assembly jobs to absorb the many product variations seems to have been emphasized more.

As a part of the Project for Future Assembly Plants, plant A's model line highlighted simple job designs to cope with increasing product variety and complexity, and it addressed the issue of group leaders and team leaders—but did not articulate the autonomy complete concept, either. The Motomachi experiment in the late 1980s did address the issue of a complete job for each component at the level of individual workers, but it did not articulate the autonomous assembly-line concept at the work group level.[40] The Motomachi trial was made on conventional assembly lines.

By the summer of 1992, the concept of a complete assembly process, as well as its main functions (morale, self-actualization, quality improvement), was articulated in the assembly-related division head meetings, as well as the plant design process for Toyota Kyushu by the Assembly Process Engineering Division. For example, the name "complete assembly line" appeared for the first time in a union document in August 1992, in which management responded that a complete line had been discussed at the assembly-related division head meetings.[41]

It was the Toyota Kyushu plant, in December 1992, that finally combined the physical, functional, and organizational elements of the new system and crystallized them as the autonomous complete as-

Takaoka #1

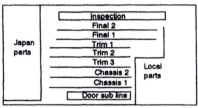

Parts	Trim 1
	Trim 2
	Inspection
	Final
	Chassis

| Engine sub line | Seat sub line |

Parts are supplied from only left side.

TMM #1

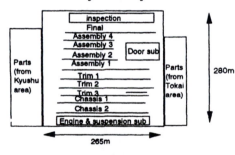

Japan parts	Inspection
	Final 2
	Final 1
	Trim 1
	Trim 2
	Trim 3
	Chassis 2	Local parts
	Chassis 1
	Door sub line

Parts are supplied from both sides.

Tahara #4

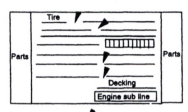

Tire

Parts ... Parts

Decking

Engine sub line

Lines are divided at ◤.
Parts are supplied from both sides.

Kyushu Miyata

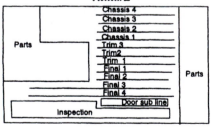

Parts (from Kyushu area)	Inspection
	Final
	Assembly 4
	Assembly 3
	Assembly 2	Door sub
	Assembly 1
	Trim 1	Parts (from Tokai area)
	Trim 2
	Trim 3
	Chassis 1
	Chassis 2
Engine & suspension sub

280m

265m

Motomachi #2 (old)

Trim	Chassis 1
Inspection	
Final 2	Chassis 2
Final 1	

Trim and Chassis 1 are connected.
There is the inspection process in the building.

↓

Motomachi #2 (new)

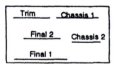

Trim	Chassis 1
Final 2	Chassis 2
Final 1	

Trim and Chassis 1 are divided.
Inspection process is in other building

TMM#2

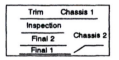

Parts	Chassis 4
	Chassis 3
	Chassis 2
	Chassis 1
	Trim 3
	Trim2
	Trim 1
	Final 1
	Final 2	Parts
	Final 3
	Final 4
	Door sub line
Inspection

Source: Interviews, bulletin of Toyota.
Note: The scale of the layouts is not consistent.

Figure 7.9 Evolution of Layouts at Toyota's Factories

sembly process. But there were many steps before the final synthesis occurred.

In-line Mechanical Assembly Automation: Trial and Error. The evolutionary pattern of in-line mechanical automation was very different. Unlike the cumulative synthesis observed in the autonomous line, this pattern is more dialectic (see figure 7.8). The trajectory started with Toyota's traditional low-cost automation concept, which did not give much attention to employee satisfaction itself. Then it swung to human-fitting off-line high-tech automation, which was a response to the employee satisfaction issue, but created a fixed-cost burden for the company.[42] Then there was another swing toward a better balance between customer satisfaction and employee satisfaction: in-line mechanical automation.

There were at least two different motivations for the previous off-line automation concept that was pursued in the assembly automation experiment, 1988 to 1991. First, there was production engineering's desire to develop and implement advanced technologies, stimulated by the European cases of FIAT and Volkswagen. Such a technology push may have been promoted by the engineering-driven culture of the tools and equipment development group (#1 Machine Making Division; now Mechatronics Systems Division), which naturally tends to be equipment oriented rather than process oriented.

The second major motivation for drastic assembly automation in the experiment of 1988 to 1991 was to absorb the excess labor demand that had been predicted then. In 1989, for example, Toyota predicted that it would need 6,000 more employees in the next five years, and that it would have to absorb half of this shortage by automation. Thus, the fear of labor shortage, by both management and the union, led to the idea of maximizing the automation ratio at any cost. Favorable financial conditions in the bubble era amplified this mood for maximizing automation. As production volume started to decrease and cash flow shrank, this motivation clearly became less important.

The assembly automation at the Tahara #4 line originated from at least three sources: rather small-scale assembly automation developed gradually by the Assembly Process Engineering Division (e.g., gas tanks, batteries, air conditioners); large-scale automation tested for the first time at the off-line automation experiment by #1 Machine Making Division (e.g., decking, tires); other sources, such as foreign automakers (e.g., windshield sealer). The second path tended to be emphasized, though.

As for assembly automation at Tahara #4, there are two different views, even among production engineers at Toyota. The first emphasizes the discontinuity between Tahara #4 and Toyota Kyushu, regards automation at Tahara #4 as a deviation from traditional Toyota philosophy, and sees the in-line mechanical automation at Kyushu as a return to the basics of Toyota's automation philosophy. The cases of engine installation and tire installation, gigantic off-line systems with expensive vision sensing for alignment are often cited as examples of the sharp difference between Tahara and Kyushu. Thus, the first view sees Tahara #4 as a "straw man," while highlighting the legitimacy of in-line mechanical automation.

The second view, by contrast, emphasizes continuity between Tahara and Kyushu, points out that Toyota constantly went through a trial-and-error process in developing its production systems in the past, sees the above case of engines and tires as just another example of such trial and error, and insists that the main stream of assembly process designs at Tahara was on an evolutionary track all along.

In a sense, the first view is a paradigm change hypothesis, while the second represents a belief in progressive evolution. Both camps, however, appreciate the value of assembly automation at the Tahara plant #4 as a precursor of in-line mechanical automation at Kyushu. Even those who criticized Tahara's automation concept usually admitted that Tahara's automation experiments enabled the new automation concept at Kyushu and Motomachi.

In any case, the lessons of off-line high-tech automation at Tahara #4 line, which had been clear by the spring of 1991, were fully taken into account in the basic design process of Toyota Kyushu's in-line automation by assembly process engineers. Note also that the experiments for in-line assembly automation were conducted by the Assembly Process Engineering Division, as opposed to the #1 Machine Making Division. This may reflect the shift from an equipment-oriented (technology push) approach to a process-oriented (demand pull) one for assembly automation at Toyota.

TVAL: Rational and Discrete Problem Solving. The case of TVAL shows a smooth pattern of ex-ante rational problem solving, however, rather than ex-post synthesis or dialectic trial and error (see figure 7.8). That is, TVAL was developed by engineers in the Assembly and Design for Manufacturing Engineering Division (VPE) in response to a clearly defined goal of developing a systematic tool for measuring workloads from a physiological or ergonomic point of view.[43] TVAL was also based partly on existing scientific knowledge in the academic community, partly on Toyota's existing measurement system (posture and weight scores), and partly on deliberate experiments that the engineers conducted. There may have been trial and error at the microscopic level, but TVAL was created basically through an ex-ante rational problem-solving cycle.

In a broader context, development of TVAL may be regarded as an evolutionary path of Toyota's systems for measuring and evaluating assembly processes and tasks. In the past, Toyota's evaluation criteria were concentrated almost exclusively in the domain of customer satisfaction—factors such as efficiency, quality, delivery, and flexibility, as well as their improvement. Advocates of the Toyota production system argued that it was human oriented, but this simply meant that the value of human activities can be enhanced by reducing non-value activities ("muda"). Thus, reducing "muda" almost automatically meant increasing productivity and human value at the same time, in the TPS tradition. There were no independent criteria that measured employee satisfaction or job attractiveness.

In the final assembly area, also, efficiency was the most important criterion for evaluating shop floor performance. There was an index that measured the workload for each task, called the work posture and weight score, developed by the Safety and Health Administration Division, but this was virtually a minimum standard from an illness point of view. In this regard, development of TVAL can be seen as the company's rational efforts to balance evaluation criteria for customer satisfaction with those for employee satisfaction in response to changes in the labor market.

Equipment for Better Work Posture: Continuous Improvements.   Recent human-friendly factories indicate that the framework for continuous and company-wide improvements, one of Toyota's traditional capabilities, can be directly applicable to tools and equipment for better work posture, better work environments, and lighter workload. Based on the objective evaluation of each job and each task by TVAL and other measures, workers, team leaders, group leaders, maintenance workers, plant engineers, and so on individually or collectively create or modify systems for better ergonomics on a continuous basis, just like Toyota's ordinary *kaizen* for quality and productivity.

For example, Toyota Kyushu, after production started in 1992, has made continuous improvements in this direction. In 1993, the plant started to introduce wagon carts, and solved an alignment problem at the tire automation equipment through *kaizen*; in 1994, it introduced four *raku-raku* seats, and increased the number of wagon carts that are designed mostly by the workers; in 1995, it adopted two-hour job rotations, and developed a tool for interior parts, both for ergonomic purposes. As a result of these and other efforts, the number of high workload jobs (TVAL score > 35 point) decreased gradually from 95 in 1993 to 89 in 1994, and to 85 in 1995.

In this way, low-cost tools for better ergonomics help the assembly shop floor achieve a better balance between customer satisfaction and employee satisfaction through a path of incremental improvements (see figure 7.8).

Path Variety and Functional Consistency

Based on this analysis, we can now identify different patterns of system evolution, which correspond to the four elements of the new Toyota assembly system: ex-post synthesis, trial and error, rational problem solving, and incremental improvements. This finding makes us infer that the new system was created through a multi-path emergent process, and that Toyota applied its evolutionary learning capability to this recent case. Consider the following three key points:

(1) *Variety in the evolutionary paths.* No single pattern can summarize the evolution of the new assembly system at Toyota. This diversity of evolutionary paths indicates that the dynamic process that created the new assembly system was a *multi-path system emergence* according to its definition in this book. This also implies that Toyota's distinctive dynamic capabilities do not lie in its specific way of controlling system changes: it is a more generic ability to harness various evolutionary patterns, including rational and discrete problem solving, continuous improvements, dialectic paths of trial and error, or more chaotic process of ex-post synthesis.

(2) *Consistency in ex-post rationality.* Despite the variety of evolutionary trajectories, the function of the resulting system seems to be quite consistent in that all the elements of the new assembly system are aimed at a better balance between customer satisfaction and employee satisfaction (the lean-on-balance system). Other Japanese firms tried various combinations of assembly automation and work organization, but as of the mid-1990s Toyota appears to be the only firm that has articulated (if not perfected) a systematic and consistent solution to the problems of the early 1990s.[44]

(3) *Essential evolutionary learning capability.* What follows from the arguments (1) and (2) is that Toyota demonstrated its *evolutionary learning capability* in building the new assembly system, including its *opportunistic learning capability.* By the latter, I mean Toyota's ability to integrate intended or unintended trials that have been already made; refine them or reinterpret them; and then make a coherent and ex-post rational system out of them. The foregoing analysis also indicates that Toyota has not always been ex-ante rational in creating the new assembly routines. Again, ex-ante rationality is not a necessary condition for explaining the ex-post rationality of a system. When we observe a variety in system change paths and consistency in the rationality of the resulting system, what matters is, after all, the evolutionary learning capability.

Anatomy of Evolutionary Learning Capability: Diversity and Convergence

One question still remains: What exactly constitutes Toyota's unique and dynamic capability in this case? Although we need further empirical research (interfirm comparative studies in particular) to answer this fully, the foregoing study identifies certain organizational patterns behind the company's dynamic capabilities. In a word, it is a certain *internal evolutionary process built into the organization*, or what Robert A. Burgelman (1991, 1994) calls "intraorganizational eco-logical process," which consists of variation, selection, retention, and propagation of new ideas.[45] According to this view, Toyota appears to have had an effective intraorganizational evolution mechanism that generated a variety of opinions, internally preselected solutions that were likely to reflect external selection environments, retained the se-lected ones as organizational memories, and diffused them through-out the company. To the extent that the criteria of the internal selec-tion reflect that of the external selection environment, the probability of creating effective organizational routines through the system emer-gence process seems to increase. Let's now examine each step of the internal evolutionary process.

Variation: Differences of Initial Opinions

Despite the stereotyped view that Toyota is a monolithic organization, there seem to have been significant disagreements inside the company throughout the transition period toward the new assembly system.

Disagreements in Interpreting the Situations.   For example, the prob-lem of assembly work attractiveness appears to have been recognized by different organizational units at different times. The problem that assembly-line work is boring, tiring, meaningless, and self-alienating apparently existed on the shop floor at least potentially or partially, but neither management nor the union recognized it as a central issue until the late 1980s. Then the union, as well as the Human Resource Division, found the problem to be critical, but the rest of the organi-zation tended to lag behind in such problem awareness.

There was also disagreement in evaluating assembly automation at the Tahara #4 line, even among production engineers. Some argue that the plant was a symbol of Toyota's mismanagement in produc-tion engineering, which was influenced by the bubble economy. For them, Tahara #4 is a temporary, but significant, deviation from Toy-ota's manufacturing tradition, and was subsequently overcome by a newer assembly concept represented by Kyushu and Motomachi. Others, however, insist that assembly technologies at Tahara #4 es-sentially belong to the mainstream of Toyota's evolutionary trajectory. For them, such trial and error is simply part of Toyota's engineering tradition.

Still another example of disagreement is found in the evaluation of the new assembly-line concept itself. For those who emphasize continuity of the Toyota production system (TPS), the new assembly concept is just another variation of TPS. For them, TPS has always pursued both efficiency and human dignity, and so does the new as-sembly system. For those who emphasize discontinuity, however, the recent trend is a departure from traditional TPS, in that the new assembly concept identified employee satisfaction as a value independent of efficiency. One manager described it as "amendment of Toyota's constitution."

Thus, the foregoing case indicated significant differences in the interpretation of external or internal environments, or what Weick (1979) calls "enactment." One of Toyota's division managers says that there are occasionally certain chaotic periods that looks like an "open tournament of new ideas," in which anyone regardless of rank may jump in. This resembles what Burgelman (1991) describes as "ecology of strategic initiatives."

Conformity in Evaluating of the Results. Despite the variety of initial opinions about the assembly concept, this study found that the evaluation of the resulting assembly system has been strikingly uniform among different organizational units: All of those interviewed, including production engineers, operations management consulting staff, human resource managers, plant general managers, union leaders, plant general managers, groups leaders, and team leaders, said they liked the new assembly system. Some may ascribe this to the Toyota's culture of strong group conformity; but then how do we explain the existence of significant disagreements in other areas, mentioned above?

There is also a striking conformity in the interpretation of the current labor environment among managers, engineers, and union leaders at Toyota: all those interviewed regarded the need for attractiveness of the workplace as a long-term objective despite a recent recession and a potential labor surplus. They all explained that the assembly-line problem was revealed by the labor shortage during the bubble economy, but the problem itself exists regardless of economic booms or recessions.

Selection and Propagation: Mechanisms for Convergence

What we can infer from this pattern of disagreement and conformity at Toyota is that this company may have an effective convergence mechanism: it can quickly convert a variety of organizational elements into a coherent system. Although this study by itself does not yield sufficient evidence, it does point to at least three elements of this organizational capability: *shared basic values, horizontal convergence,* and *vertical convergence.*

Internal Selection Criteria: Shared Values. Although they are seldom articulated, Toyota's basic values may be described as customer orientation and consciousness to manufacturing competitiveness (see chapter 4). It may be ascribed to the philosophy of Toyota's entrepreneur-founder Sakichi Toyoda or Kiichiro Toyoda, or to the heritage of the Ford production system; or it may have been shaped as a result of day-

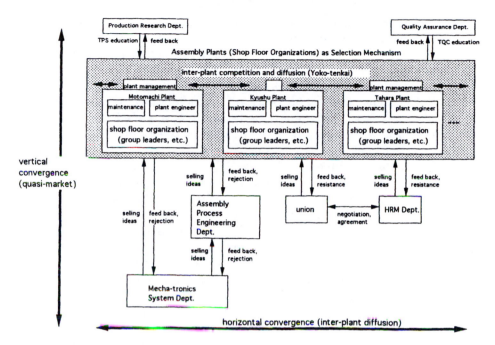

Figure 7.10 Convergence Mechanisms at Toyota's Manufacturing Organizations (Assembly)

to-day activities in TPS or TQC. In any case, it is likely that Toyota's values are deeply ingrained in its members, despite changes and specific disagreements on the surface.[46] In the evolutionary framework, it would function as consistent internal selection criteria for pre-screening of the new manufacturing routines before they face an external screening process by consumers in the product market and workers in the labor market.

Internal Selection Process: Vertical Convergence. Shared values are not enough to explain Toyota's unique organizational capabilities in system evolution. I suspect that, in addition, there are certain strong convergence mechanisms, both vertical and horizontal, at Toyota (figure 7.10). By vertical convergence I mean a quasi-market, or what Burgelman calls "internal selection environment," for screening or collecting new ideas in the production area prior to the external selection by the markets.[47] In this case, the shop floor organizations (*seisan-genba*), whose core consists of group leaders (*kumi-cho*) and team leaders (*han-cho*), appear to ultimately legitimize new production ideas, although informally.[48] The analogy that Toyota often uses, "the downstream process is your customer," can be applied to new production ideas.

In the case of new production equipment, for example, production engineers have to sell the new idea embodied in the equipment to the shop floor organization. As with customer sovereignty, the shop floor organization (*genba*) is said to make a final judgment on whether it accepts or rejects it. If the equipment does not fit their way of making things, it may literally be discarded or ignored. I have actually heard of some cases in which new equipment was scrapped. This sharply contrasts with many other manufacturers, where plant equipment, once installed, is sacred, untouchable, and, of course, not removable by shop floor people.

One important aspect of this internal selection mechanism of the new production ideas is that the shop floor organizations themselves are customer oriented, partly as a result of continuous penetration of the Toyota production System there; the Operations Management Consulting Division, TPS *shusa* at the plant, and other educators and promoters of TPS keep reinforcing this concept. In a sense, Toyota's shop floor organization represents both employee and customer interests.[49] It is likely that Toyota potentially had a screening mechanism that could be used for balancing customer satisfaction and employee satisfaction. It did not have to be activated during the high-growth era, but it existed as a potential mechanism all the same.

Facing this type of shop floor organization, production engineers tend to become "customer" (i.e., shop floor) oriented and try harder to develop production technologies that are more friendly to direct-line workers. One Toyota engineer in the VPE Division, for example, told us he is process-design oriented rather than equipment oriented, and that he emphasizes shop floor efficiency over automation ratios. Also, some plant managers say that new equipment has been thrown away much less frequently in recent years, indicating that production engineers have become shop floor oriented.

Another recent example of the shop floor sovereignty (*genba-shugi*) is the introduction of the continuous two-shift system. This system was introduced to new Toyota Kyushu in 1992 and was well received as a worker-friendly arrangement. Both the union and management at the parent company quickly agreed that it should introduce this system at other Toyota plants. But despite this consensus, it took about two years to introduce the continuous two-shift throughout Toyota. This was because the shop floor people were not persuaded easily. They were often afraid of changes in lifestyle, loss of overtime premiums, and other negative aspects of the new system. The union and the Human Resource Division, using their respective channels, approached the shop floor and tenaciously tried to persuade workers—and eventually had by 1995. Such informal shop floor power (at the levels of group leaders and team leaders, in particular), which functions as an internal selection mechanism for manufacturing routines, may facilitate the vertical convergence process.

Propagation of Selected Routines: Horizontal Convergence. Once promising production ideas have been accepted by management, union, and the shop floor, they tend to be quickly disseminated across plants through various channels, including special projects, union-management meetings, manager meetings at the corporate level (e.g., assembly division head meeting), and rotation of plant general managers. At Toyota, the horizontal convergence of new ideas, policies, and technologies across the plants is often emphasized as *yoko-tenkai* or *yoko-ten* (horizontal deployment). Indeed, I heard this word from Toyota's managers and production engineers, in my interviews with them, more frequently than most of the TPS or TQC jargons.

Retention of Routines: Standardization and Documentation

Finally, it should be noted that part of Toyota's dynamic capability may be ascribed to standardization and documentation, which are often regarded as components of bureaucracy and as counter-active. As shown in its *kaizen* activities and company rule systems, Toyota is a company that has highly standardized routine problem-solving processes and developed documentation systems (a kind of organizational memory storage). Although this may seem to contradict the notion of a dynamic capability, I would argue that standardization of regular problem solving and systematic documentation of the results are essential components for retention of routines, and thus for a company's internal evolutionary mechanism. In this sense, I do not follow a stereotyped dichotomy that simply contrasts bureaucracy and innovation. After all, repetition (i.e., standardization) and retention (i.e., organizational memory in the form of documents and others) are basic elements of the evolutionary process.[50]

An Internal Evolutionary Mechanism

The above analyses of the organizational process and culture makes it clear that this company has an effective *internal evolutionary mechanism* consisting of variation, selection, retention, and diffusion (propagation) of organizational routines inside the company. According to the evolutionary view of the firm, manufacturing companies face external selection mechanisms through which new variants of the products, services, and jobs that they offer are constantly evaluated and screened. The foregoing case of Toyota seems to indicate that there is an internal process of variety generation, screening, retention, and diffusion of new manufacturing routines, which more or less reflects this external evolutionary process.[51]

In this process, the employees of the company create various short-term solutions to a variety of manufacturing problems in a variety of ways. At this stage the solutions and intentions may be diverse and inconsistent, reflecting different environments and departmental cultures.[52] The organizational members bring the external diversity to the organization in the form of various unpolished solutions. Then, when the aggregate of problem finding and tentative solutions leads to a recognition by certain key managers that a company-wide problem has surfaced, various convergence mechanisms are triggered at multiple levels of the organization, as well as between the company and the union, like an open tournament of new ideas. Solutions from various areas of the company are brought into meetings, adjusted to other solutions, and refined as part of the total solution. The integrated solution has to be arranged so that it can pass the informal screen of shop floor leaders, who themselves are trained to be not only employee oriented but also customer oriented. More generally, awareness of customer satisfaction and competitiveness is prevalent in the entire organization, which functions as a common criterion for screening and refinement (see figure 3.5). The refined solutions are retained as standards and procedures (i.e., production routines), and are diffused quickly to the entire plant network. At this stage, we observe a remarkable uniformity and consistency in both solutions and their reasoning.

The present chapter has explored Toyota's new assembly systems, which emerged because of environmental changes since the late 1980s. I have identified the components of the system, including the autonomous complete assembly line, the in-line mechanical automation concept, TVAL, and low-cost equipment for better ergonomics, explaining the new system's ex-post rationality in terms of a balance between customer satisfaction and employee satisfaction. The foregoing historical analysis of this system seems to indicate the following points:

- Toyota's new assembly system was created through multi-path system emergence.
- Toyota's evolutionary learning capability remained robust at least into the mid-1990s.
- An intraorganizational evolutionary mechanism, including the vertical and horizontal convergence mechanisms (*genba-shugi* and *yoko-tenkai*), lies behind the company's evolutionary learning capability.
- The notion that Toyota is always a monolithic organization is a myth.
- Standardization and documentation are not always enemies of dynamic system change: they are often essential elements of the evolutionary learning capability.

Although intraorganizational evolutionary processes have already been analyzed in some of important literature (e.g., Weick, 1979; Nonaka, 1985; Burgelman, 1991), most of these authors assume that the internal selection mechanism exists at the top of the organizational hierarchy.[53] What is unique in the analysis of Toyota, by contrast, is that one of its intraorganizational selection mechanisms exists nearly at the bottom of the hierarchy, or *genba*. Whereas Toyota's executives also function as formal selectors of bottom-up proposals, the significant influence of the shop floor supervisors in the intraorganizational evolutionary process should not be overlooked.

The above propositions are by no means confirmed. However, Toyota's new assembly line seems to provide additional insights into the distinctive capabilities of this firm. Toyota appears to have an effective internal evolutionary mechanism, which reflects the diversity and changes of its external environment reasonably well. And this appears to be at least part of what is behind Toyota's overall evolutionary learning capability.

8

CONCLUSION

Toyota as a "Prepared Organization"

In the summer of 1984, Koichi Shimokawa[1] and I met Taiichi Ohno for a long interview, and then visited the new Shiga plant of Daihatsu Motor Co., a Toyota group automaker near Kyoto.[2] We had dinner with Daihatsu's plant manager, Michikazu Tanaka, then a leading practitioner of the Toyota production system and someone who had worked very closely with Ohno. Tanaka told us that evening, "What do you think is the essence of just in time? There are three possible answers. The beginner's answer would be that JIT is good simply because it reduces inventory cost. An intermediate-level answer is that JIT reveals production problems and triggers *kaizen*. But the third answer is that JIT infuses *cost consciousness* into all employees. When JIT keeps on forcing workers to face production problems one after another, the people finally start to see everything as a potential source of cost or productivity problems, and then seek problems actively. This is the level we have to reach."

In retrospect, I think Tanaka was close to describing a firm's three types of organizational capabilities: routinized manufacturing, routinized learning, and evolutionary learning. Indeed, what I have highlighted in this book—the importance of multi-path system emergence and the evolutionary learning capability—will not come as a complete surprise to the people of Toyota. When we carefully listen to what Toyota's employees say about the company and their daily working lives, and compare that with what we hear in other companies, it's not hard to identify elements of Toyota's distinctive evolutionary learning capability. And yet, to my knowledge, the concept of evolutionary learning capability has never been explicitly discussed in the public domain by company insiders, probably because it comes so naturally to them. Nor has it been articulated by outside researchers, perhaps because, unlike JIT or *kaizen*, this kind of capability building does not look unique to Toyota; it almost seems to be common sense for any learning organization.

Common sense or not, even a casual glance at business history indicates that not many organizations have developed and retained such an evolutionary learning capability over an extended period. The fact that Toyota has done so since the 1930s is not only worthy of comment; it implies a new direction that other companies—and researchers—would do well to follow.

What We Know About the Evolution of Manufacturing Systems

In *The Evolution of a Manufacturing System at Toyota*, I have reinterpreted the evolutionary, as well as the resource-capability, theories of the firm from an information point of view, which allows us to make detailed analyses of total manufacturing systems. Terms like *firm, resource, activity, product, consumption,* and *organizational routines* (or a firm's routinized manufacturing and routinized learning capabilities) were described consistently as a system of information assets.

Figure 8.1 maps the main arguments of this book in my evolutionary framework, including routines as informational patterns, their creation through a process of multi-path system emergence, and a firm's evolutionary learning capability for intervening in this process. Based on the research and analysis presented in the seven previous chapters, we can summarize these arguments as follows:

Three Layers of Manufacturing Capabilities. A firm's capabilities in product development, production, and supplier management—the basic components of its total manufacturing system—can be analyzed in three layers: routinized manufacturing, routinized learning, and evolutionary learning capabilities. The first two are routinized capabilities for repetitive information transmission or problem solving. But evolutionary learning capability is nonroutine and dynamic; it refers to a firm's ability to build a competitive set of routine capabilities as the system emerges. The long-term strength of a company like Toyota, then, comes from its overall ability to adapt and change over time—the evolutionary learning capability.

Multi-Path System Emergence and the Evolutionary Learning Capability. In the real world, effective manufacturing routines emerge through a much more complex process than straightforward competitive-rational decision making. While it's often possible to identify a total system's capabilities after the fact, each element may have emerged for reasons other than competitive advantage, such as unforeseen historical imperatives or unintended knowledge transfers. At the same time, certain firm-specific abilities for converting unintended

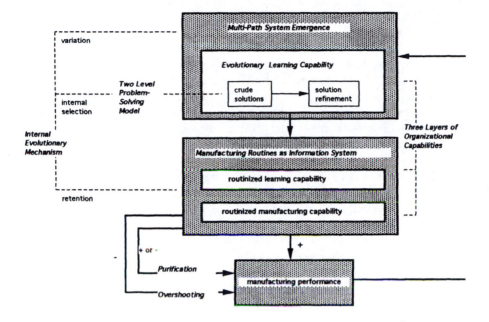

Note: Main themes are shown in *italic* style.

Figure 8.1 Overall Process of Capability Building

trials and emergent practices into competitive routines—*opportunistic* (ex-post) *learning capabilities*—may also play an important role. This complex interaction between system emergence and evolutionary learning may explain why significant interregional and interfirm differences in performance can coexist simultaneously.

A Dual-Level Problem-Solving Model. Based on the information point of view, the process of capability building can be partly explained by a modified problem-solving model that consists of (1) an emergent process of solution generation; and (2) a refinement process that converts the above solutions into competitive routines. A firm's *opportunistic learning capability* is characterized as part of this second step, or as the "preparedness" of its organizational members, who constantly associate the outcomes of the system emergence with opportunities for capability building. The model may help us understand why and how an ex-post rational approach evolves through a combination of the multi-path system emergence and the evolutionary learning capability of the firm.

Routines as Information System. Regardless of their origins and evolutionary paths, effective manufacturing routines (i.e., routinized capabilities), once selected and retained, function as a regular system that jointly creates, transmits, and enhances a bundle of product-embodied information that appeals to customers. The routinized production-related capability of the effective Japanese automakers in the 1980s, for example, can be characterized as dense and accurate transmission of value-carrying information between flexible information assets. Their routinized learning capability in both continuous improvements (*kaizen*) and product development can also be analyzed as effective patterns of interconnected problem-solving cycles. Thus, although first-time observers may find the Toyota-style manufacturing system to be an overwhelmingly complex and entangled interaction of many practices and techniques, we can map such manufacturing routines into a coherent information system to demonstrate that its functionality is quite straightforward.

Purification. When the original manufacturing system—such as the Toyota-style system in Japan—is an outcome of an emergent process, and when a competitor, such as a Western automaker, tries to adopt this system through a deliberate knowledge transfer and top-down planning, the adopting firm may first purify and systematize the original system before the transfer. That's because the emergent manufacturing system is likely to be a mixture of articulated and functional procedures, tacit but functional knowledge, and nonfunctional or dysfunctional routines. When the firm adopts only the part of the system that can be articulated and functionally explained, the result may be worse than the original, if essential tacit knowledge is missing. Yet the result may also be better if the dysfunctional parts of the original sys-·tem are effectively cleaned up. The rapid catchup of the U.S. automakers in product development performance since the late 1980s, for instance, indicates a positive effect of purification.

Overshooting. Ironically, a firm with a strong evolutionary learning capability may suffer from this problem more often than others. Overshooting, or overbuilding certain capabilities that result in dysfunctional side effects, can happen particularly when pressures for capability-building competition are intense. I regard fat product design, which Japanese automakers wrestled with in the early 1990s, a result of overbuilding product development capabilities. Yet the original set of capabilities is not the problem, but a company's response to the intensifying market pressures. In fact, overshooting may be almost inevitable for successful firms like Toyota. Given its superior evolutionary learning capability, we would expect Toyota to end up with fat design, recognize it as a problem, then adapt accordingly.

Internal Evolutionary Mechanisms. In fact, the analysis of a system change in final assembly at Toyota presented in chapter 7 indicates that this company still maintained its evolutionary learning capability in the early 1990s. Toyota also appears to have an internal evolutionary mechanism that incorporates variety generation, convergence, retention, and diffusion of manufacturing routines. The core group of shop floor leaders function as an informal intraorganizational mechanism for pre-screening the routines prior to their external selection by consumers and the labor market. Value sharing among employees in terms of basic Toyota manufacturing principles is another critical element. The company has effective processes for retention (documentation) and propagation (interplant diffusion) of selected routines. Through this internal evolutionary mechanism, Toyota copes with the complexity of multi-path system emergence, creates a diversity of ideas inside the firm, and then merges these two streams into a coherent set of routine manufacturing capabilities. This is the organizational process behind Toyota's overall evolutionary learning capability.

Overall, I have explained Toyota-style manufacturing routines as systematically as possible, arguing that the primary source of their complexity is the invisible network that connects production, product development, purchasing, marketing, and consumption—the total system of value-carrying information. The creation of such a system is too complicated a process to be explained solely by ex-ante rational decision making by top managers. At the same time, I have tried to describe the functionality of Toyota's manufacturing routines as simply as possible. Although there may be tacit knowledge, mysterious routines, and subtle skills hidden in every corner of this system, I still argue that its basic functional principle is quite straightforward and transparent: every manufacturing routine, once established as an effective one, makes some informational contribution that enhances the impact of the ultimate information—the one embodied in products and delivered to customers. In this way, we can describe Toyota-style manufacturing as an ex-post rational system without referring to its "mysterious," unknowable aspects.

The apparent paradox between structural complexity and functional simplicity is, to me, the key to understanding why the Toyota-style system emerged, and why Toyota's evolutionary learning capability has played such a crucial role. The structure of such organizational routines as the heavyweight product manager system or the black box parts practice of suppliers is too complex to have been completely designed in advance. But the functional principle of such emergent systems was simple enough to be recognized and preserved after the fact in this "prepared" organization.

While I emphasize the limits of ex-ante rationality here, it's clear that manufacturing practitioners play a role in the evolution of any system. The evolutionary process is neither totally deterministic nor stochastic. People struggle to make good decisions in the midst of multi-path system emergence. Their foresight and actions almost always influence the system change process, although they may neither fully control nor predict the processes. And even if the process is essentially emergent, there are certain firms, like Toyota, that still outperform others in the long-range competition of capability building.

Why We Need More Research

There's still much to learn about the evolution of the Toyota-style manufacturing system, as well as manufacturing systems in general. For example, systematic and comparative studies of the organizational processes and cultures that back up a firm's evolutionary learning capability would certainly add to our knowledge. We still do not understand fully the content and origins of Toyota's evolutionary learning capability, let alone the evolutionary learning capability of other firms. Most of the historical analyses presented in this book have focused on a single company. What we need to extend these analyses are comparative histories of manufacturing system evolution across firms, such as Michael Cusumano's classic comparison of Toyota and Nissan, or more recent comparative studies on the auto firm's evolutionary trajectories by Robert Boyer, Michel Freyssenet, and their colleagues at French-based GERPISA research project.[3]

Studies of other industries may also show whether this evolutionary framework can be generalized beyond automobile manufacturing. For example, the patterns of evolutionary learning capability described for Toyota and other automakers may apply to industries with similar dynamics; but the framework may not fit a more fluid industry, such as computer manufacturing or software design, in which revolutionary changes in technologies often make a company's core technology totally obsolete, or in which new businesses and product architectures emerge frequently.

The study of the evolution of manufacturing systems is by no means complete, but this book provides a good start. The foregoing historical and empirical analyses, for instance, indicate that the resource-capability view of the firm may be applied effectively to the case of manufacturing systems in a single business situation, in which both interregional and interfirm differences in competitive performance are consistently observed. Such analyses, in turn, can serve as building blocks for higher level strategic analyses of multi-industry, multidivisional manufacturing firms. In this way, the research presented in *The Evolution of a Manufacturing System at Toyota* strengthens ties between technology and operations management, on the one hand, and strategic management, and evolutionary economics, on the other.

Why We Should Link Historical and Functional Analysis

Finally, let me briefly discuss a broader issue raised by this evolutionary approach: the increasingly complementary relationship between historical and functional analysis in social science. In recent years, I have noticed renewed interest in various evolutionary approaches among social scientists—many works in evolutionary economics, as well as comparative economic institutions (Aoki, 1995), the evolutionary game theory, the regulation approach (Boyer and Freyssenet, 1995), the evolutionary approach to organizations and strategies (Nonaka, 1985; Burgelman, 1991, 1994), the evolutionary theory of cooperation (Axelrod, 1984), and so on. In my view, such proliferation of evolutionary approaches means nothing but a growing opportunity for historical and functional approaches to collaborate for explaining the same social and economic phenomenon.

In economics, for instance, equilibrium analyses (the standard functional method in this field) and historical analyses were generally regarded as *separate* approaches, dating back to the controversies during nineteenth century. For instance, a standard general equilibrium theory in microeconomics assumes a very harsh selection environment, one that allows only a single point in the system attribute space, or an equilibrium, in which economic actors can stabilize and survive. This means that a system's history does not explain why it is now a stable entity. No matter which evolutionary path the system has taken—or will take—it survives only when it hits the single equilibrium point, and knowing about the system's history adds no information at all to what we already know from equilibrium theory.[4]

However, if the selection environment is generous enough to allow a variety of points in the system space where economic actors can survive, then history *would* matter, even to rigorous equilibrium theorists. As Masahiko Aoki claims, equilibrium logic itself cannot explain which stable point an economic actor settles for; that would depend on which evolutionary path the system took historically (or "path-dependence").[5]

Since many economic researchers have shifted to studying phenomena in which a variety of systems survive and coexist—for example, comparing different economic institutions—evolutionary approaches have attracted more attention in recent years. The same logic applies to other social sciences as well. When we want to explain variety and change in the ex-post rational systems of our society, evolutionary thinking becomes more relevant. It should be emphasized again, however, that this does *not* mean a compromise between the two approaches; on the contrary, an effective evolutionary approach is based only on thorough functional analyses and detailed historical researches for the same system, as well as rigorous comparison between them.

The Evolution of a Manufacturing System at Toyota shares the spirit of this general trend. By now it's clear that empirical studies of automobile manufacturing systems since the 1980s are at a sort of disciplinary crossroads. While standing in this busy intersection for nearly twenty years, I have met people of various backgrounds — engineers, designers, business academics, historians, sociologists, anthropologists, political scientists, and economists of all sorts. In fact, some chapters of this book are based on papers that were presented in various conferences for different disciplines (management, history, engineering, and economics).

Automobile manufacturing systems provide just one of many fruitful sites for empirical research. Yet they have attracted the attention of social scientists since the early studies of the Ford assembly lines.[6] Even now that "the century of the automobile" is almost over, auto manufacturing systems remain a hot issue. Indeed, I believe this will continue to be an important topic, one where constructive collaboration among researchers from various disciplines and nations will grow and "evolve" into the next century.

APPENDIX A:
THE EVOLUTIONARY
FRAMEWORK
Generic and Specific

Since the development of modern evolutionary theory with Charles Darwin's work on living systems, such a framework has also been applied to social, economic, and managerial systems. The notion of evolution, however, has been quite elusive, and has often created various disagreements among researchers. Against this background, the purpose of appendix A is to elaborate the conceptual framework in this book, which is meant not only to share basic characteristics with the modern evolutionary paradigm in biology but also to fit the specific purpose of this book—to explain the structures, functions, and formation of a surviving manufacturing system.

For this purpose, it is important to distinguish two levels of an evolutionary framework: a *generic scheme* and a *specific scheme*. The present evolutionary approach shares its basic logical structure with many other evolutionary models of biological and social systems at the first level, while it is more or less specific to the present analytical purpose—the empirical research of manufacturing systems—at the second level.

Generic Scheme

By an evolutionary framework at this level, I do not mean any specific theories of biological or social evolution, but a general logical scheme that such theories may share. On the generic level, the present framework shares basic logical patterns with the contemporary synthetic (neo-Darwinian) theory of biological evolution, as well as other modern evolutionary theories of the firm, technologies, organizations, and strategies.[1] Here is my checklist for the generic evolutionary scheme:[2]

1. *Stability and variety.* The framework's main purpose is to explain why we observe a certain variety of stable patterns (e.g., species, routines) in the objects concerned, or relatively complex systems (e.g., organisms, organizations).
2. *Ex-post rationality.* The objects observed behave so functionally that they *look as if* someone had purposefully designed them for survival, regardless of whether such purposive motivation actually existed beforehand.
3. *History and change.* The framework tries to explain how stable patterns change over time, or how the present system formed through certain (mostly irreversible) historical paths over a long period.
4. *Genetic and functional logic.* There are three complementary explanations for a given dynamic phenomenon: system *variation* (generation of a variety of patterns), *selection* (elimination of low-performing patterns), and *retention* (preservation of the remaining patterns). In other words, the evolutionary perspective provides *genetic* and *functional* explanations separately for the same phenomenon: the former explains how the system was created and has changed to yield its present form; functional explanations demonstrate how a system's structure behaves effectively for higher performance or survival rate.
5. *Antiteleological.* Because of the above logical separation, this framework does not depend entirely on rational foresight or planning of omnipotent decision makers for explaining the formation of a system that is observed to function rationally.

The above definition of the generic evolutionary framework may seem too broad for some of the readers, but I believe it should be broad enough for us to be able to exploit the rich insights of various evolutionary theories, including biological ones, without making a mistake of adopting biological analogies from neo-Darwinian paradigm too directly to social science. In other words, the evolutionary scheme, at the generic level, should not include any assumptions specific to the neo-Darwinian notion, such as harsh selection environments and purely random system variations.

Specific Scheme: A History-Oriented Approach

At the second level, the evolutionary framework is applied specifically to the present theme, the evolution of the Toyota-style manufacturing system. At this level, the evolutionary framework is more or less "customized" to the empirical-historical analyses of a high-performing manufacturing system.

In a word, my specific evolutionary framework is *a history-oriented*

approach to manufacturing routines within a single firm, which em-
phasizes an organization's ability to learn. My specific scheme may be
summarized as follows:

1. The main purpose of this framework is to explain why we observe a distinctive pattern of organizational routines and
   their changes *within a single firm*, rather than explaining a
   pattern of diversity and changes in a population of firms
   throughout the whole industry or economy.

2. The criterion of functional rationality is the relative competitive performance of a manufacturing system, which is reinterpreted as a surrogate indicator of an individual system's
   chances of future survival; since the focus of the research is
   a single surviving firm, it is impossible to measure or estimate
   the survival ratio itself.

3. The framework tries to capture the complexity of the historical process that formed the system, rather than describing it
   as a random walk. Thus, the present framework treats changes
   in manufacturing routines as due to *multi-path system emergence,* a complex and irregular combination of rational
   plans, entrepreneurial visions, historical imperatives, and
   pure chance.

4. The present framework assumes a lenient external selection
   mechanism and an important role of internal selection. For
   the empirical analysis of today's automobile industry, it's realistic to assume that firms with lower performance can still
   survive for some time (see appendix B2); but competitive
   pressures from "best practice" rivals, which they anticipate
   or observe through revealed performance, should lead lower
   performers to change routines in the long run. In other words,
   the evolutionary process in this scheme does not assume a
   harsh selection process through which low-performing firms
   are immediately eliminated by market forces; it allows a certain moratorium period during which the firms of different
   performance levels may interpret their environments and revealed performance, learn from each other, and change routines. Thus, the main focus of the present framework is *internal selection* of routines within a surviving firm like Toyota,
   as opposed to external selection of the firms themselves. The
   impact of market force is at most indirect.

5. The framework assumes that it is a set of manufacturing-
   related routines that is retained and diffused within an organization despite the turnover of people. I reinterpret it as a
   stable pattern of information assets and flows that collectively influence levels and improvements in manufacturing
   performance. This informational pattern, or routine, may be

regarded as a "gene" in the manufacturing system.[3] Note that a reliable mechanism of routine retention, as in the case of a gene, is a necessary condition for a system's survival, even though it may also hamper its adaptive changes.[4] In this regard, I emphasize the role of Weberian bureaucracy and Taylorist standardization in effective manufacturing systems.

Overall, the evolutionary framework of the present book is by no means new, but my specific scheme is somewhat different from some other interpretations of evolutionary models. For instance, whereas the present framework shares the general logical scheme of today's synthetic theory of biological evolution, it is not a direct application of the biological model at the specific level (table A-1; see also chapter 1 for further comparison).

Connections with Existing Theories of Organization and Strategy

Let's now discuss the relationship between the present evolutionary framework and some related theories and models of business firms, including evolutionary theories of the firm, resource-based view in strategic management, organizational ecology, and the concept of emergent strategy formation. The present book adopted some aspects of these theories. In this sense, much of my own analysis is based on the previous work of economists, historians, and business researchers, including Penrose, Nelson, Winter, Dosi, Rumelt, Teece, Chandler, Mintzberg, and Burgelman.[5]

However, the specific evolutionary framework in the present book, prepared for detailed analyses of a manufacturing system, was not a direct application of these existing frameworks.

There are two streams of researches that are closely related to the present framework: resource-capability-based approaches to strategic management and evolutionary theories of the firm. Both have attracted much attention among business academics and practitioners in recent years. Their specific research agenda may be different by case (for example, the former tend to focus on firms' profitability at a given time, while the latter analyze their trajectories over time), but these theories seem to share a common view of the firm—describing a company as a collection of firm-specific, difficult-to-change, and difficult-to-imitate resources, organizational routines, capabilities, or competencies. Their proponents expect that such resources or capabilities account for interfirm differences in competitive performance, profitability, or evolutionary trajectories.[6] The present framework shares this basic view—routines and performance differ from company to company, and history matters.

Nevertheless, the existing resource-capability framework, as well

Table A.1 Comparison of Evolutionary Frameworks

	Framework of this Book	Neo-Darwinian (synthetic) Theory in Biology
Object	A manufacturing system within a single firm	A population of living systems
Criteria of ex-post rationality	Relative manufacturing performance	Survival/reproduction
Logic of retention	Object to be retained = manufacturing routines as informational patterns Routines are stored in the firm; It may be diffused across firms	Object to be retained = genes as information Genetic information is stored in the organism; It may be reproduced across generations
Logic of variation	Complex historical process changes routines Feedback from the environment may trigger routine changes (Lamarckian)	Random chance changes genetic information No feedback from the environment to gene
Logic of selection	Long-term elimination of low-performing routines by either market or organization Rather "lenient" selection environment is assumed Individual firms may select high-performing routines	Long-term elimination of low-performing genotypes by the environment Rather harsh selection environment is assumed Individual organism cannot select high-performing genes
Separation of functional and genetic explanations	Genetic Explanations = multi-path system emergence results in changes in manufacturing routines Functional Explanations = certain routines (routinized capabilities) result in relatively high performance and its improvements	Genetic Explanations = random variations of DNA result in variations of phenotypes. Functional Explanations = certain phenotypes result in higher performance for survival in the environment (natural selection)
Antiteleology	Reject the idea that omnipotent decision makers create the entire system through perfect foresight	Reject the idea that the omnipotent creator made all of the living system through predetermined plans

as the evolutionary theory of the firm, is not directly applicable to the empirical research of this book. While most of the existing resource-capability literature—found in the fields of strategic management, applied economics, and business history—analyzes the dynamics and firm-specificity of the overall systems in multiproduct firms, these studies have not been designed for detailed competitive analyses of manufacturing systems at a single plant or project level.[7] As Birger Wernerfelt points out, "'resources' remain an amorphous heap to most of us."[8]

Previous research in technology and operations management has done a much better job of analyzing the specifics of manufacturing systems, but it tended to lack either the total system perspective or a long-range historical perspective for explaining differences and changes in manufacturing performance.[9] The evolutionary framework of this book tries to fill this gap.

It should be also noted that my focus in this book is the evolution of organizational routines *within a single surviving firm* (e.g., Toyota), as opposed to that of routines diffused among firms in the entire industry or economy.[10] Also, considering this book's empirical theme, I emphasize an individual firm's *ability to learn*, adapt its internal system to the environment, and thereby survive by modifying its routines. In this sense, the present framework does not follow a strict "population ecology" version of evolutionary models,[11] which assumes that individual firms, with strong "structural inertia," are unable to adapt their routines to the environment, and that those firms with ineffective routines are likely to be weeded out eventually by the forces of external selection—a neo-Darwinian assumption that the environment selects the firms and creates a nonrandom distribution of high-performing routines in a given population of organizations.[12]

Quite simply, such a "harsh" external selection has seldom emerged in the automobile industry in the late twentieth century. Rather, individual firms have been able to change their routines in a nonrandom way, although imperfectly and slowly, which would increase their chances of survival.[13] Thus, a mechanism of *internal selection*, or what Robert Burgelman calls an "intraorganizational ecological process" (Burgelman, 1991, 1994), seems more relevant to the present case: firms may select new routines before being selected by external ecological process.

Note also that by "adaptation" I do not just mean reactive changes of the system in response to environmental changes, but also active changes of the environment itself wherever possible. Whatever the reason, better adaptation occurs when a certain new combination of a system and its environments brings about a higher chance of its survival at a given point in time.

The notion of evolutionary learning, proposed in chapter 1, is also akin to the concept of "emergent strategy," or "patterns or consistencies realized despite, or in the absence of, intentions" (Mintzberg and Waters, 1985, p. 257), in that they both emphasize the role of unintended system formation processes.[14] Note, however, that evolutionary learning assumes a situation in which managers do not even know if a deliberate strategy works or an emergent strategy leads to a success for the next occasion of system changes. Indeed, evolutionary learning capability, discussed in chapter 1, includes an ability to realize emergent strategy better than other firms (i.e., opportunistic learning), but this concept is somewhat broader than that of the emergent strategy; the former includes both intentional and opportunistic learning as possible paths. Thus, Toyota may deliberately learn at any given time, and it is always ready to do so, but it is also well prepared to take advantage of what already happened for whatever reasons.[15] No switching rule appears to exist between intentional and opportunistic learning—the company appears to be handling the two modes simultaneously.

In any case, it should be noted that, by adopting the concept of evolutionary learning capability, my main purpose is not to demonstrate the efficacy of the emergent strategy view in explaining an organization's history, but to explain why and how some firms like Toyota can outperform others in capitalizing mixed opportunities of both emergent and deliberate strategy formation. After all, my primary interest in this book is how Toyota's patterns of system formation differ from those of others.

To sum up, the present evolutionary framework shares the basic logical structure of other evolutionary and related theories in biology and social science, but it is also specific to the present research on a manufacturing system. Thus, for example, the present framework is certainly evolutionary, but it is *not* neo-Darwinian in its strict sense.

APPENDIX B:
THE BASICS OF TOYOTA-STYLE
MANUFACTURING

This appendix presents basic data and evidences on the automobile manufacturing routines and performance mainly in Japanese auto firms, particularly at Toyota. Since I have already presented basic facts on product development in chapter 6, I focus on production and supplier management here. The data presented here are based mostly on existing literature, but they also include the results of my original empirical studies in various areas, as well as other data reported for the first time in English. International comparative data are described and analyzed wherever relevant. Appendix B.1 explains basic routines of Toyota-style production systems. Appendix B.2 investigates production-related performance of the Japanese automakers of the 1980s in comparison to their Western counterparts, based mostly on existing literature. Appendix B.3 shows empirical findings about performance and practices of the Japanese supplier systems based on the three-dimensional framework proposed in chapter 4.

B.1 Practices and Techniques in the Toyota-style Production Systems

The typical volume production system of effective Japanese makers of the 1980s (e.g., Toyota) consists of various intertwined elements that might lead to competitive advantages. Just-in-time (JIT), *jidoka* (automatic defect detection and machine stop), total quality control (TQC), and continuous improvement (*kaizen*) are often pointed out as its core subsystems.[1]

Practices in Production Management

The elements of the Toyota-style production system include the following, although this is not an exhaustive list. Since there is much literature on this topic, this section makes only a brief explanation for each element. (For further details, see, for example, Toyota Motor Corporation, 1996b).[2]

Reduction of "Muda" (non-value-adding activities), "Mura" (uneven pace of production), and "Muri" (excessive workload). These are not techniques but rather principles for the so-called Toyota production system. That is, they are basic criteria through which specific choices of practices and techniques are evaluated. Elimination of "muda," or non-value activities and objects, is particularly emphasized in Toyota production textbooks. By finding and taking out "muda," the production cost is naturally reduced, according to them.

Seven types of "muda" are often cited in Ohno (1978). Among them, "muda" of the inventory is regarded as the gravest source of problems, as it not only adds additional production costs but also hides other manufacturing problems (e.g., "muda" of waiting idle time) and thereby reduces pressures for production improvements.

Inventory Reduction Mechanisms by Kanban System. Kanban refers to a production and inventory control system, in which production instructions and parts delivery instructions are triggered by the consumption of parts at the downstream process (i.e., a pull system). Standardized returnable parts containers circulate between the upstream and downstream processes, and the orders are triggered by the arrival of empty containers. A *kanban* plate, traveling with a container, automatically issues delivery and production orders. In-process inventories are reduced as the number of *kanbans* is reduced.

There are other ways of parts delivery, such as scheduled delivery and synchronized (sequential) delivery. It is important to note that synchronized delivery (i.e., supplying parts in exactly the same order as the body sequence on the assembly line) is usually more "just-in-time" than the *kanban* system. Note, also, that the *kanban* system does need a certain level of inventory to function. In other words, the *kanban* system aims at reducing inventories, but it can never achieve zero inventory by the very definition of the system.

Levelization of Production Volume and Product Mix (heijunka). Levelization means production based on a detailed production plan (e.g., assembly sequence plan) in which efforts are made to reduce fluctuations in both total output rate per process and product mix composition within the process. The latter is particularly emphasized in Toyota's textbooks. When there are numerous product variations, this means the assembly sequence is randomized in a sense that product variations to be produced are distributed as evenly as possible throughout the day, as opposed to assembly in a relatively large lot size. This may be also called the mixed model production (*konryu seisan*).[3]

The product mix levelization aims at, first, more even intervals of parts orders under the *kanban* system and, second, better line balancing when the workload is significantly different by product.

Production Plans Based on Dealers' Order Volume (genryo seisan). This is a simple principle of making exactly the same amount of products as are sold. In most cases, however, this does not mean that the assemblers are 100 percent following the final customers' firm orders. As already discussed, a majority of the Japanese domestic car sales are made from dealer stocks rather than customers' specific orders. Thus, what the above principle implies is that the assemblers should follow the aggregate volume of dealers' orders, including final users' as their part. Production cycle times (*takt* times) are determined by the demand rate in this sense, according to the textbooks.

Actual implementation may not be as simple as this. According to the order entry system, actual production plans at Toyota are determined through step-by-step negotiation and refinement between the producer issuing preliminary production plans and dealers issuing their demand forecasts and preliminary orders. Some of the dealers' monthly orders may not be accepted in that month depending upon constraints on the production system. Conversely, producers may influence dealers' order volume by using a complicated rebate system, particularly when sales of the model are slower than originally planned.

Thus, production volume, in reality, may not be determined as a result of a simple one-way information flow from the market to the dealers to the producer, but through a more subtle mutual adjustment to the extent that the actual production system is not infinitely flexible. However, the principle of *genryo-seisan* is solid as a concept, philosophy, or the ultimate goal at companies like Toyota.

Reduction of Setup Change Time and Lot Size.   Where lot production is necessary for technological and economical reasons, Toyota-style plants try to reduce setup change time to increase flexibility. For example, rather than trying to optimize the lot size with a static assumption for setup change cost and inventory carrying cost (i.e., the economic order quantity analysis), the press shops try to reduce die setup cost and thereby reduce the lot size of stamping operations without sacrificing total manufacturing cost. A rule of thumb for setup changes of major body panel dies is often referred to as less than ten minutes (single-digit setup change). Lot sizes for such press shops are relatively small accordingly: typically several hundred panels at a time.

Piece-by-Piece Transfer of Parts Between Machines (ikko-nagashi).
This is also called one-at-a-time production in some of the textbooks
(e.g., Toyota Motor Corporation, 1992, 1996b). In such areas as machining and parts subassembly, in which work-in-process transfer is
not automated, it is often advocated that continuous-flow processing
still should be pursued rather than traditional large-lot transfer of
work-in-process.

Note that one-at-a-time production is automatically guaranteed in
the case of the Ford-style assembly lines or automated transfer machines for engine cutting, in which work-in-process is automatically
transferred to the next station one by one in a synchronized way.
Thus, the argument of *ikko-nagashi* assumes that the process in question does not have automatic transfer mechanisms or moving conveyers, and that it is not economical to adopt such advanced process
technologies.

*Flexible Task Assignment for Volume Changes and Productivity Im-
provement (shojinka).* This way of flexible task assignment is proposed as a mechanism to absorb production volume changes per production line and maintain the levels of labor productivity as flat as
possible despite volume fluctuation. As production volume decreases
in a machining line, for example, workers increase the number of machines to handle, so that the number of total workers for this line can
be reduced.[4] The impact on labor productivity, if not machine productivity, is kept minimal in this way.

As discussed next, multitask job assignment, U-shape process layout, and *jidoka* are complementary practices with this *shojinka* practice.

Multitask Job Assignment Along the Process Flow (takotei-mochi).
This is also called multiprocess handling. In the case of machining,
each worker performs work using different types of machines along
the process sequence, loading, unloading, and transferring the work-
in-process, as well as turning on the machines. An important assumption here is that the machines are reliable enough not to be at-
tended and watched throughout their cycle times. It is also assumed
that the production line in question is not fully automated in terms of
loading, unloading, and transferring the work-in-process, unlike the
Detroit-type transfer machines, for some economical reasons.

*U-shape Machine Layout that Facilitates Flexible and Multiple Task
Assignment.* This is referred to as an effective layout pattern in the
flow layout without fully automated transfer mechanisms. The machines are installed in a U-shape manner along the process, as opposed to the linear layout, so that the first and the last stations are
close to each other. One multitask worker is assigned to the first and

the last stations at the same time, while others may be assigned in the middle. It is argued in the Toyota production textbooks that such a layout, together with multiprocess handling, enables flexible changes of task assignments without much loss of walking; in the linear line, "muda" for walking between stations would increase as the task assignment is enlarged as a part of *shojinka*.

Automatic Detection of Defects and Automatic Shutdown of Machines (jidoka). *Jidoka*, in the narrow sense, means a specific type of machine that can automatically detect defect inputs, processes, or outputs, and automatically shuts down itself. It is important to note that *jidoka* machines do not correct the abnormalities automatically, even when it is technologically feasible. The basic idea is that shutdown of the machine forces human intervention in the process, which in turn triggers process improvement: this would not be the case if the machine automatically corrected the defects.

In a broad sense, *jidoka* means not only the above machine designs but also nonautomated process or product designs that immediately stop work whenever abnormalities happen, which include *poka-yoke* and the line-stop cord system explained below (Toyota Motor Corporation, 1996b).

Foolproof Prevention of Defects (poka-yoke). This is a way of process and/or product design that makes defect operations physically impossible in the first place. Thus, while *jidoka* machines detect defects that just happened, *poka-yoke* goes one step further and prevents such abnormalities from happening in the first place. For example, small and inexpensive attachments to the equipment or tools, in many cases, effectively prevent wrong ways of loading the work-in-process.

Assembly Line Stop Cord. In assembly lines, where main operations are manual but material transfer is automatic (e.g., moving conveyers), a line stop cord is installed in places along the line, so that workers can manually stop the conveyer. In a sense, this is a manual version of a *jidoka* machine with a similar function. When defects or abnormalities are detected by line workers, they can pull the cord (or push a nearby button). This activates an andon signboard (explained next) and the supervisor (team leader) immediately comes to the troubled station. If the worker and/or the leader can solve the problem within the cycle time, the line continues to move; otherwise, the conveyer line has to be stopped. Just like *jidoka* automatic shutdown, this procedure dramatizes the manufacturing problems and acts as a pressure for process improvements.

Real-Time Feedback of Production Troubles (Andon Signboard). Toyota-style factories often have signboards called *andon* above the production lines, which indicate which type of troubles happened and where in real time, so that the operators and supervisors can see what is happening on the shop floor. The andon signboard is combined with *jidoka* defect detection or line stop cords to speed up human intervention when abnormalities are detected on the line.

On-the-Spot Inspection by Direct Workers. Where manual or visual inspection for quality assurance is needed, Toyota-style factories tend to emphasize inspection and minor rework performed by workers on the spot. The basic idea is for each worker *not* to give defected work-in-process to the next station. A famous slogan representing this idea is Toyota's "The downstream process is your customer." On-the-spot inspection and rework are effective in many cases for better conformance quality, but it may be also good for cost reduction and job enlargement, to the extent that this means multiple task assignments for each worker.

Building-in Quality (tsukurikomi). The common theme for *jidoka*, *poka-yoke*, on-the-spot inspection, and line stop cord is the concept of "doing things right the first time," or building in quality (*tsukurikomi*), as opposed to relying solely on ex-post inspections by specialists. In other words, preventing defects by increasing process capabilities (i.e., reducing variances in key production parameters relative to tolerances) is the key here. Statistical process control may also plays an important role.

Cleanliness, Order, Discipline on the Shop Floor (5-S). Maintaining order, cleanliness, and discipline are often called 5-S (*seiri* = arrangement, *seiton* = order, *seiso* = cleanliness, *seiketsu* = neatness, *shitsuke* = discipline). The 5-S is a collection of many small and simple things, such as keeping the floor clean, drawing white lines on the floor, keeping the parts boxes neatly inside the lines, putting tools in order in a tool display box, and so on, each of which is easy to do. As a whole, the 5-S activities help operators visualize disorder and noise in the process by contrasting them with the order of the shop floor.

Visual Management. Toyota-style factories are full of displays, charts, signboards, and other visual reminders for all the workers and managers. These visuals show the work to do, problems to be solved, results of the work, and so on. Examples include andon signboards, standard work charts hanging above the workstations, vehicle specification sheets on each body on the assembly line, color classification for the parts boxes, and various charts showing recent plant performance.

Frequent Revision of Standard Operating Procedures by Supervisors. Standard operating procedures are specified for each repetitive job on the line in basically the same manner as the traditional Taylor system, except that they are more visualized so they are easier for the workers to understand. And the procedures are fairly frequently revised for higher quality and productivity by group leaders (first-line supervisors) after they themselves demonstrate to the workers that the revised procedure is feasible.[5] Adler (1992) calls such an arrangement "democratic Taylorism."[6] In this way, the standard work procedures are fixed at any given point in time, but they are continually revised in the long run by incorporating the knowledge of the shop floor people (workers, team leaders, group leaders) for continuous improvement (*kaizen*).

Quality Circles.   A quality circle is a small group of workers who collectively find a production problem as a theme, discuss the alternative remedies, and propose a solution. The degree to which it is organized on a voluntary basis depends upon the companies. In the case of Toyota, quality circles are incorporated into the total quality control (TQC) system and conducted in a fairly hierarchical manner, more or less overlapping with the formal shop floor organization. Other firms (particularly Western plants adopting this organization) do this activity in a more voluntary basis, though.

Standardized Tools for Quality Improvement (e.g., seven tools for QC, QC story).   These are also elements of total quality control (TQC) and function as guides and analytical tools that help employees solve the production problems for continuous improvements (*kaizen*). The seven tools for quality control are a collection of charts for statistical analyses of manufacturing quality problems, which are simple enough to be made and used by all employees in the *kaizen* process. The QC story pre-specifies a standard sequence of analyses for *kaizen* activities, starting from problem recognition (theme setting) and moving on to root-cause analysis, generation of an alternative action plan, evaluation of alternatives in terms of problem-solving capabilities, recommendation of a new way of doing the task, and prevention of the same problem again. The seven QC tools are regularly used at each stage of the sequence. By combining the QC tools and the QC story, employees can perform problem solving for *kaizen* activities in a standardized manner, regardless of the nature of the problems.

Worker Involvement in Preventive Maintenance (total productive maintenance: TPM).   In a similar manner to total quality control, preventive maintenance of the production equipment is conducted on a company-wide basis by involving not only maintenance specialists and plant engineers but also direct workers, who take care of the equipment and tools that they work with. Their activities include cleaning the machines, checking the equipment periodically, performing minor repairs and tool changes, and creating and analyzing the statistics of process capabilities (statistical process control).

Low-Cost Automation or Semi-Automation with Just Enough Functions. When automation technologies are adopted, the Toyota-style factories tend to take a conservative stance, both economically and technologically. For example, these plants have tended to authorize only low-cost robots whose unit investment cost can be paid back in one or two years (i.e., equivalent of a year's labor cost). Technologically, they tend to choose simpler equipment that has "just enough" functions, rely on mechanistic automation rather than sophisticated numerical control wherever the latter does not seem to be reliable enough, and use semi-automation rather than full automation methods wherever the former seems to be more cost-effective.

In most Japanese firms, this tendency toward low-cost automation has continued until the late 1990s—except around 1990, when the labor shortage and a bubble economy made them go for more expensive and sophisticated automation technologies in the name of human-friendly factories (Fujimoto, 1997a).

Reduction of Process Steps for Saving Tools and Dies. Wherever technologically and economically feasible, efforts are made to shorten the number of production processes. By the 1980s, the Japanese press shops, for example, had reduced the number of shots for making a given panel compared to Western plants, saving both significant equipment and die investment costs.

Some Japanese companies (Honda in particular) have also concentrated on reducing the number of process steps by consolidating many jobs in one station in order to achieve better visual management. Honda's main body welding process, for example, consists of a much smaller number of workstations than most of other firms, so that operators, engineers, and managers can see the whole process at a glance. This makes each workstation complex and difficult to maintain, because many small robots have to be packed in a small space, but the benefit of sharing shop floor information was regarded more important at this company.

Practices in Human Resource Management

There are some human resource management factors that back up the above elements of production management. Again, there is much literature that focuses on this topic, so this section tries only a brief sketch of some key factors.[7]

Stable Employment of Core Workers (with temporary workers on the periphery). This is a well-known notion of "lifetime employment," but the label is not accurate, as there is a specified retirement age (sixty, in the case of blue-collar workers at Toyota).[8] We can characterize what Toyota has continued to do between the 1950s, when the company was in the middle of a financial crisis and fired many of its employees, and the late 1990s, when there were no layoff policies. When production goes down at a certain plant, overtime may be cut, temporary workers may be reduced, work days may be reduced, permanent workers may be dispatched (or permanently transferred) to busier plants or group companies to "help them," or they may be even transferred to dealers to help them sell more of what the company produces, but there have been no forced layoffs among Japanese assemblers since the mid-1950s.[9]

The stable core workforce was supplemented by temporary workers during labor shortages (e.g., late 1960s, early 1990s).[10] The temporary workers were particularly heavily used in heavy truck assemblers, which were facing significant business fluctuation.

Long-Term Training of Multiskilled (multitask) Workers.   Shop floor workers are expected to do multiple tasks across workstations, as well as between direct and indirect work, to sustain the flexible production system and to reduce "muda" in their work time. On-the-job training (OJT) through rotation and direct instruction from veteran workers and leaders are common modes of skill accumulation. In this sense, certain mechanisms of skill transfer that resemble the apprenticeship of old craft-type systems, such as direct job instructions from veteran supervisors, remain in the mass production shops.

The workers are typically expected to master the main direct jobs, as well as inspection, minor rework, improvements, and other indirect tasks within a work group. The area of rotation tends to be rather broad, but is limited to a group of functionally related jobs or processes, depending upon the rank of the worker (Koike, 1977, 1991; Asanuma, 1994, 1997). Through such career paths, workers' abilities to respond to changes and disruptions on the shop floor are enhanced.

More recently, major Japanese automakers have established a systematic and formal plan to develop multiskilled workers step by step, including both OJT and off-site education (off-JT), so that workers can have a clearer vision of their future work life (e.g., Nabeta, 1992).

Wage System Based in Part on Skill Accumulation.   Unlike the traditional U.S. system with narrow job classifications linked to different wage rates, the Japanese blue-collar workers are paid basically by their ability to perform a variety of tasks—as well as other factors such as efficiency—based on broadly defined job classifications, although the actual formula for wage calculations was quite complicated (see Nomura, 1993, and Shimizu, 1994, for example). The wage system based on wide job demarcations is consistent with multitask assignments and job rotation. Wage rates based on the width of the skills (i.e., potential capability) rather than content of the current job tends also to mean that wage rates rise as workers stay longer at the company. Thus, the wage system is consistent with stable employment and multitask job designs.

Internal Promotion to Shop Floor Supervisor.   At Toyota's assembly shops, shop floor supervisors include team leaders (leader of about five people), group leaders (leaders of about four teams), and assistant managers (head of a few groups). These posts are normally occupied by people originally hired as blue-collar workers, who graduated mostly from high schools or Toyota's training schools, and who work on the shop floor for an extended period (typically for fifteen years before becoming team leader). They become veteran multiskilled workers in their shops and eventually are promoted from inside to the supervising jobs. In fact, team leaders are in many cases "playing managers," doing both supervisory jobs off the line and relief work on the lines. They are also constantly helping workers solve their problems on the line. Group leaders are totally off the lines, but they are supposed to play key roles in process improvements (i.e., revisions of standard operating procedures), training of workers, troubleshooting on the line, and so on.

To sum up, the first-line supervisors are not only people at the bottom of the plant management hierarchy but also veteran multiskilled workers who use their extensive shop floor knowledge for process improvements (*kaizen*), education, and troubleshooting. For example, the main textbooks for the multiskilled education program at Toyota were developed by some group leaders and assistant managers, not because of their positions but because they were, after all, the core repository of shop floor knowledge.

Production Supervisors as Union Members.   Another important profile of the shop floor supervisors is that they are all union members. (Toyota's nonunion posts at the plants start from section head, which is one rank above assistant manager.) Thus, the first-line supervisors at company like Toyota have multifaceted roles—lower levels of plant management hierarchy, ex-veteran workers who still are at the core of shop floor skills and knowledge, and the influential opinion leaders in the labor union and the shop.

On the one hand, their status as union members simplifies the process of continuous improvements (*kaizen*): when a group leader takes on the task of revising standard operating procedures, for example, this does not provoke management-union negotiations because the situation does not impose changes in work rules for union members, as is the case in traditional U.S. plants. On the other hand, it is often said that it is difficult to implement an institutional change without a general consensus by the supervisor group, so both union leaders and management sometimes spend significant time getting supports when a change is envisioned (see chapter 7).

Cooperative Relationships with Labor Unions.   Since the end of the large strikes at both Toyota and Nissan in the early 1950s, management has attempted to establish cooperative relations with the unions.[11] Although the two major automakers established somewhat different patterns of union-labor relationships (Cusumano, 1985), they both built a more or less cooperative relationship by the 1960s; there have been no strikes at the major Japanese automakers since then. Frequent union-management communications and negotiations at various levels has helped maintain the generally collaborative relationships on such issues as annual wage negotiation, automation and production rationalization, construction of overseas factories, humanization of production processes, remedies for production volume decreases, and even plant shutdowns up to the mid-1990s (see chapter 7).

Communication and Worker Motivation.   Toyota's personnel managers often insist that their most important job is to promote communication between management and union, management and employees, the union and its members, and supervisors and subordinates. This task ranges from the communication of company policies to the union leaders to setting up shop floor meeting times between supervisors and workers. Managers at Toyota often point out that communication is the most important part of employee motivation.[12]

Overall Patterns: Generic Principles versus Specific Applications.   It should be noted that many of the routines described above are effective in specific production processes (e.g., final assembly, machining, stamping), rather than in generic principle (see table B.1). Generally speaking, Toyota-style production routines are often presented as a list of propositions, but the distinction between generic statements that can be applicable to any production processes and specific applications to particular production processes is not necessarily clear. Thus, empirical researchers studying the Toyota-style production systems have to identify the generic patterns that lie behind the process-specific applications, rather than simply making a "laundry list" of best practices.

B.2 Production-Related Performance: A Literature Review

Productivity and Cost

The studies conducted in the 1980s and the early 1990s repeatedly indicated that the average performance of the Japanese automobile assemblers was significantly higher than that of North American and

Table B.1 Patterns of Manufacturing at Effective Japanese Automakers in the 1980s by Processes: An Ideal Type

Process	Layout	Dedicated/ Mixed	Cycle Time	Lot Size	Automation	Material Handling	Worker	Reduction of "Muda"	Reduction of Throughput Time	Quality Improvement	Flexibility to Variety
Final assembly	product layout, continuously moving assembly line (Ford system)	platform: dedicated or mixed; variation: mixed	typically 1 to 2 minutes; fine-tuned to sales volume (in theory)	typically several dozens; mixed model	deliberately kept to low level; power assists, simple robots; low cost automation	body: continuous conveyer line (Ford system); parts: Kanban, synchronized delivery, etc.	within cycle time: multi parts tasks, but few group works; between cycle times: multi-model tasks; long-term rotation and multi-skilling	moving assembly line reveals line imbalance; Shojinka: flexible task assignment for higher value adding time ratio	relatively short assembly line with ordinary line speed; reduction of line stops and reworks	doing right things the first time; self inspection; Andon and line stop cord (visualizing problems)	general-purpose tools and equipment; multi-task assembly workers; relatively few common parts
Body spot welding	product layout, tact assembly line (intermittent)	platform: dedicated or mixed; body type: mixed	typically 0.7 to 2 minutes	typically 1 to several dozens	high ratio of automation (robots); low cost automation	body: shuttle conveyer line; parts: Kanban, synchronized delivery, etc.	mostly indirect or semi-direct work (monitoring, maintaining, inspecting, material handling, etc.)	reduction of machines' down times	reduction of line stops and reworks; Poka-yoke (fool-proof devices)	self maintenance; Poka-yoke (fool-proof devices)	mixture of fixed automation and robots; flexible jigs
Body stamping	product layout (tandem press), batch flow line	mixed (with set-up change)	typically less than 10 seconds	typically less than 1000 (rather small lot)	high ratio of automation; general purpose equipment	on both ends: inventories; in-line transfer: piece-by-piece (automated)	operators participate in set up, inspection, maintenance	reduction of set-up times with ordinary machine speed	reduction of coil and panel inventories; reduction of # of shots	quality of dies; Poka-yoke; transfer press	small lot set up changes
Engine machining	product layout (Detroit-type intermittent transfer machine)	dedicated to an engine family	typically 0.5 to 1 minutes	large lot or no change	high ratio of fixed automation	on both ends: inventories; in-line transfer: piece by piece (automated)	operators participate in set up, inspection and maintenance	reduction of machines' down times	test transfer between machines; automated inspection	self maintenance; Poka-yoke; automated inspection	low flexibility; quick set up change of tools
Low-speed parts manufacturing	product layout, dense (U-shape)	dedicated or mixed	typically 0.5 to 1 minutes	large lot or no change	semi-automation; Jidoka (automated machine stop)	in-line transfer: piece-by-piece (manual); Kanban method on both ends	an operator handles multiple machines in the line (Takotei-mochi)	reduction of machines' waiting times; Shojinka for volume changes	no inventory in the line; reduction of inventory on both ends	Jidoka visualizes quality problems; Poka-yoke; self maintenance & inspection	flexible equipment; quick set up change of tools
Overall	product layout, piece-by-piece flow	rather mixed	depends on technology and market	rather small lot	depends on technology; low cost automation	conveyer lines wherever possible; Kanban as a second best choice (invisible conveyer)	multi-tasking and multi-skilling; stable employment, broad job description, training, etc. as background	systematic reduction of non-value adding time (muda) by multi-tasking, supervisors' initiatives, etc.	systematic reduction of inventory and throughput time (JIT) by problem visualization	improvements at all levels (TQC, TPM) with Kaizen initiatives by supervisors, small group activities, suggestions, etc	flexibility for small lot high variety production; aggregate volume per line is still large

European counterparts in such indicators as assembly productivity, manufacturing quality, product development productivity and lead time, and dealer satisfaction. Although the competitive gap between Japanese and the Western (particularly U.S.) automakers narrowed or disappeared by the mid-1990s in such indicators as unit cost, manufacturing quality, and product development performance, due partly to appreciation of the yen, catchup efforts by some Western automakers, technology transfers from the Japanese through direct investment and strategic coalitions, and slowdown of productivity improvements on the Japanese side, the Japanese on average maintained their overall competitive advantage in real terms.

Because there have been books and articles that have made international comparisons of manufacturing performance in the automobile industry, this appendix will not get into the details of each analysis, but will summarize results in the 1980s and early 1990s, mainly focusing on the U.S.-Japan comparison (see also table B.2).[13]

Multiple Indicators for Productivity. Manufacturing productivity—the ratio of inputs to outputs in production processes—is a multifaceted construct. There are various ways of measuring productivity. In terms of output, we may measure it in monetary terms (e.g., value-added productivity) or in real terms (physical output productivity). As for the process, we may select a major or representative process such as assembly and measure its productivity, or we may cover the whole manufacturing process including the parts-making processes. On the

Table B.2   The Results of Major Productivity-related Indices

Productivity index	Source	Results of analysis
Manufacturing cost	Abernathy, Clark and Kantrow (1983). US Automakers Harbor (1980).	• A Japanese per vehicle advantage over American companies of $1100–$2000 at the beginning of the 1980s.
	Arthur Anderson Co.	• By latter half of 1980s, due to the strengthening yen, US productivity improvements, etc., the gap had shrunk to a few hundred dollars.
Assembly productivity	Abernathy, Clark and Kantrow (1983). Harbor (1980).	• Japanese industry had a nearly two to one advantage over the US industry at the beginning of the 1980s.
	Krafcik (in Womack, Jones and Roos, 1990)	• By latter half of 1980s, Japan averaged 17 hours/vehicle versus 25 hours for US industry and 21 hours for North American Japanese transplants.
Total industry labour output productivity (assemblers and suppliers)	US, German and Japanese Industry Census Data*	• In 1990, Japan rated 131 hours/vehicle, USA 152 hours and W. German industry at 252 hours
	Japanese Industry Census Data	• Japanese labour productivity grew at 6.3% annually in the 1970s but in 1980s moved at 0.3%.
Total industry value-added labour productivity (assemblers and suppliers)	Japan Productivity Centre (1991).	• In 1989, a 100.65 measure indicated more than a one-third advantage for the USA over Japan's industry (based on constant 1980 yen-dollar exchange rate).
		• During the 1970s, gap with USA shrank, but in the 1980s gap moved sideways, unchanging.
	Japan Productivity Centre*	• Based on a normiral exchange rate from 1989, Japan claimed more than a 10% advantage over USA. (Japan 113:USA 100)
Total factor productivity	Fuss and Weveman OSAT (Univ. of Michigan) (1992).	• Cost gap in Japan's favour from 1970s to mid-1980s; Japan claimed efficiency advantage from the mid-1970s.
		• In latter half of 1980s, Japan still held efficiency edge, but largely due to the strengthening yen, USA held 5% cost advantage
Dealer productivity	Japan Automobile Dealers Association and NADA (US National Automobile Dealers' Association)*	• Efficiency as sales/salesperson/month: Japan 4.7, USA 7.1; as measured by sales/employee/month: 1.4 for both countries' industries (1990).
		• Since 1970s, Japan sales/salesperson/month efficiency rating has moved sideways

Note: *Indicates that this is the author's analysis of this data. Other data from existing studies.

Source: Fujimoto and Takeishi (1995)

output side, we may measure one production factor as input (e.g., labor, capital, materials), or we may try to measure efficiency of total inputs (e.g., total factor productivity, unit product cost). For each case, we also face a problem of adjustment for differing conditions, such as product mix, vertical integration, automation ratio (in the case of partial factor productivity), capacity utilization, workers' skill level, and work hours. Thus, it is practically (if not theoretically) impossible to create one indicator by which we can judge the productivity level of an industry. We need to rely on multiple indicators of productivity by taking into account the merits and limits of each measure. Taking the above into consideration, let us briefly look at different indicators measured between the 1970s and the early 1990s.

Assembly Labor Productivity.   Assembly plants in a broad sense, including final assembly shops (trim, chassis, and final), body paint shops, and body welding shops, has been the focal point where international comparisons of real-term automobile productivity have been conducted since around 1980.[14] The first generation of such comparative studies included those by Abernathy, Clark, and Kantrow (1983) and Harbour (1980).[15] These comparisons done around 1981–82 and measuring person-hour per vehicle in comparable products, concluded that there existed, roughly speaking, a two-to-one advantage for the Japanese. These studies, however, tended to rely on small samples and thus may not have reflected average industry performance in each country. (The result may have been somewhat exaggerated by a sample bias, for example.)

The second generation of assembly labor productivity studies was conducted in the late 1980s by researchers of the International Motor Vehicle Program (IMVP) at Massachusetts Institute of Technology (MIT), which confirmed evidence of a Japanese advantage on an industry average basis.[16] That is, the average Japanese assembly time, adjusted for differences in product mix, automation ratio, and so on, was reported to be about 17 person-hours per vehicle; the average U.S. counterpart was 25 person-hours; the European average was 37 person-hours (Womack et al., 1990). At the same time, the author found that the gap between the United States and Japan was not as large as expected from the early 1980s studies. It may have come from sample biases of the first-generation studies, but it is also possible that efforts by U.S. firms for productivity catchup had been going on since the mid-1980s, thus narrowing the gap by the time the IMVP study was conducted.

Another important point that the IMVP data indicated is that there was a fairly wide range of performance by each regional group, so that, for example, the most productive plant among the U.S. firms was more efficient than the least productive Japanese plant. Thus, the data demonstrated that, although the interregional differences in productivity were significant, intraregional differences were also fairly large, indicating that individual firms matter to a certain extent.

It should be also noted that the average productivity of the Japanese transplants in North America—21 person-hours per vehicle—was in between that of Japanese auto plants in Japan and U.S. auto plants in North America. This seems to indicate that the Japanese manufacturing practices, which were introduced into the transplants as a system with certain modifications, would have a certain universal value as contributors to a competitive advantage even in American plants.[17]

The IMVP data in the early 1990s give us some additional insights (MacDuffie and Pil, 1996). Between 1989 and 1993, the Japanese average productivity was almost unchanged (from 17 to 16 person-hours per vehicle), while the U.S. average (from 25 to 23 person-hours), and particularly the European average (from 37 to 26 person-hours), demonstrated significant improvements. Thus, the Western catchup was obvious in the 1990s, but the interregional differences in average assembly productivity still persisted as of the mid-1990s. In any case, as the gaps between regions narrowed, the performance of individual companies, rather than that of regional groups (e.g., Japan), became increasingly important.

Total Industry Labor Productivity. Even if we have a reasonably accurate comparison of assembly labor productivities, this does not necessarily mean that we have examined the productivity of the total industry, which includes parts manufacturing. In Japan, the automobile makers incur less than 30 percent (less than 20 percent in the case of the assembly plants alone) of the unit manufacturing cost: the rest is conducted by parts suppliers. There is no guarantee that the differences in assembly productivity accurately reflect total industry productivity. While it is practically impossible to conduct comparative studies of productivity for each of the numerous parts manufacturing operations, a realistic solution is to go for industry-level data (e.g., census of manufactures and labor statistics in each country).

There is a comparative study of Japanese, U.S., and German (then West German) total industry labor productivity (measured by total employees times total labor time per units produced), which shows that Japan recorded 131 person-hours per unit versus 152 person-hours for the American industry in 1990. The German average was 252 hours per unit, falling behind the former two (For details, see Fujijmoto and Takeishi, 1995).

Thus, the data on total industry labor productivity were generally consistent with the assembly productivity data in reporting a Japanese advantage at that time. At the same time, however, it should be noted the Japanese-U.S. gap was smaller than as shown in the IMVP assembly study of the same period: Japan's average assembly person-hours per unit in the latter study was 68 percent of the U.S. average, while Japanese productivity in the former case was 86 percent of that of the United States. Thus, it would be reasonable to infer that the Japanese-U.S. gap was larger for assembly productivity than for parts manufacturing productivity.

It should be noted, however, that the total industry labor productivity data were not adjusted for differences in product mix, output besides completely built vehicles (e.g., knock-down kits), coverage of the parts industry by each government statistic, coverage of statistical samples at each statistic, capacity utilization, automation ratio, and so on. Although we have not been able to apply a systematic adjustment, Takeishi and I estimate that, after all these factors are considered qualitatively, there is a strong possibility that Japan's productivity advantage was little understated in the above studies (Fujimoto and Takeishi, 1995).

Fujimoto and Takeishi (1995) also looked at the long-term trend in Japan's total industry labor productivity over the past twenty years, and found an intriguing pattern: the average annual productivity growth rate was 6.3 percent in the 1970s; since the beginning of the 1980s, this growth had almost stopped. Throughout the 1980s, it almost leveled off, growing at a mere 0.3 percent annually. (We have to take into account that the product content of average Japanese cars significantly increased during the 1980s, making the above figure an underestimate.) Other productivity data also indicated this slowing trend in productivity growth after the 1980s (Fujimoto and Takeishi, 1994; MacDuffie and Pil, 1996). Thus, the data indicate an interesting fact that tended to be overlooked by many researchers and industry practitioners: the Japanese manufacturing system did make a remarkable productivity increase in the postwar era, but it was mostly prior to the 1980s. When the Japanese system of continuous improvements became a prevalent topic among Western practitioners in the 1980s, quite ironically, the Japanese productivity increase had already slowed significantly. The increase in product content may have been one factor, but a diminishing return from continuous improvements would be also another main reason for this apparent slow down.

Total Industry Value-Added Labor Productivity.   Another prevalent way of comparing labor productivity is to take the value added as the output measure. This is particularly useful for purposes of interindustrial comparisons, but we have to take into account the difference in profit margins caused by external conditions, the impact of exchange rates, and so on. The exchange rate is particularly important for international comparison. According to Nihon Seisansei Honbu (Japan Productivity Center, 1991), for example, the value added per worker per hour in the Japanese auto industry in 1988 was merely about two-thirds of that of an American worker's productivity, contradicting the other productivity studies discussed above. The major reason for this seems to be that the analysis used 1980 purchasing power parity (240 yen per $1). If we use the actual exchange rate in 1989 (138 yen per $1), which seems to be more relevant for current research purposes, Japan's labor value-added productivity becomes higher than the United States by 13 percent. Thus, we get a fairly consistent result of a Japanese productivity advantage by using actual exchange rate, but the U.S.-Japan difference is smaller than that measured in other ways.

As for the productivity increase, the Productivity Center's analysis shows that the Japanese industry continued to improve value-added productivity in the 1980s, unlike the case of real-term productivity discussed earlier. In relative terms, however, Japanese value-added productivity was growing faster than U.S. productivity in the 1970s, but the U.S.-Japan difference in productivity growth rate basically disappeared in the 1980s, according to this study.

Total Factor Productivity.   Total factor productivity refers to the ratio of total inputs to total outputs, although there are technical details and some theoretical background which is not discussed here. The total factor productivity analysis usually breaks down the interregional or interfirm gaps in total unit cost into two components: efficiency and factor costs.

One of the main contributions in this field is Fuss and Waverman (1990). Their study indicates a total cost disadvantage to the U.S. automobile industry compared to the Japanese industry throughout the period from 1970 to 1984. During the first half of the 1970s, the U.S. industry maintained higher efficiency, but its overall cost was higher owing mostly to wages and other factor costs. After the late 1970s, the performance of the U.S. auto industry got worse than its Japanese counterpart, in both efficiency and factor costs. Although the U.S. industry enjoyed higher economies of scale, performance in capacity utilization and country-specific efficiency (capabilities, using the terms in this book) were worse than the Japanese, which resulted in lower efficiency overall during this period.

More recently, Fuss and Waverman extended their Japanese-U.S. comparison to 1988, which indicates that, as of 1988, the U.S. auto industry held a total cost advantage of about 5 percent (Office for the Study of Automotive Transportation, 1992). It is likely that the main reason for the U.S. recovery was the increase in Japan's factor costs owing to appreciation of yen since the mid-1980s. On the efficiency side, Japan's advantage over the U.S. industry (18 percent in the period from the 1970s to mid-1980s) only slightly decreased (about 16 percent during the 1984–88 period).

Lieberman et al. (1990), on the other hand, measured the firm-level total factor productivity of six U.S. and Japanese auto companies (General Motors, Ford, Chrysler, Toyota, Nissan, Mazda) between 1950 and 1987, and found that the Japanese firms on average tended to improve their productivity faster, and that Toyota's average growth rate of total factor productivity was the highest among them.

Unit Manufacturing Costs.   Since the beginning of the 1980s, when the Japanese cost advantage was recognized by industry observers, there have been many studies trying to estimate the difference in unit manufacturing cost of comparable U.S. and Japanese cars (Abernathy, Clark, and Kantrow, 1983). Although the estimations differed depending upon the data and assumptions, the general consensus in the early

1980s was that a typical car produced in Japan held a $1100–$2000, or 20–30 percent, advantage on a U.S. port arrival basis.[18] The main contributor to the gap was unit labor costs, to which a lower labor cost per hour and a higher labor productivity on the Japanese side contributed roughly equally. Together with studies in supplier productivity and capital productivity, these researchers concluded that the Japanese cars had a significant advantage in the early 1980s. The conclusion is consistent with anecdotal evidence that the Japanese automakers in the early 1980s could make about 200,000 yen profit per vehicle from their North American sales, and that a majority of the operating profits of major Japanese firms was generated from the North American market, as opposed to the domestic market.

After the post-Plaza appreciation of the yen in 1985, the slowdown in productivity growth among the Japanese makers, and productivity improvement on the U.S. side, the cost gaps started to shrink rapidly. Two other waves of yen appreciation, in 1993 and 1994, further pushed the yen to roughly 80–110 per dollar. Although an accurate cost determination is difficult, as it depends upon various assumptions on unit labor cost, parts procurement cost, utilization ratio, and so on, some estimations by industry experts suggest that the unit cost advantage of the Japanese makers was eliminated when the yen rose to the level of 130–140 per dollar. Other estimates, however, indicate that Toyota maintained a slight advantage in unit cost over average U.S. makers even when the yen was appreciated to 100 per dollar. The difference in estimations comes partly from a difference in assumptions (e.g., unit fringe benefit cost) and partly from Toyota's cost advantages over other Japanese firms, which was estimated to be at least several hundred dollars per car in the early 1990s.

In any case, no data were found to clearly demonstrate unit cost advantages for either the Japanese or the U.S. car makers as of the late 1990s, when massive cost-cutting efforts were making progress on both sides and exchange rates were fluctuating. It is at least clear, however, that the overwhelming unit cost advantages of the average Japanese car makers that existed in the early 1980s had been basically wiped out by the mid-1990s.

Summary in Productivity and Cost Measurement. We have so far examined various measures of productivity. Although the results varied depending upon the indicators and methods selected, there seems to be a patterns that most studies agree with: First, the Japanese auto makers on average had significant productivity advantages throughout the 1980s. Even after the Japanese cost advantages eroded by the appreciation of yen, the Japanese productivity advantages were maintained, although significantly reduced, even in the mid 1990s.[19]

Second, in terms of productivity growth, the peak time for the Japanese was the 1970s or earlier; in the 1980s, they experienced a significant drop in their productivity growth rate, as well as a relative increase vis-à-vis the U.S. automakers.

Quality, Lead Time, and Flexibility

Comparison of Manufacturing (Conformance) Quality.   The recognition that Japanese import cars in the North American market tended to have higher conformance quality (reliability, fit, and finish) than their U.S. and European counterparts spread among consumers in the first half of the 1980s, as concrete data from *Consumer Reports* magazine, periodical reports from J.D. Power & Associates, and so on became widely known to the public (also partly as a result of word of mouth). The International Motor Vehicle Program also created an assembly quality index by extracting from the J.D. Power data only those factors affected by a firm's assembly activities, and this index confirmed the advantage of average Japanese quality in the late 1980s (Womack et al., 1990).[20]

Data in the early 1990s in the same indicator showed that the average assembly quality improved, not only in the United States and Europe but also in Japan—unlike the case of assembly productivity discussed earlier. The interregional difference in relative terms did narrow in this period, though.[21] Thus, the Western catchup effect was significant also in conformance quality, but the Japanese advantage on average remained into the mid-1990s (MacDuffie and Pil, 1996).

Comparison in Delivery and Production Lead Time.   There are some indicators related to each other in this category: production lead time (throughput time), distribution lead time, and customer delivery time (i.e., time elapsed between final customer's order and corresponding delivery of the product). Their relationships are different depending upon the pattern of sales. When customers buy from dealer inventories or the producer's finished goods inventories, a part of the distribution lead time and times for order processing and registration may be included, but the production lead time is excluded from the delivery time. This is usually the case in North America. When customers buy cars based on their special orders (i.e., customization), then production lead time, in addition to other lead times, is included in the delivery time. This is often the case in some parts of Europe (Sweden, Germany), particularly for high-end products. The Japanese makers tended to produce partly to dealer inventories and partly to special orders, with the former usually being a majority.

There has been little comparative data collection on customer delivery and related lead times on international scale, though. There are detailed descriptions on Toyota's order entry system and production scheduling (Monden, 1983/1993; Toyota Motor Corporation, 1992, 1996b; Shioji, 1996; Okamoto, 1996), but these studies do not compare its performance and practices to other firms. Thus, the following discussion is based partly on various internal studies conducted in the early 1990s in some auto companies and consulting firms to which the author had access, as well as the author's own interviews.[22]

Case I—Production to Dealer Inventories. In the Japanese market, delivery times to the customers are normally one to two weeks, even if they pick the cars from dealer inventory, partly because of time-consuming work related to government regulations (e.g., vehicle registration, garage certificate, etc.), which is significantly longer than in the United States and Europe (usually one day to one week). Auto manufacturers have no control over this lead time, as the production lead time is not involved here.

However, the Japanese system has an advantage here of having fewer dealer inventories to respond to customer needs. The Japanese domestic dealer inventory level is said to range from fifteen to thirty days (about three weeks in the case of Toyota) as of the mid-1990s, compared to roughly sixty to seventy days for the U.S. automakers. In the case of Toyota, its order entry system, with step-by-step refinement of production plans through frequent communication between the automaker and its dealers, facilitates higher accuracy of dealer market forecasts and thereby reduces necessary inventory levels, other things being equal. In this system, levels of product specifications get more detailed, order lot sizes get smaller as the production date approaches, and dealers are allowed to change their order specifications within a certain limit up to three or four days before production (Monden, 1983/1993; Okamoto, 1996).[23]

Case II—Production to Customers' Specific Orders. This is the case in which production lead time, as well as order processing time and distribution lead time, matters. As expected, the Japanese firms tend to have lead time advantages here. Major Japanese automakers, including Toyota, usually have a capability of delivering cars to customers within two to three weeks after receiving their orders. In Europe, the equivalent figures roughly ranged from one to three months as of the early 1990s, depending upon the country and product.

Behind this advantage are shorter order processing lead times (i.e., times between customer order and production instruction) and shorter production lead times (i.e., times between production instruction and completion). At Toyota, for example, shorter intervals of dealer orders (ten days) and opportunities for late specification changes by dealers tend to shorten order processing time. Note, however, that even Toyota appears to have many cases (roughly one-third in some cases) in which delivery times exceed one month owing in part to a production capacity shortage and in part to a mismatch between dealer orders and manufacturer's production plan.

It is also well known that production lead times tended to be short for the Japanese automakers of the 1980s. There are no international comparative studies directly dealing with this issue, but the data on work-in-process inventory levels would be a good proxy variable for the speed of production (Stalk and Hout, 1990). According to the International Motor Vehicle Program, the Japanese average levels of component inventories and painted body inventories at the assembly plants were both lower than the North American and European cases, which indirectly indicates that the production throughput times of the Japanese automakers were relatively short.

Ironically, the majority of Japanese domestic car sales (roughly two-thirds in the case of Toyota as of the mid-1990s) is from dealer inventory, where the Japanese do not have a particular lead time advantage. As a result, according to a study by the Boston Consulting Group in 1995, the average delivery lead time between customer orders and physical delivery is roughly three weeks, longer than the U.S. (about one week) and U.K. (about two weeks) cases, although it is shorter than the German (about two months) case, in which sales are predominantly based on customers' specific orders.[24]

In summary, we can characterize the Japanese industry as a middle-range situation between the two extreme patterns typically observed in the United States and Germany. First, in Germany and some other parts of Europe, customers tend to wait for the cars they specifically ordered for a long time, while car makers and dealers have low levels of finished goods inventory. Second, in North America, cars are produced, delivered to the dealers, and wait for customers to come, test drive, buy, and drive home. The cars tend to wait for a long time in the form of dealer inventories, but customers do not have to. Third, in Japan, car makers find customers relatively quickly for stock sales (compared to American dealer inventory levels), although customers have to wait for registration and other regulatory work to be completed. Alternatively, customers may order the cars they want, and get them produced and delivered relatively quickly compared to some European cases.

In this way, the Japanese automakers of the 1980s tried to compromise the tradeoff between delivery lead times and dealer inventory costs (Okamoto, 1996). A fast production throughput time for the Japanese firms, particularly at Toyota, enabled them to make such a compromise rather effectively.

Process Flexibility.   There are some studies indicating the flexibility of Japanese assemblers, directly and indirectly. One indicator of flexibility is the width of product ranges that an assembly line handles (Womack et al., 1990).[25] Another is more operational, such as the average setup change time for press dies, which enables flexible production of multiple products. The average plant shutdown time for a major model change is also an indicator that captures long-term process flexibility (Clark and Fujimoto, 1991). With most indicators, the Japanese firms of the 1980s tended to demonstrate a higher degree of flexibility.

To sum up, the Japanese assembly makers tended to show higher static and improvement performance in production in such areas as productivity, manufacturing quality, production throughput time, and flexibility, which generally contributed to their competitive advantages vis-à-vis their American and European competitors in the 1980s. Many such advantages in real terms still remain as of the mid-1990s, although the Western catchup and appreciation of the yen had eroded the overall competitiveness of the Japanese automakers by the mid-1990s.

Toyota's Firm-Specific Performance

Most of the data presented in the foregoing section dealt with the production performance of Japanese automakers in general. As we have already pointed out, in addition to interregional differences in performance (i.e., the Japan effect), there were significant intraregional performance differences among the Japanese firms (Womack et al., 1990). Thus, the question is if Toyota, the main research site of this book, is among the top performers in the Japanese group. Data for individual firms are not always available for confidentiality reasons, but there are some data that indicate that Toyota is the top-level performer among the Japanese makers in many, if not all, criteria. In labor productivity, for example, the author's separate investigation indicates that assembly productivity at one of Toyota's plants is roughly the same as that of the most productive plant reported in Womack et al. (1990). Cusumano (1985, 1988), measuring adjusted labor productivity (vehicle per employee), has shown that Toyota's productivity was consistently better than that of Nissan in the 1960s and '70s. Lieberman et al. (1990), measuring total factor productivity and value-added labor productivity, also indicated that Toyota's productivity increase between 1950 and 1987 was the highest among major U.S. and Japanese firms (GM, Ford, Chrysler, Toyota, Nissan, and Mazda) in both measures.[26]

In manufacturing quality, it is well known that Toyota of the 1980s was constantly ranked as a top rank performer, even compared to most other Japanese makers, in surveys by J.D. Power & Associates, *Consumer Reports* magazine, and so on.[27] Toyota's performance in production throughput time, estimated by the work-in-process inventory turnover, was also significantly higher than most other Japanese firms between the 1960s and 1980s, according to Lieberman, Demeester, and Rivas (1995).[28]

In addition to formal data analyses, there is anecdotal information that hints at the company's strength in production. For example, in the mid-1980s, it was said by many industry insiders that Toyota was enjoying at least a 50,000 yen advantage in manufacturing cost per ve-

hicle compared to its major competitor.[29] In using broader criteria, we
see that Toyota's domestic market share (in units of cars and trucks)
has been consistently around 40 percent in most years between the
early 1970s and the mid-1990s. Its profit ratios have been also consistently higher than most other Japanese automakers during this period.
Although there are other factors than manufacturing capabilities (e.g.,
distribution channel, size, etc.), this formal and informal evidence is
persuasive enough to believe that Toyota's production performance
was indeed high, even compared to other Japanese firms.

B.3 Basic Facts of the Supplier Systems

Although the Japanese supplier systems were empirically investigated
by many Japanese and foreign researchers in the past, particularly in
the areas of applied economics, my general impression is that various
misunderstandings have persisted, even about basic facts. This section presents selected empirical findings based on the existing literature including mine, following the three-dimensional framework proposed in chapter 4.[30] Performance of the system is discussed first;
structural patterns of the practices are discussed next.

Performance of the Japanese Supplier System

Let us first discuss the performance side of the Japanese automobile
supplier system. Since the system involves interfirm relations, we
need to examine overall efficiency and equity, as well as competitive
performance.

Efficiency of Resource Allocation (Monopoly Rent).   The traditional
industrial organization theory attempts to detect inefficiency in resource allocation by checking if there are significant interfirm differences in profit margins. Specifically, when the large assemblers enjoy
a significantly higher profit to sales ratio than the suppliers, the standard applied economics is to suspect that resource allocation is
inefficient in the sense that the former is taking monopoly rent.

Crandall (1968), for example, reports that the average profit margin
of the major U.S. automakers between 1936 and 1961 was 24 percent
and was far above that of the suppliers, at 8 percent. In the case of the
Japanese assemblers of the late 1980s (i.e., after the appreciation of the
yen in 1985), by contrast, the average operating profit to sales ratio
was less than 5 percent and was lower than that of the major suppliers
listing stocks. More generally, there has been intense domestic competition among about ten Japanese automakers since the 1960s, which
tends to lower profits from the domestic market.[31] Overall, it is hard to
demonstrate that the Japanese automakers were enjoying a high monopoly rent and thereby seriously distorting the resource allocation.

Distribution Inequity. This has been a focal point of the so-called dual structure theorists for a long time. The most important indicator in this regard is the average wage difference between large firms and small firms. According to Nishiguchi (1994), the average wage rate of small and medium manufacturing firms in general—with ten to ninety-nine employees—was about 60 percent that of the large manufacturing firms (1,000 employees or more) in the late 1950s, but the ratio went up to about 80 percent in the early 1960s (roughly equivalent of that in the United States), partly reflecting a labor shortage of the high-growth era, and stayed at around that level until the 1980s.[32] This change could be interpreted as a significant move toward better distribution equity in the 1960s or as a lack of improvement since that time, depending upon the stance of the researchers involved.

As discussed later, it should be noted that the average first-tier parts suppliers in Japan are large firms, and that the boundary between large and small to medium firms is usually between the first-tier and second-tier suppliers. This implies that the wage gap between the average assemblers and the first-tier suppliers is likely to be much smaller than the 20 percent level shown above.[33] Conversely, it should be noted that, even though we find no significant wage gap between assemblers and first-tier suppliers, that does not guarantee distribution equity throughout the supply chain, which includes second-tier, third-tier, and so on.

Static Competitive Performance. The data on static performance of the suppliers tend to be limited to first-tier suppliers. As for conformance quality, Cusumano and Takeishi (1991) reported that the Japanese firms studied significantly outperformed their U.S. counterparts. On inventory levels, Nishiguchi (1994) reported that the Japanese average was about one-fifth to one-tenth of Western counterparts. Womack et al. (1990) summarized the international comparisons for various aspects of supplier manufacturing performance and concluded that the Japanese supplier system tended to outperform its Western counterpart in the 1980s.

As for unit production cost, no systematic comparative studies are open to the public, but some studies conducted inside the Japanese auto firms in the early 1980s (prior to the appreciation of the yen in 1985 and the early 1990s) indicated that most Japanese functional components were estimated to be significantly less expensive than their U.S. counterparts.[34]

As discussed earlier this chapter, however, the Japan-U.S. difference in total industry labor productivity in the late 1980s was smaller than that of assembly productivity of the same period, which makes us infer that the productivity of Japanese suppliers at the second-tier, third-tier, and so on may not have been significantly better than Western counterparts. It would be natural from this circumstantial evidence to estimate that the source of Japanese suppliers' cost competitiveness in the 1980s would shift from productivity to wage rate as we go upstream in the parts supply chain (except raw material makers).

Dynamic Competitive Performance.   As for the improvement ratio in unit costs and conformance quality, Cusumano and Takeishi (1991) reported that the Japanese first-tier suppliers studied significantly outperformed the U.S. counterparts. Their data on the target price achievement ratio also indicate that the Japanese suppliers tended to improve component designs throughout product development, unlike U.S. counterparts.[35] In the areas of component development lead time, development productivity, and die development lead time for components, also, Nishiguchi (1993) revealed significant advantages of the sample Japanese suppliers over Western situation. Although it is likely that the U.S. and European catchup effort had been accelerated by the mid-1990s, the existing literature generally indicates the dynamic performance advantages of Japanese first-tier suppliers.

To sum up, as far as the average Japanese first-tier suppliers of the 1980s are concerned, serious problems could not be identified regarding the distortion of resource allocation or wage inequity at the industry level.[36] By contrast, their contributions to the Japanese competitive advantage in both static and dynamic senses was obvious in many indicators.[37] Based on this observation, let us shift our attention to the structural and behavioral aspects of the supplier system that may have affected the competitive performance of the Japanese supplier system of the 1980s and 1990s.

Structural and Behavioral Characteristics of the Supplier System

There are three main dimensions for analyzing the structures and behaviors of a supplier system: patterns of task partitioning, patterns of competition and transaction networking, and patterns of individual transactions. Twelve points are discussed according to these dimensions.

Patterns of Interfirm Task Partitioning

High Outsourcing Ratio (low level of vertical integration).   It is known that the outsourcing ratio (percentage of parts and material costs in total manufacturing cost) of the Japanese automakers has been over 70 percent since the mid-1970s, which was significantly higher than the U.S. average. The ratio tended to go up from the 1960s to the early 1970s, when the Japanese domestic market was at its motorization stage, when private ownership of cars started to increase rapidly (Cusumano, 1988; Nishiguchi, 1994). This coincides with the period when many first-tier suppliers started to deliver subassembly components instead of piece parts to the assemblers (called subassembly delivery or unit delivery), which was apparently a reason for the increase in outsourcing ratio.

Multilayer Supplier Network. We can classify the automobile parts suppliers into first-tier (selling parts mainly to assemblers), second-tier (selling parts mainly to first-tier suppliers), and so on, based on who the main buyers of the parts are. Around each assembler, they tend to form a hierarchical structure, with a larger number of smaller firms at the lower levels. Although the real transaction network is far from a simple hierarchy, such a classification is possible according to the main stream of transactions. Fujimoto, Sei, and Takeishi (1994), conducting a questionnaire survey in Kanagawa prefecture, showed that the first, second, and third and lower suppliers tended to be very different from each other in size, technological capability, behavioral pattern, and so on (table B.2). The study also indicated that the small suppliers at the third and lower layers tended to be more independent and floating than their stereotype images as those contained at the bottom of the *keiretsu* hierarchy.

It is known that the Japanese supplier system has been taller (i.e., more tiers) compared to Western counterparts. Such a multilayer structure was apparently built during the 1960s, when the buying companies selected higher level suppliers. Many of those that were not selected tended to survive as lower tier suppliers. In other words, the multilayer structure was a result of historical evolution.

Size Differences Between the Layers. Today's automobile industry, unlike others such as the synthetic fiber textile industry, is one in which downstream firms in the supply flow tend to be larger. As Fujimoto, Sei, and Takeishi (1994) report, first-tier suppliers are on average smaller than assemblers, but most of them are large companies (the number of average employees exceeds 1,000). A significant size gap exists between the first- and second-tier suppliers, the latter being typically small firms with fifty to one hundred employees (the average is about seventy). The third-tier and lower layer firms are normally quite small companies run by families, with fewer than ten employees.

Suppliers' Participation in Design. As discussed in the section on product development, Japanese first-tier suppliers in the 1980s on average tended to participate more in automobile product development in the form of black box parts than U.S. counterparts. In other words, the Japanese automobile manufacturers on average had a higher outsourcing ratio (i.e., a lower in-house ratio) than their Western counterparts, not only in manufacturing but also in product development. (Clark and Fujimoto, 1991, estimated the product engineering in-

Table B.3   Description of Suppliers by Tiers Summary of the Survey
Results in Kanagawa, in Japan

Attributes		First-tier	Second-tier	Third-tier
Employees	# of employees	Larger (1,200)	Middle (70)	Smaller (10)
	Average age of employees	Younger (39)	Middle (42)	Older (46)
	Production workers	Mainly fulltime male workers	Mainly fulltime male workers	Higher rate of family, female, part-time, foreign workers
Buyers	Buyers	Mainly assemblers and 1st tiers, but also 2nd and 3rd tiers	Mainly 1st and 2nd, but also assemblers and 3rd tiers	Mainly 2nd and 3rd, but also 1st tiers
	Final assemblers	Diversified	Diversified	Limited to local
	Average # of assemblers	More (5.3)	Middle (4.5)	Less (2.5)
Relations with the primary buyer	Starting year	Mainly 1950's (45%)	Mainly 60's (32%), then 70's (24%)	Mainly 70's (47%) and 80's (42%)
	Participating kyoryokukai	79% join	70% join	30% join 45% no kyoryolkukai
	Support from buyers	Equity share (41%), Directorship (33%), Equip. loan (25%) No support(38%)	Equip. loan (25%) Tech. support(19%) No support (54%)	Tech. support(11%) Equip. loan (11%) No support (79%)
Operations of the major part	Operations in charge	Subassembly, stamping machining, welding	Subassembly, stamping machining, welding	welding, machining
	Production lot size (thousand/month)	Larger (4500)	Middle(500)	Smaller (100)
	Variation of the part	More (595 types)	Middle (107 types)	Less (35 types)
	Lot size per variation	Larger (7600)	Middle(5000)	Smaller (4000)
	Engineering of the part	Own eng. (59%)	Own eng. (23%) Buyer's eng. (77%)	Buyer's eng. (100%)

Note: The sample size differs slightly across the cells, but in most cases 40 responses for the 1st tier suppliers;
60 for the 2nd; 20 for the 3rd; and 120 in total.
The numbers are either the sample means or % of the sample distribution within the group.
1st/2nd/3rd tier supplier: a supplier whose largest buyer is a vehicle assembler/1st tier supplier/2nd tier supplier
Buyers: The buyers who directly purchase the parts from the supplier.
Primary buyers: the buyer who accounts for the largest sales for the supplier.
Final assemblers: The final assembler which uses the parts the supplier manufactures.
Kyoryokukai: An association organized by the buyer to facilitate communication between the buyer and
the participating suppliers.
The major part: the type of parts which accounts for the largest amount of sales for the supplier.
This is based on a questionnaire survey conducted in 1992 summer in the Kanagawa prefecture, which is
the second largest prefecture for the automobile production in Japan.
Source: Originally from Fujimoto, Sei, and Takeishi (1994); adopted from Cusumano and Takeishi (1995).

house ratio to be roughly 40 percent in Japan, 20 percent in Europe, and 10 percent in the United States, based on their survey in the late 1980s.) In the United States, by contrast, the vast majority of parts procured from suppliers were detail-controlled parts, in which car makers not only do basic design of the total vehicle but also do detailed designs of the components.

There have been detailed studies of the black box parts practice (also called design-in or approved drawing system), in which the basic design is conducted by the car makers while the detailed engineering is done by the suppliers (Asanuma,1984, 1989; Clark and Fujimoto, 1991). Fujimoto, Sei, and Takeishi (1994) showed that this practice tended to be adopted only among the first-tier suppliers, although it is said to be gradually diffusing into second-tier firms in the 1990s. Asanuma (1989) reported that the black box practice was observed in the Japanese automobile industry rather than the electronics industry.

As discussed in more detail in chapter 6 of this book, the black box system in Japan was also an outcome of historical evolution. The peak of its diffusion is estimated to have been the 1960s.[38] Thus, the 1960s—the era of rapid growth in domestic sales and production, as well as rapid product proliferation in the Japanese auto industry—appears to be when the boundaries for assembler-supplier tasks shifted, not only in production but also in product development, toward more outsourcing to suppliers.

Patterns of Competition and Transaction Networking

Diversification of Customers-Assemblers. The prevalent image of a multilayer hierarchy in the Japanese supplier system led to misunderstandings among many researchers that it is a closed pyramid under each automaker, whereby a supplier belongs to only one hierarchy: a feudalistic hierarchy dominated by a big assembler. In reality, however, a first-tier supplier's customers-assemblers tend to be diversified in many component categories, although there are some other parts (e.g., fuel tanks, trim parts, seats) in which a supplier's sales tend to be dedicated to one assembler (figure B.1).[39] According to some existing literature, there used to be more dedicated parts transactions, but there was more diversification of customers-assemblers in the 1960s.[40] Interestingly enough, such diversification was often promoted by the assemblers themselves, which apparently expected cost reductions owing to a scope economy that additional customers would bring about. (The potential consequences of reduced negotiating power and leaks of proprietary information were apparently deemphasized in the period of rapid production growth.)[41]

As a result, the network of parts transactions tends to resemble not so much isolated mountains of dedicated suppliers as a mountain range of overlapping and open hierarchies.[42]

Examining the structure in more detail, one would find that the first-tier suppliers in the 1980s could be classified into several types, which were formed for historical reasons: (1) independent suppliers that deal with any assemblers; (2) Toyota group suppliers that deal with any assemblers *but* Nissan group assemblers; (3) Nissan group suppliers that deal with any assemblers *but* Toyota group assemblers; (4) dedicated suppliers to one assembler; (5) others.[43] Thus, it was only Toyota and Nissan—the first movers into automobile mass pro-

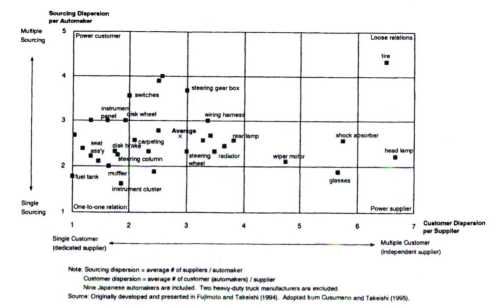

Figure B.1 Average Structure of Manufacturer-Supplier Transaction for Major Parts in Japan (1990)

duction in Japan—that have had full-scale supplier systems.[44] Other assemblers (Honda, Mitsubishi, Mazda) tended to rely on the independent, Toyota group, or Nissan group suppliers for their functional parts, supplemented by a relatively small supplier network of dedicated local suppliers that make nonfunctional parts.

As a result, as figure 5.12 shows, the overall transaction structures tend to be classified into at least three situations: (1) a network mainly of independent suppliers (e.g., lamps); (2) a mix of Toyota group, Nissan group, and other suppliers (e.g., starters, radiators); (3) a group of dedicated suppliers (e.g., seats). Thus, there is no one pattern of transactions in today's Japanese supplier industry.

Consolidation of the Supplier Base.   Conversely, past research has indicated that Japanese automobile assemblers had a smaller number of first-tier parts suppliers than their U.S. and European counterparts, as of the 1980s. There are a few reasons for this result.

First, to the extent that Japanese assemblers' outsourcing ratio is higher by relying more on the delivery of subassembled modules from suppliers, it is natural that each assembler deal with a smaller number of suppliers, other things being equal. (See figure 4.8 for this logic.)

Second, as Cusumano and Takeishi (1991) and others indicate, for each category of parts items (e.g., lamp, starter, seat), there were a relatively small number of suppliers per assembler (about three on average, according to Fujimoto and Takeishi, 1994; see figure B.1 again) compared to their Western counterparts in the 1980s. Note here that, at the level of parts categories, it is not true that Japanese assemblers usually relied on a single supplier, a rather common misunderstanding among researchers and practitioners since the 1980s. In other words, for each category, the suppliers tended to form an oligopolistic structure of competition, as opposed to a monopolistic one in most, if not all, cases. The pattern varies depending upon the category of parts, though, as figure B.1 indicates.

Third, at the level of a specific parts number or a drawing number (e.g., a head lamp for the North American version of a Toyota Corolla 1991), the Japanese assemblers do tend to rely on single sourcing. In my 1994 survey involving 201 auto parts makers in Japan (mostly first-tier suppliers), for instance, only a minority of Japanese first-tier suppliers (22 percent of the sample firms) responded that identical parts were made by multiple suppliers in over 50 percent of their transactions. This sharply contrasted the multiple-sourcing practice for a given component design commonly observed in U.S. automakers in the early 1980s. The fact that the detailed engineering of the parts are conducted in many cases by the suppliers in Japan (i.e., black box parts practice) seems to be a natural source of their monopoly status for parts from that specific drawing. In any case, we should not confuse the concept of single sourcing at the category level and that at the specific parts number level. The Japanese assemblers of the 1980s relied mostly on single sourcing in the latter case, but *not* in the former case.

Fourth, since the most of the Japanese first-tier suppliers had acquired technological capabilities as specialists in one or some parts categories, the firms tended to diversify their product items within their specialties or in related areas, using their technical resources and customer relations as sources of synergy and thereby exploiting economies of scope. As a result, the number of first-tier suppliers did not increase much during the 1980s, despite the higher complexity of cars.

Overall, it should be noted that the structure of oligopolistic competition among a relatively small number of specialist subassembly suppliers in Japan that we observed in the 1980s was largely a product of historical evolution, peaking in the 1960s (Kikuchi, 1976; Sei, Nakajima, and Omori, 1975, 1976). Also, the basic pattern has not changed much as of the mid-1990s, although there has been further consolidation of suppliers as the Japanese auto industry faced erosion of its competitiveness owing to the appreciation of the yen in the early 1990s.

Development Competition among Suppliers. As already mentioned, the Japanese first-tier suppliers tended to compete against a relatively small number of long-term competitors by parts categories. What is, then, the common pattern of competition among them? The existing literature argues that the most frequent mode of competition among Japanese first-tier suppliers has been so-called development competition (*kaihatsu konpe*), in which each candidate supplier is evaluated and screened by the assembler before the detailed component design is determined, based on not only the price that the supplier offers but also its component development capability demonstrated by a detailed design proposal, its process improvement capability, and so on (Matsui, 1988; Fujimoto, 1994a, 1995).[45] In other words, the supplier is selected for each case according to various aspects of its long-term dynamic capabilities.[46] This sharply contrasts with the case of U.S. automakers up to the mid-1980s, for which a dominant mode of supplier competition was bidding, in which the price that the supplier offers based on a drawing given by the assembler is the dominant criterion for supplier selection. According to the author's questionnaire survey of Japanese first-tier suppliers, about 50 percent of the respondents (*N* = 201) said suppliers were selected by development competition in the case of new model development; the corresponding number in the case of major model changes was about 40 percent (Fujimoto, 1995). A significant fraction of respondents (particularly in the latter case) said that one supplier was chosen from the beginning, but potential competitors are likely to have existed even in this case (see figure 5.3). In any case, only a minority (less than 20 percent) responded that the main mode of competition was bidding (i.e., price competition).

The same study also indicated that there is a correlation between adoption of development competition as a major selection mode and a option of black box parts practice as a mode of task partition (see table 5.1). In other words, there may be a strategic complementarity between the two system properties. In any case, it is important to note that bidding is not the only mode of supplier competition.

Patterns of Individual Transactions

Long-term Contractual Relations. Existing empirical studies (Asanuma, 1984; Cusumano and Takeishi, 1991) have shown that contracts between the Japanese assemblers and the first-tier suppliers tend to last as long as production of the components in question continues (usually until the next model change, or about four years). It has often been said that this kind of long-term contractual relationship in Japan contrasts with shorter contract periods in U.S. supplier relationships, but Cusumano and Takeishi (1991) indicate that U.S. contracts tend to be renewed, so that the actual transaction for a specific component is not much different between the two countries, although the average contractual period is indeed shorter in the U.S. supplier system.

In any case, Japanese first-tier suppliers enjoyed long-term (typically about four years) contracts for given transactions in the 1980s, and this tendency has not changed much. Although there are possibilities of competition for new contracts with other suppliers when model changes happen, the supplier's relationship (i.e., a bundle of the contracts) with the assembler tends to last beyond the term of each individual contract. In other words, as for a given category (e.g., lamp), the list of competing suppliers for each assembler tends to be fairly stable for a long time, except in some cases of technologically new or rapidly changing components.

Technical Assistance and Diffusion of Practices. Japanese automakers are generally known for providing both detailed technical assistance and multifaceted evaluation for first-tier suppliers. According to Wada (1991), for example, an elaborate system of evaluation and assistance did not exist in the early stages of the industry, but evolved gradually after the 1950s. In the case of Toyota, the evaluation and technical assistance of second-tier suppliers tends to be delegated to first-tier suppliers.

Also, Toyota significantly has strengthened its organizational capability of supplier assistance for total quality control and just-in-time since the late 1960s: typical events include the establishment of a Purchasing Administration Division in 1965 mainly for diffusion of TQC to suppliers, and of an Operations Management Consulting Office (*seisan chosa-shitsu*) in 1970 for diffusion of JIT.

Close Coordination and Communication. The Japanese automakers (Toyota in particular) are known for dense and face-to-face communications with suppliers, at the stages of both product development and commercial production (Dyer, 1994).

As already discussed, the production system of the postwar Japanese automobile makers (Toyota in particular) was built around JIT and TQC, which require cross-functional coordination and information sharing for a simultaneous increase in productivity, conformance quality, delivery speed, and flexibility.

Full-scale diffusion of such systems from Toyota to its first-tier suppliers appears to have started in the late 1960s and more or less was completed in the late 1970s, or after the first oil crisis. This meant the establishment of tight operational ties between the assembler and the suppliers, including *kanban* delivery (just-in-time delivery based on a pull principle using returnable containers) and elimination of receiving inspection for incoming parts (extension of the "doing things right the first time," or *tsukurikomi*, principle to supplier relations).

Sharing the Benefits from Improvements. The main Japanese assemblers in the 1980s were generally known for sharing the benefits of component cost reduction activities (value analyses, value engineering, etc.) with their suppliers by maintaining unit component prices for a certain period after the cost reduction is achieved, which gives the suppliers incentives to participate in such improvement activities (Asanuma, 1984). As Asanuma himself indicates, however, there appear some cases in which the benefit of value engineering (design improvements that aim at cost reduction for given functions) at product development are preempted by the automakers. Cusumano and Takeishi (1991), for example, report that the Japanese auto firms studied were enjoying actual unit component price on average 2 percent lower than the target component price specified at product development stage, which indicates the possibility of such preemption of benefits, at least to a certain extent.

Overall, there appears to have been no rigid rules in terms of the percentage of such quasi-rent to be given to the suppliers, although "fifty-fifty" is often referred to by the automakers as a rule of thumb. As of the mid-1990s, some practitioners in the industry are still arguing that the rules for splitting the benefits from value analysis and value engineering should be clarified.

Notwithstanding a lack of clarity in the rules, the principle of benefit sharing seems to prevail at least at the first-tier level, which is obviously key for the joint cost reduction efforts between assemblers and suppliers.

Sharing Risks of Production Fluctuation. There have been some debates on whether the assembler's share of the risks of production decrease along with the supplier's. There is a persistent hypothesis that large assemblers use suppliers as a cushion to absorb the impact of production volume reductions by switching outsourced parts to in-house production (i.e., expanding the make-or-buy boundary outward) and keeping the former's employment level by sacrificing the latter's.

Although there have been anecdotes implying this supplier-as-buffer hypothesis, recent empirical studies tend not to support it. Asanuma and Kikutani (1992), for example, conclude from their statistical analysis that there is no evidence to support the buffer hypothesis, and that it is rather consistent for the assemblers to absorb the volume risks of suppliers. Asanuma (1984) also reports that there is a certain rule for assemblers to compensate suppliers for the stamping die cost that is incurred when production volume throughout the model life falls short of the plan, and thereby absorb the volume risk for the suppliers. (Note that the die making cost is incorporated into the parts cost by using planned cumulative production volume for the product life. Shiomi (1995) reports that the production volume of the main automakers and that of consigned assemblers (i.e., suppliers of the whole vehicle) decreased almost at the same rate during the first oil crisis, contrary to the buffer hypothesis. Nishiguchi (1994) also argues that Japanese automakers are nurturing and utilizing suppliers' flexible capabilities, rather than using them as buffers.

Overall, the recent literature tends to support the hypothesis that Japanese assemblers share with suppliers not only the benefits of cost reduction but also the risks of volume fluctuation. No decisive conclusion can be drawn at this point, though. Also, there has been no systematic research on whether such risk sharing occurs between first-tier and second-tier suppliers.

NOTES

Chapter 1

1. Analysts estimate that Toyota's typical unit product cost was several hundred dollars lower than its major domestic rival in the 1980s. Toyota is also said to have enjoyed $1,000 to $1,500 profit per car in the U.S. market in the early 1980s, partly owing to its international cost advantage. Even though the yen has sharply appreciated since then (from over 200 yen per dollar in 1984 to less than 100 in 1995), industry specialists estimate that Toyota has not totally lost its cost competitiveness in the U.S. market; with quality and resale value taken into account, its overall competitiveness has remained high and stable in recent years. Toyota's market share in America, including its locally made models, reached and has stayed around 9 percent in the 1990s.

2. See Lindbrom (1959) for the concept of "muddling through."

3. See Womack et al. (1990).

4. Note that I am using the term *neo-Darwinism* broadly here—as synonymous with modern synthesis, the prevalent theory in biological evolution that includes revised Darwinism and Mendelian genetics.

5. Professor Paul Adler of the University of Southern California gave me valuable suggestions in naming this concept.

6. See, for example, Harbour (1980); Abernathy, Clark, and Kantrow (1981, 1983); Womack, Jones, and Roos (1990); Fuss and Waverman (1990); Clark and Fujimoto (1991, 1992); Cusumano and Takeishi (1991); and Fujimoto and Takeishi (1995).

7. In this book, the term *manufacturing system* stands for the total system that includes production, product development, and purchasing. It is synonymous with the *development-production system*, which also includes the supplier system. As for the history of Toyota's manufacturing system, Cusumano (1985) provides one of the most comprehensive analyses written in English.

8. Merton (1968), p. 120.

9. Giddens (1984), p. 27.

10. Mintzberg (1987). See also Quinn (1978), Mintzberg and Waters (1985), and Pascale (1984).

11. See Durkheim (1895), Popper (1957), and Levi-Strauss (1962).

12. See, for example, Weick (1979), Nelson and Winter (1982), Mintzberg and Waters (1985), Nonaka (1985), and Burgelman (1991).

13. Collins and Porras (1994), p. 9.

14. See Clark and Fujimoto (1991).

15. Alchian (1950), pp. 211–221.

16. According to von Bertalanffy (1968) and Weinberg (1975), the complexity of system behaviors stems from interactions between a "medium number" of elements of the system, rather than a random process involving a large number of objects or a mechanistic process with a small number of objects.

17. See Morgan (1927) for biological evolution, Parsons (1937) for sociology, Weinberg (1975) for general system theory, and Mintzberg and Waters (1985) for business strategy. In the fields of natural science, chaos theory tries to explain apparently disorderly, irregular, or irregular phenomena by subtle interactions between deterministic processes and random processes (see, for example, Hall, 1991), but it does not seem directly applicable to the empirical data of this book, which involves complex human interactions.

18. Neoclassical decision theory further assumes that the economic actors are equally capable and face the identical environment.

19. Note here that rationality in the present case specifically means "competitive rationality" rather than that found in the decision-making process in general. Human behavior and decision making can be guided by any goals, but I only include system changes that are driven by overt competitive objectives because the research in this book focuses on explaining a competitive manufacturing system.

20. See Merton (1968).

21. Knowledge transfer differs from rational calculation in that the decision for the former is at best based on a vague anticipation that another organization's routines are more competitive, rather than on a deliberate functional analysis of the routines.

22. See also Campbell (1970) and Weick (1979) for the variation-selection-retention framework applied to social and organizational behaviors.

23. See Burgelman (1991, 1994). Note again that, in the present book, selection occurs to manufacturing routines within a surviving company like Toyota, as opposed to the firm itself. Unlike the strict version of "organizational ecology" (e.g., Hannan and Freeman, 1989) the present framework emphasizes that an organization can select adaptive routines and thereby raise the chance of survival, rather than simply wait to be selected by the environments.

24. Note that the present definition of information, based on that found in general system theories, is broader than the Shannon-Wiener type definition in communication theory—or the computer science definition that distinguishes data from information, and knowledge. In the current

definition, data and knowledge are regarded as specific types of information.

25. *Value*, like *evolution* and *emergence*, is another equivocal term. In this book, *value-carrying information* simply means an intangible pattern that has the potential of attracting or satisfying customers.

26. Sales process is outside the main scope of this book, but it is certainly an important part of the value-carrying information cycle.

27. Nonaka (1988b) calls the two views the "information processing paradigm" and "information creation paradigm." For example, Galbraith (1973), one of the leading scholars in the former camp, argues that the amount of information input required for an organization to execute its tasks is determined by the uncertainty of its task environments. The organization then matches its information-transmission capacity to the requirements, either by reducing the need for information or by increasing the transmission capacity. Thus, Galbraith focuses on quantitative matching between requirements and capacity of information transmission. On the information-creation side, Weick (1979) argues that organizational members impose conceptual schemes on informational input (or stimuli) from objective environments and create a meaningful, though subjective, interpretation of the environment. This cognitive process is known as *enactment*. Enactment creates a perceived environment in which the organization acts. New meanings (and corresponding information) are created through the interaction between environmental stimuli and conceptual structures.

28. Nonaka (1988a), p. 60. For further discussions of this topic, also see Nonaka and Takeuchi (1995).

29. I have called these three concepts *static capability, improvement capability,* and *evolutionary capability* in my previous works (e.g., Fujimoto, 1994b). Similar evolutionary concepts include the dynamic routines of Nelson and Winter (1982) and the absorptive capacity of Cohen and Levinthal (1990, 1994), as well as the dynamic capability proposed by Teece and Pisano (1994). But my concept of evolutionary learning capability differs from these in that it emphasizes the nonroutine and/or multipath emergent nature of the process for creating routines.

30. It is important to note here that the concept of capability may be applied not only to the case of competitive performance, which is the main topic of this book, but also to other dimensions of performance. A business firm is surrounded by various stakeholders, including customers, shareholders, employees, suppliers, local communities, society at large, and so on. A firm's external performance can be regarded as its ability to attract or satisfy those stakeholders. In this context, competitive performance can be seen as an ability to attract and satisfy customers, but other types of external performance, such as an ability to attract and satisfy employees in the firm, may increase its importance in certain situations. (This topic will be discussed in chapter 7.) In general, business firms in today's society are facing higher pressures from their environments to achieve a more balanced performance profile vis-à-vis multiple stakeholders (Fujimoto, 1993, 1994c). Although such a broad perspective of a firm's external performance is mostly outside the scope of this book, it's important to keep in mind that the concept of capability could be broad-

ened and applied to other dimensions of performance and stakeholders beyond competitiveness and customers.

31. For simplicity's sake, I will also just call this *manufacturing capability* throughout the book.

32. Note that these routines may not only realize lower levels of in-process defects and field defects but also facilitate problem recognition and thereby trigger continuous improvement (*kaizen*) activities—a part of the routinized learning capability. In this way, the two types of routine capabilities tend to overlap in a real shop-floor setting.

33. Note, however, that complete stability may not be a realistic assumption. When external changes and internal disruptions do exist, stable and high performance requires coexistence of both routinized manufacturing capability and routinized learning capability.

34. See Abernathy (1978) for the concept of productivity dilemma.

35. The concept of manufacturing capability can also be applied to the interfirm situation, such as for certain Japanese companies that communicate and work closely with one another. That is, when certain steady-state patterns of information transmission between firms create higher productivity, quality, delivery, or flexibility as their joint result, we can infer that an interfirm manufacturing capability exists for the pair or group of firms in question.

36. A standard linear model of problem solving is applied here (e.g., Simon, 1945/1976, 1969; March and Simon, 1958).

37. Note that retention of solutions is a necessary condition for a high level of manufacturing capability, since it enables repetitive activation of the same information.

38. The problem-solving cycles are linked to one another so that solutions in the upstream cycles become goals for the downstream cycles (Fujimoto, 1989; Clark and Fujimoto, 1989a, 1989b, 1991).

39. Alternative frameworks, for example, include the "garbage can" model (March and Olsen, 1976; March, 1988). See also von Hippel and Tyre (1993).

40. As in the case of manufacturing capability, routinized learning capability can also apply to the interfirm relations. For example, when the information flowing between two firms facilitates both of their problem-solving cycles for faster and more effective performance improvements, interfirm routinized learning capability (that is, the ability to conduct joint problem solving) exists for the pair or group of firms in question.

41. There's always a danger that such logic leads to an infinite chain of backward explanation (a capability of capability building, and so on). The three-layer model of capabilities tries to avoid this problem by giving each construct concrete definition, rather than simply calling them meta-routines. Thus, routinized learning capabilities handle repetitive routine changes, while evolutionary learning capabilities cope with the nonroutine changes that I describe as multi-path system emergence. Since I'm well aware of this problem, however, won't go further backward in an attempt to explain why a company like Toyota developed its evolutionary learning capability in the first place. It would be impossible to explain such a rare event through the concepts of organizational learn-

ing capability. Thus, explaining the origin of Toyota's evolutionary learning capability would be a task of business historians or researchers of organizational culture; it is generally outside the scope of the present book.

42. The idea of multilayer structures in organizational capabilities, routines, programs, knowledge, learning, and so on is not particularly new in the literature of organizational studies. For example, the concepts of "initiation" for the creation of new programs (March and Simon, 1958), "double loop learning" (Argyris and Shön, 1996), and "higher level learning" (Fiol and Lyles, 1985) all assume such a multilayer structure. But the current definitions of routinized learning versus evolutionary learning capabilities are somewhat different from the above ones in that I emphasize the distinction between repetitive regular changes of a system and the irregular changes of multi-path system emergence.

Also note that the difference between routinized learning capability and evolutionary learning capability is different from the classical distinction between the ability to handle incremental innovations and to handle radical innovations (Abernathy and Utterback, 1978, Hayes and Wheelwright, 1984). The evolutionary learning capability discussed here is not an ability to perform a one-time big system change, but an ability to cope with multi-path system emergence over an extended period.

43. As in the case of the other capabilities, evolutionary capability can also apply to an interfirm situation. For example, because Toyota developed more effective interorganizational routines earlier compared to other car makers, we can infer that the company had a certain evolutionary capability that extended beyond the company's boundary.

44. See March and Olsen (1976) and March (1988).

45. To the extent that organizational learning is "encoding inferences from history into routines that guide behavior" (Levitt and March, 1988) or "improving actions through better knowledge and understanding" (Fiol and Lyles, 1985), evolutionary learning capability overlaps the concept of a higher order learning ability to change routines for learning or values (Argyris and Shön, 1996, Fiol and Lyles, 1985). For concepts and definitions of organizational learning, see, for example, Fiol and Lyles (1985), Levitt and March (1988), Argyris and Shön (1996), and Cohen and Sproull (1996).

46. Fiol and Lyles (1985) call the former "behavioral development" and the latter "cognitive development." Knowledge of the routines and their outcome is related to the concept of "theories of action" by Argyris and Shön (1996). Note also that the present definition of organizational learning basically agrees with the routine-based concept of organizational learning presented by Levitt and March (1988).

47. Pisano (1997), analyzing organizational learning in process development and commercial production, examines the spectrum between "learning by doing" (process capability building through repetitive production experience) and "learning before doing" (capability building through experimentation prior to commercial production).

48. See Simon (1945/1976, 1969).

49. The original phrase was made famous statement by Louis Pasteur: "Fortune favors the prepared mind." The relevance of this phrase was suggested to me by David A. Hounshell of Carnegie Mellon University, as well as in a paper by Cohen and Levinthal (1994).

Chapter 2

1. Since this historical study itself gradually emerged over about fifteen years, accurate interview dates are not always available. All the interviews were recorded in the form of interview notes, some of which were checked by the interviewees themselves.

2. See also appendix B for detailed data backing up these facts.

3. See, for example, Womack, Jones, and Roos (1990), and Clark and Fujimoto (1991).

4. See, for example, Cusumano (1985), and Clark and Fujimoto (1991).

5. For further details on the history of the Japanese automobile industry and of the Toyota manufacturing system, see Jidosha Kogyokai (1967), Ohno (1978), Nakamura (1983), Cusumano (1985), Ohshima and Yamaoka (1987), Shimokawa (1994), Sato (1994), Ogawa (1994), Kawahara (1998), as well as official corporate histories of the Japanese automobile firms (e.g., Toyota Motor Co., Ltd., 1967, 1978; Toyota Motor Corporation, 1987).

6. Jidosha Kogyokai (1967).

7. Direct transfer of the Ford system by Ford itself was observed in other countries such as the United Kingdom. See, for example, Lewchuk (1987), Tolliday and Zeitlin (1986), and Fujimoto and Tidd (1993).

8. See, for example, Hounshell (1984).

9. Oshima and Yamaoka (1987).

10. The original Japanese name was Toyota Jidosha Kogyo Kabushiki-gaisha (Toyota Motor Co., Ltd.); it was renamed to Toyota Motor Corporation or Toyota Jidosha Kabushikigaisha since 1982 when it merged its sales company.

11. Note that the concept "craft-type system" is defined rather broadly in this book as a pre-mass-production indigenous system that depends on hand skills, general-purpose equipment, a job shop setting, and indirect shop floor control where foremen-craftsmen enjoy significant autonomy. Strictly speaking, the craft system with strong trade unions and institutionalized craft controls never existed in the Japanese auto industry. In order to avoid confusion with the craft system in this rigid sense, I call the indigenous automobile production system described in this chapter "craft-type."

12. Toyota Motor Co., Ltd. (1978), p. 95.

13. Toyota Motor Co., Ltd. (1978), p. 93.

14. Wartime anecdotes are mostly omitted here, as their impact on the subsequent systems and capabilities are regarded as rather limited, as far as manufacturing is concerned. The wartime production of trucks was stagnant. (Domestic production of four-wheel trucks dropped from the prewar peak of 45,502 units in 1941 to 21,743 units in 1944 and 8,187 units in 1945 (see table 2.1). Physical damage of production facilities by air raids was relatively small. See, for example, Toyota Motor Co., Ltd. (1978), pp. 111–130.

15. Interview with Taiichi Ohno by K. Shimokawa and T. Fujimoto, July 16, 1984 at the headquarters of Toyoda Gosei Co., Ltd. (Fujimoto and Shimokawa, 1997).

16. Interview with Taiichi Ohno by Shimokawa and Fujimoto, July 16, 1984 (Fujimoto and Shimokawa, 1997). See also Cusumano (1985), p. 306.

17. Clark and Fujimoto (1990, 1991).

18. The consolidation of first-tier suppliers was particularly obvious at Nissan, rather than Toyota, whose number of suppliers was more stable.

19. Consider, for example, Honda's CVCC, Mitsubishi's MCA Jet, Toyota's three-way catalytic converter.

20. Womack et al. (1990).

21. The definition of these nonsedan passenger vehicles (often called recreational vehicles or RV) is not clear, but one Japanese auto company reported that the share of such vehicles (including station wagons) in Japan increased from about 10 percent in the mid-1980s to about 30 percent in the mid-1990s. In the U.S. market, sales of truck-based passenger vehicles (minivans, sport utility vehicles, pickup trucks) reached nearly half of total passenger vehicle sales as of the late 1990s.

22. See, for example, Ohno (1978), Abernathy, Clark and Kantrow (1983), Shimokawa (1991), and Fujimoto and Tidd (1993).

23. Fujimoto and Shimokawa (1997).

24. The discussion in this section is based mainly on Fujimoto and Tidd (1993).

25. For a comprehensive historical analysis of production systems at such British firms as Morris and Austin, see Tolliday and Zeitlin (1986).

Chapter 3

1. Toyota Motor Co., Ltd. (1978), p. 64.

2. See Shimokawa (1990) for this comparison. For the experiments with the early Ford System, see, for example, Hounshell (1984).

3. Toyota Motor Co., Ltd. (1978), pp. 179–180.

4. Toyota Motor Co., Ltd. (1978), p. 180.

5. Ohno (1978); see chapter 5 in particular.

6. Ohno (1978), 190.

7. Shimokawa (1990) and Satake (1995) also emphasize continuity from the Ford system (Henry Ford version) to the Toyota system in terms of synchronization, as well as discontinuity in terms of production lot sizes.

8. Shioji (1994) also argues that Toyota's adoption of the Ford system was "limited and selective."

9. Wada (1995) points out that there was another source for the synchronized production idea—the prewar aircraft industry. Shioji (1994) also points out that an article on Lockheed's attempt of the "supermarket production system" in fuselage assembly, which appeared in a trade journal in 1954, inspired Ohno's group, although they did not know the details of the Lockheed system. See also Toyota Motor Corporation (1987).

10. For labor movements at this stage, see, for example, Cusumano (1985), chap. 3.

11. Interview with Taiichi Ohno by Shimokawa and Fujimoto, July 16, 1984 (Fujimoto and Shimokawa, 1997).

12. See Ohno (1978).

13. The term *kanban* was coined when Toyota tried to win the Deming Prize in 1965.

14. Interview with Taiichi Ohno by Shimokawa and Fujimoto, July 16, 1984 (Fujimoto and Shimokawa, 1997).

15. For the chronology of main elements in the Toyota production system, see also Cusumano (1988).

16. The following descriptions are based on the author's interview with Mr. Kaneyoshi Kusunoki on April 17, 1996 (see Fujimoto and Matsuo, 1997).

17. Cusumano (1988).

18. Suppose there are two variations: a high-content one that needs a long time for assembly work (e.g., with air conditioner and sunroof) and a low-content one (e.g., a standard package without such options). If the high-content variation is assembled in a large batch, then the assembly-line speed has to be set for the assembly time needed for the high-content one; otherwise the workers cannot keep pace with the line and production stops eventually. This arrangement, however, lowers the assembly pace and efficiency owing to the line balancing loss created by idle times when the low-content versions are assembled. To avoid the line balancing loss and the line stops at the same time, companies like Toyota randomize the body sequence (e.g., alternating the high-content and low-content variations with the batch size of one). Such randomization levelizes the workload of not only assembly workers but also suppliers of the option parts, reduces the loss, and increases efficiency. This method is called levelization (*heijunka*), and many companies worldwide have adopted this system as of the mid-1990s. See, also, appendix A.

19. Cusumano (1985), pp. 61 and 75.

20. Interview with Taiichi Ohno by Shimokawa and Fujimoto, July 16, 1984 (Fujimoto and Shimokawa, 1997).

21. This was based on his estimate in 1935 that U.S. productivity in spinning operations would have been nine times as high as that of the Japanese.

22. See Fujimoto and Tidd (1993) for details of the UK–Japan comparison in this regard.

23. Toyota Motor Co., Ltd. (1978), pp. 92–95.

24. Interview with Taiichi Ohno by Shimokawa and Fujimoto, July 16, 1984 (Fujimoto and Shimokawa, 1997).

25. On the transformation of the Ford system from dynamic experimentation to a static system of fragmented jobs, see, for example, Abernathy, Clark, and Kantrow (1983), chap. 6; and Shimokawa (1990).

26. Interview with Ohno, by Shimokawa and Fujimoto, July 16, 1984 (Fujimoto and Shimokawa, 1997).

27. Interview with Taiichi Ohno by Shimokawa and Fujimoto, July 16, 1984 (Fujimoto and Shimokawa, 1997).

28. Toyota Motor Co., Ltd. (1978), p. 41.

29. According to Abernathy (1978, p. 138), the capacity of a standard Ford assembly plant was 400 to 500 units per eight hours, or about a 1-minute cycle time, since the mid-1910s.

30. Toyota Motor Co., Ltd. (1978), p. 60.

31. Toyota Motor Co., Ltd. (1978), p. 85.

32. Toyota Motor Co., Ltd. (1978), p. 160.

33. See, for example, Fujimoto (1997a).

34. As for the change in machine layout in the early Ford system, see, for example, Hounshell (1984), pp. 221–222. Wada (1995) points out that

the prewar aircraft industry may be another source of the product-focused layout and semiflow production system.

35. For example, the number of boring machines increased from 50 to 200. Interview with Taiichi Ohno by Shimokawa and Fujimoto, July 16, 1984 (Fujimoto and Shimokawa, 1997).

36. For development and diffusion of Detroit-type automaton, see Hounshell (1995).

37. For the concept of *jidoka*, see, for example, Monden (1983/1993).

38. Interview with Taiichi Ohno by Shimokawa and Fujimoto, July 16, 1984 (Fujimoto and Shimokawa, 1997).

39. Toyota Motor Co., Ltd. (1978), p. 181.

40. See Robinson and Schroeder (1993) for a detailed illustration of TWI.

41. See Nemoto (1992).

42. See, for example, Udagawa (1993), Nonaka (1995), and Udagawa et al. (1995).

43. According to Akira Kawahara, former managing director of Toyota, the quality and performance of Toyota's large trucks had already reached the level of U.S. products by 1956, when the APA told five Japanese makers to prototype U.S. standard military trucks. All of the prototypes passed APA's tests, and Toyota won the order from the APA. This indicates that Toyota's SQC efforts had already brought about internationally competitive quality (if not cost) as far as large trucks were concerned.

44. Toyota Motor Co., Ltd. (1978), p. 251.

45. Masao Nemoto, the first head of the Purchasing Administration Division, as well as Taiichi Ohno, played a central role in this diffusion process.

46. See also Nishiguchi (1994), Wada (1991), Oshima (1987), Sato (1980), and so on. Note that this book avoids using a word that often characterizes the Japanese supplier system—*keiretsu*—because it tends to have multiple meanings or connotations, and is sometimes misleading.

47. For further details, see Fujimoto (1994a, 1995).

48. See Fujimoto (1994a).

49. Hasegawa (1993). See also Maema (1993).

50. As for the concept of product integrity, see Clark and Fujimoto (1990, 1991).

51. See Simon (1945/1976), March and Simon (1958).

52. See March and Olsen (1976) and March (1988).

Chapter 4

1. Note that manufacturing systems are defined broadly in this book, covering not only production but also product development and supplier management. Also, the Toyota-style manufacturing system includes not only the so-called Toyota production system (TPS) but also other aspects of production management, such as total quality control (TQC). In this sense, the coverage of this book may be somewhat similar to that of Womack et al. (1990), in that both cover production (assembly in particular), product development, and supplier systems. Womack et al. also deals

with sales and overall corporate strategies, which the current book does not, but it is often said that the lean production concept in Womack et al. does not cover TQC.

2. Womack et al. (1990) does advocate this totality, but the interactions of production, product development, and procurement were not discussed explicitly as a coherent system in the book.

3. Davis and Olson (1974/1985), p. 200.

4. For further details of the definition, see Fujimoto (1989), p. 70.

5. It is important to note that the Shannon and Wiener-type definition of information, which assumes that information can be created by selecting signals from a finite set of prefabricated forms and combining them, is too narrow for the current analysis. See, for example, Gregory (1987), p. 369.

6. The present problem solving model is a modification of Herbert Simon's original framework (1969). For further detail of the model, see Fujimoto (1989), and Clark and Fujimoto (1989b).

7. *Value* is defined here as a marketing sense: "the consumer's estimate of the product's capacity to satisfy a set of goals" (Kottler, 1967/1984, p. 6). In this regard, the present system may be viewed as a version of a "value chain" (Porter, 1985). A major difference between the two is that the present system tracks information flows while Porter's value chain basically tracks physical flows. While the latter is an effective approach in analyzing oligopolistic competition and transaction, the former seems to be a more appropriate view for the current research purpose: analyzing functions and structures of a manufacturing system. Lawrence and Dyer (1983), pp. 268-269, on the other hand, explicitly describe productive activities of a producer from the point of view of "information value added."

8. Although sales and marketing is another indispensable function for delivery of the value-carrying information, it was omitted in this paper for simplicity.

9. The information-processing approach is a prevalent model in the field of consumer behaviors. See, for example, a standard textbook by Robertson, Zielinski and Ward (1984). Some economists, such as Lancaster (1966), also analyze a product as a bundle of intangible service. For further details of this discussion, see Fujimoto (1989), p. 97.

10. See Penrose (1959).

11. Note that this expression is exaggerated for simplicity of explanation. In today's auto industry, for example, raw materials such as sheet steel and plastic compound already contain certain structural patterns (i.e., information) specific to the product. In other words, even raw materials contain product-specific information in many cases.

12. The information processing approach has been adopted by much of the important literature in the field of R&D management or innovation studies (Myers and Marquis, 1969; Allen, 1966, 1977; Morton, 1971; Freeman, 1982; Clark and Fujimoto, 1991).

13. This list may include apparently physical, rather than informational, assets. This book, however, treats them as chunks of information embodied in tangible media. Allen (1977), p. 4, calls them "physically encoded information."

14. As for stages of product development or innovations, a widely ac-

cepted view has been a three-stage model with the phases of idea generation, problem solving, and implementation (Myers and Marquis, 1969; Utterback, 1974; Rosenbloom, 1978). It roughly matches the four-stage
model adopted in this book, although the latter is more or less specific to
this particular industry.

15. This is a rather broad definition of product development. For example, many manufacturing firms regard process engineering as part of
production and exclude it from product development. Also, concept generation and product planning are sometimes considered part of marketing, corporate planning, and so on. Because the unit of analysis in this
study is a major development project, however, all the activities that a
project covers are included in product development here.

16. Clark and Fujimoto (1991) chap. 2. A standard model of problem
solving, such as Simon (1945/1976, 1969) and March and Simon (1958), is
applied here.

17. Clark and Fujimoto (1991), chap. 2.

18. See, for example, Hayes and Wheelwright (1984), Monden (1983/
1993), Schonberger (1982), Jaikumar (1986), Jaikumar and Bohn (1992),
and Hayes, Wheelwright, and Clark (1988).

19. Information processing or communication views in marketing have
been prevalent in the mainstream literature of marketing. As Kottler summarizes it, for example, "Marketers must know how to use advertising,
sales promotion, publicity, and personal selling to communicate the
product's existence and value to the target customers" (Kottler, 1967/1984,
p. 633).

20. For example, "A product is, to the potential buyer, a complex cluster of value satisfaction" (Levitt, 1983, p. 77); "We will use the term product to cover all vehicles that are capable of delivering satisfaction of a
want or need" (Kottler, 1967/1984, p. 5).

21. This framework may be regarded as an extension of the classic
differentiation-integration perspective (Lawrence and Lorsch, 1967) to the
case of multiple-firm situations.

22. For the concept of task partitioning in the case of innovation
processes, see von Hippel (1990).

23. For the concept of boundary spanning units, see Thompson (1967),
Aldrich and Harker (1977), and so on. The idea that differentiated environments need to be handled by differentiated organizational units, which
in turn needs a strong internal integrator, stems from Lawrence and
Lorsch (1967).

24. In the case of labor productivity, the following simple identity applies

$$\frac{\text{work hours}}{\text{unit}} = \frac{\text{work hours}}{\text{value-adding time}} \times \frac{\text{value-adding time}}{\text{unit}}$$

(factor productivity) (density of transmission) (speed of transmission)

where work hours = value-adding time + non-value-adding time
= average cycle time x number of units produced

25. Note that the density approach applies to both labor productivity
and capital productivity: reducing workers' idle time waiting for the next
material to come, walking time for picking up parts and tools, machine

breakdown time, tool change time, die setup time, air-cutting time, and so on.

26. Note that the speed approach applies to both labor and capital productivity: increasing the worker's standard speed of motions; assembly-line speed; stamping strokes per hour; the cutting and feeding speed with improved tools, materials, and machines; and so on.

27. As in the case of factor productivity, total throughput time corresponding to a given process flow is divided into value-receiving time (= value adding time), during which transformation of the work in process goes on, and non-value-receiving time (figure 4.11).

28. Integrating multiple process steps into one can be included in this category.

29. Conway et al. (1988) also point out that "perhaps the most important cost of WIP (work-in-process inventory) is the effect on manufacturing 'lead time' or 'flow time.'"

30. For the concepts of product quality, see also Juran, Gryna, and Bingham (1975); Garvin (1984); Groocock (1986).

31. For the concept of flexibility in general in manufacturing, see, for example, Browne et al. (1984), as well as Upton (1995). Note that the concept of flexibility in the section is narrow in that it focuses on flexibility of mass production processes and products against variety.

32. For definitions and facts on individual manufacturing practices and overall performance, see the appendix B.

33. See, for example, Ohno (1978), p. 38.

34. Womack, Jones, and Roos (1990).

35. Note that I call the production subsystem of the total Toyota-style manufacturing system the "Toyota-style production system," which is a broader concept than the so-called Toyota production system (TPS), which Toyota itself defines strictly. For example, total quality control is included in the former but not in the latter.

36. See, for example, Shingo (1980).

37. It is possible, however, that the view of industrial engineers and that of production engineers on this priority is very different within, for example, Toyota. The literature about Toyota's production system has been written predominantly by industrial engineers, but this does not necessarily mean that industrial engineers always dominated the plant management. Further empirical investigation is needed on the cross-functional power relations within Toyota factories (see also chapter 7 of this book).

38. Imai (1986).

39. See, for example, Leonard-Barton (1992b).

40. Schonberger (1982) explicitly explains the core system as a combination of JIT and TQC.

41. For the role of supervisors and team leaders in continuous improvements, see Nemoto (1992).

42. For the concept of knowledge conversion, see Nonaka and Takeuchi (1995).

43. See also Fujimoto (1989, 1993) and Clark and Fujimoto (1991).

44. See Clark and Fujimoto (1992) and Sheriff (1988).

45. Clark and Fujimoto (1992).

46. Another important aspect of the product development capability is that at the multiproject level. For example, Nobeoka (1993) argues that rapid transfer of product design information across the projects was identified as one of the core capabilities in product improvements. Continuity of product managers and working engineers between old and new projects also helped interproject knowledge transfer (Aoshima, 1996). Although this chapter concentrates on product development capabilities at the individual project level, chapter 6 briefly touches on the issue of multiple project management.

47. See Clark and Fujimoto (1991), chapter 7.

48. For general discussions, see Williamson (1979), Monteverde and Teece (1982), Dore (1987), MacNeil (1983), Imai et al. (1982).

49. This is one of the main propositions of the pioneer of transaction cost economics, Oliver E. Williamson (1979, 1985, 1991). Transaction cost economics postulates that economic actors choose a governance structure (e.g., markets, hierarchies, hybrid) that minimizes the cost of creating and maintaining transactions despite opportunism and bounded rationality. See also Dyer (1996) for the case of automobile supplier systems.

50. Nishiguchi (1994) contains a critical survey of past literature on supplier management, including such relational transaction hypotheses.

51. Nishiguchi's book on the Japanese supplier system takes a similar stance in that it emphasizes the historical evolution of the system (Nishiguchi, 1994).

52. *Quasi-rents* means an excess over returns that a certain production factor creates in its next best use. For example, when certain relation-specific assets between a car maker and a supplier create cost advantages and thereby above-normal returns for them, we call such an excess relational quasi rent.

53. See Cusumano and Takeishi (1991) for empirical evidence.

54. It is important, however, to distinguish outsourcing in action (capacity) and outsourcing in knowledge (Fine and Whitney, 1996) . Effective supplier management firms, such as Toyota, may rely on bundled outsourcing in manufacturing activities, but they may retain technical-manufacturing knowledge in house, partly by tapered vertical integration and partly by keeping technical staff in house for effectively guiding and evaluating the suppliers' developmental activities.

55. See also Clark (1989a).

56. Ito's "face-to-face competition" assumes that long-term relational transactions and rank order tournament exist, that competitors can observe rivals actions, that Hirschman's voice relations (customers complains to suppliers but do not quit from the transaction unilaterally) prevail, and that criteria for competition are multifaceted, including not only price but also suppliers' long-term capabilities for improving quality and technologies.

57. Itami's "competition by visible hands" assumes that there are a small number of firms that are visible to each other, that entry and exit are not totally free owing to *keiretsu* relations, that Hirschman's voice relations prevail, that both parties recognize the existence of relational quasi-rent (improvements of productivity and technology by working together), that nonprice information is shared between buyers and sellers, and that

buyers control the transaction in multiple dimensions. Thus, the characteristics of this concept are in many senses similar to those of Ito's.

58. See, for example, Nishiguchi (1994), Cusumano and Takeishi (1991), Fujimoto (1994a, 1995), and Lieberman and Demeester (1995).

Chapter 5

1. This chapter is essentially a significantly expanded and modified version of Fujimoto (1994a, 1995).

2. One important exception is the official company history of a Japanese parts supplier (Kojima Press Industry Co, Ltd., 1988), which has a short description on the development of the black box parts (*shoninzu*) system.

3. Note that, to the extent that the Japanese supplier system is shared by more than one assembly maker, as discussed in chapter 3, the routine capabilities in supplier management are likely to be not only firm specific but also region specific or country specific because suppliers tend to form geographical agglomerations.

4. Clark and Fujimoto (1991).

5. On the strength and weakness of each category, see Clark and Fujimoto (1991), chap. 6.

6. In Toyota's *Supplier's Guide* (1996a), written primarily for U.S.-based suppliers, approved drawings (*shoninzu*) are expressed as "supplier-generated drawings." The brochure explains that "suppliers prepare detailed drawings based on overall layouts and basic specifications provided by Toyota. We use this approach when suppliers have demonstrated ample capabilities in developing designs on their own" (p. 48).

7. For example, a manager of a Japanese parts manufacturer (company A) points out that Chrysler's Outdoor Design (ODD) program is based on the consigned drawings. According to a Chrysler's manager, 70 percent of Chrysler's manufacturing cost is procurement parts and 40 percent are already black box parts as of 1993 (a presentation by Thomas T. Stallkamp, Vice President Procurement and Supply, General Manager Large Car Operations, Chrysler Corporation, on December 7, 1993, in the "1993 Global Automobile Conference," Management Centre Europe, Brussels, Belgium). According to him, though, whether the parts drawings are owned by Chrysler or by suppliers depends upon the types of parts. Further investigation is needed for this issue.

8. See Mitsubishi Research Institute (1987), p. 7.

9. Mitsubishi Research Institute (1987), p. 11.

10. For example, nearly ten suppliers of plastic resin competed to win contracts with Toyota for its new-generation bumpers in the early 1990s. A supplier that had been rejected by Toyota in the previous generation got the first and most lucrative contract, as it was the first company to meet the technical requirements set by Toyota.

11. For further details of the survey, see note 13 of chapter 5.

12. At Nissan, such drawings are simply called parts drawings (*buhinzu*). At Mazda, it is called manufacturing drawings (*seizozu*). Thus, the name of this concept may differ from company to company.

13. The questionnaire was mailed to 438 companies, of which 199 made valid responses (45 percent response rate). One company made three responses for three different product groups, so the total number of the sample is 201. Actual sample size differs, depending upon the questions. On average, annual sales of the sample companies was 73 billion yen (sample size 201), the number of employees was about 1900. The author appreciates the efforts and cooperation of Mr. Akito Ozeki (JAPIA), Mr. Ryuji Fukuda (Japan Association for the Research on Automotive Affairs), and Ms. Keiko Shiroki (research assistant to the author).

14. This result is also consistent with the one in Clark and Fujimoto (1991), although the method of measurement is not identical.

15. See Asanuma (1989).

16. Clark and Fujimoto (1991).

17. Regarding the component divisions as inside the companies, Mitsubishi Research Institute (1987) estimated average U.S. outside parts ratio to be from 52 to 55 percent.

18. See Ellison et al. (1995). Also, Cusumano and Takeishi (1991) studied the parts suppliers of four different component categories, and found that the Japanese car makers relied more on black box parts system in the parts studied.

19. Fujimoto, Sei, and Takeishi (1994).

20. Supplier proprietary parts (i.e., purchasing of generic parts) is a more extreme case of bundled outsourcing, as figures 5.1 and 5.4 indicate, but this is a rather rare in the case of the car because it is essentially a closed architecture product, in which adjustment and optimization of component designs to the total product design is needed at least partially to maintain product integrity (Clark and Fujimoto, 1990).

21. This observation is also consistent with a prediction by Asanuma (1989) that the black box parts system needs higher levels of transaction-specific skills than the other types of transactions.

22. In the prewar aircraft industry, Japanese military authorities gave specifications to potential aircraft makers, ordered them to make prototypes, and selected aircraft suppliers on the basis of evaluations of the prototypes (see, for example, Maema, 1993). There is no clear evidence that such a practice influenced purchasing systems in the early automobile industry in Japan.

23. Fujimoto and Tidd (1993).

24. Abernathy, Clark, and Kantrow (1983).

25. See, for example, Fujimoto and Tidd (1993).

26. Toyota Motor Co., Ltd. (1957), p. 108.

27. Toyota Motor Co., Ltd. (1967), pp. 172–182.

28. Toyota Motor Co., Ltd. (1967), p. 277.

29. Toyota Motor Co., Ltd. (1967), p. 182.

30. In 1943 an organization of Toyota suppliers, Kyoho-kai, was established. Actual controls and assistance from Toyota to the suppliers was not significant at that time, though.

31. Toyota Motor Co., Ltd. (1967), pp. 253–254.

32. Toyota Motor Co., Ltd. (1967), p. 277. There is a hint that Kiichiro Toyoda had planned to encourage separate electric parts specialists, while Toyota Motor Co. (1957), (p. 300), indicates that the electric parts unit of

Toyota was losing money and was separated for better management. Which was the stronger motive for the separation is not clear.

33. This paragraph is based on interviews with Yoshihiko Furuya, director, and Michihiro Ohashi, general manager, of Nippondenso on September 16, 1993.

34. This fact was confirmed by Kazuyoshi Yamada, former engineer of Nippondenso.

35. The contents of this paragraph are based on an interview with Toshihito Kondo, Masami Komatsu, and Shoji Kasama, Purchasing Planning Division of Toyota, August 4, 1993.

36. For the unification of Toyota's document format, see Toyota Motor Co., Ltd. (1957), pp. 253-254.

37. Another possibility is that Toyota Auto Body, separated from Toyota in 1945, built cabs for Toyota based on the approved drawings. The appendix of the 1953 Approved Drawings Rule specifies how to handle the cabs by Toyota Auto Body as an exceptional case, though. This makes us suspect that approved drawings from Toyota Auto Body did not become an issue prior to 1953.

38. One of the surveyed companies was established after the war, so its response is excluded from the analysis here.

39. I am grateful for some valuable insights from Haruhito Takeda and Kazuo Wada of Tokyo University on this issue.

40. This path was already predicted by Asanuma (1989).

41. See, for example, Sei, Omori, and Nakajima (1975); and Kikuchi (1976).

42. Clark and Fujimoto (1992).

43. The development workload was estimated by using a model change history chart of Toyota that the author made (figure 5.2) and converting this into workload estimation by using certain coefficients. It was assumed that the development lead time was four years, that the model was introduced at the end of the year, and that the development workload was 0.3 in the year of full model change or new model introduction, 0.3 in the previous two years, and 0.1 three years prior to the model change. The workload index was calculated by simply adding up the estimated workload of all models and dividing it by the estimated number of engineers at Toyota for each year. Thus, it should be noted that this is a very rough estimate of the time-series patterns of total development workload for the company. The estimation of the number of Toyota's engineers was made by using various sources, including Yano (1985) and Nomura (1993).

44. An interview with Ryo Hatano, general manager of the Material Purchasing Department, Nissan, May 8, 1993.

45. The data that follow were provided by a former executive of company A in an interview on September 17, 1993.

46. Note that these data are based on the number of engineering draw-· ings. The fraction of approved drawings in terms of purchasing cost is much higher, as parts cost per drawing is much higher in the case of approved drawings (mostly subassembly) than for provided drawings (mostly piece parts). See also Clark and Fujimoto (1991).

47. Another survey that the author conducted in 1993 among several product managers working for Japanese automakers also shows that most

of the respondents felt that the auto companies increased their dependence on suppliers' engineering resources between the mid-1980s and 1993, and that the fraction of approved drawing parts in the total number of parts procured also increased during the same period.

48. This section is based mainly on the interview with Ryo Hatano, general manager of the Material Purchasing Department, Nissan, May 8, 1993.

49. Note that the black box parts transactions at Nippondenso at the initial stage were also based on such drawings, or *shiyozu*, supplied by the automakers. The inputs from the automobile makers were subsequently simplified to specification documents, though.

50. Nissan's purchasing staff were not concerned about the possibility that early selection of suppliers would deprive them of their price negotiation power because they were confident of the reliability of their target cost system.

51. The average fraction of black box parts in procurement cost among the Japanese samples ($N = 12$) was 62 percent, with a standard deviation of 17 percent. Toyota was not among the highest in this figure; Nissan was above the Japanese average. For the regional average data, see Clark and Fujimoto (1991).

52. Note that some Nissan suppliers started the approved drawings system before the war. Considering that many of the Nissan suppliers are located in the eastern part of Japan, where there were some major aircraft makers (e.g., Nakajima), they may have been aircraft parts suppliers before and during the war. Further investigation is needed on this point.

53. Among the fifteen respondents that said they introduced the formal approved drawing parts system between 1951 and 1955, two were supplying mainly to Toyota, two were mainly for Nissan, five were neutral in supplying both, and six were dealing mainly with other Japanese companies such as Honda, Suzuki, Daihatsu, Mitsubishi, and large truck companies. In other words, there is no particular concentration in the Toyota group suppliers.

54. The author greatly appreciates the cooperation of anonymous managers of company B.

55. Toyota holds a minority share of company B's stock. Virtually all of company B's business is related to the Toyota group.

56. There are two major parts categories that company B is engaged in: X and Y. X occupies a majority of company B's sales.

57. As for parts X, company B was one of several suppliers (and one of two major ones) for Toyota.

50. Such a specification is called structural planning, which consists of a number of documents and rough drawings and is made by translation of product planning, an upstream document.

59. For the influence of the Ford system on the Toyota-style system, see Fujimoto and Tidd (1993).

Chapter 6

1. This chapter is based on previous papers by the author (Fujimoto, 1997d, 1997e) with significant modification.

2. See, for example, Clark and Fujimoto (1991).

3. *Capability* is defined here as a consistent pattern of a firm's activities and resources that brings about distinctive competitive advantages. See also Fujimoto and Tidd (1993) and Fujimoto (1994a, 1994b). For the concept of dynamic capabilities, see, for example, Teece, Pisano, and Shuen (1992).

4. Sheriff, 1988; Clark and Fujimoto, 1992.

5. For the concept of rapid incrementalism, see Clark and Fujimoto, 1991. For dematurity, see Abernathy, Clark, and Kantrow, 1983.

6. The Harvard study did not disclose the name of the firms in this high-performing category. It is a general consensus among many industry observers, however, that Toyota was one of the better product development performers among the Japanese automakers of the 1980s.

7. See also Clark, Chew, and Fujimoto (1987).

8. See, for example, Clark and Fujimoto (1991). Note also that I use the words *routines* and *routine capabilities* (or *routinized capabilities*) interchangeably henceforth for simplicity, assuming that the product development routines discussed here contribute to the distinctive performance advantages of a group of automakers.

9. Clark and Fujimoto (1989, 1991).

10. For this particular analysis, the coordination with suppliers was not included as the case of external integration. See also Clark and Fujimoto (1991) and Fujimoto, Iansiti, and Clark (1996).

11. See, for example, Fujimoto (1989; 1991), Clark and Fujimoto (1990; 1991).

12. This situation did not change much at the individual product level in the early 1990s. For example, one of the Japanese firms known for its strong emphasis on project management reported that it co-located only around 10 percent of its R&D personnel by products as of the mid-1990s.

13. This inference is based on the author's conversation with various Japanese managers and engineers in the early 1980s, when they quite often expressed concerns of insufficient specialization.

14. See Clark and Fujimoto (1994) for a brief summary of the case.

15. For organizational learning through this catchup process, see Ellison (1996).

16. See Ellison et al. (1995) for the data analysis on this catchup process.

17. "Building Successful Supplier Relationships." Presentation by Thomas T. Stallkamp of Chrysler Corporation at the 1993 Global Automotive Conference, "Megatrend and the Auto Industry," December 6–7, 1993. See also Dyer (1996).

18. For the schedule data indicating increased overlapping in U.S. projects, see figure 6.14. This, however, has not affected the length of engineering lead time, as explained later. More detailed case studies would be needed in order to examine what exactly was happening to the product-process interface of the U.S. projects. What is puzzling in the same figure is that Japanese makers on average decreased their degree of product-process overlap. Note, however, that this happened because the lengths of both product and process engineering themselves became shorter in the

Japanese case, and that overall engineering lead times were almost un-changed (roughly thirty months) despite the decreased overlap.

19. For further details, see Ellison et al. (1995). With the participation of Professor Young-suk Hyun of Han-Nam University , the study added three Korean projects as our sample. An important finding is that the av-erage Korean project performance in terms of development productivity and lead time was basically as good as that of Japan as of the early 1990s, although they lagged behind the other regions in total product quality index. The study needs further investigation on how Korean automakers, as newcomers, achieved this performance.

20. For the methods of lead time adjustment for project content, see the appendix of Ellison et al. (1995).

21. For the methods of engineering hours adjustment for project con-tent, see the appendix of Ellison et al. (1995).

22. Clark and Fujimoto (1991).

23. Clark and Fujimoto (1992).

24. Takeishi and Kawahara (1994) showed that the impact of a model change was different depending upon the type of the models by analyzing Japanese automobile sales data by models.

25. Also, it is said that one of Toyota's new models in the mid-1990s re-duced the number of bolts from about 5,000 in the previous generation to roughly 4,000 without sacrificing product attractiveness.

26. Kuhn (1970).

27. The idea that overbuilding strength turns to weakness is not new. Non-Darwinian evolutionists, for example, proposed a theory of overdevel-opment, which argued that "evolutionary growth of certain once-useful or-gans would gain a 'momentum' that would eventually lead to excessive growth and finally, extinction" (Bowler, 1988, p. 101). Similar ideas have been found in social science. See, for example, the "competence trap" (Levitt and March, 1988), "core rigidity" (Leonard-Barton, 1992a), and so on.

28. For the concept of element-focused strategy, see Iansiti (1993).

29. For the limit of technologies as a source of competitive advantages, see, for example, Clark (1989b).

30. For the concept of product integrity, see Clark and Fujimoto (1990, 1991); Fujimoto (1991); and Fujimoto, Iansiti, and Clark (1996). For system-focused strategy, see Iansiti (1993).

31. For this mechanism, see Clark and Fujimoto (1992).

32. Detailed discussion on implementation toward lean product design is beyond the scope of this paper. See, for example, Fujimoto and Takeishi (1994) and Fujimoto (1996) for further details on the implementation issues.

33. Clark and Fujimoto, 1994.

34. See, for example, Fujimoto (1997b), for the load time cutting efforts by some Japanese automakers.

35. For further details, see Fujimoto (1997b).

Chapter 7

1. This chapter is a modified version of Fujimoto (1997f). Takashi Mat-suo, doctoral student of Tokyo University, assisted the author in the field researches and creation of figures 7.3, 7.4, 7.5, 7.6, 7.7, 7.9, and table 7.2.

2. More generally, such attempts by the Japanese automakers to modify so-called lean production system (Womack et al., 1990) were referred to by some industry observers as postlean system, Toyotism II, and so on. See, for example, Nomura (1993), and Shimizu (1995).

3. For the concept of the lean-on-balance system, see Fujimoto, 1994c; 1997a, and Fujimoto and Takeishi, 1994; 1997.

4. For the trend of assembly automation in Japanese automakers, see Shimokawa, Jürgens, and Fujimoto (1997).

5. It is not the intention of this book to demonstrate that this is the best assembly system to handle the current competitive and labor problems, compared to alternative assembly process designs (e.g., Volvo's Uddevalla concept). Instead, this section describes how the new system at Toyota was recognized internally as a rational system after it was established.

6. Fujimoto (1997a).

7. See Fujimoto (1993, 1994c); and Fujimoto and Takeishi (1994).

8. For these new assembly lines, see Kawamura et al. (1993); Toyota Motor Corporation (1994); Kojima (1994); Ogawa (1994); Shimizu (1995); Niimi and Matsudaira (1997); Berggren and Nomura (1997).

9. Note that such body buffers between the line segments are essentially different from component inventories at the line side. That is, the existence of the body buffers does not necessarily mean relaxation of just-in-time principle.

10. Since the 1970s, Toyota began to assign different assembly subtasks for completing one assembly task for a given component (e.g., setting, bolting) to different workers in order to maximize productivity by eliminating non-value-adding time ("muda") since the 1970s. Toyota's assembly line originally followed the parts-complete principle. Thus, the reestablishment of a parts-complete principle means a back-to-basics effort for Toyota.

11. See Niimi et al. (1994); and Niimi and Matsudaira (1997).

12. See Niimi et al. (1994); Toyota Motor Corporation (1994); and Niimi and Matsudaira (1997).

13. See Kawamura et al. (1993).

14. It is important to note here that the basic philosophy behind this work organization was somewhat close to the sociotechnical approach (Benders, 1996). The autonomous and complete line also resembled work organization designs implemented by some of European automakers, such as FIAT and Renault, in the early 1990s. Although there was no sign that Toyota adopted these Western theories or practices directly, it would be reasonable to infer that the Japanese environment during this period (i.e., labor shortages and worker dissatisfaction) and the European environment, in which sociotechnical ideas first became popular, were similar, so that Toyota's response naturally resembled the sociotechnical work designs of some European automakers.

15. Kawamura et al. (1993).

16. For the concept of residual work, see Jürgens et al. (1986).

17. Shibata et al. (1993).

18. Toyota Kyushu Miyata plant had adopted this shift pattern in 1994.

19. For further details, see Nabeta (1992).

20. Assistant managers (general group leaders), group leaders, and

team leaders are normally selected from veteran workers. The section head (*kacho*) may be also from among the shop floor leaders, but is more likely to be a college graduate. In any case, the section head usually is the highest rank to which blue-collar workers are promoted, in most cases at Toyota.

21. There is a paper by former personnel manager at Toyota reporting that the adversarial atmosphere persisted on the shop floor even after the strike and that personnel managers had to make tenacious efforts to visit the shops one by one for better communications for many years before a cooperative atmosphere emerged (Tanaka, 1982).

22. New assembly plants of this period are as follows: Motomachi, 1959; Takaoka, 1966; Tsutsumi, 1970; Tahara #1, 1979. See table 2.2.

23. Typical plant planning and construction lead time is said to be roughly two years, but it varies widely depending upon the case.

24. Exceptions in Japan include, in fact, Tsutsumi plant, Tahara #4 plant, and Toyota Kyushu plant, where the paint building was separated.

25. FIAT's Cassino plant, another new and highly automated final assembly line, was another plant that Toyota paid much attention to. Some of Toyota's production engineers also paid some attention to the experiments of Volvo (e.g., Uddevalla plant), but they did not adopt this concept at this point because they were not convinced of its competitive potential in terms of productivity.

26. Plant A is one of Toyota's existing assembly plants in Japan.

27. Separately, certain automated equipment that was based on the concept of the experiment was selectively introduced at Tahara #4 line in 1991.

28. More accurately, the main assembly line at Tahara #4 was cut into thirteen segments with buffer zones, because five of the eight lines were cut in the middle into two segments. Three of them were cut because of assembly automation, but two of them were cut to separate functionally different parts (e.g., carpet and brake).

29. Also, TMM's assembly line segments were much longer, as the overall length of the main assembly line was about 1.3 times as long as that of Toyota's domestic assembly lines.

30. A leader of the union, in our interview (July 1995), said that it was recognizing the existence of the assembly problem when it was making the action plan between 1986 and 1988, but it did not highlight this problem at that point.

31. Evaluation of Tahara #4 line had already started in the spring of 1991 prior to its startup, when the basic planning of the Toyota Kyushu plant was going on, according to Nobuyoshi Hisada, a leading process engineer for both Tahara #4 and Kyushu.

32. For example, Kiyotoshi Kato, plant general manager of the Kyushu plant, was a former assembly division head of the Motomachi plant when Takahashi was Motomachi plant general manager.

33. It is said that the basic layout of the Kyushu plant was supervised by Jagawa, and then the task was succeeded by Kitano and Shiramizu, in this order.

34. Shiramizu took charge of the plant planning of both Kyushu and TMM #2.

35. The new Motomachi #2 line is said to have been designed under supervision of Shiramizu, and then handed over to Kitano, Motomachi plant general manager then.

36. For example, Toyota's Motomachi Crown assembly line was renovated in the same spirit in 1995. The Tahara #1 line is also under renovation as of 1995.

37. Criticism of Toyota's assembly job was not new (See, for example, Kamata, 1973). Thus, it is likely that the problem was recognized by certain organizational members for a long time. Here, however, we focus only on the process that such problems became issues to be discussed on a company-wide basis.

38. Assembly division heads of seven factories, as well as heads of the Human Resource Division, Assembly Process Engineering Division, Safety and Health Administration Division, Production Control Division, and Operations Management Consulting Office were the members of the assembly-related division head meeting as of 1990.

39. Note that this diagram is not based on objective measurement of consumer satisfaction and employee satisfaction, but on my subjective · judgment from the foregoing historical cases. Note, also, that it is assumed that balanced improvements of CS and ES are regarded as key, based on my arguments about the lean-on-balance system (Fujimoto, 1994c; Fujimoto and Takeishi, 1994; 1997).

40. Note that the origin of the parts-complete concept and the autonomous complete concept are different.

41. The Motomachi plant took the initiative in this theme.

42. For the concepts of low-cost automation and human-fitting automation, see Fujimoto (1997a).

43. Kosuke Shiramizu, Division head and director in charge of assembly process engineering since 1992, took a clear leadership role in the development of TVAL. He insists that current TVAL, as of 1995, is only 60 percent complete, as it does not capture full aspects of assembly workload and fatigue. TVAL needs further development, according to him. For further details of TVAL, see Shibata et al. (1993).

44. For the assembly automation and work organizations at Toyota and other Japanese makers of this period, see Shimokawa, Jürgens, and Fujimoto (1997).

45. The foregoing case seems to be rich enough to be interpreted by various concepts of organization studies, such as organizational learning, organizational culture, and organizational development, but I limit my analysis to the evolutionary approach to organizational learning. See also Weick (1979), Nonaka (1985).

46. See also Mishina (1995).

47. See Burgelman (1991, 1994).

48. The reason why the shop floor organization possesses such informal power is not well known, but there is a possibility that the tradition of pre-Taylor foremen-craftsmen, who enjoyed significant power in shop floor management up to the late 1940s, may still remain in a subtle way.

49. Burgelman (1994), interpreting the case of Intel's strategic exit from the memory business, emphasized that "firms whose internal selection criteria accurately reflect external selection pressures are more likely" to

make effective strategic choices than the others (p. 50). However, what is unique in the present case of Toyota, compared to Burgelman's case of Intel, seems to be the fact that one of the former's critical internal selection mechanisms existed nearly at the bottom of the intraorganizational hierarchy, or *genba*.

50. The present argument is consistent, for example, with the concept of learning bureaucracy proposed by Adler (1992).

51. Burgelman (1994), for example, interprets "dynamic competence" as a pattern of intraorganizational ecological (evolutionary) processes with effective mechanisms for the generation of variations, selection, and recognition-retention of strategic initiatives. For the external evolutionary process, see, for example, Nelson and Winter (1982). For the internal evolutionary process, see also Weick (1979) and Nonaka (1985).

52. See, for example, Lawrence and Lorsch (1967).

53. See also Bower (1970) for a model of intraorganizational resource allocation process in which top managers influence bottom-up strategic initiatives.

Chapter 8

1. Koichi Shimokawa is a professor at Hosei University and one of my senior research colleagues. The interview took place on July 16,1984, at Daihatsu.

2. Toyota has owned a minority share in Daihatsu since 1968.

3. Cusumano, 1985; also see Boyer and Freyssenet, 1995; Freyssenet et al., 1997. GERPISA (Groupe d'Etudes et de Recherches Permanent sur l'Industrie et les Salariès de l'Automobile, or Permanent Group for the Study of the Automobile Industry and its Employees) is an international network of automobile industry researchers, which I have participated in since 1993.

4. Suppose that we can list all the system types (or "species") generated historically, and call this set G, and that we can also list all the system types that can survive in the environment we are observing, and call this set S. Naturally, the system types or "species" that we observe as stable entities are the ones that were generated and survived up to now, or G«S (a product of G and S). The standard equilibrium theory allows only one element in S, so $S \overline{\bigcirc} G$ (S is included in G). In this situation, what we observe, or G«S, is nothing but S itself, regardless of the content of G. What we observe is what survived, and therefore history (G) does not matter. On the contrary, history matters whenever $S \grave{A} G$ (S is not included in G). The evolutionary framework becomes useful in the latter case.

5. See Aoki (1995), Chapters 1 and 3.

6. Jürgens, 1997.

Appendix A

1. Note that I am using the term neo-Darwinism broadly here as synonymous with so-called modern synthesis, the prevalent theory in biological evolution that includes revised Darwinism and Mendelian genetics.

2. As for general discussions of the concept of evolution, see, for example, Bowler (1983, 1988) and Laszlo (1987).

3. For this analogy, see also Nelson and Winter (1982), p. 14.

4. The concept of structural inertia in population ecology of organizations (Hannan and Freeman, 1989), emphasizes the role of such retention mechanisms for a system's survival.

5. Penrose (1959); Nelson and Winter (1982); Dosi (1982); Chandler (1990); Teece, Rumelt, Dosi, and Winter (1994), pp. 1–30; Mintzberg and Waters (1985), pp. 257–272; Burgelman (1994), pp. 24–56.

6. For the concepts of resource, organizational routine, capability, and competence, see, for example, Penrose (1959); Nelson and Winter (1982); Dosi (1982); Wernerfelt (1984); Itami (1984); Chandler (1990, 1992); Prahalad and Hamel (1990); Grant (1991); Leonard-Barton (1992a); Teece, Pisano, and Shuen (1992); Kogut and Kulatilaka (1992); Iansiti and Clark (1993); and Teece, Rumelt, Dosi, and Winter (1994). For evolutionary aspects of the intraorganizational processes, see, also, Weick (1979), Nonaka (1985), Mintzberg (1987), and Burgelman (1991, 1994).

7. Such recent literature as Chandler (1990); Prahalad and Hamel (1990); and Teece, Rumelt, Dosi, and Winter (1994) mainly analyze the multiproduct or multi-industry situations.

8. Wernerfelt (1995), p. 172.

9. Abernathy (1978); Hayes and Wheelwright (1984); and Hayes, Wheelwright, and Clark (1988) are among the exceptional cases that included both total system and dynamic perspective, but they did not make an explicit connection to evolutionary theories of firms or organizations.

10. See Hannan and Freeman (1977), and Barnett and Burgelman (1996), for this distinction.

11. See, for example, Hannan and Freeman (1977, 1989).

12. Note that, if numerous random variations and strict selection of optimal routines are assumed, the neo-Darwinian model can be compatible with equilibrium models of microeconomics. See Alchian (1950) and Hirshleifer (1977).

13. Population ecology models may be applied more effectively to the case of earlier phase of automobile industrial evolution, in which many births and deaths of individual automobile manufacturers were observed. See, for example, Abernathy (1978) and Carroll et al. (1996) for the case of the U.S. auto industry.

14. See also Quinn's concept of "logical incrementalism" (Quinn, 1978).

15. Mintzberg's metaphor of "crafting strategy" (Mintzberg, 1987) is quite insightful in this sense. Extending his analogy of pottery, I would add an example of potters of some Japanese earthenware (e.g., Bizen) whose baking process is highly uncertain. On the one hand, the potters try to control the baking process; at the same time, they appreciate unintended results of the process, which often becomes a core of the pottery's artistic value. One of their critical skill is to judge good ones and bad ones, destroying the latter—a skill of internal selection.

Appendix B

1. TQC emphasized clarification of quality goals, communication of the goals to the shop floor, involvement of all the employees, education of shop floor supervisors, diffusion of quality and cost consciousness, making good product the first time (*tsukurikomi*), cross-functional coordination, coordination with suppliers and dealers, smooth implementation of model changeover, and so on.

2. For standard explanations of the production system at Toyota and other effective Japanese automakers of the 1970s and 1980s, see, for example, Ohno (1978); Nihon Noritsu Kyokai (1978); Shingo (1980); Schonberger (1982); Monden (1983/1993); Imai (1986); Toyota Motor Corporation (1987, 1996b); Womack et al. (1990), and Coriat (1991).

3. Note, however, that not all of the Japanese auto firms are following this principle. Honda, for example, is known for making thirty or sixty assembly batches in principle, as opposed to randomizing the assembly sequence. This does not necessarily mean that Honda's manufacturing performance is lower than that of firms following the levelization principle. It may be an alternative way of making cars effectively without relying strictly on the levelization principle.

4. It is assumed that the workers pulled out from this line are not laid off but are transferred to other production lines under the stable employment policies of the postwar large Japanese firms.

5. See also Adler and Cole (1993). In some Western auto factories that introduced this standard operating procedure system, the process was more democratic, in that workers themselves can revise the procedures after getting reviews from the specialists.

6. See also Jürgens et al. (1993); and Nomura (1993) for similar arguments.

7. For the human resource management policies and labor relations of the postwar Japanese automakers, see, for example, Koike (1977), Yamamoto (1981), Cusumano (1985), Totsuka and Hyodo (1990), Nomura (1993), Asanuma (1994).

8. First-line supervisors used to retire from management work when they reached fifty-five, while staying with the company, but this rule was abolished in the early 1990s.

9. When Nissan announced it was closing its Zama assembly plant, it started negotiating with the union and the workers; it made a plan to distribute the employees to other facilities, and it shut down the plant without layoffs or terminations, according to the Nissan union. This was the first case of a major plant shutdown in Japan since continuous growth started in the 1950s

10. Many temporary workers were subsequently hired as permanent workers. Nomura (1993), for example, estimates that, back in 1982, about 40 percent of Toyota's blue-collar workers (*gino-in*) were originally hired as temporary workers.

11. On the labor side, in some cases, relatively moderate unions superseded older and militant unions as the main negotiators after the strikes.

12. Generally egalitarian policies for corporate welfare and networks of

employee clubs also supplement the above efforts for better communication and motivation.

13. Some of the indicators discussed in this section may include non-production performance (e.g., sales), but they are presented here as long as they are related to the production performance of the assemblers (performance of the suppliers are discussed later in this chapter).

14. Most of the Japanese plants, as well as in many recently built Western assembly plants, include press (stamping) operations in the assembly plant. The existing assembly labor productivity study tended to exclude this process, though. In the 1990s, the International Motor Vehicle Program (IMVP) at MIT started to measure productivity in stamping shops as a separate project.

15. Another important area of in-house production by the assembly makers is engine production, but there were no comparative productivity studies in this area until the mid-1990s, with the International Motor Vehicle Program's first study (e.g., a presentation, "IMVP Engine Plant Study" by D. Whitney and G. Paschard, at IMVP Sponsors Meeting, San-Paulo, Brazil, June 1996).

16. John Krafcik of IMVP conducted pioneering work for the first comprehensive comparisons of assembly productivity in the Japanese, North American, and European factories, as well as those of newly industrialized countries. The study was continued by John Paul MacDuffie and Frits Pil in the 1990s; see Krafcik (1988) and MacDuffie and Pil (1996).

17. As for the activities and performance of the Japanese transplants, see, for example, Abo (1994), Florida and Kenny (1991), Adler and Cole (1993).

18. Freight from Japan to the U.S. West Coast was estimated to be about $500 at that time.

19. Although sales productivity is outside the scope of the research in this book, we also found that sales productivity in Japan was lower or at best similar to the U.S. level, depending upon the definition. See the bottom part of table B.1, and also Fujimoto and Takeishi (1995).

20. See also Initial Quality Study (IQS) of *Power Report* by J.D. Power & Associates.

21. We should keep in mind that conformance quality is ultimately determined by the customer's mind. As the customer accumulates product experience and his or her discernment or sensitivity to detect subtle product problems evolves, the definition of a defect (i.e., definition of conformance quality) may change. Thus, we have to constantly check if the quality indicators reflect changing customer expectations reasonably accurately.

22. For example, the author had frequent contact with the Boston Consulting Group, which conducted an international comparative study in this field. For a part of their research result, see Stalk, Stephenson, and King (1996).

23. Note, however, that this type of elaborate order entry system still does not solve the problems inherent in the sales from dealer stocks (i.e., push sales). Mismatches between dealer orders and customer demands do exist, particularly in the case of relatively unpopular models, and large discounts and other sales costs tend to incur with the dealers' efforts to

match what they have with what customers request. The existence of a chronic price discount among the Japanese dealers is circumstantial evidence of such a mismatch. See also Fujimoto and Takeishi (1994; 1997).

24. Part of this research is reported in Stalk, Stephenson, and King (1996).

25. Note that this type of indicator may be measured at various levels, such as platforms, models, body types, and variations (options, colors, body and engine types), and that the result may be different depending upon the definition.

26. See also Lieberman (1994) for more recent labor productivity statistics.

27. For example, according to Initial Quality Study (IQS) by J.D. Power & Associates (The Power Report, June 1994), seven out of the top ten models were made by Toyota or its joint venture (NUMMI).

28. For the relationship between inventory reduction and productivity growth in the Japanese automobile industry including Toyota, see also Lieberman and Demeester (1995) and Lieberman and Asaba (1997).

29. There are other cost estimations by industry experts that indicate Toyota had a unit cost advantage of at least several hundred dollars over other Japanese makers as of the early 1990s.

30. See, for example, Sei, Omori, and Nakajima (1975); Asanuma (1984, 1989, 1997); Oshima (1987); Matsui (1988); Nishiguchi (1989, 1993); Cusumano and Takeishi (1991); Clark and Fujimoto (1991); Fujimoto, Sei, and Takeishi (1994); Dyer (1994); Fujimoto (1994a, 1995); Helper and Sako (1995).

31. In the early 1980s, it is said that the majority of operating profits for the major Japanese automakers originated from the U.S. market, due partly to their productivity advantages then, a relatively low exchange rate, supply constraints in part by voluntary Japanese export restrictions to the U.S. market, and the relatively high U.S. retail price levels as a result of this.

32. The specific data in the automobile industry are not available.

33. For example, members of the Japan Automobile Workers' Unions (JAW) include not only all assemblers but also many first-tier suppliers, but few second-tier suppliers. Thus, there seems to be constant pressure toward wage levelization between the assemblers and first-tier firms.

34. Even with freight costs taken into accounted, some Japanese auto firms in the early 1980s were estimating that most of the functional parts, except very bulky parts, could be imported from Japan, to their U.S. transplants at lower prices than those from U.S. suppliers.

35. Lieberman and Asaba (1997) also indicated that the pace of inventory reduction by the U.S. parts suppliers was much slower than that by U.S. assembly makers.

36. We should not forget, however, that the classic problems of resource allocation and income distribution may still exist in the more upstream part of the supply chain.

37. Theoretically, this implies that the impact of relation-specific quasi-rent (Aoki, 1988) was more important than monopoly rent, and that X-inefficiency (Leibenstein, 1966) was more important than inefficiency in resource allocation in explaining the performance of the Japanese supplier system of the 1980s.

38. Helper (1991) also indicates that adoption of the detail-controlled parts system by the U.S. big three was also an outcome of historical evolution. She argues that many major U.S. suppliers in the early stages of the industry's history had component development capability, but the technological capability started to concentrate with the car makers as they moved to oligopoly, vertical integration, and monopoly rent-seeking by excising negotiation power over parts suppliers.

39. It should be noted that one assembler may still be a dominant customer in terms of sales share, even if there are multiple customers.

40. See, for example, Kikuchi (1976).

41. Nobeoka (1996) indicated that the Japanese auto suppliers with diversified customer bases tended to outperform other Japanese suppliers with fewer customers, which is consistent with this view.

42. See also Nishiguchi (1987).

43. The barriers between Toyota group and Nissan group suppliers have been slowly lowering in the 1990s.

44. There are, however, different types of suppliers within the category of Toyota group or Nissan group suppliers in terms of the closeness of their connections to their assemblers (e.g., equity ownership, exchange of managers, degree of information sharing in product development). See, for example, Sato (1988), Ueda (1989, 1990, 1991), Kamath and Liker (1994).

45. As for development competition, the *Supplier's Guide* published by Toyota, prepared mainly for its U.S.-based suppliers, explains as follows: "We ordinarily work with prototype suppliers on the assumption that they will become mass production suppliers unless they fail to complete development work on schedule. But we sometimes choose a larger number of prototype suppliers than we need for mass production and cull their numbers to one or two on the basis of performance in development work" (Toyota Motor Corporation, 1996a, p. 45). Note, however, that this discourse might not accurately reflect its real practices with the Japanese suppliers.

46. Toyota's Supplier's Guide explains one of its basic policies of purchasing as: "We evaluate the overall strength of prospective suppliers, including their quality, cost, technological capabilities, and reliability in delivering the required quantities on time. In addition, we evaluate their potential strength, as evidenced in such ways as their amenability to continuous, improvements" (Toyota Motor Corporation, 1996, p. 6.).

REFERENCES

Abernathy, W. J. (1978). *The Productivity Dilemma.* Baltimore: Johns Hopkins University Press.

Abernathy, W. J., Clark, K. B., and Kantrow, A. M. (1981). "The New Industrial Competition." *Harvard Business Review*, September–October: 68–81.

Abernathy, W. J., Clark, K. B., and Kantrow, A. M. (1983). *Industrial Renaissance: Producing a Competitive Future for America.* New York: Basic Books.

Abernathy, W. J., and Utterback,W. J. (1978). "Patterns of Industrial Innovation." *Technology Review* 80, no. 7 (June-July 1978): 2–9.

Abo, T., ed. (1994). *Hybrid Factory: The Japanese Production System in the United States.* New York: Oxford University Press.

Adler, P. S. (1993). "The Learning Bureaucracy: New United Motors Manufacturing, Inc." In B. M. Staw and L. L. Cummings, eds., *Research in Organizational Behavior*, vol. 15 (pp. 111–194). Greenwich, Conn.: JAI Press.

Adler, P. S., and Cole, R. E. (1993). "Designed for Learning: A Tale of Two Auto Plants." *Sloan Management Review*, Spring: 85–93.

Alchian, A. A. (1950). "Uncertainty, Evolution, and Economic Theory." *Journal of Political Economy* 53, no. 3: 211–221.

Aldrich, H., and Herker, D. (1977). "Boundary Spanning Roles and Organization Structure." *Academy of Management Review*, April 1977: 217–230.

Allen, T. J. (1966). "Studies of the Problem-Solving Process in Engineering Design." *IEEE Transactions on Engineering Management EM-13*, no. 2 (June): 72–83.

———. (1977). *Managing the Flow of Technology.* Cambridge: MIT Press, 1977.

Aoki, M. (1988). *Information, Incentives, and Bargaining in the Japanese Economy.* Cambridge, UK: Cambridge University Press.

————. (1995). *Keizai system no shinka to tagensei - hikaku seido bunseki josetsu* [Evolution and diversity of economic systems: An introduction to comparative institutional analysis]. Tokyo: Toyo Keizai Shinposha (in Japanese).

Aoshima, Y. (1996). "Knowledge Transfer across Generations: The Impact on Product Development Performance in the Automobile Industry." Unpublished Ph. D. dissertation, MIT Sloan School of Management.

Argyris, C., and Shön, D. A. (1996). *Organizational Learning II: Theory, Method, and Practice.* Reading, Mass.: Addison-Wesley.

Asanuma, B. (1984). "Jidosha sangyo ni okeru buhin torihiki no kozo" [Structures of parts transactions in the automobile industry]. *Kikan Gendai Keizai,* Summer: 38–48 (in Japanese).

————. (1989). "Manufacturer-Supplier Relationships in Japan and the Concept of Relation Specific Skill." *Journal of the Japanese and International Economies 3* (March): 1–30.

————. (1994). "Shokuba no rodo soshiki to zensha no jinteki shigen kanri" [Shop labor organization and company-wide human resource management]. Kyoto University Working Paper Series J-1 (in Japanese).

————. (1997). *Nihon no kigyo soshiki; kakushinteki tekio no mechanism* [Organizations of the japanese firms: the mechanism of innovative adaptation]. Tokyo: Toyo Keizai Shinposha.

Asanuma, B., and Kinutani, T. (1992). "Risk Absorption in Japanese Subcontracting: A Microeconomic Study of the Automobile Industry." *Journal of the Japanese and International Economies 6* (March): 1–29.

Axelrod, R. (1984). *The Evolution of Cooperation.* New York: Basic Books.

Barnett, W. P., and Burgelman, R. A. (1996). "Evolutionary Perspectives on Strategy." *Strategic Management Journal* 17: 5–19.

Benders, J. (1996). "Leaving Lean? Recent Changes in the Production Organizations of Some Japanese Car Plants." *Economic and Industrial Democracy* 17, no. 1: 9–38.

Berggren, C., and Nomura, M. (1997). *The Resilience of Corporate Japan.* London: Paul Chapman.

Bowen, H. K., Clark, K. B., Holloway, C. A., and Wheelwright, S. C., eds. (1994). *The Perpetual Enterprise Machine.* New York: Oxford University Press.

Bowler, P. J. (1983). *Evolution: The History of an Idea.* Berkeley: University of California Press.

————. (1988). *The Non-Darwinian Revolution.* Baltimore: The John Hopkins University Press.

Bower, J. L. (1970). *Managing the Resource Allocation Process: A Study of Corporate Planning and Investment.* Boston: Harvard Business School Press.

Boyer, R., and Freyssenet, M. (1995). "The Emergence of New Industrial Models." *Actes du GERPISA,* Universite' d'Evry-Val d'Essonne, no. 15: 75–142.

Browne, J., Dubois, D., Rathmill, K., Sethi, S. P., and Stecke, K. E. (1984). "Classification of Flexible Manufacturing Systems." *FMS Magazine,* April: 114–117.

Burgelman, R. A. (1991). "Intraorganizational Ecology of Strategy Making and Organizational Adaptation: Theory and Field Research." *Organizational Science 2*, no. 3: 239–262.

———. (1994). "Fading Memories: A Process Theory of Strategic Business Exit in Dynamic Environments." *Administrative Science Quarterly 39*: 24–56.

Campbell, D. T. (1970). "Natural Selection as an Epistemological Model." In R. Naroll and R. Cohen (eds.), *A Handbook of Method in Cultural Anthropology* (pp. 51–85). Garden City, N. Y.: Natural History Press.

Carroll, G. R., Bigelow, L. S., Seidel, M. L, and Tsai, L. B. (1996). "The Fates of De Novo and De Alio Producers in the American Automobile Industry 1885–1981." *Strategic Management Journal 17*: 117–137.

Chandler A. D. (1990). *Scale and Scope*. Cambridge, Mass.: Harvard University Press.

———. (1992). "What Is a Firm?" *European Economic Review 36*: 483–492.

Clark, K. B. (1989a). "Project Scope and Project Performance: The Effect of Parts Strategy and Supplier Involvement on Product Development." *Management Science 35*, no. 10: 1247–1263.

———. (1989b). "What Strategy Can Do for Technology." *Harvard Business Review*, November-December: 94–98.

Clark, K. B., Chew, W. B., and Fujimoto, T. (1987). "Product Development in the World Auto Industry." *Brookings Papers on Economic Activity 3*: 729–771.

Clark, K. B., and Fujimoto, T. (1989a). "Lead Time in Automobile Product Development: Explaining the Japanese Advantage." *Journal of Technology and Engineering Management 6*: 25–58.

———. (1989b). "Overlapping Problem Solving in Product Development." In Ferdows, K., ed., *Managing International Manufacturing* (pp. 127–152). Amsterdam: North Holland.

———. (1990). "The Power of Product Integrity." *Harvard Business Review*, November–December: 107–118.

———. (1991). *Product Development Performance*. Boston: Harvard Business School Press.

———. (1992). "Product Development and Competitiveness." *Journal of the Japanese and International Economies 6*, 101–143.

———. (1994). "The Product Development Imperative: Competing in the New Industrial Marathon." In P. B. Duffy, ed., *The Relevance of a Decade* (pp. 287–322). Boston: Harvard Business School Press.

Cohen, M. D., and Sproull, L. S., eds. (1996). *Organizational Learning*. Thousand Oaks, Calif.: Sage Publications.

Cohen, W. M., and Levinthal, D. A. (1990). "Adaptive Capacity: A New Perspective on Learning and Innovation." *Administrative Science Quarterly 35*: 128–152.

———. (1994). "Fortune Favors the Prepared Firm." *Management Science 40*, no. 2: 227–251.

Collins, J. C., and Porras, J. I. (1994). *Built to Last*. New York: Harper Business.

Conway, R., Maxwell, W., McClain, J. O., and Thomas, L. J. (1988). "The Role of Work-in-Process Inventory in Serial Produiction Lines." *Operations Research 36*, no. 2 (March-April): 229–241.

Coriat, B. (1991), *Penser à l'Envers*. [The Reverse Thinking] Christian Bourgois Editeur, Paris (in French).

Crandall, R. (1968). "Vertical Integration and the Market for Repair Parts in the United States Automobile Industry." *Journal of Industial Economics 16*: 212–234.

Cusumano, M. A. (1985). *The Japanese Automobile Industry*. Cambridge, Mass.: Harvard University Press.

———. (1988). "Manufacturing Innovation: Lessons from the Japanese Auto industry." *Sloan Management Review* 30, no. 1 (Fall): 29–39.

Cusumano, M. A., and Takeishi, A. (1991). "Supplier Relations and Management: A Survey of Japanese-Transplant, and U.S. Auto Plants." *Strategic Management Journal 12*: 563–588.

Davis, G. B., and Olsen, M. H. (1974/1985). *Management Information Systems*. New York: McGraw-Hill.

Dore, R. (1987). *Taking Japan Seriously*. London: Athlone Press.

Dosi, G. (1982). "Technological Paradigms and Technological Trajectories." *Research Policy* 11: 147–162.

Dumas, A., and Mintzberg, H. (1989). "Managing Design Designing Management." *Design Management Journal 1*, no. 1 (Fall): 37–44.

Durkheim, É. (1895/1938). *Les Règles de la méthode sociologique* [The rules of sociological method]. Glencoe, Ill.: Free Press.

Dyer, J. H. (1994). "Dedicated Assets: Japan's Manufacturing Edge." *Harvard Business Review*, November-December: 174–178.

———. (1996). "How Chrysler Created an American Keiretsu." *Harvard Business Review*, July-August:42–56.

Ellison, D. J. (1996). "Dynamic Capabilities in New Product Development: The Case of the World Auto Industry." Unpublished PhD. dissertation, Harvard University.

Ellison, D. J., Clark, K. B., Fujimoto, T., and Hyun, Y. (1995). "Product Development Performance in the Auto Industry: 1990s Update." Harvard Business School Working Paper 95–066.

Fine, C. H., and Whitney, D. E. (1996) "Is the Make-Buy Decision Process a Core Competence?" MIT Center for Technology, Policy, and Industrial Development Working Paper.

Fiol, C. M., and Lyles, M. A. (1985). "Organizational Learning." *Academy of Management Review 10*, no. 4: 803–813.

Florida, R., and Kenny, M. (1991). "Transplant Organizations: The Transfer of Japanese Industrial Organization in the U.S." *American Sociological Review 56* (June): 381–398.

Freeman, C. (1982). *The Economics of Industrial Innovation*. Cambridge, Mass.: MIT Press.

Freyssenet, M., Mair, A., Shimizu, K., and Volpato, G. (1998). *One Best Way? Trajectories and Industrial Models of the World's Automobile Producers*. Oxford: GERPISA Books, Oxford University Press.

Fujimoto, T. (1989). "Organizations for Effective Product Development— The Case of the Global Automobile Industry." Unpublished D.B.A. dissertation, Harvard Business School.

———. (1991). "Product Integrity and the Role of Designer as Integrator." *Design Management Journal 2*, no. 2 (Spring): 29–34.

———. (1993). "At a Crossroads." *Look Japan 93*, no. 450 (September): 14–15.

———. (1994a). "The Origin and Evolution of the 'Black Box Parts' Practice in the Japanese Auto Industry." University of Tokyo Research Institute for the Japanese Economy Discussion Paper 94-F-1.

———. (1994b). "Reinterpreting the Resource-Capability View of the Firm: A Case of the Development -Production Systems of the Japanese Auto Makers." University of Tokyo Research Institute for the Japanese Economy Discussion Paper 94-F-20. An abridged version is in A. D. Chandler, P. Hagström, and Ö. Sölvell (1998), *The Dynamic Firm. The Role of Technology, Strategy, Organization, and Regions* (pp. 15–44). Oxford: Oxford University Press.

———. (1994c). "The Limits of Lean Production." *Politik und Gesellschaft*, Friedrich-Ebert-Stiftung, Germany, January: 40–46.

———. (1995). "Note on the Origin of the 'Black Box Parts' Practice in the Japanese Auto Inudstry." In H. Shiomi and K. Wada, eds., *Fordism Transformed: The Development of Production Methods in the Automobile Industry* (pp. 184–216). Oxford: Oxford University Press.

———. (1997a). "Strategies for Assembly Automation." In K. Shimokawa, U. Jürgens, and T. Fujimoto, eds. (1997), *Transforming Automobile Assembly* (pp. 211–237). Berlin: Springer Verlag.

———. (1997b). "Shortening Lead Time through Early Problem Solving— A New Round of Capability-Building Competition in the Auto Industry." University of Tokyo Research Institute for the Japanese Economy Discussion Paper 97-F-12.

———. (1997c). "The Japanese Automobile Supplier System: Framework, Facts, And Reinterpretation." *Proceedings of the 3rd International Symposium on Logistics*. SGE-Servizi Grafici Editoriali, Padova.

———. (1997d). "Capability Building and Over-Adaptation—A Case of 'Fat Design' in the Japanese Auto Industry." *Actes Du GERPISA*, Reseau International, no. 19, Fevrier.

———. (1997e). "The Dynamic Aspect of Product Development Capabilities: An International Comparison in the Automobile Industry." In A. Goto and H. Odagiri, eds., *Innovation in Japan* (pp. 57–99). New York: Oxford University Press.

———. (1997f). "Evolution of Manufacturing Systems and Ex-post Dynamic Capabilities—A Case of Toyota's Final Assembly Operations." Forthcoming in R. Nelson, G. Dosi, and S. Winter, eds. *Nature and Dynamics of Organizational Capabilities*. Oxford University Press. (The original version was presented at the Third International Workshop on Assembly Automation, Ca' Foscari University of Venice, October 1995.)

Fujimoto, T., Iansiti, M., and Clark, K. B. (1996). "External Integration in Product Development." In T. Nishiguchi, ed., *Managing Product Development* (pp. 121–161). New York: Oxford University Press.

Fujimoto, T., and Matsuo, T. (1997). "Toyota Jidosha ni okeru body buffer kanri no hensen: Hino jidosha Kusunoki kaicho kojutsu kiroku" [Changes in management of body buffers at Toyota: Interview with Mr. Kusunoki, chairman of Hono Motors, Ltd.]. University of Tokyo Research Institute for the Japanese Economy Discussion Paper 97-F-12.

Fujimoto, T., Nishiguchi, T., and Sei, S. (1994). "The Strategy and Structure of Japanese Automobile manufacturers in Europe." In M. Mason and D. Encarnation, eds., *Does Ownership Matter?* (pp. 367–406). New York: Oxford University Press.

Fujimoto, T, Sei, S., and A. Takeishi (1994). "Nihon jidosha sangyo no supplier system no zentaizo to sono tamensei" [The total perspective and multifaceted nature of the supplier system in the Japanese auto industry]. *Kikai Keizai Keknyu* [Research in Machinery Economy] 24, Kikai Keizai Kenkyu-sho: 11–36 (in Japanese).

Fujimoto, T., and Shimokawa, K. (1997). Toyota jidosha moto fukushacho Ohno Taiici-shi kojutsu kiroku. [An interview with Taiici Ohno, July 16, 1984]. University of Tokyo Research Institute for the Japanese Economy Discussion Paper 92-J-4.

Fujimoto, T., and Takeishi, A. (1994). Jidosha sangyo 21 seiki he no shinario [The automobile industry: A scenario toward the 21st century]. Tokyo: Seisansei Shuppan.

———. (1995). "An International Comparison of Productivity and Product Development Performance in the Auto Industry." In R. Minami, K. S. Kim, F. Makino, and J. Seo, eds., *Acquisition, Adaptation and Development of Technologies* (pp. 249–280). New York: St. Martin's Press.

———. (1997). "Automobile Industry." In Japan Commission on Industrial Performance, ed., *Made in Japan* (pp. 71–95). Cambridge, Mass.: The MIT Press.

Fujimoto, T., and Tidd, J. (1993). "The U.K. and Japanese Auto Industry: Adoption and Adaptation of Fordism." Imperial College Working Paper. Presented at Entrepreneurial Activities and Corporate Systems Conference, Tokyo University, January.

Fuss, M., and Waverman, L. (1990). "The Extent and Sources of Cost and Efficiency Differences between U.S. and Japanese Motor Vehicle Producers." *Journal of the Japanese and International Economies 4*: 219–256.

Galbraith, J. R. (1973). *Designing Complex Organizations*. Reading, Mass.: Addison-Wesley.

Garvin, D. A. (1984). "What Does 'Product Quality' Really Mean?" *Sloan Management Review*, Fall: 25–43.

Giddens, A. (1984). *The Constitution of Society*. Berkeley: University of California Press.

Granovetter, M. S. (1985). "Economic Action and Social Structure: The Problem of Embeddedness." *American Journal of Sociology 91*, no. 3: 481–510.

Grant, R. (1991). "The Resource-Based Theory of Competitive Advantage: Implications for Strategy Formulation." *California Management Review*, June: 114–135.

Gregory, R. L., ed. (1987). *The Oxford Companion to the Mind*. Oxford: Oxford University Press.

Groocock, J. M. (1986). *The Chain of Quality*. New York: John Wiley & Sons.

Hall, N., ed. (1991). *Exploring Chaos: A Guide to the New Science of Disorder*. New York: W. W. Norton.

Hannan, M. T., and Freeman, J. (1977). "The Population Ecology of Organizations." *American Journal of Sociology. 82*: 929–964.

———. (1989). *Organizational Ecology*. Cambridge, Mass.: Harvard University Press.

Harbour, J. (1980). "Comparison and Analysis of Manufacturing Productivity." Final consulting report, Harbour and Associates, Dearborn Heights, Mich.

Hasegawa, T. (1993). "Nihon ni okeru jidoshagijutsu no okori to tenkai: Watakushino keiken" [Origin and development of automobile technologies in Japan: From my experience]. Kagaku Gijutsu Seisaku Kenkyusho (NISTEP) Research Material. Seminar note 43 (in Japanese).

Hayes, R. H., and Wheelwright, S. C. (1984). *Restoring Our Competitive Edge*. New York: John Wiley & Sons.

Hayes, R. H., Wheelwright, S. C., and Clark, K. B. (1988). *Dynamic Manufacturing*. New York: Free Press.

Helper, S. R. (1991). "How Much Has Really Changed between U.S. Automakers and Their Suppliers? " *Sloan Management Review*, Summer: 15–28.

Helper, S. R., and Levine, D. I. (1994). "Long-term Supplier Relations and Product-market Structure." *Journal of Law, Economics, and Organization 8*, no. 3: 561–581.

Helper, S. R., and Sako, M. (1995). "Supplier Relations in Japan and the United States: Are They Converging?" *Sloan Management Review*, Spring: 77–84.

Hirshleifer, J. (1977). "Economics from a Biological Viewpoint." *Journal of Law and Economics 20*, no. 1: 1–52.

Hounshell, D. A. (1984). *From the American System to Mass Production 1800–1932: The Development of Manufacturing Technology in the U.S.* Baltimore: Johns Hopkins University Press.

———. (1995). "Planning and Executing 'Automation' at Ford Motor Company, 1945–1960: The Cleveland Engine Plant and its Consequences." In H. Shiomi and K. Wada, eds., *Fordism Transformed: The Development of Production Methods in the Automobile Industry*: 49–86. Oxford: Oxford University Press.

Iansiti, M. (1993). "Real World R&D: Jumping the Product Generation Gap." *Harvard Business Review*, May-June: 138–147.

Iansiti, M., and Clark, K. B. (1993). "Integration and Dynamic Capability: Evidence from Product Development in Automobiles and Mainframe Computers." Harvard Business School Working Paper 93-047.

Ikari, Y. (1985). *Toyota tai Nissan: Shinsha Kaihatsu no Saizensen* [Toyota versus Nissan: The Front Line of New Car Development]. Tokyo: Diamond.

Imai, K., Itami, H., and Koike, K. (1982). *Naibu soshiki no keizaigaku* [The economics of internal organizations]. Tokyo: Toyo Keizai Shinpo Sha (in Japanese).

Imai, M. (1986). *Kaizen*. Random House, New York.

Itami, H. (1984). *Shin keieisenryaku no ronri* [The logic of business strategy: Revised]. Toyko: Nihon Keizai Shinbunsha (in Japanese).

Itami, H. (1988). "Mieru te no kyoso: Buhin kyokyu taisei no koritsu-sei" [Competition by visible hands: Efficiency of parts supply systems]. In H. Itami, T. Kagono, T. Kobayashi, K. Sakakibara, and M. Ito, eds., *Kyoso to kakushin: Jidosha sangyo no kigyo seicho* [Competition and innovation: Company growth in the automobile industry] (pp. 144–172). Tokyo Keizai Shinpo Sha (in Japanese).

Ito, M. (1989). "Kigyo-kan kankei to keizoku-teki torihiki" [Inter-firm relations and continual contracts]. In K. Imai and R. Komiya, eds., *Nihon no kigyo* [The Japanese firms] (pp. 109–130). Tokyo: Tokyo University Press (in Japanese).

Jaikumar, R. (1986). "Postindustrial Manufacturing." *Harvard Business Review,* November-December: 69–76.

Jaikumar, R., and Bohn, R. E. (1992). "A Dynamic Approach to Operations Management; An Alternative to static Optimization." *International Journal of Production Economics vol. 27.* No. 3, October: 265–282.

J. D. Power & Associates (1994). *The Power Report,* June, J. D. Power & Associates.

Jidosha Kogyokai [Japan Automobile Manufacturers Association]. (1967). *Nihon jidosha kogyo shiko* [A manuscript of the history of the Japanese automobile industry], Parts 1–3. Tokyo: Jidosha Kogyokai [Japan Automobile Manufacturers Association] (in Japanese).

Jürgens, U. (1997). "Rolling Back Cycle Times: The Renaissance of the Classic Assembly Line in Final Assembly" (pp. 255–273). In K. Shimokawa, U. Jürgens, and T. Fujimoto, eds., *Transforming Automobile Assembly.* Berlin: Springer Verlag.

Jürgens, U., Dohse, K., and Malsch, T. (1986). "New Production Concepts in West German Car Plants" (pp. 258–281). In Steven Tolliday and Jonathan Zeitlin, eds., *The Automobile Industry and Its Workers: Between Fordism and Flexibility.* Cambridge: Polity Press.

Jürgens, U., Malsch, T., and Dohse, K. (1993). *Breaking from Taylorism.* Cambridge, UK: Cambridge University Press.

Juran, J. M., Gryna, F. M., Jr., and Bingham, Jr., R. S., eds. (1975). *Quality. Control Handbook.* New York: McGraw-Hill.

Kamata, S. (1973). *Jidoha zetsubo kojo.* [*The automobile plant of desperation*]. Tokyo: Gendaishi Shuppankai.

Kamath, R. R., and Liker, J. K (1994). "A Second Look at Japanese Product Development." *Harvard Business Review,* November-December: 154–170.

Kawahara, A. (1998). *The Origin of Competitive Strength: Fifty Years of the Auto Industry in Japan and the U.S.* Tokyo: Springer-Verlag Tokyo.

Kawamura, T., Niimi, A., Hisada, N., and Kuzuhara, T. (1993). "Korekara no hito ga shuyaku no kumitate rain zukuri" [Coming worker friendly factory]. *Toyota Technical Review, 43,* no. 2 (November): 86–91.

Kikuchi, H. (1976). *Wagakuni ni okeru gaichu shitauke kanri no tenkai* [Development of outsourcing and subcontracting management in Japan]. Tokyo: Chusho Kigyo Kenkyu Center [Research Institute for Small and Medium Size Firms] (in Japanese).

Kogut, B., and Kulatilaka, N. (1992). "What is a Critical Capability?" Paper presented at the Joseph A. Schumpeter Society, Kyoto, August.

Koike, K. (1977). *Shokuba no rodo kumiai to sanka.* [Shop union and participation]. Tokyo: Toyo Keizai Shinposha (in Japanese).

———. (1991). *Shigoto no keizaigaku.* [The economics of work]. Tokyo: Toyo Keizai Shinposha (in Japanese).

Kojima T. (1994). *Cho lean kakumei* [The ultra-lean revolution]. Tokyo: Nohon Keizai Shinbun-sha (in Japanese).

Kottler, P. (1967/1984). *Marketing Management.* Englewood Cliffs, N.J.: Prentice-Hall.

Krafcik, J. (1988). "Triumph of the Lean Production System." *Sloan Management Review,* Fall: 41–52.

Kuhn, T. B. (1970). *Structure of Scientific Revolutions.* Chicago: University of Chicago Press.

Lancaster, K. (1966). "A New Approach to Consumer Theory." *Journal of Political Economy,* 74: 132–157.

Laszlo, E. (1987). *Evolution: The Grand Synthesis.* Boston: New Science Library.

Lawrence, P. R., and Dyer, D. (1983). *Renewing American Industry.* New York: Free Press.

Lawrence, P. R., and Lorsch, J. W. (1967). *Organization and Environment.* Homewood, Ill.: Richard D. Irwin.

Leibenstein, H. (1966). "Allocative Efficiency vs. 'X-Efficiency.'" *American Economic Review 56*: 392–415.

Leonard-Barton, D. (1992a). "Core Capabilities and Core Rigidities: A Paradox in Managing New Product Development." *Strategic Management Journal 13*: 111–125.

———. (1992b). "The factory as a Learning Laboratory." *Sloan Management Review, 34,* no. 1 (Fall): 23–38.

Levi-Strauss, C. (1962). *La pensée sauvage,* Paris: Librairie Plon, [*The Savage Mind*] London: Weidenfeld & Nicolson, 1966.

Levitt, T. (1983). *The Marketing Imagination.* New York: Free Press.

Levitt, B., and March, J. G. (1988). "Organizational Learning." *Annual Review of Sociology 14*: 319–340.

Lewchuk, W. (1987). *American Technology and the British Vehicle Industry.* Cambridge, UK: Cambridge University Press.

Lieberman, M. B. (1994). "The Diffusion and Lean Manufacturing in the Japanese and U.S. Automobile Industry." Working paper prepared for the conference on New Imperatives for Managing in Revolutionary Change. Shizuoka, Japan, August 28–30.

Lieberman, M. B., and Asaba, S. (1997). "Inventory Reduction and Productivity Growth: A Comparison of Japanese and US Automobile Sectors." *Managerial and Decision Economics 18*: 73–85.

Lieberman, M. B., and Demeester, L. (1995). "Inventory Reduction and Productivity Growth; Evidence from the Japanese Automotive Sector." The John E. Anderson Graduate School of Management at UCLA Working Paper S&O 95-6.

Lieberman, M. B., Demeester, L., and Rivas, R. (1995). "Inventory Reduction in the Japanese Automobile Sector 1965–1991." Working paper, MIT International Motor Vehicle Program, Cambridge, Mass.

Lieberman, M. B., Lau, L. J., and Williams, M. D. (1990). "Firm-Level Productivity and Management Influence: A Comparison of U. S. and Japanese Automobile Producers." *Management Science 36*, no. 10: 1193–1215.

Liker, J. K., Kamath, R. R., Wasti, S. N., and Nagamachi, M. (1995). "Integrating Suppliers into Product Development." In J. K. Liker, J. Ettlie,

J. C. Campbell, eds., *Engineered in Japan: Japanese Technology Management Practices* (pp. 152–191). New York: Oxford University Press, 1995.

Lindblom, C. E. (1959). "The Science of 'Muddling Through.'" *Public Administration Review 19* (Spring): 79–88.

MacDuffie J. P., and Pil, F. K. (1996). "Assembly Plant Performance." In Office of Technology Policy, U.S. Department of Commerce, *The U.S. Automobile Manufacturing Industry*, December, U.S. Department of Commerce: 25–31.

MacNeil, I. R. (1983). "Values in Contract: Internal and External." *Northwestern University Law Review 78*, no. 2: 341–418.

Maema, T. (1993). *Man-machine no showa densetsu* [The legend of man-machine in the Showa era], Vols. 1 and 2. Tokyo: Kodansha (in Japanese).

March, J. G. (1988). *Decisions and Organizations.* Oxford: Basil Blackwell.

March, J. G., and Simon, H. A. (1958). *Organizations.* New York: John Wiley & Sons.

March, J. G., and Olsen, J. P. (1976). *Ambiguity and Choice in Organizations.* Bergen, Norway: Universitetsforlaget.

Matsui, M. (1988). *Jidosha buhin* [Automobile parts]. Tokyo: Nihon Keizai Shinbun-sha.

Merton, R. (1968). *Social Theory and Social Structure.* New York: Free Press.

Mintzberg, H. (1987). "Crafting Strategy." *Harvard Business Review*, July–August, 1987: 66–75.

Mintzberg, H., and Waters, J. A. (1985). "Of Strategies, Deliberate and Emergent." *Strategic Management Journal*, 6, no. 3: 257–272.

Mishina, K. (1995). "What is the Essence of Toyota's manufacturing Capability? Self-Manifestation by the Transplant in Kentucky, 1986–1994." Paper presented at GERPISA Third International Colloquium, Paris, June 1995.

Mitsubishi Research Institute (1987). *The Relationship between Japanese Auto and Auto Parts Makers.* Tokyo: Mitsubishi Research Institute.

Miwa, Y. (1989). "Shitauke kankei: Jidosha sangyo" [Subcontracting relationship: The case of automobile industry (pp. 163–186)]. In K. Imai and R. Komiya, eds., *Nihon no kigyo* [The Japanese firms]. Tokyo: Tokyo University Press (in Japanese). See also Y. Miwa (1994), "Subcontracting Relationship (Shitauke Relationship)—The Case of the Automobile Industry," University of Tokyo Research Institute for the Japanese Economy Discussion Paper 94-F-16.

Monden, Y. (1983/1993). *Toyota Production System.* Norcross, Ga.: Industrial Engineering and Management Press.

Monteverde, K., and Teece, D. J. (1982). "Supplier Switching Costs and Vertical Integration in the Automobile Industry." *Bell Journal of Economics 13*: 206–213.

Morgan, C. L. (1927). *"Emergent Evolution: The Gifford Lectures Delivered at the University of St. Andrews in the Year 1922* (2nd edition). London.

Morton J. A. (1971). *Organizing for Innovation.* New York: McGraw-Hill.

Myers, S., and Marquis, D. G. (1969). *Successful Industrial Innovations*. National Science Foundation, NSF 69-17.

Nabeta, S. (1992). "Jinji seido minaoshi de ginokei no miryoku takameru Toyota jidosha" [Toyota improving attractiveness of blue-collar worker by modifying its personnel policies]. *Rosei Jiho, 3059*, no. 4.3.6: 36–42 (in Japanese).

Nakamura, S. (1983). *Gendai jidosha kogyoron* (The theory of modern automobile industries). Tokyo: Yuhikaku (in Japanese).

Nelson, R. R., and Winter, S. G. (1982). *An Evolutionary Theory of Economic Change*. Cambridge, Mass.: Belknap, Harvard University Press.

Nemoto, M. (1992). *TQC seiko no hiketsu 30-kajo* [30 secrets of successful TQC]. Tokyo: Nikka Giren Shuppansha (in Japanese).

Nihon Noritsu Kyokai, [Japan Management Association], ed. (1978). *Toyota no genba kanri* [Shop floor management at Toyota]. Tokyo: Nihon Noritsu Kyokai.

Nihon Seisansei Honbu [Japan Productivity Center] (1991) Rodo Seisansei no Kokusai Hikau 1991 Nen Ban [International Comparison of Labor Productivity: Version 1991] Tokyo: Nihon Seisansei Honbu (in Japanese).

Niimi, A., and Matsudaira, Y. (1997). "Development of a New Vehicle Assembly Line at Toyota: Worker-oriented, Autonomous, New Assembly System" (pp. 82–93). In K. Shimokawa, U. Jürgens, and T. Fujimoto, eds., *Transforming Automobile Assembly*. Berlin: Springer Verlag.

Niimi, A., Miyoshi, K., Ishii, T., Araki, T., Uchida, K., and Ota, I. (1994). "Jidosha kumitate rain ni okeru jiritsu kanketsu kotei no kakuritsu." [Establishment of autonomous complete process planning for automobile assembly line]. *Toyota Technical Review 44*, no. 2 (November): 86–91 (in Japanese).

Nikkan Jidosha Shinbun-sha [Daily Automobile News] (1996) *Jidosha Sangyo Handbook: 1996 Nen Ban* [Automobile Industry Handbook: Version 1996] Tokyo: Nikkan Jidosha Shinbun-sha.

Nishiguchi, T. (1987). "Competing Systems of Automotive Component Supply: An Examination of the Japanese 'Clustered Control' Model and the 'Alps' Structure." Presented at the First Policy Forum, International Motor Vehicle Program, May.

———. (1993). "Competing Systems of Auto Component Development." Presented at the Annual Sponsors' Briefing Meeting, International Motor Vehicle Program (MIT), June.

———. (1994). *Strategic Industrial Sourcing*. New York: Oxford University Press.

Nobeoka, K. (1993). "Multi-Project Management: Strategy and Organization in Automobile Product Development." Unpublished Ph.D. dissertation, MIT Sloan School of Management.

———. (1996). "The Influence of Customer Scope on Supplier's Performance in the Japanese Automobile Industry." Discussion Paper Series, No. 56, 1995, RIEB, Kobe University.

Nomura, M. (1993). *Toyotism*. Tokyo: Minelva (in Japanese).

Nonaka, Ikujiro (1985). *Kigyo shinkaron* [The theory of corporate evolution]. Tokyo: Nihon Keizai Shinbunsha (in Japanese).

————. (1988a). "Creating Organizational Order Out of Chaos: Self-Renewal in Japanese Firms." *California Management Review 30*, no. 3 (Spring): 57–73.

————. (1988b). "Toward Middle-Up-Down Management: Accelerating Information Creation." *Sloan Management Review 29*, no. 3 (Spring):. 9–18.

Nonaka, I., and Takeuchi, H. (1985). *The Knowledge-Creating Company.* New York: Oxford University Press.

Nonaka, Izumi (1995). "The Development of Company-Wide Quality Control and Quality Circles at Toyota Motor Corporation and Nissan Motor Co. Ltd." Presented at the 21st Fuji Conference, January.

Office for the Study of Automotive Transportation (OSAT). University of Michigan. (1992). *The Competitiveness of the North American Automobile Industry.* Ann Arbor: OSAT.

Ogawa, E., ed. (1994). *Toyota seisan hoshiki no kenkyu* [A study on Toyota production system]. Tokyo: Nihon Keizai Shinbunsha (in Japanese).

Ohno, T. (1978). *Toyota seisan hoshiki* [Toyota production system]. Tokyo: Diamond (in Japanese).

Kojima Press Industry Co., Ltd. (1988). *Okagesamade 50-nen minna genkide* [We have been well thanks to you for 50 years]. Toyota City, Aichi: Kojima Press Industry Co., Ltd. (in Japanese).

Okamoto, H. (1996). *Seihan togo to seisan system seihan togo* [Integrating production and sales]. Tokyo: Nihon Keizai Shinbunsha (in Japanese).

Okochi, A. (1979). *Keiei kosoryoku* [The capability of business conceptualization]. Tokyo: Tokyo University Press (in Japanese).

Oshima, T. ed. (1987). *Gendai Nihon no jidosha buhin kogyo* [The automobile parts industry in modern Japan]. Tokyo: Nihon Keizai Hyoronsha (in Japanese).

Oshima, T., and Yamaoka, S. (1987). *Jidosha* (The automobile). Tokyo: Nihon Keizai Hyoron-sha (in Japanese).

Parsons, T. (1937). *The Structure of Social Action.* Glencoe, Ill.: Free Press.

Pascale, R. T. (1984). "Perspectives on Strategy: The Real Story Behind Honda's Success." *California Management Review 26* no. 3: 47–72.

Penrose, E. T. (1959). *The Theory of the Growth of the Firm.* Oxford: Basil Blackwell.

Pisano, G. P. (1997). *The Development Factory.* Boston: Harvard Business School Press.

Popper, K. R. (1957). *The Poverty of Historicism.* London: Routledge & Kegan Paul.

Porter, M. E. (1985). *Competitive Advantage.* New York: Free Press.

Prahalad, C. K., and Hamel, G. (1990). "The Core Competence of the Corporation." *Harvard Business Review,* May-June:79–91.

Quinn, J. B. (1978). "Strategic Change: 'Logical Incrementalism.'" *Sloan Management Review 1*, no. 20 (Fall): 7–21.

Robertson, T. S., Zielinski, J., and Ward, S. (1984). *Consumer Behavior.* Glenview, Ill.: Scott, Foresman.

Robinson, A. G., and Schroeder, D. M. (1993). "Training, Continuous Improvement, and Human Relations: The U.S. TWI Programs and the

Japanese Management Style." *California Management Review*, Winter: 35–57.

Rosenbloom, R. S. (1978). "Technological Innovation in Firms and Industries: An Assessment of the State of the Art." In P. Kelly and M Kranzberg, eds., *Technological Innovation* (pp. 215–234). San Francisco: San Francisco Press.

Sako, M. (1992). *Prices, Quality and Trust: Inter-Firm Relations in Britain and Japan.* Cambridge, UK: Cambridge University Press.

Satake, H. (1995). *Shohikanketsu-gata seisan hoshiki* [Consumption-complete production system]. Tokyo: Hakuto Shobo.

Sato, Yoshio, ed. (1980). *Teiseichoka ni okeru gaichu shitauke kanri* [Outsourcing and subcontracting management in a low-growth period]. Tokyo: Chuo Keizaisha (in Japanese).

Sato, Yoshinobu (1988). *Toyota group no senryaku to jissho bunseki* (Strategy and empirical analysis of Toyota group). Tokyo: Hakuto Shobo (in Japanese).

———. (1994) *Toyota keiei no genryu: Sogyo-sha Kiichiro no hito to jigyo.* [The origin of Toyota management: Personality and business of Kiichiro Toyoda]. Tokyo: Nihon Keizai Shinbunsha (in Japanese).

Sawai, M. (1985). "Senzenki Nihon tetsudo sharyo kogyo no tenkai katei" [Development of the Japanese locomotive manufacturing industry in the prewar era]. *Shakai Kagaku Kenkyu* [Studies of a Machine Economy] *37*, no. 3: 1–200 (in Japanese).

Schonberger, R. J. (1982). *Japanese Manufacturing Techniques.* New York: Free Press.

Sei, S., Omori, H., and Nakajima, H. (1975, 1976). "Jidosha buhin kogyo ni okeru seisan kozo no kenkyu" [A study of production structure in the auto parts industry]. *Kikai Keizai Kenkyu* [Studies of a machine economy] 8: 72–113; 9: 34–83 (in Japanese).

Seki, T. ed. (1980) *Jidosha no Kihon Keikaku to Design* [Basic Planning and Designing of the Automobile]. Tokyo: Sankaido.

Sheriff, A. M. (1988). "Product Development in the Automobile Industry: Corporate Strategies and Project Performance." M.S.M. dissertation, Sloan School of Management, Massachusetts Institute of Technology.

Shibata, F., Imayoshi, K., Eri, Y., and Ogata, S. (1993). "Kumitate sagyo futan no teiryo hyokaho (TVAL) no kaihatsu" [Development of assembly load verification]. *Toyota Technical Review 43*, no. 1 (May): 84–89 (in Japanese)

Shimada, H. (1988). *Humanware no keizaigaku* [The economics of humanware]. Tokyo: Iwanami Shoten (in Japanese).

Shimizu, K. (1994). "Toyotism-teki chingin kettei yoshiki—Jirei kenkyu." [Toyotism wage formation—a case study]. *Okayama Economic Review 25*, no. 4 (March): 241–263 (in Japanese).

———. (1995). "Toyota jidosha ni okeru rodo no ningenka (I) (II)." [Humanization of work at Toyota Motor Co. (I) (II)]. *Okayama Economic Review 27*, no. 1 (June): 1–24; *27*, no. 2 (September): 293–315 (in Japanese).

Shimokawa, K. (1990). "Ford system kara just-in-time systeme" [From the Ford system to the just-in-time system]. In K. Nakagawa, ed., *Kigyo keiei no rekishiteki kenkyu* [A historical study of corporate management]. Tokyo: Iwanami Shoten:284–303 (in Japanese).

————. (1994). *The Japanese Automobile Industry: A Business History*. London: Athlone.

Shimokawa, K., Jürgens, U., and Fujimoto, T., eds. (1997). *Transforming Automobile Assembly*. Berlin: Springer Verlag.

Shingo, S. (1980). *Toyota seisan hoshiki no IE-teki kosatsu*. (An industrial engineering analysis of Toyota production system). Tokyo: Nikkan Kogyo Shinbunsha (in Japanese).

Shioji, H. (1994). "Toyota system keisei katei no sho-tokushitsu." [Various characteristics in the formation process of Toyota system]. *Kyoto Daigaku Keizaigakkai Keizai Ronso 154*, no. 5: 467–479 (in Japanese).

Shioji, H. (1996). "The Order Entry System in Japan." Paper presented for Automotive Fellowship International, February 29.

Shiomi, H. (1995). "The Formation of Assembler Networks in the Automobile Industry: The Case of Toyota Motor Company (1955–1980)." In H. Shiomi, and K. Wada, eds., *Fordism Transformed: The Development of Production Methods in the Automobile Industry*. Oxford University Press: 28–48.

Simon, H. A. (1945/1976). *Administrative Behavior*. New York: Free Press.

————. (1969). *The Science of the Artificial*. Cambridge: Cambridge, Mass: MIT Press.

Somu-cho Tokei-kyoku [Management and Coordination Agency, Statistics Bureau] (1970–1997) *Kagaku Gijutsu Kenkyu Chosa Hokoku* [Repport on the Survey of Research and Development] (in Japanese).

Stalk, G. Jr., and Hout, T. M. (1990). *Competing Against Time*. New York: Free Press.

Stalk G. Jr., Stephenson, S., and King,T. (1996). "Searching for Fulfillment: Breakthroughs in Order and Delivery Processes in the Auto Industry." Discussion Paper, The Boston Consulting Group.

Suzuki, N. (1991). *America shakai no nakano nikkei kigyo* [Japanese companies in American society]. Tokyo: Toyo Keizai Shinposha (in Japanese).

Takeishi, A., and Kawahara, E. (1994). "Shisutemu antei to dealer shisutemu" [System stability and the dealer system]. *Business Review, Hitotsubashi University 41*, no. 3: 37–50 (in Japanese).

Tanaka, H. (1982). "Nihon-teki koyo kanko wo kizuita hitotachi—Moto Toyota jidosha kogyo senmu Yamamoto Keimei-shi ni kiku" [The people who created Japanese employment practices—Interview with Mr. Keimei Yamamoto, former senior managing director of Toyota Motor Corporation], Parts 1–3. *Nihon Rodo Kyokai Zasshi*, July: 38–55; August: 64–81; September: 25–41 (in Japanese).

Teece, D. J., and Pisano, G. (1994). "The Dynamic Capabilities of Firms: An Introduction." *Industrial and Corporate Change* 3, no. 3: 537–556.

Teece, D. J., Pisano, G., and Shuen, A. (1992). "Dynamic Capabilities and Strategic Management." University of California at Berkeley Working Paper. Revised.

Teece, D. J., Rumelt, R., Dosi, G., and Winter, S. (1994). "Understanding Corporate Coherence: Theory and Evidence." *Journal of Economic Behavior and Organization 23*: 1–30.

Thompson, J. D. (1967). *Organization in Action*. New York: McGraw-Hill.

Tolliday, S., and Zeitlin, J. (1986). *The Automobile Industry and its Workers.* Cambridge, UK: Polity Press.

Totsuka, H., and Hyodo, T. eds. (1990). *Roshi kankei no tenkan to sentaku* [Changes and choices in industrial relations]. Tokyo: Nihon Hyoronsha (in Japanese).

Toyota Motor Co., Ltd. (1957). *Toyota Jidosha 20-nenshi* [20 years of Toyota Motor Co., Ltd]. Toyota City, Aichi: Toyota Motor Co., Ltd. (in Japanese).

Toyota Motor Co., Ltd. (1967). *Toyota Jidosha 30-nenshi* [30 years of Toyota Motor Co., Ltd]. Toyota City, Aichi: Toyota Motor Co., Ltd. (in Japanese).

Toyota Motor Co., Ltd. (1978). *Toyota no ayumi* [History of Toyota]. Toyota City, Aichi: Toyota Motor Co., Ltd. (in Japanese).

Toyota Motor Corporation (1987). *An Introduction to the Toyota Production System.* Toyota City, Aichi: Toyota Motor Corporation.

Toyota Motor Corporation (1996a). *Suppliers Guide.* Toyota City, Aichi: Toyota Motor Corporation.

Toyota Motor Corporation (1992/1996b). *The Toyota Production System.* Toyota City, Aichi: Toyota Motor Corporation.

Toyota Motor Corporation. (1994). "Atarashii jidosha kumitate rain no kaihatsu" [Development of new vehicle assembly system]. *Dai 40-kai Okochi-sho Jusho Gyoseki Hokoku-sho* [Reports of Achievements in Industrialization Awarded the Okochi Memorial Prize 1994], Okochi Memorial Foundation: 99–109.

Udagawa, M. (1993). "Nihon jidosha sangyo ni okeru hinshitsu kanri katsudo—Nissan to Toyota" [Quality control activities in the Japanese automobile industry: Nissan and Toyota]. Hosei University Center for Business and Industrial Research Working Paper No. 36 (in Japanese).

Udagawa, M., Sato, H., Nakamura, K., and Nonaka, Izumi (1995). *Nihon kigyo no hinshitsu kanri* [Quality control in Japanese firms]. Tokyo: Yuhikaku.

Ueda, H. (1989–1991), "Jidosha sangyo no kigyo kaiso kozo—Jidosha maker to ichiji maker no ketsugo kankei" [The hierarchical structure in the automobile industry—Linkages between the automobile makers and first-tier suppliers], Parts 1–3. *Kikan Keizai Kenkyu* [Economic Research Quarterly, Osaka City University] *12*, no. 3: 1–30; *13*, no. 1: 29–60; *14*, no. 2: 1–38.

Upton, D. M. (1995). "Flexibility as Process Mobility: The Management of Plant Capabilities for Quick Response Manufacturing." *Journal of Operations Managemnt* 12: 205–224.

Utterback, J. M. (1974). "Innovation in Industry and Diffusion of Technology." *Science* 183 (February 15): 658–62.

von Bertalanffy, L. (1900). *General System Theory: Foundations, Development,* Applications. New York: George Braziller.

von Hippel, E. (1990). "Task Partitioning: An Innovation Process Variable." *Research Policy.* 19: 407–418.

von Hippel, E., and Tyre, M. (1993). "How 'Learning by Doing' is Done: Problem Identification in Novel Process Equipment." M.I.T. Sloan School Working Paper.

Wada, K. (1991). "The Development of Tiered Inter-Firm Relationships in the Automobile Industry: A Case Study of the Toyota Motor Corporation." *Japanese Yearbook on Business History 8*: 23–47.

———. (1995). "The Emergence of 'Flow Production' Methods in Japan." In H. Shiomi and K. Wada, eds., *Fordism Transformed: The Development of Production Methods in the Automobile Industry*. Oxford: Oxford University Press.

Weick, K. (1979). *The Social Psychology of Organizing*. Reading, Mass.: Addison Wesley.

Weinberg, G. M. (1975). *An Intrduction to General Systems Thinking*. New York: John Wiley & Sons.

Wernerfelt, B. (1984). "A Resource-Based View of the Firm." *Strategic Management Journal 5*: 171–180.

Wernerfelt, B. (1995). "The Resource-Based View of the Firm: Ten Years After." *Strategic Management Journal 16*: 171–174.

Williamson, O. (1979). "Transaction-Cost Economics: Governance of Contractual Relations." *Journal of Law and Economics 22*: 233–261.

Williamson, O. (1985). *The Economic Institution of Capitalism: Firms, Markets, Relational Contracting*. New York: Free Press.

Womack, J., Jones, D. T., and Roos, D. (1990). *The Machine that Changed the World*. New York: Rawson Associates.

Yamamoto, K. (1981). *Jidosha sangyo no roshi kankei* [Industrial relations in the automobile industry]. Tokyo: Tokyo University Press (in Japanese).

Yano, S., ed. (1985). *Hito, gijustu, soshiki* [People, technology, organization]. Tokyo: Yuhikaku (in Japanese).

INDEX